INTERNATIONAL SERIES OF MONOGRAPHS IN
EXPERIMENTAL PSYCHOLOGY

GENERAL EDITOR: H. J. EYSENCK

VOLUME 14

Homosexual Behaviour:
Therapy and Assessment

Homosexual Behaviour: Therapy and Assessment

BY

M. P. FELDMAN

AND

M. J. MacCULLOCH

PERGAMON PRESS

OXFORD · NEW YORK · TORONTO
SYDNEY · BRAUNSCHWEIG

Pergamon Press Ltd., Headington Hill Hall, Oxford

Pergamon Press Inc., Maxwell House, Fairview Park, Elmsford,
New York 10523

Pergamon of Canada Ltd., 207 Queen's Quay West, Toronto 1

Pergamon Press (Aust.) Pty. Ltd., 19a Boundary Street,
Rushcutters Bay, N.S.W. 2011, Australia

Vieweg & Sohn GmbH, Burgplatz 1, Braunschweig

First edition 1971

Library of Congress Catalog Card No. 77-151943

Printed in Great Britain by A. Wheaton & Co., Exeter

08 016244 4

CONTENTS

PREFACE

THE work which is described in this book had its origin in the idea that co-operation between an experimentally oriented clinical psychologist and a clinical psychiatrist, trained in the phenomenological tradition of Germany psychiatry, and with a strong sympathy for the scientific method, would be fruitful. Inter-disciplinary co-operation in research is all too rare, yet it is at the border-areas of subjects that progress will be most rapid. Research into deviant sexual behaviour demands the methods and concepts of several disciplines and we have tried to cast our therapeutic, measurement and theoretical nets as widely as possible within the limitation of our joint professional competence.

Our original intention was to explore the extent to which principles derived from the experimental psychology of learning could be applied to the treatment of a variety of behaviours, such as smoking, excessive drinking and over-eating, which have both pleasurable and distressing consequences to the individual displaying them. Deviant sexual behaviour, the area in which we have made much of our major effort, was added at the suggestion of our clinical director who had found, over many years, that such behaviours were both highly distressing to many of those displaying them and particularly resistant to existing methods of treatment. We began with the notion that homosexual behaviour was very much more than a simple "symptom" which could be "unlearned", as a phobia can be desensitized, but involved a total way of life. To our great surprise it began to seem that the learning technique described in this book was effective where the passage of time, psychotherapy of any variety and physical methods were relatively ineffective. However, it has also become clear to us that while a sound learning technique is probably necessary for the *acquisition* of homosexual avoidance and heterosexual approach behaviour, additional principles derived from the social and cognitive areas of psychology are needed to provide a complete account of the process of behaviour change. Moreover, we are strongly of the view that behaviour therapy techniques are most effective in a therapeutic setting of concern and support.

Throughout this book, and in particular by means of the large number of case histories which form Appendix A, we have attempted to provide the reader with as much data as possible so that he can form his own view as to the backgrounds and response to treatment of the patients. The last chapter is a frankly speculative attempt to weave together a variety of sources of evidence in order to account for the development and maintenance of homosexual behaviour, the motivation for, and the response to, treatment. These speculations are intended to stimulate research, particularly of an inter-disciplinary kind.

We have been greatly assisted by psychiatrists, psychologists, secretaries and technicians. In particular we would like to record our great debt to Northage J. de V. Mather and Pauline Snow who not only tolerated but encouraged a research effort which must have seemed at times somewhat esoteric. Valerie Mellor and John Pinschof have spent many hours treating many patients and their assistance is gratefully acknowledged, as is that of Sheila Glazier who typed many of our earlier papers, and Elaine Grainger who typed the bulk of this book. In addition, we must thank our editors, particularly D. S. B. Inglis, for their patience and sound advice.

Finally, it is true that many homosexual individuals are content with their way of life and do not seek treatment. It is equally true that many are not content and do seek treatment. As citizens we respect the right of the former to live their lives on equal terms with heterosexual members of society. As therapists we equally respect the right of the latter to seek help in changing their sexual orientation. To deny the right of either to the way of life of their choice is a denial of a vital human freedom.

GLOSSARY

THE definitions given below should not be thought as having the status of standard definitions appearing in a textbook of experimental psychology. Although broadly accurate they are primarily intended to enable the reader to translate the technical terms used in this book to the events which occur in treatment.

Classical conditioning (CC). The sequence of events is independent of the subject's behaviour. CC is used in Chapter 5 as follows: the presence of the unconditioned stimulus (UCS) shock evokes an unconditioned response (UCR), e.g. jerking of the leg to which the shock has been applied together with unpleasant bodily sensations. A conditioned stimulus (CS1), a slide of a person of the same sex, is repeatedly visually displayed just prior to the UCS and both cease together. A second conditioned stimulus (CS2), a slide of a person of the opposite sex, is displayed immediately afterwards and is then removed by the therapist. Eventually the CS1 will evoke a conditioned response (CR) such as a feeling of unpleasantness when it is displayed without the occurrence of the UCS.

Instrumental conditioning. There is by no means a complete separation between classical and instrumental conditioning, but a broad definition of instrumental conditioning would be as follows: rewards and punishments are made to occur as a consequence of the learner's motor response or failure to respond. Reinforcement, which can be either positive such as food, or negative such as shock, plays a central role. The subject makes verbal or motor responses to stimuli.

Anticipatory avoidance (AA). The AA learning technique referred to throughout this book is an example of instrumental conditioning. The following abbreviations are used, some being the same as those used above for classical conditioning:

CS1   A slide of a person of the same sex as the patient.
CS2   A slide of a person of the opposite sex to that of the patient.
UCS   See above; the ultimate power source is a motor-car battery.
CR   The avoidance response to CS1 made by pressing a switch to remove the slide of the same sex from the screen.
CR2   The approach response to CS2 made by pressing another switch to bring the slide of the opposite sex on to the screen.

(N.B.—CS1 always *precedes* CR1, which is an avoidance response. CS2 always *follows* CR2, an approach response.)

Trial. In classical conditioning this means the sequence CS1–UCS–CS2 (see above and Chapter 5). This occurs independently of the behaviour of the patient. The length of time taken by the trial is the same for each trial. In anticipatory avoidance, *trial* means a sequence of events which always begins with CS1 and then takes a variable form depending on the type of trial (see Chapters 3 and 5) but which *always* includes at least one CR1. Hence the simplest example would be:

CS1–CR1

Same sex slide projected by therapist   Same sex slide removed by patient

Additional aspects could be: more than one CR1, a number of CR2s, a number of CS2s, and a UCS. The end of a trial could be marked either by a CR1 or by the removal by the therapist of the last CS2 allowed for that particular trial.

Inter-trial interval. A period of time between trials during which the screen is blank, varying randomly in both CC and AA, and lasting between 20 and 40 sec.

Session. A circumscribed group of trials, usually between 20 and 30 in number, and lasting between 20 and 30 min. Sessions were held twice daily, or daily, etc., depending on the circumstances of the individual case.

Abbreviations relating to physiological measures:

EEG   Electro-encephalography. A measure of spontaneous electrical activity of the brain measured using a high-gain amplifier.
EMG   Electromyography. A measure of the electrical activity of muscle groups using the same kind of high-gain amplifier as is used for EEG recording.
ECG   Electrocardiography. A measure of the electrical activity of the heart in relation to its contraction; in this instance used as an index of heart rate and measured by the EEG high-gain amplifier.

CHAPTER 1

TREATMENT: A REVIEW OF TECHNIQUES AND RESULTS

INTRODUCTION

The beginnings of the treatment of homosexuality coincide with an increasing medical interest in sexual deviations around the turn of the century (Kraft-Ebbing, 1934). For the last 30 years, treatment has usually meant one form or other of psychotherapy. The criticism that psychotherapists provided little evidence for or against the efficacy of their techniques (Eysenck, 1952) applies to the area of sexual deviations as widely as to other disorders of behaviour. Since Eysenck's powerful attack, several attempts have been made to evaluate, in a controlled manner, the efficacy of psychotherapy, as compared with behaviour therapy, in the treatment of phobias and other neuroses, e.g. Gelder (1968a). Prior to the research reported here in Chapter 5, no such comparisons had been made in the treatment of sexual deviations. The result is that only indirect comparisons can be made, and inevitably these must be between widely differing samples of patients, treated by different therapists, and using often unstated variations of the various possible techniques. Anyone attempting to review the literature on treatment is thus circumscribed by the unsatisfactory nature of almost the entire published literature.

In order to compare the results of different methods, or of the same method as carried out by different workers, we must be able to compare the patients receiving treatment, the type of treatment, and the way in which it was carried out. Initially, there must be a clear and unequivocal statement of the proportion of patients presenting for help who actually received treatment. If selection was involved (and usually it is), the criteria for this should be stated. If the patients who are reported on in the published paper represent only a sample of all those treated by the therapist, the reason for this possible further selection must also be stated. In addition to these basic needs, the following information is also relevant in assisting the reader to compare the various series of patients reported upon.

1. The full history of sexual behaviour and the nature of the sexual activities at the time of presentation for treatment. These data will lead to the assignation of Kinsey ratings (Kinsey *et al.*, 1947) to the sample.

2. The patient's motivation for treatment and future aspirations—both sexually and maritally.

3. The manner of presentation for treatment, i.e. whether of the patient's own accord, on an order of the court or because of some other separate or related psychiatric disturbance.

4. The present psychiatric status and the psychiatric and medical history of the patients in the sample.

5. The occurrence of other sexual deviations such as transvestism, fetishism, etc.

6. The proportion of the series who mix in the homosexual subculture and the extent to which they do so as a proportion of their total social life.

7. The proportion of the sample who have made appearances in court for homosexual and other offences and the number of such offences.

8. The manner in which the information given in the report was obtained, e.g. hearsay, surmise, or direct statement by the patient. If the latter, whether this was obtained in interview or by letter. This last point is particularly relevant to follow-up information on the patient. All too often this consists solely of a letter from the patient to the therapist in which he states that he is doing well but does not wish to return for further interviews. Whether or not the patient's unchecked claim is accepted makes a considerable difference to the degree of success reported.

9. Information is needed concerning the treatment: (a) a clear-cut description of the form of treatment; (b) the length of time over which the treatment was received; and (c) the number of treatment sessions involved together with the length of each session.

10. The mode of assessment of change in sexual behaviour and interest. This may have been obtained by the patient's own testimony, and this in turn may or may not have been confirmed by others. Alternatively, the change of behaviour may have been indexed by direct observations, by some form of assessment procedure such as an attitude scale (Feldman *et al.*, 1966), or by direct objective measurement such as the phallo-plethysmograph (Bancroft *et al.*, 1966).

11. A statement as to whether the assessment of change, as reported, was made immediately after treatment or after follow-up, and, if the latter, the length of the follow-up.

There is considerable evidence (Goldstein, 1962) that the expectations patients have concerning psychotherapy play a considerable part in determining the outcome of treatment. It is relevant, therefore, that the vast majority of a non-patient sample of 127 homosexuals who gave voluntary interviews to Westwood (1960) were pessimistic as to the likelihood of treatment altering their sexual orientation. It seems possible that at least a considerable proportion of those who do seek help are pessimistic about the likelihood of a successful outcome. This cannot help the chances of a successful response to treatment. In addition, it is worth pointing out that whereas the majority of those who seek psychiatric help for their problems do not gain from the nature of the problem behaviour and are relieved when these problems ease, this is not entirely true in the case of homosexuality. As well as leading to considerable distress and unhappiness, homosexuality has at the same time enjoyable consequences for many of those who practise it, leading as it does to sexual—and in some cases—social gratification. The prospect of a successful outcome of treatment is not an unmixed blessing. It both implies giving up something which, however distressing, has also produced satisfaction and the need for the individual to learn new social skills, or at any rate re-learn skills that have been long dormant. About 20% of Westwood's sample had received some kind of treatment for their homosexuality, mainly by psychiatrists, and of these, one-half left their treatment within 3 months and before it had been completed. Nearly one-half of those who had received treatment had been followed up (from 6 to 18 months) and none reported any change in the direction of their sexual urge. A further 20% had had a desire to change, usually in their late teens or early twenties, but had never done anything about it.

Westwood's sample was drawn largely from the homosexual subculture: possibly an even larger proportion of solitary homosexuals would seek treatment, or at any rate might seriously contemplate doing so, if a reasonable expectation of success could be held out to them. No such optimism is justified by the reported results of treatment reviewed in the rest of this chapter. However, recent developments, both in techniques of aversion and of desensitization, described in Chapters 3 and 5, are rather hopeful. If these hopes are confirmed by the experience of other workers, it is likely (short of a revolution in the social climate) that the numbers of homosexuals seeking treatment will vastly increase.

A. TREATMENT BY PSYCHOTHERAPY OR PSYCHOANALYSIS

1. CURRAN AND PARR (1957)

Curran and Parr found 128 male cases of homosexuality out of a series of 5000 seen in the first author's private practice. Out of the original 128, 100 were selected for further study because of adequate documentation. Of the sample, 30 had been referred following a charge or on an order of the court. Another 22 had appeared because of psychiatric problems other than homosexuality. Only 25 came out of direct personal anxiety concerning their homosexuality; another 12 did so because of pressure from friends or relatives and 5 because of marital problems. One-fifth of those aged under 35 had been charged with a homosexual offence as compared with twice that proportion of those aged over 35. As is usual in samples of those treated privately, the educational and occupational status of the group was high; 51 had been to public (fee-paying) school and 19 to grammar (high) school, while 41 had had a university education. Of the sample 30 had abnormal personalities; in 23 there was a previous history of nervous trouble, and 26 had received a psychiatric diagnosis. The authors concluded that no fewer than 51 % were to be considered free from gross personality disorder, neurosis, or psychosis during their adult lives. In addition, the series included a number of important and talented individuals of high integrity. Only 2 had been on any criminal charge other than homosexuality.

Seventeen of the series were paedophiliacs—defined as those who were sexually attracted to pre-pubertal boys. The paedophiliac section was significantly more likely to appear because of a criminal charge concerned with their sexual behaviour (12 out of 17 as compared with 18 out of the remaining 83); a significantly higher proportion were married, and they also tended to be older. When the patients were originally seen they were not assigned a Kinsey rating; the assignation of a rating was made at the time of the analysis of the data. There is, therefore, a possibility of criterion contamination in that the outcome of treatment was known at the time the Kinsey rating was made. Unfortunately, Curran and Parr did not separately report Kinsey 5's and 6's, so that 42 of their sample are described as Kinsey 5 and 6 (defined as "100% homosexual or nearly so"). Another 29 were "bi-sexual but predominantly homosexual", receiving a Kinsey rating of 4. Finally, 16 received a rating of 1–3 ("bi-sexual but predominantly heterosexual"), 3 a rating of "somewhere between 2 and 5", and 10 were not classified. Little data is provided on heterosexual activity, but, as Curran and Parr point out in partial extenuation of this omission, many homosexuals indulge in intercourse with women out of curiosity or in an attempt at self-diagnosis or treatment, so that for assessment purposes the subjective aspect of heterosexual experience—whether it is enjoyed or desired or not—is at least as important as what physically takes place.

Eleven of the series were advised to seek in-patient care, psychotherapy was recommended for 23, and for the remaining 66 treatment was limited to discussion at the initial interview, simple counselling, prescription of medicines, or environmental adjustment. Follow-up was carried out to only a limited extent, 15 of the sample being personally seen by one of the authors, while documentary information was available on the sex life of the patient for a further 44. Nine of the 59 (15 + 44) reported less intense homosexual feelings or an increased capacity for heterosexual arousal; 6 of these were assigned a pre-treatment Kinsey rating of between 1 and 3, 2 a rating of 4, and only 1 a rating of 5 or 6. Three became more homosexual in preference, and no change, even of a minor order, was found in the sexual orientation of the other 47. However, nearly one-half reported improved subjective adjustment and general well being. This seems a useful secondary outcome of treatment for homosexuality. It is rather too easy to sneer at treatment only producing "happy" homosexuals as compared with a state of previous distress. If one of the objectives of any therapy is the alleviation of human suffering, then if it has not proved possible to change a person's sexual orientation as he desires, helping him to lead a happier though sexually unchanged life, appears a reasonable therapeutic objective.

Finally, Curran and Parr report on the 25 patients who were treated by psychotherapy of any kind. These were compared with a matched group who had not received psychotherapy. The mean duration of follow-up was 4½ years. No difference could be found between the 2 groups as regards change in sexual orientation, increased discretion, or control. The only slight change was that rather more of the treated patients appeared to come to better terms with their problem at a subjective level, but even this difference was not statistically significant.

2. WOODWARD (1958)

A slightly more optimistic, though still very far from satisfactory, picture of the outcome of psychotherapy is provided by two papers reporting homosexuals treated at the Portman Clinic (the Portman, now called the ISTD, specializes in the study and treatment of delinquency, so that a large proportion of the homosexuals treated there are referrals from the courts). The first series consist of those cases discharged from the Portman Clinic in 1952 and 1953, and the initial sample consisted of 113 cases. Woodward's report on this series, though lacking in certain important respects, is one of the few which comes near to meeting the criteria for reporting, outlined earlier in this chapter.

A Kinsey rating was available for 104 of the series, and of these 14% received a rating of 6, 26% one of 5, 35% 3 or 4, and 26% 1 or 2. These figures are rather similar to those of Curran and Parr. Slightly more than one-half of the 88 who received a rating of between 1 and 5 had had some sexual intercourse with females at some time in the past. The patients had been referred for treatment following a court appearance, and represented an unknown percentage of those who had made such appearances. Some selection had therefore been made by the referring agency, and while the criteria for such a selection are quite unknown, it is a reasonable inference that an attempt was made to select those who were felt to be more likely to respond to treatment. Some psychiatric disorder was noted in 55 of the series. In the majority of cases this was a personality disorder of some type.

Ninety-two of the total series of 113 were eventually recommended for treatment at the Portman Clinic and 5 for treatment elsewhere. The recommendation was made on the basis of the prognosis attached to the case by the examining psychiatrist. The major prognostic factors were a Kinsey rating of 4 or less, a preference for homosexual practices other than anal intercourse, and a high motivation for treatment. Age and degree of incidence of homosexual acts were unrelated to prognosis. Eighty-one of the 97 recommended for treatment actually began to receive treatment. The others did not do so on account of various factors, including being sent to prison and failure to attend for treatment. Seventeen of the group of 81 left treatment without making headway, 14 of these after 5 sessions or less. There was a slightly greater tendency for those who left without any good reason to be exclusively homosexual, to have homosexual convictions, and also convictions for offences other than homosexuality. But all of these tendencies were only slight. Sixty-four patients either completed treatment or interrupted it for some good reason. Of these, 48 were regarded as having satisfactorily completed their treatment: 33 of the 48 received 29 sessions of psychotherapy or less, and many psychotherapists would regard this as a surprisingly small number of sessions. The mode of assessment of outcome is not stated, but presumably it was by interview. Twenty-one of the 48 are described by Woodward as having "no homosexual impulse" on completion of treatment. Neither, however, did they have any heterosexual impulse. (It has been our experience that patients relapse unless it has been possible to replace homosexual by heterosexual interest.) A successful outcome of treatment, in terms of the reorientation of sexual interest, was obtained in only 7 out of the 48 who completed treatment and in none of those in whom it was interrupted. From figures given by Woodward it would seem that all 7 were bisexual, i.e. had a pretreatment Kinsey rating of 5 or less, and 3 of the 7 had a rating of 1 or 2. Six of the 7 were aged under 30 and 5 were not homosexually active until their late teens. The outcome of treatment appeared worse for those who were not on probation than for those who were. The possibility is raised of patients making a more favourable report on themselves when this might have appeared to relate to their successful completion of the probationary period.

The emphasis of interest during the follow-up period tended to be on whether or not the patient had offended against probation by being re-convicted. Woodward was able to conclude that there were only 11 convictions for homosexuality and another 3 for offences connected with property; "the remaining cases may be presumed to have been successful—at least to the extent of avoiding further Court appearances." As has already been pointed out, failure to re-attend may well be tantamount to relapse. Woodward was able to trace reports of only 19 of the total sample with whom there had been recent contact and who had not been in any further trouble. Ten of the 19 had completed their treatment; 5 of the 10 reported no homosexual impulse, and 5 reported that the impulse was still present. The incompleteness of the follow-up data prevents more than the very tentative conclusion that in a series of patients referred by the courts and treated by psychotherapy, only a small proportion responded to treatment with both reduced homosexuality and increased heterosexuality.

3. COATES (1962)

A further series of 45 male homosexuals referred to the Portman Clinic between 1954 and 1960 was reported by Coates in 1962. One psychiatrist sent all his homosexual cases, and these comprised 38% of the 45 referrals, the remainder being sent by 12 other psychiatrists. The sample was rather different from that of Woodward (1958) in that 26 of the 45 were self-referred, only 19 being referred by the courts. Data on Kinsey ratings are available for 33 of the sample, only 9 of which were assigned a rating of 6. No data are provided on the length of the follow-up, but "many were still in treatment". No distinction was made in presenting the follow-up data between those who had completed and those who were still undergoing treatment. The sample was divided into those aged over and those aged under 21, there being 33 of the former and 12 of the latter. Five of the adults and 2 of the boys were considered to have improved in that they were displaying active heterosexual behaviour not necessarily leading to intercourse, although they might still have had homosexual phantasies. A further 5 adults and 6 boys reported no sexual activity of any kind. Once again we must regard the latter group as having a somewhat poor long-term prognosis. The remainder of the sample (23 adults and 4 boys) were either unchanged or were worse in the sense of being more actively homosexual. Data on length of treatment are provided for 33 of the sample, 14 having had 300 sessions of treatment or more and 19 less than 300 sessions. Five of those having more than 300 sessions were definitely improved as compared with none of those who had had less than 300. No data are provided on the length of the follow-up, so that the 5 who definitely improved, having received 300 sessions or more, might still have been receiving treatment. The data in this paper are either incomplete or inconclusive. At best it seems that 15% (5 adults and 2 boys) were definitely improved after treatment by psychotherapy following an unspecified period of follow-up. Oddly enough, it is stated that there was no relation between outcome and court appearance—a rather different finding from that of Curran and Parr (1957).

The remaining reports all tend, in varying degrees, to a rather more optimistic outlook for the effect of psychotherapy on homosexuality.

4. OVESEY *et al.* (1963)

This is a series of only 3 cases, and the major interest of the report lies in the explicit statement of psychoanalytical theory underlying the treatment approach used. Perhaps the most interesting aspect of the theory is that an important source of homosexuality is said to reside in the avoidance of self-assertion by the male child who fears to take on the masculine role. This fear spreads to all aspects of behaviour, so that in adult life heterosexual desires revive the earlier fear and normal heterosexual behaviour is inhibited. Fear of heterosexual stimuli is associated with the perception of homosexual stimuli as being safer. Hence, deviant sexuality of any kind is a defence against the anxiety raised by the female sexual organs; the anxiety is initially reduced by heterosexual avoidance, and this in turn is further strengthened by homosexual approach behaviour. The last two sentences have deliberately phrased the psychoanalytical theory in behavioural language, giving an indication of the possibility of uniting psychoanalytical and behavioural notions (Dollard and Miller, 1950). The primary focus of therapy is seen to be that of any phobia: "sooner or later the patient must attempt to approach the phobic object, that is, he must attempt intercourse." Ovesey *et al.* go on to state that this end is to be achieved through gaining insight into the unconscious phantasies which convert the vagina into a symbol of danger. They do not state how much of the emphasis in their therapeutic efforts was on the interpretation of dreams and how much on the desensitization of anxiety (Wolpe, 1958) to females.

Ovesey *et al.* describe 3 cases, all of whom were aged under 30, and received psychoanalytical therapy for 250 hours or more. All 3 responded successfully and showed a good heterosexual adaptation following treatment. In 2 of the 3 cases the follow-up was for 5 years. No details are given of the length of follow-up of the other case. Finally, Ovesey *et al.*

say that they have used their 1963 paper to describe their successful cases. They promise a further paper to describe their unsuccessful ones and the probable reasons for lack of success. To our knowledge this has not yet appeared.

Another psychoanalyst, Rubenstein (1958), was rather cautious about the likelihood of success: "psychoanalysis can help to a certain extent and for a fair number. Some improve well beyond the original expectations." This recalls the 1938 statement of Freud, quoted in Jones (1964): "in a certain number of cases we succeed . . . in the majority of cases it is no longer possible . . . the results of our treatment cannot be predicted" (p. 624).

Similar caution is shown by Hadfield (1958). Although he quotes several cases of successful analytical treatment, he considers that the technique "is a long one . . . and cannot be considered . . . a practical answer to . . . homosexuality". Interestingly enough, Hadfield—like Ovesey *et al.* (1963)—has a good deal to say on heterosexual avoidance in homosexuality, quoting, as an example, a patient whose avoidance he was able to trace back to choking whilst feeding at the breast. This, Hadfield claims, leads to a fear of the sexual aspect of women. He discussed the fear with the patient for between 15 and 20 interviews and found that the emotional reaction of anxiety was evoked on each occasion. This seems to be a form of desensitization, and is a further example of common ground between psychoanalysis and behaviourism.

No such doubts and cautions as those expressed by Hadfield and Rubenstein are met in the report of the next 2 series of homosexuals, both of which were treated by psychoanalytically orientated psychotherapy.

5. ELLIS (1956)

Ellis reports on 28 males and 12 females treated for "homosexual problems" rather than for homosexual desires or activities *per se*. However, 36 of the series were having overt homosexual relations. Ellis states that the emphasis "is not that of inducing the patient to forego all homosexual activity or desire . . . [it is] the exclusiveness or . . . obsessive . . . compulsiveness . . . the aim of psychotherapy is to free the confirmed homosexual from the fear of antagonism towards heterosexual relations and to enable him to have a satisfying love sex involvement with members of the other sex". It seems, then, that Ellis puts the emphasis on desensitizing heterosexual avoidance rather than averting the patient from his interest in his own sex. Ellis reports that his results with his female patients were better than with his males, and suggests that this was because they were treated by a male therapist. "The therapist shows by his manner and verbalizations that he himself was favourably prejudiced towards heterosexual relationships." He does not explain what this entailed. Ellis states that 64% of his male patients were improved or considerably improved, and that 100% of his female patients fell into these two categories. He does not state the meaning of these terms nor does he give any data either on length of follow-up or of selection of patients. Ellis differs markedly from most other therapists in finding that 18 out of 26 patients who prior to treatment had "little or no" heterosexual activity showed either improvement or considerable improvement. However, he does not define "little or none" nor, as has been pointed out above, does he define improvement. One possible interpretation is that the increase in heterosexual activity may have been accompanied by the continuance of homosexual activity. For Ellis the aims of treatment are to free the patient from his inhibitions concerning heterosexuality, and are therefore more restricted than those of most other therapists, which include, in addition, the cessation of homosexual behaviour. Nevertheless, an increase in heterosexual behaviour occurred in a much higher proportion of patients than in any other series described in this chapter, and from the description given by Ellis it is tempting to consider that some form of desensitization was involved.

6. ALLEN (1958)

Allen is similarly optimistic. He gives a list of cases which he collected for the Royal Commission on Homosexuality and Prostitution (set up in 1954), adding a few whom he had seen after the commission had completed its work. He states that he had not treated all these cases himself, raising the possibility of bias in selection over and above the usual problems of self-selection. Allen describes 12 cases who were successful and another 3 who were unsuccessful in response to psychoanalytically orientated psychotherapy. From the data which he gives it seems that at least 9 of these cases merited a Kinsey rating or 4 or less. Moreover, 6 out of the 12 displayed no overt homosexual behaviour prior to treatment. In view of the paucity of the data presented by Allen and of the rather polemical tone of his book, very little weight can be attached to his results.

7. BIEBER *et al.* (1963)

Much the largest scale psychoanalytical study is that reported by Bieber and his colleagues. They report the work of a special research committee of the Society of Medical Psychoanalysts which, over a 9-year period, collected a large amount of questionnaire data from 77 American psychoanalysts on 206 men (106 homosexual males and a comparison group of 100 heterosexual males, all of whom had been treated by the responding analysts). The response to treatment was only one aspect examined in this study; others included family relationships during childhood and adolescence, early sexual experiences, sexual development and attitudes, choice of homosexual partners, and attitudes to women. Several qualifications concerning sampling bias must attach themselves to the results of the study as a whole; for instance, as in the case of most psychoanalytical samples, all were fee-paying, all were self-referring, and most were of a high level of education (nearly 70% were college graduates). It is not, however, our purpose at the present time to evaluate research other that that concerned with response to treatment, and, when compared with other work in this field, Bieber's study is of considerable merit. A good deal of factual data is given concerning the pre-treatment sexual behaviour of the sample. For example, only 28 of the 106 homosexual patients had never had a heterosexual genital experience and 55 had had successful heterosexual intercourse at some stage prior to treatment. It would seem that if we translate such data into Kinsey ratings, the series is rather less loaded on the Kinsey 5 and 6 side than most of those discussed so far. Of the total sample, 74 had terminated psychoanalysis, whilst 32 had not yet done so at the time the data were collected. For purposes of data analysis, all 106 were considered together. Twenty-eight of the patients had fewer than 150 psychoanalytical sessions, of whom only 2 were exclusively heterosexual at the time of report: of these, one had died in an automobile accident whilst still in treatment, but was reported to have been actively heterosexual at the time of his death. The second patient was a 16-year-old adolescent who discontinued treatment after having rapidly established heterosexual relationships. He was reported to have been exclusively heterosexual at follow-up 4 years later. Forty patients received between 150 and 350 sessions and 38, 350 or more.

Seventy-two of the patients were described as being initially exclusively homosexual; of these, 42 had the same status at the time of report, 2 were described as inactive, 14 were bisexual, and 14 (19%) had become exclusively heterosexual. Thirty patients were initially described as bisexual, and at the time of report none were exclusively homosexual, 2 were inactive, 13 were still bisexual, and 15 (50%) were exclusively heterosexual. The remaining 4 patients were "inactive" at the beginning of treatment, and on report none were exclusively heterosexual. The proportion finishing exclusively heterosexual increased as the number of sessions increased. Bieber *et al.* present interesting and important data comparing the 27 patients who had had 150 hours of treatment or more and who terminated as being exclusively heterosexual with the 26 who, despite having a similar amount of treatment, remained exclusively homosexual (the remainder, 25 of the 78 who received 150 hours or more of treatment, finished bisexual). Significant differences between the groups were found for degree of motivation—the successful patients having a higher degree of motivation, for age on entering treatment—the successful patients being younger and for previous heterosexual genital experience. This last comparison is particularly interesting. Thirteen of those who finished treatment exclusively homosexual had never tried heterosexual genital contact, whilst none of those who terminated as exclusively heterosexual fell in this category. Highly significant differences were also found in several aspects of pre-treatment heterosexual attitudes, the successful group generally displaying more favourable attitudes than the unsuccessful group. It is clear that the 19% of the total series described by Bieber as exclusively homosexual at the onset of treatment but who finished exclusively heterosexual, had all had *some* heterosexual experience in the past. The description of exclusive homosexuality refers to their status at the *beginning* of treatment only and not to their behaviour throughout their total life history. The total failure with those who had *always* been Kinsey 6's is in accord with our own experience recorded in Chapters 3 and 5.

To recapitulate, 27% of Bieber's total sample of 106 were exclusively heterosexual at the time of report. This is a rather higher proportion than was found by either Curran and Parr (1957), Woodward (1958), or Coates (1962). The relative degree of success possibly reflects both the highly selected nature of a fee-paying sample and the great deal of effort represented by several hundred hours of treatment. Unfortunately, Bieber *et al.* do not state precisely what bisexuality at the end of treatment means. The fact that a person is practising both homosexuality and heterosexuality does not necessarily mean that he enjoys the latter, which may have the function of a social cover. We are left with the conclusion that 27% of 106 homosexual patients treated privately by psychoanalysis and followed up for an unstated period of time had become exclusively heterosexual in behaviour at the time of the report. A degree of improvement had occurred in at least another 12% of the sample in that 14 patients who were exclusively homosexual at the onset of treatment were bisexual at the time of the report.

With the exception of the series reported by Allen (1958) and Ellis (1956)—samples which were smaller in number and rather biased in reporting—the Bieber series is the most optimistic in outcome reported to date by psychoanalysts or psychotherapists. It appears to represent the best result that can be expected in a series of psychoanalytically treated patients, particularly when these are self-selected and fee-paying .The favourable prognostic signs are much the same as those in the two samples of patients reported in Chapters 3 and 5, namely a prior heterosexual interest and a tendency to be in a younger age group (under

35). As no attempt is made in any psychoanalytical approach to increase avoidance of males, whilst a good deal of attention is paid to increasing approach to females—made most explicit in the paper by Ovesey *et al.* (1963)—some sort of desensitization, to use the behavioural language, may have been responsible at least in part for the degree of success obtained by psychoanalysis. As was pointed out in the discussion of the Ovesey paper, it is not clear whether this is due to a direct attempt at desensitization, or occurs indirectly, through lengthy discussions of material concerning the nature and origins of attitudes unfavourable to females as sexual partners. However, the very explicit emphasis on heterosexual avoidance throughout the Bieber book, and the conclusion of these authors that it is one of the major features of homosexuality, is very much in accord with our views, which are amplified in Chapter 8.

B. TREATMENT BY BEHAVIOUR THERAPY

Although aversive techniques have been used for many years in the treatment of alcoholism (Franks, 1960) prior to the 1950's, there appears to be only one reference (Max, 1935) to the treatment of sexual deviations by aversion therapy. Max used a classical conditioning approach in that his patient phantasized the attractive sexual stimulus in conjunction with electric shocks. Max reported "a diminution of the emotional value of the sexual stimulus" which lasted for several days after each experimental period, the effect being cumulative over 3 months. Four months after treatment the patient reported a 95% degree of success, but no further details are given.

The majority of the reports of the use of aversion therapy are confined to small numbers of patients, and few series of a satisfactory size have yet appeared in the literature. Those which have so far been reported are described below, following which brief reference will be made to the individual case studies.

1. FREUND (1960)

Freund used a mixture of caffeine and apomorphine in order to produce nausea and vomiting (the unconditioned response). Slides of males were shown to the patient to coincide with the aversive effects of the chemical stimuli. Freund also tried to increase approach behaviour to females by means of a second phase of treatment; the patient was shown films of females 7 hours after he had been administered testosterone propionate.

Freund reported on a series of 67 patients treated in this manner; treatment was refused to none of those referred to him. Twenty of his patients were referred by the courts, and only 3 of these made any kind of heterosexual adaptation, in no case lasting more than a few weeks. The first follow-up occurred after 3 years. Of the 47 remaining patients, 12 had shown some long-term heterosexual adaptation, and the second follow-up, 2 years later, further reported on the history of these 12 patients. None of them were able to claim complete absence of homosexual desires, and only 6 a complete absence of homosexual behaviour. In fact 3 of the group were practising homosexuality fairly regularly. Although 10 did have sexual intercourse at least once a fortnight, only 3 found females other than their wives sexually desirable.

2. SCHMIDT et al. (1965)

This paper is headed "A retrospective study of 42 cases of behaviour therapy". The cases, which were treated by various techniques of behaviour therapy, ranged from phobias through sexual deviations of various kinds including homosexuality to obsessional symptoms, alcoholism, and writer's cramp. Sixteen of the 42 were diagnosed as displaying homosexuality, and of these, 13 were treated by "aversion relief therapy" (see Feldman, 1966, for a detailed critique. The work of this group is further referred to in Chapter 2). Ten of the 16 were described as practising homosexuals and 6 as latent homosexuals, the latter term being defined as "those patients who considered themselves as homosexuals and feel attracted to men but who have never really indulged in homosexual practices"; no definition is given of the term "really". Seven of the 10 practising homosexuals refused to continue with treatment before it was judged to have been completed. The remaining 3 patients were described as being markedly improved on discharge from treatment. Five of the 6 latent homosexuals were described on discharge as being markedly improved and 1 as moderately improved. Follow-up data (an average of 14 months elapsed between the completion of treatment and final follow-up) is provided on 19 out of the 32 patients of the original sample of 42 who completed treatment. These 19 are not broken down by original diagnosis, so that no separate data are available for the patients who were diagnosed as homosexual, whether practising or latent. No data are provided concerning the nature and duration of pre-treatment and post-treatment homosexual practices. The incompleteness of the data provided in this paper prevents any other observation being made except, perhaps, that any treatment technique which leads to 7 out of 16 patients leaving treatment before its conclusion is capable of considerable improvement.

3. BRIERLEY (1964)

For the sake of completeness the above paper, which was read to a psychiatric meeting in the north of England, will be briefly described. Brierley used what he called "rough shock" (Brierley, personal communication, 1965) in the context of a conditioning technique which involved the patient being shown slides of homosexual stimuli and simultaneously receiving an electric shock. He treated a total of 34 cases of indecent exposure, fetishism, and assault, as well as homosexuality. Ten of the series were homosexuals, 6 of whom completed the course of treatment; of the latter group of 6, 4 appeared to have improved over a follow-up period of unspecified length. Brierley assigned the majority of his sample a Kinsey rating of 5 or 6. However, he provided no data on the basic sexual behaviour which would support or otherwise the particular rating given. Nor did he give detailed data on the length of the follow-up period; but from the information provided it seems that this was a year on average. No data were available on the nature of the improvement or whether this was confined to an apparent cessation of homosexual practice, or, in addition, included an increase in or a return to heterosexual behaviour. No further reports have been provided by Brierley on this series.

4. SOLYOM AND MILLER (1965)

This paper reports on a series of 6 homosexual patients treated by what appears to be a classical conditioning technique. Solyom and Miller did not assign Kinsey ratings to their patients, but from the descriptions of the sexual behaviour which they do provide, 4 of them at least merit a Kinsey rating of 6, and the other 2 one of 4 or 5. The treatment appeared to be unsuccessful with all 6 patients, 1 of whom discontinued treatment before it was completed. In discussing their relative lack of success, the authors point out that 3 of the patients had had extensive psychotherapy prior to entering upon aversion therapy, and 1 had been diagnosed as schizophrenic.

5. McGUIRE AND VALLANCE (1964)

These authors present treatment results for a variety of patients who were treated by a classical conditioning technique and self-administered electric shock; the latter feature of their technique is further discussed in Chapter 2. Of their patients, 6 were homosexuals, 3 of whom discontinued treatment and 3 showed an improvement which is listed under the heading "mild, good and symptom removed", no further details being given. In most cases the follow-up time was a month. In a later paper (McGuire *et al.*, 1965) this group claim "at least as good results as the more elaborative mimes and cues provided by other aversion therapists". Unfortunately, they provide no data to support their claims. In a personal communication, McGuire has informed the authors that he is continuing to apply his technique, but regards it as a clinical approach, and is not collecting data for analysis as a series.

6. LEVIN *et al.* (1967)

This paper is of interest in that, although it only reports upon 2 patients, 1 of whom was a transvestite, and therefore outside the bounds of the present review, the treatment technique used combined aversion and desensitization. A very full description of the previous sexual and social behaviour of the homosexual patient is given, and it is stated that he had had a year of traditional psychotherapy prior to entering upon behaviour therapy. The patient received 40 reciprocal inhibition sessions over a period of 16 weeks, the hierarchies used being concerned with assertive behaviour, competition with men, rejection by women, and demands by women. The aversive technique used was a more or less precise reproduction of that described by Feldman and MacCulloch (1965). Levin *et al.* report both a decreased avoidance of females and a decreased attraction to males, both appearing to be related to the particular technique used. In Chapter 8, reference is made to the possible future desirability of combining aversion and systematic desensitization within the same treatment setting.

Finally, there are a number of papers reporting the use in treatment of imaginal stimuli; i.e. the patient was required to visualize a scene verbally described by the therapist.

7. STEVENSON AND WOLPE (1960)

The authors report the treatment of 3 patients displaying sexual deviations, 2 of whom were homosexual, treated by desensitization, which was intended to encourage assertive behaviour towards other people in general and to females in particular. The first homosexual patient received 10 sessions of desensitization, and the second 21 sessions. Both were followed up for at least 3 years, and in both cases a complete success is recorded. It is of interest that in both cases treatment involved very little discussion of homosexual behaviour, being largely confined to attitudes to females. The explanation for the anxiety towards females displayed by their 2 patients which was given by Stevenson and Wolpe is related in many ways to that of Ovesey et al. (1963), described earlier in the chapter. We have therefore a considerable degree of similarity of rationale between a psychoanalytically orientated approach and a behaviourally orientated one.

8. GOLD AND NEUFELD (1965)

The technique of covert sensitization is related both to desensitization and to aversion therapy and was used by Gold and Neufeld (1965) to treat a 16-year-old homosexual. The patient was relaxed and then asked to visualize a succession of images, each of which included homosexual stimuli, but in an unpleasant rather than a pleasant setting. In later sessions, treatment included requests to imagine both attractive females associated with pleasant suggestions, and men associated with unpleasant suggestions. Follow-up over a year showed clear evidence of a change of sexual orientation. Further reports, each on one or two cases, have been given by Kolvin (1967) and Cautela (1967).

9. BARLOW et al. (1969)

A recent study by Barlow et al. (1969) on 2 patients, one a case of paedophilic behaviour (the sexual object being small girls), the other homosexual behaviour, provides further support for the possible usefulness of covert sensitization. They paired sexually arousing scenes with nauseous scenes for a number of sessions, followed by a series of extinction sessions, in which sexually arousing scenes were presented alone, and finally, a return to the former type of trial for the last few sessions (re-acquisition). Response was measured both by a card-sort measure of descriptions of sexually arousing scenes, and GSR (considered to indicate sexual arousal, and recorded prior to every second session during treatment). Both the card-sort measures and the GSR measures rose during extinction and declined during re-acquisition. Both patients showed some evidence of improvement in self-reported behaviour outside treatment, but no follow-up data are given. Barlow et al. consider that their study provides evidence "that pairing a noxious scene with a sexually arousing scene is a crucial procedure in covert sensitization" (demonstrated by response during extinction when the noxious scene was omitted). They also consider that imaginal noxious stimuli can replace physical aversive stimuli such as shock. The advantage in ease of administration is indeed obvious, and Barlow and his colleagues are carrying out further research into the technique. Further research is also needed in the indexing both of the occurrence of visual imagery and of sexual arousal. One advantage of aversion therapy is that it may be administered by a junior psychologist using largely automated apparatus; sensitization appears to make more demands on the interpersonal skills of the therapist.

Unfortunately, prior to the study reported in Chapter 5, there had been no direct attempts to compare psychotherapy and aversion therapy, although the next paper to be described promises, at first sight, to provide such a comparison.

10. MEYER (1966)

The title of this paper is somewhat misleading, in that it seems to promise a controlled trial of psychoanalysis and behaviour therapy. In point of fact, what Meyer has done is compare the series separately published by Freund (1960) and by Bieber *et al.* (1963). The latter series is added to by a number of cases separately reported to Meyer by Bieber. Meyer concluded that whether the criteria of success adopted by Bieber, or those adopted by Freund are used, the results of psychoanalysis are very much superior to those of aversion therapy. It will be recalled that 5 years after treatment, only 6 out of the 47 of Freund's patients who presented other than due to court referral could claim complete absence of homosexual practices, and only 3 others found females other than their wives sexually desirable. That is, only 9 out of 47, or 16.2%, could be considered successful. By way of contrast, using the same rather loose criteria, Meyer reports that 36.8% of Bieber's series were successful. The two samples are not, of course, in any way comparable. Bieber's subjects were fee-paying, and were selected by their therapist for report to Bieber and his colleagues. Freund's patients were neither selected nor fee-paying. The psychoanalytical patients were all in treatment for a minimum of 150 sessions; Freund's patients in no case had more than 24 sessions of treatment. Perhaps most important is the fact that the length of follow-up of the Bieber sample is unknown, and in most instances the assessment of outcome appears to have been made immediately after treatment. On the other hand, the follow-up on Freund's patients was made 5 years after completion of treatment. It is also worth pointing out that Freund used apomorphine as the aversive stimulus in the context of a classical conditioning technique. Several authors, e.g. Rachman (1965) and Feldman (1966), have argued that electrical aversion is likely to be considerably more effective than is chemical aversion in view of the increased ease of control of timing. More detailed support for the superiority of electrical aversion is given in Chapter 2. What Meyer has done is to compare a sample of fee-paying American patients treated by highly trained analysts, self-selected, and probably selected for reporting by their analysts, with a sample of patients from eastern Europe, probably unselected, receiving less than one-sixth the amount of treatment time and treated by a technically unsound form of aversion therapy. These differences are so great that Meyer's comparison is invalid, and no weight can be attached to his conclusion that psychoanalysis is superior to aversion therapy. It is concluded that prior to the controlled trial reported in Chapter 5, there had been no direct comparison between psychotherapy and behaviour therapy, and that the one indirect comparison was completely unsatisfactory.

C. HORMONAL METHODS OF TREATMENT

For the sake of completeness, brief reference will be made to hormonal methods of treatment. Swyer (1954) cited evidence that the capacity for sexual response is not primarily dependent upon the sexual hormones, and that the direction of development of sexual interest is influenced mainly by psychological and environmental conditioning. He concluded from a review of the reports of treatment using endocrines, that hormones do little more than modify the intensity of sexual activity and that the use of sex hormones in treatment had been largely disappointing. A recent review of the results of hormonal methods by West (1968) also refers to various other occasionally used and ineffective physical methods such as electro-convulsive therapy and castration. West found little evidence for the use of hormones in the treatment of homosexuality, the major finding being that androgenic hormones stimulate sexual desire without altering the direction of sexual interest. Conversely, oestrogenic hormones reduce the level of desire without altering the direction of interest.

D. CONCLUSION

This review of the results of treatment of homosexuality has revealed a lamentable lack of information both on patients under treatment and the outcome of that treatment in most of the reported series and single cases. Nor is there a single instance of a controlled trial in which the different techniques are systematically compared. However, there is some evidence that a proportion of the homosexual patients made a satisfactory response to treatment, both by psychotherapy/psychoanalysis and behaviour therapy. A major sign found to be prognostic of success was a previous history of sexual attraction to the opposite sex. There are suggestions that *both* the increase of attraction to females and the decrease of attraction to males are relevant to successful therapy. Finally, the fact that both psychoanalysts and the behaviourists emphasize the importance of fear of female sexual stimuli both in establishing and maintaining male homosexual behaviour, suggests the existence of a common ground between the two apparently opposed standpoints, and the value of directing research towards heterosexual as well as homosexual attitudes and behaviour.

CHAPTER 2

THE DEVELOPMENT OF A TREATMENT TECHNIQUE

A. INTRODUCTION

At the time when the research reported in this book began, that is at the end of 1962, the major effort in the behaviour therapy field had been in such problems as phobias and obsessions (Wolpe, 1958). With the exception of the large series reported by Freund (1960), only a small number of single case studies had been reported on the application of behaviour therapy to sexual deviations, and these were reviewed by Rachman (1961). No doubt more concerned to make a case for the clinical usefulness of such approaches, Rachman made little attempt to assess them critically. A detailed critique of the aversion therapy techniques which had been described by the middle of 1965 was undertaken by Feldman (1966), and some of the points made in that paper are repeated in this chapter.

We felt that there were two main arguments in favour of applying learning techniques to the treatment of sexual deviations. Firstly, the outcome of treatment by various psychotherapeutic techniques was rather poor—a point amply made in Chapter 1. Secondly, there was the intrinsic interest of applying laboratory-derived learning theory principles to a field in which the problem was one of real life behaviour. It was felt that sexual behaviour could be described as consisting of two components—an intrinsic mediational component and an extrinsic behavioural component. The possibility of directly manipulating the latter, and hence of influencing the former, was theoretically, at any rate, quite evident. Unfortunately, of course, most of the overt responses involved in homosexual behaviour could not be reproduced in a laboratory setting and would not, therefore, be available for manipulation. However, it was considered that homosexual behaviour could be thought of as a chain of responses beginning with the visual response of looking at an attractive sexual object. At least one sexual response was thus available for laboratory manipulation, and it is this response which has been utilized by most of the behavioural approaches reviewed in Chapter 1. The majority of aversion therapists have used classical conditioning, i.e. the attempt is made to associate anxiety or fear (consequent on the application of an aversive stimulus) with the previously attractive homosexual stimulus, the patient being the passive recipient of stimuli. We have preferred to use instrumental conditioning, in which escape or avoidance from the punishing stimulus is contingent on the performance of a specific operant response —the avoidance of the previously attractive stimulus. In all the conditioning techniques used, the underlying aim (although this has frequently not been specifically stated) has been to suppress the visual response of looking—in reality or phantasy—at an attractive but socially inappropriate stimulus. The intention has been that this effect would generalize over the chain of homosexual responses which are not available for laboratory manipulation.

Although very little information existed concerning the practical application of learning techniques in the field of sexual deviations, a good deal of laboratory data concerning the probable relevance of many variables was available from nearly half a century of research work. Matters have improved considerably in recent years, but the criticism made by Eysenck (1965a) concerning the very limited extent to which behaviour therapy techniques in general had been derived in any logical way from the general body of the experimental psychology of learning, very much applied when we began our research work. Eysenck made the following general statement: "For all the attention that is being paid to them by practitioners in the field, the theoretical and experimental advances in learning and conditioning methodology might just have well not taken place." We decided to make as serious an attempt as possible to base whatever technique we decided upon very firmly on findings made in experimental psychology. The most important consideration in designing a learning technique for the treatment of homosexuality appeared to be the securing of a high degree of resistance to extinction. It was thought vital that, once established, the new pattern of sexual interest should persist for as long as possible. We anticipated that the use of an aversive technique would win a breathing space within which the patient might acquire (or re-acquire) an interest in heterosexual behaviour. Obviously, the longer the breathing space the better for the patient. Hence, in selecting a learning technique we needed to concern ourselves not only with the ease of acquisition of avoidance responses to homosexual stimuli and approach responses to heterosexual stimuli, but also with the extent to which these newly acquired responses would resist relapse outside the treatment situation. It has been pointed out by Kimble (1961) that the explanation of resistance to extinction is largely related to the conditions of acquisition of the response concerned. We needed a training technique which led both to reasonably quick acquisition and, more important, to very strong resistance to extinction. The most useful review of the various techniques of avoidance learning has been given by Solomon and Brush (1956). This is summarized in Feldman and MacCulloch (1965), and our conclusion was that the technique of anticipatory avoidance learning (Solomon *et al.*, 1953) produces both reasonably good acquisition and has a very high resistance to extinction. Solomon and Wynne (1953) used dogs as their subjects, one dog being placed in a cage separated by a fence from a second cage. Eight seconds after the onset of a buzzer, the dog received a shock. Leaping over the fence terminated both the buzzer and the shock. It was usual for several trials to be required before the dog learned to anticipate the shock and to leap over the fence before it ensued, hence terminating the buzzer and avoiding the shock. Once established, the response showed no tendency to extinguish. Solomon *et al.* (1953) experienced very great difficulty in extinguishing the avoidance response of their dogs, which persisted over many hundreds of trials after the shock had been removed. Solomon introduced the concepts of conservation of energy and partial irreversibility of responses acquired in this manner, in order to account for his findings. More recently, Turner and Solomon (1962) have extended the anticipatory avoidance technique to humans, and have demonstrated that it is readily possible to set up fairly quickly stable avoidance responses to a neutral conditioned stimulus (CS) which were strongly resistant to extinction. They also showed that the most effective variety of anticipatory avoidance learning involved the subject performing an operant response rather than a reflexive one. That is, one in which the subject had to move a shuttle from side to side in order to switch off a sound stimulus rather than one in which a toe flexion, originally conditioned as a reflex response to shock, switched off the sound. Solomon *et al.* (1968) have carried out further research on avoidance behaviour in dogs, but instead of the neutral stimulus of a buzzer they used an attractive and very strongly learnt stimulus, namely meat, as the CS. They found that punishing the dogs (swatting with a rolled newspaper) just as they approached the food, was more successful in setting up and maintaining the response of not eating meat than punishing them after they had either begun to eat or finished eating. Instead of eating the meat, the dogs turned to an initially less-sought-after dish of bone-meal, emphasizing the importance of providing an alternative outlet for the drive concerned—in this case hunger. The nearest situation to the one involved in the treatment of homosexuality was also reported in the literature after we had begun our research. Aronfreed and Reber (1965) have shown that for child subjects playing with dolls, administering the aversive stimulus (verbal disapproval) as they were about to touch the doll, was more effective in setting up an avoidance response than administering it after they had picked it up and had begun to play with it. Aronfreed (1965) has, in fact, built rather an impressive theory of the development of moral behaviour, using the notion of anticipatory avoidance as one of the main learning paradigms.

It was decided to design a technique which would reproduce, with appropriate variations for human subjects and homosexual stimuli, that used by Solomon and his colleagues with animal subjects. It was also decided to build into this technique all the variables which have been shown to increase resistance to extinction. It might well have been that a simple reproduction of the anticipatory avoidance paradigm would have been sufficient in itself, but it seemed advisory to optimize the likelihood of success.

B. THE RELEVANT VARIABLES

1. INTER-STIMULUS INTERVAL

The too frequent occurrence of training trials might be expected to lead to the rapid build-up of reactive inhibition, and thence to the possibility of permanent decrement of the avoidance response through the development of conditioned inhibition (Feldman, 1963). Trials should therefore be well distributed rather than massed.

2. THE INTENSITY OF THE UNCONDITIONED STIMULUS

Kimble (1955) showed that avoidance response time shortened as shock increased, up to an asymptote, beyond which increasing the shock had no further effect. From this it can be deduced that there is little point in bombarding the patient with very high levels of shock. All that is required is one sufficiently intense for him to find it more unpleasant than he finds the CS (e.g. a male stimulus) to be pleasant.

3. CONDITIONED STIMULUS—UNCONDITIONED STIMULUS INTERVAL

Solomon and Brush (1956), discussing the results of their technique of avoidance training, concluded that it is particularly important that contiguity should occur throughout. That is, the performance of the instrumental avoidance response should be contiguous with CS offset, and on those trials on which the subject fails to perform the avoidance response, hence receiving a shock, the offset of the shock and of the CS should both occur contiguously with the eventual performance of the escape response. They further concluded that the importance of the shock was not the length of its duration but the fact of its occurrence.

4. MODE OF INTRODUCTION OF SHOCK

Miller (1960) has demonstrated that gradually increasing the strength of the shock enabled successful habituation to high-level shocks and resulted in less avoidance learning in rats than when they immediately received a high-level shock with no gradual habituation. From personal discussions with several psychologists working in the field of aversion therapy, it seems that quite often patients are subjected to gradually increasing shocks so that they have the opportunity of habituating to them. The result in some cases has been that patients have adapted to the strongest available shock, the aversive power of which is thus lost.

5. PERCEPTUAL SALIENCE

It is a general rule that learning is most effective when the CS stands out clearly from the visual and auditory background. Hence avoidance training should as far as possible be carried out in rooms which are darkened and sound-proofed.

6. PARTIAL REINFORCEMENT

Humphreys (1939) demonstrated that a random alternation of reinforcement and non-reinforcement in eyelid conditioning led to a very considerably increased resistance to extinction. This fact has been demonstrated on many occasions since. Whatever the explanation of the finding (Lewis, 1960), the fact of its occurrence is undoubted. In an instrumental avoidance training situation, this implies that some attempts to avoid should succeed (reinforcement) and others should fail (non-reinforcement). That is, on the latter type of trial, despite making the avoidance response, the patient should be shocked. Reinforced and non-reinforced trials should be alternated randomly.

7. DELAY OF REINFORCEMENT

There are many data on the effect of delay of positive reinforcement on the acquisition and resistance to extinction of an approach response. As summarized by Renner (1964), the results suggest that while constant delay will retard acquisition and may retard resistance to extinction, variable delay may or may not retard acquisition but will lead to considerably increased resistance to extinction. Further, variable delay is essentially the same phenomenon as partial reinforcement. Unfortunately, there are comparatively few data on the effect of delay of negative reinforcement (e.g. shock) on the acquisition and resistance to extinction of an avoidance response. However, Crum et al. (1951) have demonstrated that varied delay of punishment leads to greater resistance to extinction than immediate punishment.

The work discussed above is concerned with learning situations in which the criterion response is emitted only once on each trial, such as a rat moving down a runway across a barrier. In the aversion therapy situation, the avoidance response might well be that of a patient pressing a switch to remove a picture (CS) which has acquired noxious qualities by association with shock. In this case, therefore, the avoidance response is such that it could easily be performed several times within a few seconds. The delay would thus consist of the failure of the picture to leave the screen immediately the patient presses the switch. Work by Amsel (1958) on frustrative non-reward suggests that frustration by delay results in increased motivation with the result that the rate of performance on the next trial is increased. He has also produced evidence that frustrative non-reward has the effect of increasing resistance to extinction, and has speculated that this phenomenon is rather similar to that of partial reinforcement, which also has the effect of increasing resistance to extinction (Amsel, 1962). It would seem, therefore, that the effect of randomly varying the delay time (i.e. the interval between the appearance of the picture and the eventual removal of the picture) would be further to increase the resistance to extinction of the avoidance response. The assumption here is that the first avoidance attempt is made very shortly after the appearance of the picture, thus providing sufficient time before shock onset for "delay" to have a perceptible effect.

8. VARIATION DURING TRAINING

McNamara and Wike (1958), Crum *et al.* (1951), and McClelland and McGowan (1953) have shown that the greater the variation of stimulus conditions during training, the greater the resistance to extinction. The explanation for this finding appears to involve the concept of generalization decrement. That is, the more the training situation and the real life situation differ, the more rapidly will extinction occur. Hence one should try to make the training situation both as realistic as possible and as varied as possible, thus simulating real life in so far as one is ever able to do so in a therapeutic situation. It follows, for instance, that varying the interval of time between successive trials would also be expected to increase resistance to extinction, although there appears to be no direct evidence upon this point.

9. QUANTITY OF REINFORCEMENT

McClelland and McGowan (1953) showed that varying the quantity of reinforcement in a random fashion also increased resistance to extinction. In the present situation, randomly varying the level of shock, administered on non-reinforced trials, would therefore be expected to have this effect. (Reinforcement, in the present context, is given by the relief of anxiety consequent upon shock avoidance.)

To summarize, the variables relevant to conditioned avoidance are as follows:

(1) Learning trials should be distributed rather than massed, and the inter-trial interval should vary randomly.
(2) Contiguity of stimulus and response, particularly at offset, should be maintained throughout.
(3) Shock should be introduced at whatever level has been found to be unpleasant to the patient rather than gradually increased, thus possibly enabling the patient to habituate.
(4) Partial reinforcement should be used in conjunction with instrumental techniques.
(5) Reinforcements should be variable rather than fixed, both in ratio and in interval schedules.
(6) Delaying a proportion of the patient's attempts to avoid should lead to greater resistance to extinction than immediate reinforcement.

(7) In general, the greater the variation in the conditions of training, the more will these approximate to the real-life situation. This avoids, as far as possible, generalization decrement, which is probably the most potent source of rapid extinction.

C. THE AVERSIVE STIMULUS: CHEMICAL OR ELECTRICAL?

The animal evidence on avoidance conditioning has almost all been based on the use of an electrical aversive stimulus. By way of contrast, prior to the beginning of our research, avoidance conditioning of human patients had, for the most part, used apomorphine as the aversive stimulus. This has been particularly so in the case of the aversion treatment of alcoholism (Franks, 1960). Franks has pointed out that it is extremely difficult to control the time relationship between CS and the UCS in chemical aversion, despite the strong evidence for the importance of this relationship if successful avoidance learning is to be achieved (Kimble, 1961). There are considerable individual differences in reactivity to the various nausea-producing drugs. People differ both in the speed and the extent of their reaction to the various drugs, and, moreover, the same person may react differently to the same quantity of drug on different days, and even at different times on the same day. The use of chemical noxious stimuli also makes it very difficult to carry out accurate measurements of the responses which are being elicited, whilst the physical movement that often attends nausea and vomiting further increases the difficulty of carrying out recordings. Particularly important is the fact that the arduous and complicated nature of the chemical aversive conditioning situation makes it impracticable to provide frequent repetitions of the association between the CS and the UCS. The number of trials within any one session is therefore considerably restricted. A further restriction is the heavy demands that are made on the nursing staff. These demands are not only in terms of time, but also of the unpleasantness of the situation, which has frequently led to reports of nursing staff complaining about the distastefulness of the treatment (Rachman and Teasdale, 1969). By way of contrast, electrical stimulation can be precisely controlled. The shock can be given for a precise period of time, at a measured intensity, and at exactly the desired moment. These variables can all be manipulated as the therapist desires, so that the treatment situation becomes much more flexible. Moreover, it is easier to use partial reinforcement, and this is particularly important from the point of view of increasing resistance to extinction. It is also possible to make more accurate measurements of the progress of treatment. In connection with this last point, a good deal of objective measurement data are reported in other chapters of this book, none of which would have been possible with the use of chemical aversive stimuli. The use of an electrical aversive stimulus does not require more than one therapist to be present, and hence it is less arduous to administer. The likelihood of physical side-effects, particularly of a dangerous kind, is also rather less than in the case of chemical aversion.

Rachman and Teasdale (1969) have very rightly drawn attention to some of the disadvantages of electrical aversion. For instance, the administration of electrical aversive stimuli in laboratory experiments has been shown to give rise to aggressive behaviour (Ulrich et al., 1965). Similar reports have been given of aggressiveness, negativism, and hostility in clinical practice. People sometimes have an initial fear of electric shocks even before experiencing them in the clinical situation. This point emphasizes the importance of using a level of shock no higher than that which is just necessary to lead to avoidance behaviour. Bombarding the patient with very high levels of shock may only result in his leaving the treatment situation prematurely—it is possible that something of this kind happened in the series treated by Schmidt *et al.*(1965); 7 of the 10 practising homosexuals in this series left treatment before completion (see Chapter 1).

McGuire and Vallance (1964) described a classical conditioning technique in which the patient was required to signal to the therapist when the image of his usual phantasy was clear. When he did so, a shock was administered. The procedure was repeated throughout the 20–30-minute session, which was held up to 6 times per day. The next stage was that the small and completely portable electrical apparatus used in the treatment was handed over to the patient so that he could treat himself in his own home. He was told to use the apparatus whenever he was tempted to indulge in the phantasy concerned. One problem here lies in the interpretation of the term "clear". If this meant that the patient had achieved a complete representation of his usual phantasy, the point is raised that the authors may have been carrying out a variety of punishment learning (Estes, 1944). In this paradigm, the noxious stimulus occurred following the *completion* of the undesirable response. Estes showed extinction of a newly acquired avoidance response to be particularly rapid with this technique.

A further point of importance is that it was left to the patient himself to set the level of the shock, and this raises a problem discussed by Sandler (1964). He has provided a most useful discussion on the concept of masochism, defined as the situation in which a noxious stimulus does *not* result in the subject receiving it displaying avoidance. Conversely, the noxious stimulus appears to be not only tolerated but even sought after. Sandler described a large number of experimental analogues to various clinical forms of masochistic behaviour, so that, in the most dramatic examples, organisms have been found actually working for punishing results. The end result may be that "the aversive stimulus becomes positively reinforcing in the same process" (Skinner, 1953). This view is in accordance with psychoanalytical thinking. For instance, Fenichel (1945) states: "Certain experiences may have so firmly established the conviction that sexual pleasure must be associated with pain, that suffering has become the prerequisite for sexual pleasure." It is always possible that self-treating patients will use a fairly low level of shock: this level then becomes associated with a very well-reinforced event. Thus, far from electrical shock being averting, it might become part of the normal phantasy situation.

D. THE CHOICE OF THE CONDITIONAL STIMULUS

It seems clear that the treatment should be carried out in the presence of the therapist and under controlled conditions. It is still possible that it might be desirable to use the patient's own phantasies as the CS rather than stimuli introduced by the therapist. However, the patient may not always be able to reproduce his phantasy, and merely handing him pictures to look at may not be sufficient to hold his attention in face of the distractions of the treatment room. A mechanically projected picture has the advantages of clarity of reproduction and ease of control. Should it become possible for the occurrence of phantasy to become indexed in some objective way—work by Antrobus *et al.* (1967) raises this as a distinct possibility—then its use may become more practicable. At the time we designed our treatment set-up, the work of the Antrobus's had not been published. We decided to use slides of the relevant sexual stimuli; wherever possible, the patient provided his own photographs of satisfying real life stimuli in order to reduce the problem of generalization decrement.

E. THE INTRODUCTION OF AN ALTERNATIVE (HETERO-SEXUAL) RESPONSE

One of the major problems was to substitute for the deviant sexual behaviour a form of sexual outlet that was both desired by the patient and was socially possible. Ideally, this would involve overt heterosexual behaviour; in the context of the laboratory, only the use of heterosexual pictorial stimuli was possible. At the time our research began there were two publications concerning aversion therapy, both using apomorphine as the aversive stimulus, and both using pictorial stimuli in order to increase approach to females as well as attempting to set up sexual aversion to males. Freund (1960) showed his series of homosexual patients films of nude or semi-nude women 7 hours after the administration of testosterone propionate. James (1962) used a particularly intensive form of apomorphine aversive conditioning, and, in addition, during the 3 days following aversion treatment, photographs of sexually attractive young females were placed in the patient's room. Each morning the patient received an injection of testosterone propionate and was told to retire to his room whenever he felt any sexual excitement.

Rather than separating out the conditioning of aversion to males and of approach to females, we felt it desirable to try to carry out the two processes at more or less the same time. The fact that subjects exposed to aversive conditioning report feeling relief when the stimulus which had been associated with aversion is removed, suggested a method of doing so. There is experimental evidence (Kimble, 1961) concerning the desirability of introducing the female stimulus contiguous with the removal of the male stimulus, as follows: "stimuli associated with a cessation of shock are secondary reinforcers. Looking at it another way, they take on a value seemingly opposite of that acquired by stimuli which accompany shock onset." That is, the fact that the female slide is associated with the cessation of pain increases the likelihood that it will acquire positive reinforcing qualities. Thorpe *et al.* (1964) similarly used a relief stimulus; their technique can be criticized on the grounds of its predictability—the relief stimulus always appeared as the last presentation of each session, indicating the end of the session rather than the association, within the session, of the appearance of the female stimulus with the cessation of pain. Another method of increasing the strength of approach to female stimuli has been used by McGuire *et al.* (1965). They instructed their patients that whatever the initial stimulus to masturbation, the phantasy in the 5 seconds just prior to orgasm should be of normal sexual intercourse. Thorpe *et al.*, (1963) criticized their own somewhat similar technique on the grounds that its failure probably was due to backward conditioning (Kimble, 1961). A further objection can be made. It became clear during the course of our own work that several patients, of their own accord, attempted to phantasize females late in the masturbatory sequence. A frequent consequence was detumescence, thus adding a further increment of strength to the habit of not approaching females. It was decided that the most effective combination was to introduce female photographs as relief stimuli in order to initiate approach responses to females, and then gradually to shape these in the manner described by Ferster (1965). He argued that it was desirable to start with a response which was relatively likely to be reinforced, such as that of speaking to females, and then to proceed along the hierarchy of responses which are increasingly less likely to be reinforced, not moving to the next one in the hierarchy until the preceding one had been very well established. Our experience has been that it might well take as long as 6 months before sexual approach responses to females are really well established, particularly in those patients in whom such behaviour has been dormant for long periods of time—perhaps 10 years or more.

F. THE USE OF STIMULUS HIERARCHIES

Many of the aversion therapy techniques reviewed by Feldman (1966) have introduced male or female stimuli quite unsystematically, without regard to their relative degrees of attractiveness or repulsion to the patient. At the outset of treatment, the dominant sexual response is a homosexual one, the heterosexual response being non-dominant. The problem is to design the treatment so as to reverse this situation. We felt that the order of presentation of CS was a variable of considerable importance. Wolpe (1958) has emphasized the importance for the desensitization of avoidance behaviour of the patient beginning treatment by exposure to a situation which was only slightly anxiety-evoking, moving on to a more difficult situation when the previous step in the hierarchy was no longer evoking anxiety. Applying this principle to avoidance learning in the treatment of homosexuality, it seems logical to begin with a male stimulus which is only mildly attractive and to which an avoidance response may be set up with relative ease. It follows that if a female stimulus is introduced contiguous with the off-set of the male stimulus, it should be as attractive to the patient as possible. This both increases the ease of setting up an avoidance response to the male stimulus (Kimble, 1961, see above) as well as increasing the strength of approach to the female stimulus. Once the avoidance response to the first male stimulus is well established, one moves on to the next male slide, and, in a similar manner, when the approach response to the first female stimulus is well established, one moves to the next one. The patient is taken along hierarchies of ascending attractiveness of male stimuli and descending attractiveness of female stimuli. Indeed, the principles underlying the use of stimulus hierarchies are so well established in experimental psychology that their neglect by aversion therapists is rather surprising.

G. CLINICAL AND PERSONALITY FACTORS

Some of the aversion therapy reports are marked by rather moralistic overtones. This is particularly clear in the single case reports by Cooper (1963) and Clarke (1963), in both of which the authors used tape recordings which stressed the "disgusting and unpleasant" nature of the patient's sexual deviations. Apart from the fact that this might render the whole situation so unpleasant to force the patient into a "flight into health", a further factor should also be mentioned; this is the unsuitability, in our view, of the therapist expressing strong negative opinions concerning the patient's practices, particularly in the absence of evidence that such a degree of hectoring condemnation is essential to the effective outcome of treatment.

Westwood (1960) has pointed out that therapists tend to see an atypical sample of homosexuals. It is possible that this atypicality resides in the marked incidence of psychiatric disturbance displayed by homosexuals presenting themselves at psychiatric centres. As was pointed out in the previous chapter, people tend to appear for treatment when their behaviour results in them suffering in some way, frequently with anxiety or depression. The majority of the reported series and single cases described in Chapter 1 are marked by an inadequate psychiatric description of the patients concerned. This point is expanded in Chapter 7, in which evidence is presented of the importance for the outcome of treatment of pre-existing personality and psychiatric factors. The implication of this view is that it is most important for there to be full psychiatric participation in aversion therapy treatment to enable the diagnosis to be made of coexisting psychopathology, as well as treatment of this where necessary and possible. We would argue very strongly for behaviour therapists maintaining their links with, on the one hand, general experimental psychology, and, on the other, with clinical psychiatry. This is not to argue for a "kitchen sink" approach to treatment. None of the patients described in Chapters 3 and 5 and Appendix A received either drug therapy or psychotherapy as the sole or even major portion of their treatment (with the exception of the psychotherapy group— see Chapter 5 for a description of a controlled trial). However, some have received adjuvant drug therapy and most have received supportive psychotherapy of a superficial kind. This leads on to the problem of the patient–therapist relationship. Inevitably, the question arises of the degree of importance of this over and above the specific technique used. Coates (1964) has argued that in all of the conditioning techniques used thus far, the patient–therapist relationship has played a major if not always recognized part. The degree of importance attached to it by behaviour therapists has varied. Meyer and Gelder (1963) state: "those who wish to make use of learning theory to treat their patients should not ignore the relationship between the patient and the therapist." On the other hand, Wolpe (1962) has claimed to have specifically demonstrated the lack of importance of the patient–therapist relationship. Half-way through he handed over the treatment of a phobic patient to a junior psychiatrist. The patient made a complete recovery. Wolpe claims that this implies that the relationship between himself and the patient was not relevant to the outcome of the treatment. However, the patient was throughout in contact with *a* therapist, and the degree to which he perceived his therapists as providing support, re-assurance, and so on, is quite unknown. While behaviour therapists might prefer to regard the situation as a purely experimental one, the patient himself has a reinforcement history of having a "supportive" type of relationship with doctors and others associated with thera-peutic work, or at any rate a socially learned expectation of such relationships. Without accepting in any way the analytical insistence on the importance of this relationship being "transference" in type, it is impossible for us to ignore the fact that many of our homosexual patients treated by aversion therapy liked to talk about their problems, however superficially, and appeared to welcome the opportunity of doing so. We did not, however, at any time, make special attempts to encourage them to talk, nor have we in any way "interpreted" what they have said. Perhaps the simplest way to look at the question of the patient–thera-pist relationship in the context of aversion therapy is to understand that we are dealing with a form of behaviour which is socially unacceptable, and about which most patients feel guilty and anxious. It follows that the therapist has to reassure the patient that he is not being judged, but helped, or at any rate that an attempt at help will be made. Moreover, it seems unnecessarily rigid to decline to make any comments on the patient's reports of increasing success; throughout our work, therefore, we have expressed satisfaction and plea-sure with our patients' reports of progress, whilst refraining from adverse comment on lack of progress. At the same time, as will become clear in the course of this book, and particular-ly so from the case-history evidence in Appendix A, our criteria for accepting the occurrence of change are severe, and we have attempted to prove patients' claims to be false rather than accepting them at face value. It is in this connection that we have not relied solely on the clinical interview, which is subject to error, however searching it may be. Instead, we have developed as an additional and complementary tool for the assessment of change, a simple but effective questionnaire technique which is described in Chapter 4, together with supporting evidence concerning the reliability and validity of the technique.

H. THE TREATMENT TECHNIQUE

The technique which is described below was the one used for the series of 43 patients, which is described in Chapter 3. A more advanced and complex form of the technique was developed for the controlled trial, which is described in Chapter 5.

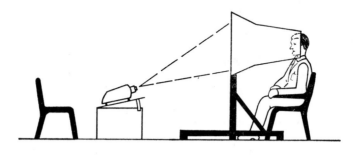

FIG. 2.1.

I. APPARATUS

1. SLIDE PRESENTATION

The patient sat in a wooden armchair. Six feet in front of him there was a ground-glass screen, 3 ft 6 in. by 2 ft 6 in., whose centre was at eye-level. The screen formed one end of a viewing box whose sides tapered as they approached the patient's face to form an oblong apex, 12 in. tall by 9 in. broad. The patient sat with his face just inside this, and the interior surface had a semicircle cut out to accommodate his neck. The apparatus was lined with matt black paper.

The slides were projected from an Aldis, magazine-loaded semi-automatic projector. It was found desirable to run the projector so that the patient could not see the light source directly. This was achieved by projecting from a low position so that the lens of the projector was below the level of the bottom rim of the glass screen. A diagrammatic sketch of the whole set-up is shown in Fig. 2.1. In order that, theoretically at any rate, the patient's only sensory input was visual, he was provided with ear-muffs manufactured by one of us (M.J.M.). The ear-muffs were attached to a perspex headband and consisted of two cloth-covered sponge-foam ear-pads of 3 in. diameter. They were subjectively found to reduce auditory acuity markedly when used upon ourselves and our patients.

2. THE ELECTRICAL STIMULUS

It was decided to use a battery-run induction coil for presenting the electrical stimulus (i.e. the UCS). Apart from the fact that it is psychologically sounder, electrical stimulation was also felt to be physiologically safer than chemical methods such as apomorphine. The batteries had a low capacitance, so that the chance of a serious mishap was very small.

The electrical stimulus was derived from a self-oscillatory induction coil with vibrating contact, similar in type to those on the market for entertainment purposes. The unit is battery-driven and consists of a magnetic/mechanical make–break circuit as used in an electrical buzzer. The current passed from the battery to the contacts adjacent to the magnetic core, and then through the primary winding of the induction coil back to the battery. The time integral of the induction coil was such that when the contacts opened, due to the magnetic attraction of the core, a high peak back e.m.f. was produced into what was, in effect, an exceedingly high resistance on open circuit. It was this pulse to which the patient was subjected.

The primary was fed from an 18-volt multi-tap battery, and there were two switches in this circuit. The first closed the circuit; the second enabled the battery to be tapped for preselected voltages. It was found that some patients' shock threshold was so high that 18-volt primary potential was sometimes required. The secondary circuit was connected to the patient via two nickel electrodes, $1\frac{1}{2}$ in. in diameter, cloth covered, and always soaked in saline. It was considered important to standardize the "sweat resistance" by adding physiological saline to the pads. In this way the patient's resistance was kept constant at successive sessions. The saline, although subject to an electrophoretic effect, was not dangerous. The application of naked electrodes could have resulted in the tattooing of nickel to the skin, and for a similar reason electrode jelly was avoided. The electrodes were placed over the posterior tibial group of muscles, avoiding the tibia and the lateral peroneal nerve. The positive and negative electrodes were randomly interchanged from right to left, and both legs were used randomly. It was thus impossible for the patient to habituate to set electrode positioning. Because of the cloth covers over the electrodes, sufficient saline was retained throughout the session to obviate drying for up to about 30 minutes. Both electrodes were applied to the same limb, thus avoiding current flow through the body itself.

The strength of the current applied was varied by the operator via a variable resistor. An alternative circuit was provided, so that a fresh pre-set stimulus could be introduced in order to avoid habituation. On the final circuit to the patient there was a cut-out switch which was operated by the patient. When he used this switch, the CS (CS1) was always switched off. The cut-out switch was "mastered" by a control switch on the therapist's control panel, so that on some occasions, as described earlier, the patient's attempt to remove the CS (CS1) was delayed. The intervals between slide presentations and the duration of the CS presentations were both measured by a stop-watch.

J. SEQUENCE OF EVENTS

We first presented the patient with a large series of slides of males, both clothed and unclothed. He was asked briefly to assess these for their degree of attractiveness. A number of them were selected and were then presented to him using the paired comparisons technique (Woodworth and Schlosberg, 1960), in order to arrange them in a hierarchy of attractiveness. The hierarchy obtained usually comprised about 8 slides, and provided as wide a range as possible of homosexual stimuli and behaviour. We started with a slide which was only mildly attractive, thus beginning at a relatively low point on the gradient of approach, so that it was as easy as possible to set up an avoidance response. (In much the same way, of course, Wolpe and his colleagues began to decondition a phobia by presenting a situation which evokes relatively little anxiety.) A hierarchy of female slides was set up in the same way but in the reverse order of attractiveness. That is, we began with the most attractive (for some patients this was more accurately described as the least unattractive) working up to the least attractive. We accumulated a large number of slides, some in colour and some in black and white. The pictures from which the male slides were made came both from magazines for the general public and from those which appear to have been specifically designed for homosexuals. If patients had any pictures in their possession of which they were particularly fond, then these were also used. The female pictures were also taken from magazines. In the case of both male and female pictures, we attempted to acquire a wide range of stimuli, varying from the totally clothed to the fully nude. We also used pictures which suggested various types of homosexual activity, although we have not yet used any of heterosexual activity. It was found particularly helpful to use pictures of males and females known to the patient in real life. In one case we were provided with pictures of a recent homosexual "affair", and in many cases we used pictures of wives or girl friends.

We then established that level of shock which the patient described as very unpleasant. Shock was increased up to this point in a step-wise manner so as to reduce the possibility of habituation.

We presented slides by back projection on to a viewing box. The room was in darkness and was in a quiet corner of the department.

The patient was told that he would see a male picture, and that several seconds later he might receive a shock. He was also told that he could turn off the slide by pressing a switch, with which he was provided, whenever he wished to do so, and that the moment the slide left the screen the shock would also be turned off. Finally, he was told that he would never be shocked when the screen was blank. It was made clear to him that he should leave the slide on the screen for as long as he found it sexually attractive. The first male slide was then presented. The patient had the choice of switching it off or leaving it on the screen. If switched off within 8 seconds, he was not shocked; this was termed an avoidance response. If he did not switch off within 8 seconds, he received a shock. If the shock strength was not sufficiently high to cause him to switch off immediately, it was increased until he did so. In practice this was hardly ever necessary. The moment the patient performed the switching-off response, the slide was removed and the shock terminated. This was termed an escape response. In addition to switching off, the patient was told to say "No" as soon as he wished the slide to be removed. It was hoped that a further increment of habit strength would accrue to the avoidance habit by means of this further avoidance response.

The usual course of events was as follows:

(i) Several trials in all of which escape responses were made.
(ii) A sequence of trials in some of which the patient escaped and in some of which he avoided.
(iii) A sequence of trials in which the patient avoided every time.

When he had avoided on three successive trials, we placed him on a predetermined schedule of reinforcement which had had built into it the variables which had been shown to increase resistance to extinction, as described earlier. There were three basic types of trial:

(i) Reinforcement (R) trials. One-third of all attempts to avoid were allowed to succeed immediately.

(ii) Non-reinforced (NR) trials. One-third of all attempts to avoid were not allowed to succeed; that is, in spite of the patient's attempts to switch off and to say "No", he had to sit out the 8 seconds and receive a brief shock. The shock and the slide terminated simultaneously.

(iii) Delayed (D) trials. One-third of all trials were delayed; that is, for a period of time within the 8-second period, the patient's attempts to switch off failed to succeed. He did eventually succeed before 8 seconds had elapsed. The length of time for which he was delayed, either $4\frac{1}{2}$, 6, or $7\frac{1}{2}$ seconds after the onset of the slide, varied randomly.

The three types of trial—reinforced, non-reinforced, and delayed—appeared in random order, and the inter-trial interval was also randomly varied.

When the patient both (i) reported that his previous attraction to the slide had been replaced by indifference, or even actual dislike, and (ii) attempted to switch off within 1 to 2 seconds of the slide appearing, we proceeded to the next male slide and repeated the process.

As well as attempting to increase the gradient of avoidance of male stimuli, we also attempted to decrease the gradient of avoidance of female stimuli. (Strictly speaking, we could not attempt to make females more attractive. All we could do was to attempt to make them less unattractive.) Several references were made in Chapter 1 to suggestions that many homosexuals are not merely indifferent to females, but frequently fear sexual contact with them. Hence it was necessary to attempt to reduce this anxiety. In order to do so, we used observations made during pilot experiments on colleagues, using neutral slides as the CS. When the pilot subjects were regularly performing avoidance responses, they reported experiencing considerable relief when the slide left the screen. Our patients also reported this in the clinical situation. We therefore made the introduction of the female slide contiguous with the removal of the male slide. That is, we attempted to associate relief of anxiety with the introduction of the female slide. However, a female slide was not introduced at every trial, thereby preserving the principle of attempting to reduce generalization decrement. Moreover, we allowed the patient to request the return of the female slide after it had been removed. (The female slide was always removed by the therapist and not by the patient, so that his habit of avoiding females was not strengthened in the training situation.) When wishing to request the return of the female slide, he was told to do so by clicking a switch and by saying "Yes" immediately after the female slide had been removed. The situation was such that the absence of a female slide meant that a male slide, by now associated with shock and hence anxiety-provoking, might reappear. Hence the patient gradually became motivated to request the return of the female slide. However, this request was met in an entirely random manner, sometimes being granted and sometimes not, so that the patient could not predict what would be the consequences of his attempting to switch off the male slide nor of his asking for the return of the female slide. The whole situation was designed to lead to the acquisition of two responses; firstly, attempts to avoid males, and, secondly, attempts to approach females.

We began by pairing the least attractive male picture with the most attractive (or least unattractive) female picture, and proceeded to the next female picture when the patient was regularly requesting the return of the first one. As has been explained earlier, we proceeded to the next male slide when the patient was both regularly and quickly rejecting the first one. The object of pairing slides in this manner was to reduce as far as possible the disparity between the degree of attractiveness of the male and female pictures, thus making easier

TABLE 2.1. PROGRAMME FOR AVOIDANCE TRAINING

Trial	Type	Shock intensity	Delay time (sec)	Time to next stimulus (sec)
1	D		$4\frac{1}{2}$	20
2	R_F			
3	D_{FF}		6	
4	R			25
5	NR			15
6	D		$4\frac{1}{2}$	35
7	D		$4\frac{1}{2}$	25
8	NR	Down		
9	NR	Up		30
10	R_F			
11	D_{FF}		$7\frac{1}{2}$	
12	R			25
13	NR	Down		
14	R			25
15	R			15
16	D_F		6	
17	D_{FF}		$7\frac{1}{2}$	
18	NR	Up		15
19	D		6	35
20	R_{FF}			
21	NR	Same		30
22	R_F			
23	NR	Up		30
24	NR	Down		15
25	D_{FF}		6	

Start at any point in the programme. Then proceed in circular manner: e.g. start at trial 6, proceed to 25, restart at trial 1.
Key: R = reinforced. NR = non-reinforced. D = delayed. F = female. FF = female reappears if requested.

the acquisition of avoidance to male sexual stimuli and the reduction of avoidance to female sexual stimuli.

The treatment schedule is shown in Table 2.1. This was rigidly adhered to, and in order to avoid the subject learning the schedule and thus being able to anticipate the nature of the next trial, we started at different points in the sequence for each session. About 25 trials per session were given, and each session lasted about 20 minutes: in-patients received two sessions of treatment per day. With out-patients, the length of time between sessions varied according to the patient's convenience.

CHAPTER 3

THE RESULTS OF AVERSION THERAPY
ON A SERIES OF HOMOSEXUAL PATIENTS

In this chapter we describe the results of the treatment by the technique described in Chapter 2 of a series of 43 homosexual patients, a brief account of which was previously given by MacCulloch and Feldman (1967a). The first patient was treated in July 1963, and the last in August 1965. All patients were followed up at various intervals of time after the end of treatment, and all were finally followed up in August and September 1966. There is a minimum follow-up on all patients of at least 12 months and a maximum one of over 3 years. The results of treatment are those which were reported by the patient at the time of the latest follow-up, i.e. at least a year after the end of treatment. We were able to follow-up all patients who completed treatment except for 3—2 who failed to appear for any follow-up after treatment and 1 who failed to appear after 3 months had elapsed after treatment. The remainder, apart from 7 who failed to complete treatment (of whom more below), have all been followed-up for the minimum period of a year.

Treatment was offered to all who appeared for interview; no selection criteria other than self-selection (two potential patients declined the offer) have been used. It was thought that unless all patients were accepted for treatment, no true assessment of criteria prognostic of success could be made. Thirty-six patients completed the full course of treatment and 7 failed to complete it. Six of the 7 terminated the treatment after 1 or 2 sessions, and 1 did so after 6 sessions. The remainder received a course of treatment which lasted from 5 sessions at one extreme to 38 sessions at the other. The average number of sessions received was 20. In all cases, treatment was continued until either a change of interest occurred or it became clear that no change was likely. The data which are given in this chapter refer, except where indicated, to the entire sample of 43. It is intended to present data in sufficient detail for the reader to compare this series with other previously published ones, as described in Chapter 1. It has been assumed that the 3 patients who, despite finishing treatment, failed to return for follow-up, have all relapsed and this assumption is made irrespective of any apparent improvement immediately after the completion of treatment. It has also been assumed that the 7 who failed to complete treatment had not changed spontaneously by September 1966, and are included, for purposes of analysis, in the failure group.

A. SOCIAL AND PERSONALITY FACTORS

The ages of the patients when they first appeared for treatment are shown in Table 3.1; it can be seen that there is no marked preponderance of young patients, 9 of the series being over the age of 40. The 7 patients who failed to complete treatment were fairly evenly distributed throughout the age range. Seven of the 43 patients, including 1 of those who

31

failed to complete treatment, were married. Two were females and were mutual partners in a lesbian "affair"; both were aged 18 and both completed treatment. All other patients were male homosexuals.

TABLE 3.1. AGE AT REFERRAL

Age range	No.
15–20	5
21–25	8
26–30	10
31–35	8
36–40	3
40+	9
Total	43

We now present data on the early histories of the patients. Two of the 43 had spent a period in an approved school and one had been to Borstal. Three had a considerable record of truancy whilst at school, and of these 3, 1 failed to complete treatment and 1 failed to respond.

Eight of the series had had an alcoholic father; of these, 4 themselves drank 5 pints of beer, or the equivalent, per day either when first interviewed or in the past, and all 4 drank for personality reasons (e.g. the reduction of social anxiety). In addition, 2 of the remaining 4 with an alcoholic parent also drank for personality reasons, although less than 5 pints per day. Of the remaining 35 only 5 reported that they drank 5 pints a day or the equivalent, either when first interviewed or in the past, and of these 5, 3 drank for personality reasons. There is thus a significant association ($p = < 0.01$) between a personal history of drinking and having an alcoholic father.

TABLE 3.2. ONE OR BOTH PARENTS ABSENT IN
PERIOD PRIOR TO PRESENTATION

Age during parental absence	No.
0–5	2
5–10	7
10+	10
Never	24
Total	43

Table 3.2 shows the numbers of patients who had one or both parents absent during the period in which they lived in the parental home, where "absence" is defined as a period of at least 6 months. It can be seen that only 2 patients had 1 parent absent before the age of 5, and 1 parent or both was absent between the ages of 5–10 in only 7 more. Slightly over half the series had grown up in a parentally intact home.

The educational history of the patients is shown in Table 3.3. Nearly half the series had passed the 11-plus examination or an equivalent, leading to a grammar school education,

TABLE 3.3. SCHOOL PERFORMANCE

Performance	No.
Poor (in the context of a secondary modern school)[a]	5
Average (in the context of a secondary modern school)[a]	13
Good (in the context of a secondary modern school)[a]	4
11+ or equivalent	21
Total	43

[a]Until recently the majority of British schoolchildren who failed to pass the 11+ examination were educated until the age of 15 in a secondary modern school.

as compared with the proportion in the population at large, which is probably around 20%. It seems, then, that whilst it may or may not be correct to say that homosexuality is more frequent amongst the better educated, those asking for help do appear to come more frequently from the better educated group. This imposes a limitation on generalizations made from those appearing for treatment in psychiatric centres to the population of homosexuals at large.

We also looked at the family histories of the patients in terms of mental illness and family criminal record. These data are shown in Table 3.4. Only 6 of the 43 patients had a definite history of psychiatric illness (psychosis or personality disorder) in the family and only one a family criminal record. Once again, as in the data concerning the extent to which their homes as children had survived intact, it seems likely that our patients came from backgrounds which were not markedly different from those of any other sample of the population.

TABLE 3.4. FAMILY HISTORY

(a) Psychiatric illness in the family	No.
Present	6
Absent	37
Total	43

(b) Family criminal record	No.
Present	1
Absent	42
Total	43

Seven of the series were married; 2 had 3 children, 2 had 2 children, 1 had 1 child and the other 2 married patients had no children. The proportion of the 7 who had children (5) probably did not differ from that in the population at large. It is a truism worth repeating that being married and having children does not necessarily indicate that the sexual preference is heterosexual.

TABLE 3.5. REASONS FOR APPEARING FOR TREATMENT

Reason	No.
On an order of the court	11
As sequel to court appearance (not on an order)	7
Pressure by wife or girl friend	2
Originally referred to psychiatric illness	4
Entirely on own accord	19
Total	43

Table 3.5 gives the reasons why patients appeared for treatment. Eighteen (42%) did so either on an order of the court, as a sequel to a court appearance or prior to a court appearance. This may have been due, to some extent, to the fact that the Director of the Department of Psychiatry at the hospital where this work was undertaken is a distinguished forensic psychiatrist. Four patients presented symptoms other than their homosexuality; all of them asked for treatment when they learnt that it was available. It is of some interest that of the 7 who failed to complete treatment, 5 presented either on an order of the court or in some way connected with a court appearance. This fact throws into some relief the results of treatment obtained in the series reported by Woodward (1958) and Coates (1962). It will be recalled that the proportion of success in both series was markedly lower than that reported by Bieber *et al.* (1963), despite the fact that all 3 series of patients were treated by some form of psychotherapy and that, at least in the case of the Coates series, a very large number of sessions of treatment was given. Table 3.6 shows the degree of association (non-significant) between age on presentation and mode of referral. Ten of the 13 who were aged 25 or under appeared entirely of their own accord. The fact that 3 of the over 40's also did so is indicative of the extent to which homosexuals may persist in a desire for treatment for many years.

TABLE 3.6. AGE ON PRESENTATION AND MODE OF REFERRAL

Referral	Age						No.
	15–20	21–25	26–30	31–35	36–40	40+	
Court order	1	1	3	2	0	4	11
Following court appearance (no court order)	0	0	2	3	0	2	7
Pressure by wife or girl friend	0	1	1	0	0	0	2
Other psychiatric condition	0	0	2	1	1	0	4
Own accord	4	6	2	2	2	3	19
Total	5	8	10	8	3	9	43

At the first interview we assessed the motivation for treatment, and the outcome of this assessment is shown in Table 3.7. The motivation for treatment was described as strong in just over half the series. All but 1 of those who failed to complete treatment were in the "low" or "equivocal" sections of Table 3.7. A further indication of the importance of age in

TABLE 3.7. MOTIVATION FOR TREATMENT

Level of motivation	No.
Low	4
Equivocal	14
High	25
Total	43

assessing a series of patients seeking treatment is provided in Table 3.8, which shows the relationship between age on presentation and the motivation for treatment. In 5 of the 9 over 40's, this was absent or equivocal, whereas in 10 of the 13 under 25's, motivation was strong. Once again, however, the fact that 4 of the over 40's had strong motivation for treatment is indicative of the extent to which some homosexuals struggle against their homosexual tendencies for many years.

TABLE 3.8. AGE ON PRESENTATION AND MOTIVATION FOR TREATMENT

Motivation	Age						No.
	15–20	21–25	26–30	31–35	36–40	40+	
Low	0	0	0	0	0	4	4
Equivocal	2	1	6	2	2	1	14
High	3	7	4	6	1	4	25
Total	5	8	10	8	3	9	43

We next turn to the extent to which our series of patients had been in trouble with the legal authorities because of their homosexual practices. Table 3.9 shows that slightly over one-half of the series had been charged and found guilty of at least one homosexual offence.

TABLE 3.9. CHARGED AND FOUND GUILTY OF HOMOSEXUAL OFFENCES

Number of offences	No.
0	21
1	17
2	4
3 or more	1
Total	43

It is worth noting, however, that in no single instance had any patient been on a charge concerned with homosexual practices carried out in private. The nearest to this which any of our patients had come, was one who had appeared on a charge arising from homosexual behaviour whilst in a van parked in a semi-public place (a quiet backstreet). It is clear, therefore, that the recent (1967) change in the law concerning homosexual offences would not have reduced by even 1 the number of charges which had been attracted by our series of patients. Table 3.10 shows the relationship between the age of presentation and the number of convictions for homosexuality. Not surprisingly, only 1 of those aged under 25 had such a conviction as opposed to all 9 of the over 40's.

TABLE 3.10. AGE ON PRESENTATION AND NUMBER OF CONVICTIONS FOR HOMOSEXUALITY

No. of convictions	Age						No.
	15–20	21–25	26–30	31–35	36–40	40+	
0	5	7	5	2	2	0	21
1	0	1	4	5	0	7	17
2	0	0	0	1	1	2	4
3 or more	0	0	1	0	0	0	1
Total	5	8	10	8	3	9	43

Considerable care was taken to make as full as possible an examination of the psychiatric status and the personality features of the patients. A more detailed discussion of the latter is given in Chapter 7, in which a description will be found of the personality classification described by Schneider (1959)—the descriptive system which is in use throughout this book. Table 3.11 shows the psychiatric status of our sample on presentation for treatment. It can

TABLE 3.11. PSYCHIATRIC STATUS ON PRESENTATION

	No.
(a) *Current chronic disorder*	
Schizophrenic defect state	1[a]
Personality disorder	25[a]
Nil	17
Total	43
(b) *Acute psychogenic reaction*	
Present	15
Absent	28
Total	43
(c) *Abnormal psychogenic development*	
Present	13
Absent	30
Total	43

[a]Combined in Tables 3.43 and 3.44.

be seen that 25 of the series had a personality disorder on presentation. In most cases, this was of the kind which causes the patient to suffer rather than causing other people to suffer. One patient was displaying a post-schizophrenic defect state. Fifteen patients, on presentation, were displaying an acute psychogenic reaction to either their homosexuality itself or to a connected court appearance. Thirteen displayed an abnormal psychogenic development throughout the course of their lives; that is, the development of unusual self-perceptions based either on their homosexuality or on other people's real or imagined reactions to it. Further psychiatric data are given in Table 3.12. The incidence of those who drank for personality reasons has already been commented on in an earlier section of this chapter. It is of interest that the majority of the 32 (25 + 7) who had experienced a reactive depression at some stage of their lives had done so as a consequence of their homosexuality. This finding demonstrates the extent to which people suffer from their homosexuality, and provides an important argument for an attempt to give help to those who ask for it. The majority of those who were under current psychiatric therapy for other conditions were suffering from anxiety states or depressions.

TABLE 3.12. FURTHER PSYCHIATRIC DATA

Nature of datum	No.
Drinks for personality reasons	9
Previous or present reactive depression *re* homosexuality	25
Previous or present reactive depression for other reasons	7
Previous or present endogenous depression	2
Under current psychiatric therapy for other conditions	9

B. SEXUAL PRACTICES PRIOR TO TREATMENT

We now present data concerning the nature and degree of our patients' sexual practices. Forty-one of the sample had begun masturbating by the time they appeared for interview. The source of the instigation of the initial masturbation is shown in Table 3.13. It is of

TABLE 3.13. INSTIGATION OF INITIAL
MASTURBATION

Instigation	No.
Male over 16	2
Male under 16	21
Self	18
None	2
Total	43

interest that only 2 of the 41 had been initiated by a male over the age of 16. This apparently demonstrates the very limited extent to which direct seduction by male adults had been associated with the onset of homosexual behaviour in our patients. However, these data are not entirely satisfactory as an index of the extent of seduction, as a child, by a male adult. When we look at the direct evidence in answer to this question, it is found that 10 of the series had a sexual relationship with an adult male when they were under the age of 16. However, of these 10, only 1 became a paedophiliac; the other 6 of the total number of 7 who were paedophiliacs (Table 3.14) did not have a sexual relationship with an adult male before the age of 16.

TABLE 3.14. AGE OF PREFERRED SEXUAL
PARTNER

Preference	No.
Under 16	7
Over 16	36
Total	43

Twenty-four of the series had been practising homosexuality overtly for more than 10 years (Table 3.15) and only 2 had never practised overtly, but instead had exclusively utilized strong homosexual phantasy. The fact that 35 of the series had been practising overtly for five years or more is indicative of the strength of the homosexual habit in the series.

TABLE 3.15. DURATION OF HOMOSEXUAL
PRACTICE

Years of practice	No.
0	2
1–2	5
3–4	1
5–6	4
7–8	1
9–10	6
10+	24
Total	43

TABLE 3.16. HOMOSEXUAL PRACTICES
ON PRESENTATION

Practices	No.
Phantasy only	8
MM only	9
AI only	3
MM and AI	10
F only	0
MM and F	3
AI and F	0
MM, AI and F	10
Total	43

MM, mutual masturbation. AI, anal intercourse. F, fellatio.

At the precise time of presentation, 8 of the series were using homosexual phantasy only and were not actively practising homosexuality (Table 3.16). It can be seen from this table that the majority of the series used mutual masturbation either as their sole mode of homosexual activity or in addition to another mode. Only 3 of the series used anal intercourse, and none used fellatio, exclusively.

TABLE 3.17. AGE ON PRESENTATION AND HOMOSEXUAL PRACTICES

Practice	Age						No.
	15–20	21–25	26–30	31–35	36–40	40+	
Phantasy only	0	4	2	2	0	0	8
MM only	2	1	1	1	2	2	9
AI only	1	0	1	0	0	1	3
MM and AI	1	0	4	2	0	3	10
MM and F	0	0	0	1	1	1	3
MM, AI and F	1	3	2	2	0	2	10
Total	5	8	10	8	3	9	43

Table 3.17 shows the relationship between the age on presentation and the type of homosexual practice. There was no special tendency for any particular practice to be confined to any particular age group with the possible exception that none of the over 35's were using phantasy exclusively at the time of presentation. There was a strong tendency ($p = <0.001$) for an association between failure to complete treatment and the use of all three homosexual practices, namely mutual masturbation, anal intercourse, and fellatio, 5 of the 7 who failed to complete treatment falling into this category. By contrast, only 5 of the 36 who did complete treatment used all three practices. In Table 3.18 we further examine the data on

TABLE 3.18. MAJOR HOMOSEXUAL
PRACTICE ON PRESENTATION

Practice	No.
Strong phantasy only	8
MM	9
Buggery*	26
Total	43

homosexual practices by looking at the major homosexual practice. By way of contrast with Table 3.16, it is now clear that the major practice (i.e. of *choice*) is anal intercourse, so that mutual masturbation becomes of secondary importance. The important point to note here is that our series did not consist largely of rather shy, anxious individuals who were unable to enter into a full sexual relationship, preferring fleeting contacts, but were the homosexual equivalent of a normal heterosexual sample. Further support for this argument is provided by the data on the incidence of homosexual "affairs" in the series (Table 3.19). Only 13 of the series had never had a lasting homosexual relationship, where "lasting" is defined as

* English term meaning anal intercourse.

TABLE 3.19. HOMOSEXUAL AFFAIRS

Number of affairs	No.
0	13
1	15
2	7
3 or more	8
Total	43

existing for more than a month. Seven of the series had 2 such affairs and 8 had had 3 or more. The relationship between the number of homosexual affairs and the age of presentation is shown in Table 3.20. It is of interest that 3 of the 8 patients who had had 3 or more

TABLE 3.20. AGE ON PRESENTATION AND HOMOSEXUAL AFFAIRS

Number of affairs	Age						No.
	15–20	21–25	26–30	31–35	36–40	40+	
0	0	5	2	2	1	3	13
1	0	2	4	5	1	3	15
2	2	0	1	1	1	2	7
3 or more	3	1	3	0	0	1	8
Total	5	8	10	8	3	9	43

affairs were under the age of 20 and 7 were under the age of 30. By way of contrast, only 1 of those aged over 30 had had 3 or more affairs and only 4 had had 2 affairs, whilst 6 had had none. The suggestion is that while young people will seek treatment despite a vigorous socio-sexual life, in older people a history of continued loneliness is associated with seeking help. Some further data on the homosexual social life of the series are provided by the proportion of the series who described themselves as frequenting homosexual pubs and clubs; slightly under one-half of the sample doing so (Table 3.21). There was no significant association between membership of an age group and mixing in homosexual coteries. (Visiting pubs and clubs is not necessarily an indication of a full social life, and there is no contradiction between the last statement and the earlier one concerning the higher proportion of "affairs" in those aged under 30.)

TABLE 3.21. AGE ON PRESENTATION AND SOCIAL MIXING IN HOMOSEXUAL COTERIES

Mixing	Age						No.
	15–20	21–25	26–30	31–35	36–40	40+	
Present	3	3	5	4	1	5	21
Absent	2	5	5	4	2	4	22
Total	5	8	10	8	3	9	43

We now look at the developmental data concerning the heterosexual behaviour. The first aspect of these is the extent of sexual interest in females when the patients were between the ages of 5 and 10. Thirty-five of the series showed no sexual interest in females when between these ages as compared with 8 who did so. Between the ages of 10 and 15, a marked development occurred in that 20 of the series had by then a sexual interest in females; this number includes all those who showed such an interest when they were aged between 5 and 10. Superficially, therefore, 20 patients showed the normal development of the young person (Schofield, 1965a). We next looked at the data on overt sexual behaviour with females when aged between 10 and 15, and it is found that 16 of the sample (that is the majority of those who showed sexual interest in females when aged between 10 and 15), did engage in overt heterosexual behaviour.

TABLE 3.22. HETEROSEXUAL BEHAVIOUR WHEN AGED
10–15

Behaviour	No.
Dating and kissing (even once)	7
Petting (even once)	3
Sexual intercourse (even once)	5
Nil	28
Total	43

The nature of the sexual behaviour with females between the ages of 10 and 15 is shown in Table 3.22. However, heterosexual behaviour continued to develop after the age of 15 and it was found that 33 of the series did engage in heterosexual behaviour with females at some time between the age of 15 and the time of presentation (accompanied by satisfaction in all cases but one). The nature of this behaviour is shown in Table 3.23; perhaps somewhat surprisingly, slightly more than half the series had had sexual intercourse with females at least once. It seems, therefore, that at the outset of treatment, about three-quarters of the patients had prior experience of pleasurable overt heterosexual behaviour, and hence of the behaviour responses involved.

However, at the time when they appeared for treatment only 18 of the 33 who had experienced some form of overt heterosexual behaviour in the past were engaged in some form of heterosexual behaviour (even if only in phantasy—Table 3.24). Twenty-five of the patients

TABLE 3.23. NATURE OF HETEROSEXUAL BEHAVIOUR
FROM THE AGE OF 15 TO PRESENTATION

Heterosexual behaviour	No.
Dating and kissing (even once)	6
Petting (even once)	4
Sexual intercourse (even once)	23
Nil	10
Total	43

TABLE 3.24. MAJOR HETEROSEXUAL PRACTICE ON
PRESENTATION

Practice	No.
Weak phantasy	7
Strong phantasy	2
Dating	0
Kissing	1
Petting	1
Sexual intercourse	7
Nil	25
Total	43

were displaying no heterosexual practice or phantasy of any kind. Of the 9 patients who used heterosexual phantasy, only 2 did so to a marked extent. There were 9 patients in all who were heterosexually active on presentation. Seven of these were having sexual intercourse, in 5 cases with their wives. All 5 of these patients had to utilize homosexual phantasy on at least some occasions in order to maintain an erection. In these instances, therefore, the behaviour was that of masturbation *per vaginam* (Curran and Parr, 1957). Frequent overt homosexual behaviour was displayed by all 5 of these (apparently) heterosexually active married patients. The other 2 patients who were practising heterosexual intercourse were the 2 female homosexuals, both of whom did so with a variety of partners. Neither patient found this pleasurable, and both felt a considerable degree of contempt for their male partners. In fact, these 2 patients, one perhaps to a more marked extent than the other, appeared to be using heterosexual intercourse in order to reinforce their contempt for the male sex.

TABLE 3.25. PRE-TREATMENT
KINSEY RATING

Kinsey rating	No.
0	0
1	0
2	0
3	5
4	7
5	12
6	19
Total	43

The above data on sexual practices and phantasies on presentation were combined to yield a pre-treatment Kinsey rating. The Kinsey ratings for the series are shown in Table 3.25, 19 of the sample having Kinsey ratings of 6, and 12 one of 5, giving a total of 31 patients (72%) with a Kinsey rating of 5 or 6. A relevant comparison is with the Curran and Parr (1957) series, in which 42% had a Kinsey rating of 5 or 6. Only 12 of our series were rated as Kinsey 3 and 4, in whom at the time of interview there was felt to be a reasonably strong heterosexual component. As might be expected (Table 3.26), there was a tendency for the

TABLE 3.26. AGE AND PRE-TREATMENT KINSEY RATING

Kinsey rating	Age						Total
	15–20	20–25	25–30	30–35	35–40	40+	
3	0	2	1	1	1	0	5
4	2	0	1	1	0	3	7
5	1	4	3	2	1	1	12
6	2	2	5	4	1	5	19
Total	5	8	10	8	3	9	43

older age groups to have a higher representation in the high Kinsey ratings than the younger age group, 5 of the 9 over 40's having a Kinsey rating of 6. However, 3 of the over 40's had a Kinsey rating of 4, showing the extent to which some homosexuals continued to display an appreciable degree of heterosexual interest until at least early middle age. The Kinsey rating is assigned on the basis of the sexual practices during the 3 years prior to presentation, and not on those over the whole life-span of the patient. The fact, therefore, of being assigned a Kinsey rating of 6 on presentation does not necessarily imply a total absence throughout the life-span of any interest or practice with females.

Perhaps the most revealing insight into the content of sexual life is provided by the examination of the masturbatory phantasies used by our patients. This is shown in Table 3.27, in

TABLE 3.27. MASTURBATORY PHANTASY

Phantasy	No.
Boys under 16 only	7
Boys under 16 only and men	4
Boys and girls under 16	1
Men only	20
Men and women	8
Nil	3
Total	43

which it can be seen that 7 of the sample used exclusively males under the age of 16 as their phantasy, whilst another 4 used males under 16, together with those over 16. It is of interest that only 4 of the series of 43 used males both over and under 16 with equal ease, supporting the frequently reported finding (e.g. Curran and Parr, 1957) that homosexuals are attracted either by adults, or by children, but not by both. Only 8 of the series used females as a masturbatory phantasy, and all 8 also used males. One patient used both boys and girls under the age of 16. A breakdown of masturbatory phantasy in terms of age is given in Table 3.28. It was not unexpected that 6 of the 8 patients who phantasized both adult males and females would be under the age of 30, nor that none of those under the age of 25 phantasized males under the age of 16 only. The latter finding should not be used to support the observation made by Curran and Parr (1957) that paedophilia is confined to those over the age of 40. An equally plausible explanation for the finding is that it is relatively rare for

TABLE 3.28. AGE ON PRESENTATION AND MASTURBATORY PHANTASY

Phantasy	Age						No.
	15–20	21–25	26–30	31–35	36–40	40+	
Male under 16 only	0	0	2	2	1	2	7
Male under 16 and male over 16	0	0	1	1	1	1	4
Male under 16 and female under 16	0	0	0	0	1	0	1
Male over 16 only	2	6	4	4	0	4	20
Male and female over 16	2	2	2	1	0	1	8
Nil	1	0	1	0	0	1	3
Total	5	8	10	8	3	9	43

paedophiles either to be apprehended and sent for treatment or to ask for help of their own accord, and that both reasons for presentation have an increasing likelihood of occurrence with increasing age.

Finally, we have some data on the extent of homosexual prostitution in our series both as client and as prostitute, and this is shown in Table 3.29. Only 9 of the series had had experience of homosexual prostitution, 34 never having served as either client or prostitute. There is a very strong association between age and prostitution ($p = <0.001$), 6 of the 7 patients who had been a client were over the age of 40 (9 of the series were aged 40 or over), whilst both those who had been paid for prostitution were under the age of 30. The former finding throws an additional light on the rather sad and lonely situation of the ageing homosexual.

TABLE 3.29. HOMOSEXUAL PROSTITUTION

	No.
As client	7
As prostitute	2
Neither	34
Total	43

C. THE RESULTS OF TREATMENT

As stated at the beginning of this chapter, all patients but 3 were followed up for at least a year, and these 3 were assumed to have relapsed. The 7 who failed to complete treatment were not, by definition, followed up, although almost by chance we did come into further contact with one of them who, not surprisingly, showed no change in his sexual practices. Thirty-three of the 36 patients who completed treatment were followed up several times during the period of time after treatment, and interviews lasting at least 30 minutes—and very often up to 60 minutes—were carried out on each occasion. Inevitably, these partook to some extent of the nature of supportive psychotherapy in that a fair degree of verbal communication of an approving sort took place, i.e. if patients described facts indicative of improvement, this was met with encouraging remarks or nods, thereby further reinforcing their own satisfaction at their progress. It would have been impossible to treat our patients as laboratory subjects, both because they had a reinforcement history of experiencing something rather different from therapists, and also because to do so might not have been sufficient either to support them during the early period of treatment before change became noticeable, or to assist them through the difficult period immediately after treatment. It was in this latter period, when the patient was learning to employ new, or at best dormant social skills in the heterosexual area, that relapse seemed particularly likely. The maximum length of follow-up was 38 months and the mean length slightly under 20 months.

Throughout this section on the results of treatment it is assumed that the 7 patients who failed to complete treatment were engaging, at a period of time equivalent to a year after treatment, in the same sexual practices as at first interview, and the data concerning them are therefore combined with those on the 36 patients who did complete treatment.

TABLE 3.30. RESPONSE TO TREATMENT
OF 43 HOMOSEXUAL PATIENTS

Response	No.
Improved	25
Unimproved	11
Failed to complete	7
Total	43

The overall results of treatment are set out in Table 3.30; of the 36 patients who completed treatment, 25 improved to a sufficient degree for their treatment to be described as successful, 11 were unimproved, and, as stated previously, 7 failed to complete treatment.

The detailed evidence concerning the nature of the sexual behaviour after treatment follows.

TABLE 3.31. MAJOR HOMOSEXUAL
PRACTICE POST-TREATMENT

Practice	No.
Weak phantasy	5
Strong phantasy	4
MM	5
Buggery	9
Nil	20
Total	43

The major homosexual practice after treatment is shown in Table 3.31. It can be seen that 20 of the series were neither using homosexual phantasy nor displaying overt homosexual practice. Nine patients were using homosexual phantasy; 5 of them, however, to only a weak extent and then only occasionally. The 14 remaining patients were still displaying overt homosexual activities. The relationship between age and pre- and post-treatment homosexual behaviour is shown in Table 3.32 in which it can be seen that after treatment there was a

TABLE 3.32. AGE ON PRESENTATION AND MAJOR PRE- AND POST-TREATMENT HOMOSEXUAL PRACTICE

Practice	Age			
	Under 30		Over 30	
	Pre-treatment	Post-treatment	Pre-treatment	Post-treatment
Phantasy	5	4 (2 weak)	2	4 (2 weak)
MM	4	0	6	5
AI	10	1	9	2
Nil	0	14	0	6
(Failed to complete treatment)	4	4 (3 AI; 1 phantasy)	3	3 (3 AI)
Total	23	23	20	20

significantly stronger tendency ($p = <0.025$) for the under 30's to be neither using homosexual phantasy nor engaging in overt homosexual behaviour after treatment, than for those aged over 30. This finding is further reinforced by the fact that of the total group of 20 with either overt homosexual behaviour, or phantasy, after treatment, only 1 of the 14 under 30's experienced mild interest in directly observed males as compared with 4 out of the 6 over 30's in this category. It is assumed that the 7 patients who failed to complete treatment were engaged in the same homosexual behaviour a year after leaving treatment as when they began treatment. The major heterosexual practices after treatment are shown in Table 3.33. It can

TABLE 3.33. MAJOR HETEROSEXUAL
PRACTICE POST-TREATMENT

Practice	No.
Weak phantasy	2
Strong phantasy	5
Dating	2
Kissing	4
Petting	3
Sexual intercourse	13
Nil	14
Total	43

be seen that 13 patients were engaging in heterosexual intercourse, and in all cases this was unaccompanied by homosexual phantasy or practice. Seven other patients were actively heterosexual short of intercourse. Two were mixing socially with females (this appears under the heading "dating") and were beginning to approach active heterosexual practice. Finally, 3 patients out of the 5 shown as using strong phantasy were also improved in the homosexual area. The numbers in the above categories add up to the 25 patients described as improved. Two patients in the failed group continued to use strong heterosexual phantasy, as they had done prior to treatment, together with overt homosexual activity. There were 14 patients, as compared to 25 prior to treatment, who had no heterosexual phantasy or practice of any kind. The association between pre- and post-heterosexual behaviour and age is shown in

TABLE 3.34. AGE ON PRESENTATION AND MAJOR PRE- AND POST-HETEROSEXUAL PRACTICE

Practice	Age			
	Under 30		Over 30	
	Pre-treatment	Post-treatment	Pre-treatment	Post-treatment
Phantasy	5	0	3	6
Dating	0	2	0	0
Kissing	0	3	0	0
Petting	1	3	0	0
Sexual intercourse	3	9	3	3
Nil	10	2	11	8
(Failed to complete treatment)	4	4 (1 kissing; 3 nil)	3	3 (1 phantasy, 1 SI, 1 nil)
Total	23	23	20	20

Table 3.34. As in the case of homosexual activity, the improvement was more marked in the under 30's than in those over 30. Whereas prior to treatment there were only 3 of the under-30 group who were practising heterosexual intercourse, 2 of whom were female homosexuals and 1 a married patient who had to use homosexual phantasy to maintain an erection, after treatment there were 9 who were practising such intercourse. None of the 8 male patients in the latter group (7 of whom were unmarried prior to treatment) had to use homosexual phantasy in order to maintain an erection. The other patient was one of the 2 female homosexuals. She had practised heterosexual intercourse, even prior to treatment, but after treatment she did so with satisfaction and had a high regard for her partner whom she later married.

In the over-30 age group, improvement manifested itself very much more in phantasy life than in overt behaviour; 6 of the 9 over-30 group who were either using heterosexual phantasy or engaging in heterosexual practice after treatment were confining their heterosexual activity to their phantasy life. This reflects the increasing difficulty in making social contacts with increasing age. All 3 of the over-30 group who were practising sexual intercourse after treatment were married, the difference being that, after treatment, they were able to do so without the use of homosexual phantasy to achieve and maintain an erection. Unless the over-30 age group of patients are prepared to confine their sexual activities after treatment to phantasy, then it is always possible that they may relapse to their previous

TABLE 3.35. COMBINED DATA ON POST-TREATMENT HETEROSEXUAL AND HOMOSEXUAL PRACTICES OF SUCCESSFUL PATIENTS

Heterosexual practice	Homosexual practice			Total
	Nil	Weak phantasy	Strong phantasy	
Strong phantasy	0	4	0	4
Dating, kissing, and petting	8	1	0	9
Sexual intercourse	12	0	0	12
Total	20	5	0	25

homosexual behaviour (see series patient no. 2, Appendix A). Age emerges as an important prognostic factor for the possibility of developing overt heterosexual behaviour as opposed to covert heterosexual interest and phantasy.

The marked relationship between the nature of heterosexual and homosexual practices is shown in Table 3.35. None of the 12 patients who were having heterosexual intercourse after treatment either engaged in homosexual practices or used homosexual phantasy. By way of contrast, all 4 of the patients whose heterosexual activities were confined to strong phantasy also used homosexual phantasy, although of weak intensity. Once again it is assumed that the failed-to-complete group were unchanged a year after leaving treatment. Table 3.35 refers to the 25 patients in the series who are described as successful, and it can be seen that the appellation "success" was only used where the patients had actually ceased homosexual practice, even though some did still display some weak homosexual phantasy. This is seen in contrast to the practices of the authors of other series, such as Bieber *et al.* (1963) and Ellis (1956), both of whom have tended to regard the establishment of bisexuality, i.e. the increase in or the establishment of heterosexual behaviour even in the continued presence of homosexual behaviour, as evidence of success.

The data on sexual practices after treatment have been combined as Kinsey ratings, and are shown in Table 3.36. It can be seen that there were 14 patients with a rating Kinsey 0, 9 with one of Kinsey 1, and 2 one of Kinsey 2 (making up the 25 improved patients), the remainder all being Kinsey 3–6. The 2 patients who were rated as Kinsey 2 are included in the

TABLE 3.36. POST-TREATMENT KINSEY
RATINGS

Kinsey rating	No.
0	14
1	9 improved
2	2
3	2
4	3 unimproved and failed
5	3 to complete
6	10
Total	43

improved group because before treatment they were Kinsey 6 and had therefore shown a very considerable improvement. Moreover, neither was engaged in overt homosexual activity after treatment. The fact that 20 patients were displaying neither homosexual activities nor phantasy (Table 3.31) but only 14 could be rated as Kinsey 0, is accounted for by the fact that the other 6 had an occasional and very slight degree of homosexual interest in directly observed males (Table 3.32) without, however, any subsequent phantasy. Because we have been trying to make our criteria as strict as possible, it was decided to rate these patients as Kinsey 1.

In order to supplement the qualitative data on sexual practices and phantasies obtained by interview, we have developed an attitude scale for the qualitative measurement of the direction and intensity of sexual interest before, during, and after treatment. This is known as the Sexual Orientation Method (SOM), and is described in detail in Chapter 4 together with the results of its application to the majority of the 36 patients who completed treatment. (For obvious reasons, no SOM data was available for the 7 patients who failed to complete their treatment, nor was the research on the use of the SOM completed in time to include the data on 4 of the 36 patients who did complete their treatment.) The results of the use of the SOM amply confirm and supplement the results of the interview-obtained reports of sexual practices.

D. FACTORS PROGNOSTIC OF SUCCESS

We have attempted to pick out a number of factors, recorded in the pre-treatment interviews, which might be prognostic of success in response to treatment. Several objectively measured variables recorded during treatment, also related significantly to outcome, and these are discussed in Chapter 6. Table 3.37 relates the pre-treatment Kinsey ratings to

TABLE 3.37. PRE-TREATMENT KINSEY RATINGS AND RESPONSE TO TREATMENT OF IMPROVED VERSUS UNIMPROVED AND FAILED-TO-COMPLETE GROUPS

Response	Kinsey rating				Total
	3	4	5	6	
Improved	3	5	8	9	25
Unimproved and failed to complete	2	2	4	10	18
Total	5	7	12	19	43

response to treatment. There appears to be a tendency for ratings of Kinsey 6 to occur more often in the failed-to-improve and the failed-to-complete groups than in the improved group, and for ratings of Kinsey 3 and 4 to occur less frequently. However, neither tendency is statistically significant. A rating of Kinsey 6 is not necessarily a bar to a successful outcome of treatment. Nine of the 19 Kinsey 6 patients did respond successfully. At this point we return to the point made earlier in the chapter, namely that the Kinsey rating is assigned on the basis of interest, practice, and phantasy in the 3 years prior to presentation for treatment as opposed to the entire lifetime of the individual. Of the 9 Kinsey 6 patients who made a satisfactory response to treatment, 6 had experienced pleasurable heterosexual behaviour at some stage in their lives, prior to the 3 years immediately preceding presentation for treatment, and of the other 3 none had started actively practising heterosexually by the time of the latest follow-up. By way of contrast, only 2 of the 10 patients with a rating of Kinsey 6 who either failed to improve, or failed to complete treatment, had experienced pleasurable heterosexual behaviour in the entire course of their lives. In both instances the patients were very well integrated into the homosexual world. The 19 Kinsey 6 patients were divided into those who had experienced pleasurable heterosexual behaviour at some stage in the past and those who had never done so. When this distinction was made, it was found that 8 Kinsey 6 patients had displayed prior heterosexual interest or practice; 6 of these improved as a result of treatment and 4 of the 6 were engaging in overt heterosexual practice at least a year after treatment.

Of the other 11 Kinsey 6's who had never at any stage in the past experienced pleasurable heterosexual behaviour, only 3 improved in response to treatment, and none of these 3 have displayed overt heterosexual behaviour after treatment. Twenty-two of the total improved group of 25 did engage in pleasurable heterosexual behaviour at some time prior to treatment, and of these 20 have done so after treatment. Table 3.38 demonstrates that a major variable ($p = < 0.025$) prognostic of success in response to treatment by aversion therapy is a pre-treatment history at some stage in the patient's life of overt heterosexual activity. While such a history does not guarantee success, it makes it very much more likely. A corollary is that a successful response is highly unlikely where there is no such previous history. The development of techniques to incorporate heterosexual responses into the sexual repertoire of such patients represents an important future area of research. This point is developed more fully in Chapter 8.

TABLE 3.38. PRIOR HETEROSEXUAL INTEREST AND RESPONSE TO TREATMENT

	Improved	Unimproved	Total
Prior heterosexual interest	22	10	32
No prior heterosexual interest	3	8	11
Total	25	18	43

$\chi^2 = 5.02. p = < 0.025.$

Table 3.39 shows the relationship between the age on presentation and response to treatment. Of the 23 patients under the age of 30, 16 made a successful response to treatment, whereas of the 20 patients over the age of 30, 9 did so, indicating a tendency (which is not, however, statistically significant) for the younger patients to respond better than the older ones. This was, of course, expected. However, what was not expected was that 4 of the 9 patients who were aged over 40 made a satisfactory response to treatment. Two of these patients were married, and therefore had an available heterosexual partner. It was pointed out earlier that the older patients find it much more difficult than do the younger ones to translate their increased heterosexual interest into overt practice, so that it is likely that they will continue to be at risk. It seems, therefore that while being over the age of 40 tends to result in a less successful outcome, there are no grounds for complete pessimism.

TABLE 3.39. AGE ON PRESENTATION AND RESPONSE TO TREATMENT

Age range	Improved	Unimproved and failed to complete
15–20	3	2
21–25	6	2
26–30	7	3
31–35	4	4
36–40	1	2
40+	4	5
Total	25	18

TABLE 3.40. AGE ON PRESENTATION AND PRE- AND POST-TREATMENT KINSEY RATINGS

	Age																
	Under 30 Post-treatment Kinsey rating								Over 30 Post-treatment Kinsey rating								
Pre-treatment Kinsey rating	0	1	2	3	4	5	6	Total	0	1	2	3	4	5	6	Total
3	1	1	0	0	0	0	0	2	0	1	0	1	0	0	0	2
4	3	0	0	0	0	0	0	3	1	1	0	0	0	0	0	2
5	7	0	0	0	0	0	0	7	1	1	0	0	0	2	0	4
6	2	2	1	0	0	0	2	7	0	3	1	0	1	0	4	9
(Failed to complete treatment)	0	0	0	1	0	1	2	4	0	0	0	0	2	0	1	3
Total	13	3	1	1	0	1	4	23	2	6	1	1	3	2	5	20

TABLE 3.41. AGE OF PREFERRED SEXUAL PARTNER AND RESPONSE TO TREATMENT

	Age of partner		
Response	Under 16	Over 16	Total
Improved	4	21	25
Unimproved	3	15	18
Total	7	36	43

In Table 3.40 we look at the relationship between the pre- and post-treatment Kinsey ratings and age group. As was pointed out earlier in the chapter, there is no very marked tendency for an over-representation of Kinsey 3's and 4's in the younger age groups nor for the Kinsey 5's or 6's to be similarly over-represented in the older age groups. However, there is a stronger tendency for pre-treatment Kinsey 5's and 6's to make a satisfactory response to treatment when under 30 than when over 30. No fewer than 11 of the 13 pre-treatment Kinsey 5's and 6's who were under 30 received a post-treatment Kinsey rating of 0 or 1; in contrast, only 5 of the 11 over 30's with a pre-treatment rating of 5 or 6 had a post-treatment Kinsey rating of 0 or 1. This is simply another way of looking at the data presented earlier in this chapter, which showed that whereas it was only slightly more difficult for the older patients than for the younger ones to lose their homosexual interest, it was considerably more difficult for them to acquire (or more precisely re-acquire) overt heterosexual practice. The age of the patient on presentation therefore emerges as a significant factor in response to treatment, even when the initial Kinsey rating is controlled for.

The association between the nature of the sexual object and improvement (Table 3.41) is well short of statistical significance, indicating that paedophiles respond to treatment as well as do other homosexuals. Nor does the association between the mode of referral and improvement, though suggestive, reach an acceptable level of significance. Seventeen improved out of the 25 patients who were self-referred, came under pressure from wife or girl friend, or were originally referred for other psychiatric conditions. By comparison, only 8 of the 18 patients who appeared on an order of the court, as a sequel to a court appearance, or prior to a court appearance, showed an improvement. It would be reasonable to expect that the motivation of those referred through the courts was likely to be less than that of those who were self-referred. Nevertheless, nearly half of the 18 patients who appeared for treatment in connection with a court appearance improved. Whilst we feel that therapists should not be called upon to act as the agents of society in order to alter individuals who are not conforming to its norms, it is worth while pointing out that some at least of those referred through the courts (e.g. series patient no. 3, Appendix A) were grateful for the opportunity to have treatment, an opportunity which they never previously had either because of shyness or because treatment was not available.

Evidence of the importance for treatment outcome of the initial level of motivation is provided in Table 3.42, which shows the highly significant association ($p = < 0.001$) between these two variables.

Table 3.43 shows the relationship between pre-treatment personality disorder and the outcome of treatment. While the presence of personality disorder did tend to militate against a successful outcome, in that only 12 improved of the 26 suffering from a disorder of personality, as compared to 13 of the 17 who did not ($p = < 0.05$), Table 3.44 shows that this

TABLE 3.42. MOTIVATION FOR TREATMENT AND RESPONSE TO TREATMENT

| Response | Level of motivation | | | Total |
	Low[a]	Equivocal[a]	High	
Improved	0	4	21	25
Unimproved	4	10	4	18
Total	4	14	25	43

[a]Combined for statistical analysis.

TABLE 3.43. PRE-TREATMENT PERSONALITY DISORDER IN IMPROVED VERSUS UNIMPROVED AND FAILED-TO-COMPLETE GROUPS

| Personality disorder | Response | | Total |
	Improved	Unimproved	
Present	12	14	26
Absent	13	4	17
Total	25	18	43

TABLE 3.44. TYPE OF PERSONALITY DISORDER AND RESPONSE TO TREATMENT

Personality disorder	Improved	Unimproved
Nil	13	4
Self insecure	11	2
Other disorders	1	12
Total	25	18

association depends, very significantly, on the *type* of personality disorder. If the disorder was of the self-insecure type, the prospects for a successful outcome were very much better ($p = < 0.001$) than for the other disorders, taken as a group. In fact, for the latter group of patients, mainly suffering from personality disorders of the attention-seeking type, the prospects for a successful outcome are extremely poor. Three of the 4 patients (17 − 13) who, despite not suffering from a personality disorder made an unsuccessful response to treatment, were very well integrated in the homosexual social world, and all were rated as Kinsey 6. One of the patients who suffered from a self-insecure personality disorder failed to complete treatment, having been discharged from the ward by another psychiatrist due to a misunderstanding over ward discipline. The other patient with a self-insecure disorder who is included in the failure group, made a successful response to treatment, but is presumed to have relapsed because of failure to keep follow-up appointments. This patient, in addition to suffering from a self-insecure disorder, also suffered from an attention-seeking disorder.

All 7 of those suffering from a disorder of the self-insecure type, uncomplicated by any other disorders or abnormalities of personality, made a satisfactory response to treatment. However, only 2 of the 13 patients who suffered from disorders of types other than self-insecure, made a satisfactory response to treatment. Five of the 7 patients who failed to complete treatment were in the group of 13 suffering from disorders other than the self-insecure type. Of the other 2 patients who failed to complete treatment, 1 was very well integrated into the homosexual world, working as a barman in a homosexual pub, and the other was the patient who was discharged from the ward by another psychiatrist. A much more detailed analysis of the relationship between clinically assessed personality and response to treatment—as measured by SOM scores—is presented in Chapter 7, together with a considerable quantity of data on psychometric measures of personality and other quantitative measures.

E. CONCLUSIONS

In this chapter we have described the treatment of the initial series of 43 homosexual patients. We have shown that despite the fact that this series of patients was unselected other than the fact that 2 of those who were originally offered treatment refused the offer, nearly 60% made a satisfactory response to treatment. This is a rather better outcome than was obtained by any of the series described in Chapter 1. The best previous outcome was that obtained by the psychoanalytically treated series of Bieber *et al.* (1963). Our results are clearly somewhat better than his; even if they were no better, and without allowing for the fact that a substantial proportion of our series were referred for treatment in connection with a court appearance, the method of choice would still be the form of aversion therapy used for our series of patients and described in Chapter 2. The reason concerns the length of time taken for treatment. Our patients received an average of 18–20 sessions, each lasting 20–25 minutes. Seventy-five per cent of the Bieber sample had 150 sessions or more, and 35% had 350 sessions or more; in each case a session lasted 1 hour.

The results reported in this chapter provide encouraging support for a behavioural approach to the treatment of homosexuality. However, it still remained possible that at least some of the success obtained was due to the fact that we were carrying out a piece of research, and that we were increasingly hopeful about the likely success of the technique used. Despite the fact that we made considerable efforts not to raise our patients' expectations, it is possible that some of our enthusiasm may have communicated itself to the patients. It is likely that we put sufficient effort into the care of our patients to persuade them to continue with treatment during the difficult early days before change became noticeable; it is also probable that we gave them considerable reinforcement on their follow up visits through the expression of our satisfaction with their improvement. However, as shown by the data reported on in this chapter, our criteria for accepting the occurrence of change have been rather severe, and we have attempted to prove patients' claims to be false rather than accepting them at face value. Further, the results of the application of the SOM, a technique on which it is rather difficult to "fake good", have strongly supported the interview-obtained data. Where they have not, we have found that further interviewing has resulted in the patient modifying his report towards a more modest conclusion. We have also tended to bias the results of treatment against success by assuming that patients had relapsed if they failed to appear in person for follow-up appointments, but instead either made no communication at all or replied only in writing, and they have all been included in the failure group.

The figure of 58 % improved after the follow-up period of a year* is unusually high for this very difficult problem, and we tentatively concluded that this was due to the appropriateness of the learning technique used. The next step was to carry out a controlled trial of anticipatory avoidance learning in the treatment of homosexuality under conditions which would be as stringent as was compatible with the well-being and care of the patients.

*Contact was maintained with a number of patients even after the last round of follow-up interviews was carried out in September 1966. While the majority of the patients in the improved group maintained, or even advanced on the degree of change previously attained, 2 patients relapsed. These were series patient no. 2 who relapsed 4 years after treatment, and series patient no. 17 who relapsed 2 years after treatment. The histories of both, up to and after final follow-up, are described in Appendix A. Both had improved despite showing features which had a significantly poor prognosis for success. Patient no. 2 had had no prior heterosexual experience or interest (see Table 3.38); patient no. 17, though not lacking such experience, was judged at his pre-treatment interview to be equivocal in his motivation for treatment (see Table 3.42). In addition, patient no. 17 had a number of abnormalities of personality, one of which, attention-seeking, was not far short of attaining the level of a disorder of personality, in which case it would have been prognostic of failure (see Table 3.44).

CHAPTER 4

THE SEXUAL ORIENTATION METHOD

ONE of the problems in the treatment of homosexuality is the assessment of changes in sexual orientation during the course of treatment. It is customary to give patients a Kinsey rating (Kinsey *et al.*, 1947) at the beginning of treatment. The Kinsey rating has the merit that it conceives of homosexuality as a graded form of behaviour and not as something which is present in an all-or-none manner. However, it does have the serious shortcoming that it is based on the clinical interview and is therefore subjective. In the last few years several reports have appeared of methods which might solve this problem. Freund (1963) has described a laboratory method which involves the continuous recording of volume changes in the male genitalia while the subject is viewing projected pictures of potentially erotic stimuli. Bancroft *et al.* (1966) have described a similar device, and Marks and Gelder (1967) have demonstrated its usefulness in monitoring the treatment of transvestism. Brown (1964) has reported a technique in which the number of times a subject operates a shutter to reveal a picture is used to index the relative levels of sexual interest. A critique of some of these techniques has been given by Koenig (1965). A possibly promising method, though one requiring much development, is that of Hess *et al.* (1965) who have reported that pupil responses relate to sexual arousal. More recently, Scott *et al.* (1967) have thrown some doubt on this claim, suggesting that the pupillary response is to arousal in general rather than to sexual arousal in particular.

None of the above techniques were available when we began our research. Accordingly, a specially designed and very simple technique was constructed and a description of this follows.

The technique, which is a questionnaire one, is intended to indicate the relative levels of homo- and hetero-erotic orientation at the outset of treatment and to show any changes on these relative levels as treatment proceeds. It combines features of the semantic differential technique of Osgood *et al.* (1957) and the personal questionnaire technique of Shapiro (1961). We have followed the basic approach of the former, but have changed the method of presentation so as to gain the advantage of detecting departures from internal consistency afforded by the latter, as well as basing our scoring system on Shapiro's.

CONSTRUCTION

Six adjectives from the list provided by Osgood *et al.* (1957) were chosen because they all have a sexual connotation. They are: interesting, attractive, handsome (beautiful when applied to the concept "women"), hot, pleasurable, and exciting. The concepts for which scores are derived are: "men are sexually to me" and "women are sexually to me", and the patient has to choose the scale position of the particular adjective which is more true for him when taken in conjunction with the concept. Five scale positions are used for each adjective, e.g. (a) very attractive, (b) quite attractive, (c) neither attractive nor unattractive, (d) quite unattractive, and (e) very unattractive. Each of these scale positions is compared with each of the others, making ten pairs in all, as shown below:

Pairs

1	2	3	4	5	6	7	8	9	10
a	a	a	a	b	b	b	c	c	d
b	c	d	e	c	d	e	d	e	e

This is the standard pattern for the questionnaire, so that in each case the no. 1 pair compares the most favourable level with the next most favourable; the no. 2 pair compares the most favourable with the middle-most one, and so on. The scale positions within each pair were then randomized, as follows:

1	2	3	4	5	6	7	8	9	10
b	a	d	a	b	d	e	c	c	e
a	c	a	e	c	b	b	d	e	d

Six adjectives are used to measure attitudes to the concept "men are sexually to me", and six to the concept "women are sexually to me", making twelve in all. As there are ten pairs for each adjective, 120 pairs in all are set out in the printed questionnaire. Pairs 1–60 concern the attitude to men and 61–120 concern the attitude to women.

Pairs	*Adjective*
1–10 and 61–70	interesting
11–20 and 71–80	attractive
21–30	handsome (men)
81–90	beautiful (women)
31–40 and 91–100	hot
41–50 and 101–110	pleasurable
51–60 and 111–120	exciting

These 120 pairs are set out in random order but, in order to assist in scoring, the original numbers from 1 to 120 are printed beside the relevant pairs. The pairs of adjectives are presented, 6 per foolscap page, with a double-space between each pair member, and each member of a pair appears immediately above and below the concept concerned. A sample appears below:

3. Men are sexually to me   quite boring............................
                                          very interesting.......................

81. Women are sexually to me   quite beautiful......................
                                          very beautiful...........................

The result is that each pair presents a fresh discrimination problem to be approached separately, so that response sets are broken up.

SCORING

A score of 8 on the standard pattern (see below) is obtained by preferring the bottom (B) pair member to the top (T) on pair 1; the top to the bottom in pair 2; the bottom to the top in pair 3, and so on, so that the pattern would then run:

1	2	3	4	5	6	7	8	9	10
B	T	B	T	T	B	B	T	T	B

In each case, the more favourable of the two pair members is being preferred as being nearer the patient's true feelings. This pattern of B's and T's, together with the other possible seven patterns, are shown below:

1	2	3	4	5	6	7	8	9	10	Score
B	T	B	T	T	B	B	T	T	B	8
T	T	B	T	T	B	B	T	T	B	7
T	B	B	T	T	B	B	T	T	B	6
T	B	T	T	B	B	B	T	T	B	5
T	B	T	B	B	T	B	T	T	B	4
T	B	T	B	B	T	T	B	T	B	3
T	B	T	B	B	T	T	B	B	B	2
T	B	T	B	B	T	T	B	B	T	1

A score of 7 is obtained by a pattern which is similar to that which receives a score of 8 except in one respect. In pair 1, that is the one in which the patient is asked to choose between the highest intensity and the next highest, the patient has preferred "quite attractive" (b) to "very attractive" (a): order of choice (b), (a), (c), (d), (e). Similarly, a score of 6 is obtained in the same way as a score of 7 except that in pair 2 the patient has preferred the bottom member (B) to the top one (T); that is, he has preferred "neither attractive nor unattractive" (c) to "very attractive" (a): order of choice (b), (c), (a), (d), (e). The remaining scores are derived in the same manner.

The upper part of the score sheet is reproduced below, and instructions are given for entering patients' choices on to the score sheet.

The letter B or T is inserted in the blanks provided. The vertical numbers refer to the tens and the horizontal numbers to the ones, so that pair no. 29 would concern the concept "men are . . . ", and in order to fill in the patient's choice one simply finds the vertical 2, that is the one next to the adjective "handsome", and then looks along the line until the square underneath the horizontal no. 9 is reached. The result is a matrix of 120 letters which will be either B or T. By reference to the standard score patterns set out above, one can assign a score to the responses given by the patient.

In most cases patients' choices are consistent, that is they exactly represent one of the eight standard score patterns. In some cases, however, they are inconsistent. For instance, the pattern T B B T T B B T B B may be produced. The nearest standard pattern to this is one which yields a score of 7, namely T B B T T B B T T B. In this case the subject is assigned a score of 7. (It can be seen that the B produced by the patient in pair 9 is, in fact, appropriate to a pattern yielding a score of 1 or 2.) When a patient produces a pattern which is only slightly inconsistent and which could be altered to yield one of two scores, say 5 or 6,

S	Word		1	2	3	4	5	6	7	8	9	10	Score
M	Interesting	0											
M	Attractive	1											
M	Handsome	2											
M	Hot	3											
M	Pleasurable	4											
M	Exciting	5											
													_____
F	Interesting	6											
F	Attractive	7											
F	Beautiful	8											
F	Hot	9											
F	Pleasurable	10											
F	Exciting	11											
													_____

then he is scored as $5\frac{1}{2}$. The technique therefore borrows from Shapiro's personal questionnaire approach in that it allows one to make consistency out of inconsistency and so assign a score to the patient's responses. Moreover, by revealing inconsistency, the technique allows the patient who is trying to present himself in an untrue light to be spotted. Several patients do, in fact, attempt to "fake good"; that is, they attempt to minimize the extent of their homosexual orientation and maximize the extent of their heterosexual orientation. Data on consistency appear in the next section.

The questionnaire was administered to all new patients when they presented for treatment for homosexuality. It was again administered to them midway through treatment, at the end of treatment, and at intervals of 2 weeks, 6 weeks, 3 months, 6 months, and 1 year after treatment. We attempted, therefore, to indicate both change—or lack of it—during treatment as well as the trend which took place after treatment.

STATISTICAL DATA

A. INTERNAL CONSISTENCY

Table 4.1 shows data on the internal consistency of the responses of 32 homosexual patients whose treatment had been completed, and for whom at least a 3-month follow-up was available. Data are shown for questionnaire administrations prior to treatment, midway through treatment and post-treatment. As there were 32 patients giving scores on each of 6 adjectives, there are 192 adjective scores available for each occasion. There were 10 paired comparisons to be made by each patient, so that a dominant trend allowing a score of from 1 to 8 to be assigned could not appear unless at least 6 out of the 10 choices were consistent

TABLE 4.1. THE SEXUAL ORIENTATION METHOD. INTERNAL CONSISTENCY OF THE RESPONSES OF 32 HOMOSEXUAL PATIENTS (%)

No. of inconsistencies	Homosexual measure			Heterosexual measure		
	Pre-treatment	Mid-treatment	Post-treatment	Pre-treatment	Mid-treatment	Post-treatment
0	58.85	53.13	50.00	48.96	64.58	71.87
1	30.72	34.37	36.46	33.33	29.17	23.44
2	7.82	8.87	10.42	12.50	4.69	4.17
2–4	2.61	3.63	3.12	5.21	1.56	0.52
More than 4	0.00	0.00	0.00	0.00	0.00	0.00
	100.00	100.00	100.00	100.00	100.00	100.00

with each other. In practice, in no single case did the number of inconsistencies obtained from any one patient on any one adjective exceed 4. All responses, therefore, could be assigned a score. It can be seen that in well over 80% of the cases, on all occasions and on both the homosexual and the heterosexual concepts, the number of inconsistencies out of 10 was either 0 or 1. The number of inconsistencies tended to increase for the homosexual measure and to decrease for the heterosexual measure between pre- and post-treatment. However, the changes are not particularly marked and it is not proposed to embark on a discussion of this finding at the present time. What can be concluded is that the technique gives a high degree of internal consistency of response.

B. UNIDIMENSIONALITY

We thus had a measuring device consisting of six separate adjectives, each of which yields a score of from 1 to 8. Should it be possible to add these scores together, we would have had a scale which would range from 6 to 48, giving a wide range of scores, and thus a fairly high degree of discrimination of changes in sexual interest. We therefore carried out principal components analyses on the Atlas computer of Manchester University of the adjective scores of the 32 patients and of 26 female controls not selected for their known sexual interest. These controls were aged between 18 and 29, and all were born in Great Britain.

Data are shown for the controls of the results of testing on two occasions separated by a 1-month interval, and for the pre-, mid-, and post-treatment scores of the 32 patients. For ease of presentation, the latent roots which were extracted by the principal components analyses, numbering up to 5 at most, are shown for each group of subjects on each occasion of testing. The data shown in the body of Table 4.2 consists of the percentage variance accounted for by

TABLE 4.2. PRINCIPAL COMPONENTS ANALYSES OF SEXUAL ORIENTATION METHOD SCORES OF CONTROLS (26 UNSELECTED FEMALES) AND 32 HOMOSEXUAL PATIENTS

| Group | Measure | Occasion | Latent roots | | | | |
			1st	2nd	3rd	4th	5th
Controls[a]	Hom.	First	78.30	10.27	6.48	2.86	2.09
		Second	90.93	5.46	3.61		
	Het.	First	84.12	7.46	3.26	3.05	2.10
		Second	90.75	3.54	3.13	2.58	
Homosexuals	Hom.	Pre-treatment	85.83	6.82	4.74	2.60	
		Mid-treatment	89.90	5.13	3.04	1.93	
		Post-treatment	96.44	3.56			
	Het.	Pre-treatment	82.52	7.49	5.57	2.38	2.04
		Mid-treatment	90.47	3.98	3.51	2.04	
		Post-treatment	91.40	3.61	2.77	2.22	

Data expressed as percentages of the total variance accounted for by each latent root.
[a]Twenty-six female controls aged 18–29 were administered the scale twice, the test–re-test interval being 1 month.

each latent root. It can be seen that the first latent root accounted for the vast majority of the total variance in each case, the lowest proportion being 78%. It was not possible to rotate any of these principal components analyses, as after the first latent root had been extracted the proportion of the sums of squares which still remained in no case reached 0.9. This is the minimum required by the Atlas principal components programme for rotation. None of the 6 adjectives loaded consistently on any of the roots more than did any of the others. It could be concluded that one latent root accounted for the vast proportion of the total variance for both groups and for all occasions on which they were tested. It was reasonable, therefore, to assume the unidimensionality of the questionnaire, and it followed that it was permissible to add the scores obtained on each adjective to yield two total scores, each of which had a possible range of 6 (1 × 6) to 48 (8 × 6). One score related to the concept "men are sexually to me" and the other to the concept "women are sexually to me". The remainder of the data discussed below consisted of scores treated in this manner.

C. RELIABILITY

Table 4.3 presents the test–re-test reliabilities of 2 samples of control subjects. The first consisted of 26 females referred to above who were re-tested after an interval of 1 month. The reliabilities of both measures for this group are around 0.8 and are significant at well beyond the 0.1% level. It is of interest that of the 26 female controls, the 9 who had the lowest heterosexual score ("men are . . .") on the first occasion were also the 9 who had the lowest score on the second occasion. Similarly, of the 9 who had the highest homosexual ("women are . . .") score on the first occasion, 8 were in the top 9 on the second occasion also. This provides further evidence of the reliability of the scale even in control subjects who had no particular reason to be honest about themselves.

TABLE 4.3. TEST–RE-TEST RELIABILITY ON THE TWO MEASURES OF THE SEXUAL ORIENTATION METHOD OF 26 UNSELECTED FEMALES (TEST–RE-TEST INTERVAL = 1 MONTH) AND 14 MALE CONTROLS (TEST–RE-TEST INTERVAL = 9 MONTHS)

		Measure			
		Homosexual		Heterosexual	
Group	Occasion	Mean	SD	Mean	SD
Unselected females	First	16.54	8.44	42.15	5.79
	Second	14.15	9.50	42.80	6.04
		$r\ 1.2 = 0.80^a$		$r\ 1.2 = 0.82^a$	
Heterosexual males	First	9.43	4.77	46.71	3.97
	Second	7.57	2.53	47.64	1.35
		$r\ 1.2 = 0.85^a$		$r\ 1.2 = 0.94^a$	

[a] $p = < 0.001$.

The second sample consisted of the 14 subjects out of a larger initial sample of 24 males who were available for re-testing after an interval of 9 months. The total sample of male controls was deliberately selected for their known active heterosexuality. It can be seen that in this sample also, the reliability of the test is extremely high, being 0.85 on the homosexual and 0.94 on the heterosexual measure. Both of these are significant at well beyond the 0.1% level.

D. VALIDITY

It is clear from Table 4.4 that the pre-treatment mean homosexual score of the patient group is very significantly higher than those of both control groups. Conversely, on the heterosexual measure, the mean score of the patient group is significantly less than those of the 2 control groups. A further examination of these results shows that the female group is significantly more homosexual than is the male control group, and that it is also significantly less interested in the opposite sex. The female control group consisted, of course, of unselected subjects, some of whom, by chance alone, would be expected to have some degree of homosexual orientation. By way of contrast, the male group was specially selected for its known heterosexuality. The difference between the 2 groups is therefore entirely explicable.

The next question was to ascertain whether patients who showed an improvement after treatment, as clinically assessed (Feldman and MacCulloch, 1965), showed a similar change on the questionnaire measures. In all cases the clinical assessment of improvement was made independently. Of the group of 32 patients (all but 4 of the 36 patients who completed treatment, as described in Chapter 3), 23 had shown a marked clinical improvement in their

TABLE 4.4. SEXUAL ORIENTATION METHOD SCORES OF 26 UNSELECTED FEMALES, 24 HETEROSEXUAL MALES, AND 32 PRE-TREATMENT HOMOSEXUAL PATIENTS

Group	Measure							
	Homosexual				Heterosexual			
	Mean	SD	Comparison	t	Mean	SD	Comparison	t
1. Unselected females	16.54	8.44	1 vs. 2	3.61[a]	42.15	5.79	1 vs. 2	3.85[a]
2. Heterosexual males	9.24	5.50	2 vs. 3	19.13[a]	47.16	2.92	2 vs. 3	6.93[a]
3. Homosexual patients	40.42	6.62	1 vs. 3	13.52[a]	31.21	9.83	1 vs. 3	4.52[a]

[a]$p = < 0.001$.

sexual orientation in that they had entirely ceased homosexual practices and had ceased, or almost entirely ceased to use homosexual phantasy. In addition, the majority had engaged in active overt heterosexual practice, or at the very least, used strong heterosexual phantasy.

TABLE 4.5. SEXUAL ORIENTATION METHOD SCORES OF PRE- AND POST-AVERSION THERAPY TREATMENT FOR HOMOSEXUALITY OF 23 IMPROVED AND 9 UNIMPROVED PATIENTS

Occasion	Measure									
	Homosexual					Heterosexual				
	Improved		Unimproved			Improved		Unimproved		
	Mean	SD	Mean	SD	t	Mean	SD	Mean	SD	t
Pre-treatment	39.71	6.95	42.33	5.55	1.02 N.S.	32.83	10.03	26.84	9.37	1.57 N.S.
Post-treatment	22.08	10.34	39.00	8.01	4.46[a]	42.75	6.71	32.77	10.75	3.25[b]

[a]$p = < 0.001$.   [b]$p = < 0.01$.

Table 4.5 shows the scores on the 2 measures of 23 improved and 9 unimproved patients. It can be seen that, prior to treatment, the mean scores of these 2 groups did not differ significantly on either measure. Post-treatment, the groups do differ very significantly on both the homosexual measure ($p = < 0.001$) and on the heterosexual measure ($p = < 0.01$).

It is necessary to show that the changes in the improved patients were not due to an expectation effect of the kind described by Goldstein (1962) which might be displayed because of their exposure to the possibility of receiving help. Data are available on 8 patients who first appeared for interview at a time when the waiting list was such that an immediate start to treatment was not possible. This group were the first 8 patients who participated in the controlled trial described in Chapter 5. They were, therefore, re-tested immediately before they started their treatment. The mean interval between first interview and the start of treatment was 9.75 weeks, with a standard deviation of 3.28 and a range of 4–16 weeks. The mean score on the homosexual measure on the first occasion was 45.62 and on the second was 44.63, the difference not being significant. The mean score on the heterosexual measure on the first occasion was 26.76 and on the second occasion 27.25; again, the difference is not significant.

During the 6 months following treatment, the improved patients continued to improve, albeit slowly; in some cases the unimproved patients showed poorer scores, particularly on the heterosexual measure. Table 4.6 shows the 6 and 12 months post-treatment scores of 20 improved and 6 unimproved patients. It is clear from Table 4.6 that there were no significant changes for either the improved or the unimproved patients on either measure between 6 and 12 months post-treatment. There is, therefore, good evidence that improvements on the scale are not random and do not occur as a function either of time alone or of an expectation effect.

TABLE 4.6. SEXUAL ORIENTATION METHOD SCORES OBTAINED 6 AND 12 MONTHS POST-TREATMENT FROM 20 IMPROVED AND 6 UNIMPROVED HOMOSEXUAL PATIENTS

Group	Occasion	Measure			
		Homosexual		Heterosexual	
		Mean	SD	Mean	SD
Improved patients	6 months' post-treatment	20.90	10.95	44.35	5.50
Improved patients	12 months' post-treatment	17.25	9.34	45.95	3.98
		$t = 1.127$ (NS)		$t = 1.024$ (NS)	
Unimproved patients	6 months' post-treatment	43.33	5.91	22.33	5.73
Unimproved patients	12 months' post-treatment	43.33	5.62	18.00	9.67
		$t = 0$		$t = 0.86$ (NS)	

DISCUSSION

We have described a technique, termed the Sexual Orientation Method* (SOM) for assessing the relative levels of homo- and heteroerotic interest in patients known to display homosexual behaviour. It is intended for the purpose of plotting changes, or the absence of changes, in these relative levels, as treatment proceeds. It is *not* intended for the purpose of detecting homosexuality in those otherwise not presenting with it, as no attempt is made to disguise the overall purpose of the SOM.

We have demonstrated that the SOM provides results which are internally consistent, exhibit unidimensionality, and have a satisfactorily high reliability and validity. It provides a wide range of scores, and hence is a means of picking up relatively small changes in sexual orientation.

Qualitative data are provided by the clinical interviews which are carried out before and after treatment. For instance, we might wish to know the extent to which an increase in score on the heterosexual measure, following treatment, has been translated into overt behaviour. Conversely, a high score on the homosexual measure, marked by much inconsistency, throws considerable doubt on a verbally stated claim by the patient to be less

*Phillips (1968) has recently described a development of the SOM which appears to represent a technical advance.

interested in males. His claim can then be probed in interview until the patient feels able to accept his true lack of change, thus providing a realistic basis for continued treatment. The SOM is thus not intended to supplant the clinical interview but to provide complementary quantitative data.

Finally, it should be relatively simple to design questionnaires similar to this which would be specific to individuals displaying sexual deviations which present relatively infrequently for treatment. For instance, one of our fetishist* patients had a strong degree of sexual interest in women much older than himself and only a small degree of interest in females of his own age. Treatment for him consisted of a modification of the anticipatory avoidance learning technique described in Chapter 2. His progress was recorded in much the same way as for our homosexual patients except that the concepts used were "older women are sexually to me" and "women of my own age are sexually to me".

*Described in Feldman *et al.* (1968).

CHAPTER 5

A CONTROLLED TRIAL OF ANTICIPATORY AVOIDANCE, CLASSICAL CONDITIONING, AND PSYCHOTHERAPY

THE results of the treatment of the series of 43 homosexual patients, given in Chapters 3 and 4, provided substantial support for the hypothesis that the anticipatory avoidance learning technique had a considerable degree of effectiveness in the treatment of homosexuality. However, it was possible to interpret the particular form of avoidance learning that had been used in terms of the active element of the learning technique being subsumable under the heading of classical conditioning. This is because the patient received a shock on one-third of all trials irrespective of his attempts to remove the slide. In classical conditioning proper the patient would be shocked on every trial, and he would not be provided with a response lever. The trials on which shock was received are perhaps best described as un-avoidable shock trials; however, the resemblance to standard classical conditioning was sufficiently close to require examination. A further possible interpretation of the results obtained was that the enthusiasm of the therapist was being communicated to the patient; this, together with the fact that a good deal of reinforcement was given in the form of reassurance and praise for reported improvement, could be construed as constituting a form of psychotherapy. In addition, there seemed to us to be a standard requirement for any treatment technique to be evaluated in the form of a controlled trial. It was, therefore, decided to carry out a further piece of therapeutic research, taking the form of a controlled trial, in which successive homosexual patients asking for treatment would be randomly assigned to one of three treatment groups—anticipatory avoidance, classical conditioning, and psychotherapy.

A number of changes were made in the stimulus presentation system, in the patient response system, and in the recording system. These changes were partly in order to achieve a greater flexibility in the anticipatory avoidance treatment system and partly to enable a wider range of responses to be recorded.

CHANGES IN THE STIMULUS PRESENTATION SYSTEM

(1) The range of stimuli used, both male and female, was increased. In the series of patients described in Chapter 3, all the stimuli were stills. Several movie clips of both male and female persons were now incorporated; it was hoped that these would increase the verisimilitude of the treatment situation.

(2) Only one still-projector was used in the original system. Two such projectors were now used both in order to reduce the mechanical burden on the therapist and also to allow the

patient increased operant control in the manner described below. In addition, because of the incorporation of movie stimuli, two movie projectors were now used, giving four projectors in all.

(3) In the previous system the patient sat in a chair, viewing slides presented by back-projection on to a viewing box. At times, however, patients complained of discomfort, and a more relaxed position was thought necessary. In the Trial to be described, the patient lay on a bed in order to view the slide, which was projected by an angled mirror on to a ceiling screen.

(4) The arrangements for presenting the electrical aversive stimulus were duplicated, so that it could now be given to either leg using a preselector switch. The shock strength was controlled by individual rheostats on the output circuits (see below).

CHANGES IN THE PATIENT RESPONSE SYSTEM

(1) In the series of 43 patients, the female slide was introduced by the therapist immediately following the removal of the male slide. The patient was allowed operant control only of the *reappearance* of the female slide. This system was changed so that both the *initial* appearance *and* the subsequent reappearance of the female slide were under the control of the patient with therapist override.

(2) The control system was re-designed to allow the patient's operant response directly to switch off the male stimulus and the shock (when this was administered). Previously, the patient merely signalled his wish that the male slide be switched off.

These changes necessitated two separate patient switches. The patient's male stimulus avoidance switch automatically broke the UCS (electrical aversive stimulus) circuit; his female approach switch automatically caused the female slide to appear in a manner described below.

THE ANTICIPATORY AVOIDANCE TREATMENT SYSTEM

As described in Chapter 2, there was much experimental evidence that the greater the variation in stimulus conditions during training, the greater the resistance of a newly acquired response to post-training extinction. The corollary of this was that the transition between training and real life condition should be as gradual and imperceptible as possible. The reinforcement schedule used for the series of patients described in Chapter 3 could be criticized as somewhat rigid (Feldman, 1966), in that one-third of all trials, in all sessions, were non-reinforced. It was felt preferable gradually to reduce the proportion of these non-reinforced (shock) trials so as to allow the patient the experience of performing avoidance responses during a long sequence of stimulus presentations from which shock was absent. The single programme of one-third reinforced, one-third delayed, and one-third non-reinforced trials was replaced by a series of 4 programmes, through which the patient proceeded in turn. The proportion of reinforced and delayed trials gradually increased from programme 1 to programme 4, and the proportion of non-reinforced trials was gradually decreased from one-third in programme 1 to nil in programme 4. There were several other ways in which greater flexibility of technique was sought, all being specifically connected with the occurrence of the female (relief) slide and all exemplifying the working out in practice of the major theoretical principle of the desirability of avoiding generalization decrement (Kimble, 1961). They were as follows:

(1) The frequency of the initial appearance of the female slide (when requested by the patient) now varied from 100% on non-shock trials in programme 1—as before—to 33% in programme 4. The purpose of this was to establish the response of requesting the female slide (programme 1) and then gradually to accustom the patient to performing this response despite his decreasing rate of reward (programmes 2–4).

(2) The number of trials on which a female slide reappeared was gradually reduced from 16 (programme 1) to 3 (programme 4). Once again, the aim was to establish the initial operant response of requesting the reappearance of the female slide and then to maintain this response despite relatively infrequent rewards.

(3) The next variable concerned the maximum number of reappearances a female slide made per trial. This gradually increased from 1 in programme 1 to 3 in programme 3, and then decreased to 2 in programme 4. Once again, the aim was to first establish and maintain,

TABLE 5.1. FOUR PROGRAMMES USED IN SUCCESSION IN THE TREATMENT OF THE GROUP TREATED BY ANTICIPATORY AVOIDANCE LEARNING (AA)

A	Programme 1			Programme 2			Programme 3			Programme 4		
	B	C	D	B	C	D	B	C	D	B	C	D
			(secs)			(secs)			(secs)			(secs)
1.	D4½	2	20	D4½	3	20	R	–	20	R	3	20
2.	R	2	35	D4½	–	35	R	1	35	R	–	35
3.	D6	2	20	D6	1	20	R	1	20	D4½	1	20
4.	R	2	25	R	3	25	D4½	4	25	D6	–	25
5.	NR	–	15	NR	–	15	NR	–	15	R	1	15
6.	D4½	2	35	D7½	–	35	R	–	35	R	–	35
7.	D7½	2	25	D6	–	25	D4½	–	25	D4½	–	25
8.	NR	–	40	NR	–	40	D6	1	40	D4½	–	40
9.	NR	–	30	R	1	30	D7½	–	30	R	1	30
10.	R	2	40	R	3	40	D6	4	40	R	–	40
11.	NR	–	20	R	–	20	D4½	–	20	R	–	20
12.	R	2	25	D4½	1	25	R	–	25	R	–	25
13.	NR	–	35	NR	–	35	D4½	1	35	D7½	1	35
14.	R	2	25	R	–	25	R	–	25	R	–	25
15.	R	2	15	R	1	15	R	4	15	R	–	15
16.	D6	2	40	D4½	3	40	D6	–	40	D7½	–	40
17.	D7½	2	30	D6	–	30	R	–	30	D6	–	30
18.	NR	–	15	D7½	3	15	R	4	15	D7½	–	15
19.	D4½	2	35	R	–	35	R	–	35	D4½	3	35
20.	R	2	20	R	3	20	R	1	20	R	–	20
21.	NR	–	30	NR	–	30	NR	–	30	R	1	30
22.	R	2	40	R	–	40	D7½	–	40	D6	–	40
23.	NR	–	30	D7½	3	30	D7½	4	30	D6	3	30
24.	D7½	2	15	R	3	15	D6	–	15	D7½	–	15
	(Female stimulus time 4 sec both for initial appearance and reappearance)			(Female stimulus time 8 sec)			(Female stimulus time 12 sec)			(Female stimulus time 12 sec)		

A, trial no.
B, trial type: D, delayed; R, reinforced; NR, non-reinforced (shock).
C, no. of female requests granted.
D, inter-trial interval.

TABLE 5.2. SUMMARY OF VARIATIONS IN THE FOUR PROGRAMMES USED FOR AA LEARNING

Variable	Programme			
	1	2	3	4
Non-reinforced trials	8	4	2	0
Reinforced trials	8	10	11	12
Delay trials	8	10	11	12
Trials on which initial F allowed	16	12	10	8
Exposure of initial F	4 sec	8 sec	12 sec	12 sec
No. of reappearances of F per trial	1	2	3	2
No. of trials on which F reappears	16	8	5	3
Exposure of return F	4 sec	8 sec	12 sec	12 sec

Patient must avoid within 4 seconds on 3 trials in succession at the beginning of each new slide before going on to a programme.

despite relative non-reward, the developing habit of performing approach responses to female stimuli.

(4) In order to accustom the patient to the presence of the female slide, the length of the initial presentation was gradually increased from 4 seconds (programme 1) to 12 seconds (programme 4).

(5) Similarly, as in (4), the length of reappearance of the female slide gradually increased from 4 seconds (programme 1) to 12 seconds (programme 4).

Programmes 1–4 are set out in Tables 5.1 and 5.2. It will be seen that these programmes varied along several dimensions simultaneously. When this system is used in its most flexible way, the change over between programmes is contingent upon the patient responding satisfactorily to the previous programme—that is performing avoidance responses with short latencies (2 seconds or less) and also making at least as great a number of requests for the female slide as the particular programme allowed. By the time the patient is exposed to programme 4, he is both avoiding the male slide, in the absence of shock, and also making a considerable number of requests for the appearance and reappearance of the female slide even though these were only granted infrequently. As in the case of the previous treatment system, hierarchies of male and female slides are simultaneously traversed in opposite directions. It might be that both slides and programmes are changed in mid-session. Overall, the system is now more flexible than previously, giving increased control over the patient's responses and an increased theoretical likelihood of avoiding generalization decrement. The situation is also very much more of a "dialogue" between patient and therapist in that there is a constant feedback from the patient which the therapist matches by the appropriate combination of slide and programme. However, because the trial was to be carried out in as controlled a manner as possible, very considerable constraints were imposed upon the flexibility of the new treatment system for anticipatory avoidance learning, as will be described shortly.

CLASSICAL CONDITIONING (CC)

Patients receiving CC had the same number of sessions of treatment as those having anticipatory avoidance (AA), with the same number of trials per session. The interval between trials varied randomly, again as in the case of the AA patients. Each of the CC trials consisted of the following sequence of events. The male slide was displayed for 2 seconds and in the last half-second of this 2-second period the patient received a shock, the strength of which varied randomly about a point previously determined as being unpleasant for the patient. The male slide and shock were removed simultaneously, and a female slide was shown immediately for a period of 10 seconds precisely and then removed. The female slide was shown on every trial of every session, hence those receiving CC were shown a female stimulus irrespective of their own wishes in this respect.

In the CC situation patients were the passive recipients of stimuli, and were not provided with any response manipulanda in contrast to the patients receiving AA conditioning. The female slide was exposed for 10 seconds on each trial, giving a total exposure of female slides of 4 minutes per session. This figure was calculated as representing approximately the same total exposure to female stimuli as that experienced by AA patients receiving all the exposures of the female slides allowable in programmes 1–4. Because of the nature of CC, those receiving CC treatment would, of course, be exposed to a considerably greater number of shocks than those receiving AA treatment.

PSYCHOTHERAPY (P)

The third group of patients were treated by psychotherapy given by a consultant psychiatrist (M. J. MacCulloch—M.J.M.) who had had previous training and experience in psychotherapy. These patients received their treatment resting on the same bed in the same treatment room used for the patients receiving the two learning treatments. The number of hours of psychotherapy was the same as the number of treatment hours in the two learning techniques. Psychotherapy consisted of the exploration and discussion of the patients' sexual and associated personality difficulties. In all cases, a considerable proportion of the psychotherapy time was spent in discussing the patient's attitudes to females, particularly attitudes of aversion and fear, but formal systematic desensitization (Wolpe, 1958) was not used.

THE REVISED APPARATUS SYSTEM

Summary of functions required in the system.

Therapist:

    (a)   Switches on and off male still slides.
    (b)   Switches on and off female still slides.
    (c)   Switches on and off male movie loops.
    (d)   Switches on and off female movie loops.
    (e)   Administers electrical aversive stimuli to the patient.
    (f)   Overrides the patient's attempts to remove the male stimuli.
    (g)   Regulates the strength of the shock and the site of shock administration.

Patient:

    (a)   Switches off male slide and shock concurrently, either before the onset of the UCS or during its time of administration.
    (b)   Switches on female still or movie stimuli.

Permanent record requirements:

    (a)   Temporal record of CS onset and offset, both still and movie.

    (b)   Temporal record of onset and offset of female stimuli.

    (c)   Onset and offset of UCS.

    (d)   Onset and offset of patient's avoidance or escape responses.

    (e)   Onset and offset of patient's requests for female stimuli.

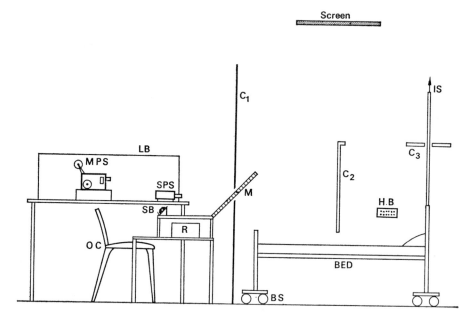

Fig. 5.1. Controlled trial of treatment of homosexuality: laboratory layout. BS, ballistic mechanism for the bed. C_1, C_2, C_3, black curtains which enclose the patient. HB, headboard for connecting ECG and EMG. IS, inertial switch for recording bed movement. LB, light box. M, mirror. MPS, movie projectors (2). OC, operator's chair. R, recorder. SB, operator's switchboard. SPS, still projectors (2).

APPARATUS FOR THE REVISED SYSTEM

Two pairs of projectors (one movie and one still) were set to project via a mirror on to a ceiling screen. This was placed immediately over the patient's bed. The projection apparatus was thoroughly light-screened from the patient.

The projectors were set to run continuously; their light sources were obscured by cardboard discs which were carried on the semaphore arms of four car-direction indicators. The 12-volt d.c. source for activating the indicators was supplied via a 2-pole 5-position switch which, when operated, fed current in parallel to appropriate time markers.

Thus the stimuli were presented by an electrically safe system, avoiding a 250-volt circuit; these switching events were capable of temporal recording using a 12-volt marker system. Figure 5.1 shows the layout of the treatment system.

The recorders were electromagnets and were attached to fibre-write pens. The write-out deck contained 10 pens, all of which operated vertically on to a standard 4-in. wide kymograph, running at 1.5 cm/sec.

The main CS1 presentation circuit was modified by including a break-switch loop which allowed the patient to avoid (i.e. to switch off the male stimulus). The therapist was provided with an override switch which short-circuited the patient's control loop on delayed and non-reinforced trials.

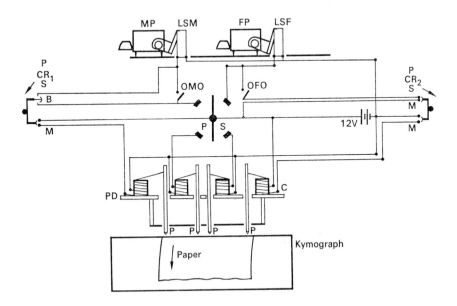

FIG. 5.2. Controlled trial of treatment of homosexuality: wiring diagram for therapy and recording apparatus. *Stimulus presentation circuit:* Anti-clockwise operation of operator's presentation switch (PS) supplies power to light shutter male (LSM) via the patient's CR1 switch (PCR$_1$S). This activation of LSM uncovers the light source of the male projector (MP). Clockwise operation of the PS activates female light shutter (LSF), thus uncovering light source of the female projector (FP). *Patient's response system:* (a) *Avoidance.* During the operation of LSM by the operator, the patient may inactivate the light shutter LSM by pressing switch PCR$_1$S which breaks the circuit to LSM. The operator is able to override this avoidance switching by closing the operator's male override switch (OMO). (b) Female request switching is achieved by the patient pressing switch PCR$_2$S which, when the operator's female override (OFO) is closed, will activate light shutter female (LSF) and provide the patient with a female stimulus. *Recording Apparatus:* The 4 electromagnetic coil/pen units (C) are set on a pen deck (PD) allowing the pens (P) to write on the kymograph paper. The central 2 units are operated simultaneously (in parallel) when the operator's PS is moved to either clockwise or anti-clockwise position recording onset, duration, and offset of female and male stimuli respectively. During patient's avoidance switching using PCR$_1$S, a second switch labelled M linked in mechanical parallel to B is simultaneously operated and activates left-hand pen unit marking the patient's avoidance responses. An identical method is employed at PCR$_2$S to mark patient's female requests via the right-hand pen unit.

The patient was provided with a second hand-switch whose operation shorted the therapist's female presentation switch. This allowed the patient to obtain a female stimulus. The circuit (Fig. 5.2) was also mastered on the operator's switchboard by the inclusion of an operator's break switch on one arm of the patient's circuit.

Both operant response switches were mechanically linked to temporal marker switches.

THE DESIGN OF THE CONTROLLED TRIAL

Thirty patients were randomly assigned to the three treatment groups on the basis of a random numbers table drawn up previously. The assignation was completely automatic as the patient presented for treatment and was in no way dependent upon clinical or other features of the patient. The criteria for inclusion in the trial were as follows:

(1) Aged under 40.
(2) No current psychosis.
(3) No current organic psycho-syndrome.
(4) Assuming that this was detectable in the initial interview, no severe personality disorder other than one of the self-insecure type.
(5) No epilepsy.
(6) No alcoholism or drug addiction.
(7) IQ above 80.

Only 5 patients of the total number who presented for treatment in the year during which the trial patients were selected and treated were excluded on the grounds of the above criteria.

When they first appeared, all patients received a lengthy interview schedule which they completed themselves and which was then gone over with the patient in order to fill in any gaps where amplification was needed. In addition, all patients completed the Cattell 16 personality factors questionnaire, the Eysenck personality inventory (Eysenck and Eysenck, 1964), the Mill Hill vocabulary scale, and the sexual orientation method questionnaire (Feldman *et al.*, 1966). The results of these measures were coded on to punch cards. Each patient was given a trial number and assigned to one of the three treatment groups by J. F. Orford (J.F.O.) on the basis of a random numbers table. J.F.O. knew nothing about the patients whatsoever apart from their identification number and the treatment which they received. Both learning treatments were carried out by J.F.O. for the majority of the patients and for the last few patients by Mrs. Valerie Mellor, another probationer psychologist at the hospital. As previously stated, psychotherapy was carried out by M.J.M. The involvement of M. P. Feldman (M.P.F.) was restricted to the initial interview and to interviews carried out after each batch of treatment sessions. Throughout, M.P.F. did not know the composition of the three treatment groups. M.J.M. did not know to which learning technique the non-psychotherapy patients had been assigned.

For both the AA and the CC group, 8 male stimuli and 8 female stimuli were used. Prior to the administration of the learning techniques, both groups of patients were shown by J.F.O. a series of 30 male and 30 female stills, and a number of male and female movie clips. To each of these they assigned a score from 0 to 10 to indicate the degree of sexual attractiveness which the slide or still picture had for them. J.F.O. then selected for each patient 8 male and 8 female stimuli to give a range of scores from 0 to 10. Each group of 8 were then shown to the patient in pairs, so that each member of a series of 8 was paired with each other member. In each case the patient was required to indicate which of the two was more attractive to him. By the use of this paired comparison method, which had also been used for the series of patients described in Chapter 3, hierarchies of slide attractiveness were constructed.

On the basis of the experience obtained with the series patients, it was decided that 24 sessions of learning treatment would be sufficient to indicate whether or not the patient was likely to make a satisfactory response to treatment; accordingly, both learning groups received 24 sessions of treatment. Because of the unreality of giving psychotherapy for the relatively short period of 30 minutes, psychotherapy patients received 12 one-hour sessions.

In order to match as precisely as possible the treatment received by the 2 learning groups, each of the 8 slides was used for 3 sessions exactly. This meant that the AA patients might be moved from one slide to another, even though they were still showing long avoidance latencies. Similarly, they might be moved from one female slide to another, even though they were not making a large number of requests for the return of the female slide. Anticipatory avoidance patients started on programme 1 for session 1, moving on to programme 2 for session 2, and on to programme 3 for session 3. For session 4, they then moved on to male and female slides number 2, and moved back to programme 1, proceeding through programmes 2 and 3 for sessions 5 and 6. This sequence of events was repeated for the next 6 sessions, so that for sessions 1–12 programmes 1–3 were used. For sessions 13–24 the first programme to be used was programme 2; the second programme 3, and the third programme 4. Once again, there were 3 sessions per slide. The sequence of events for sessions 13–24 was: session 13, slide 5, programme 2; session 14, slide 5, programme 3; session 15, slide 5, programme 4. The sequence began again with session 16, as follows:

Session 16, slide 6, programme 2.
Session 17, slide 6, programme 3.
Session 18, slide 6, programme 4, and so on, to session 24.

There was, therefore, the possibility that the patients would be moved from programme 3, on which they received two non-reinforced trials, to programme 4, on which no shocks were received at all despite still showing long latency responses to the slide in use. That is, we were not using the AA method in the flexible manner ideally allowed by the new system of 4 programmes, described earlier in this chapter. However, it was felt essential to control the trial as rigidly as possible, even though this meant using one of the learning techniques in a less than optimal manner.

On the basis of the data obtained on the series of patients described in Chapter 3, it was decided that a shift on the SOM homosexual measure of 12 points or more, using the immediately pre-treatment score as the base line, would be sufficient to indicate that a successful response to treatment had been achieved and that treatment could, therefore, cease after 24 sessions. Having completed 24 sessions (or 12 hours of treatment in the case of the psychotherapy patients), patients again filled in the SOM, and their scores on this were compared by J.F.O. with the score obtained prior to treatment. A post-treatment interview was held with the patient by M.P.F. This consisted of a brief assessment of the patient's self-reported sexual interests and behaviour. At the conclusion of the interview, J.F.O. informed M.P.F. whether or not the patient had met the criterion for successful response. Should the SOM score have indicated that the patient had failed to reach the criterion laid down, he was informed by M.P.F. that it had been decided to continue his treatment, but that something rather different was to be done. On the basis of the review of literature described in Chapter 1 concerning the efficacy of psychotherapy, it was decided that patients who had had a learning treatment should not be exposed to psychotherapy, but that those who had had psychotherapy should have the opportunity of receiving a learning treatment. Those patients who had had psychotherapy, but who had failed to reach the criterion of change, were randomly assigned by J.F.O. to either AA or CC. Those patients who had been treated by one of the two learning techniques and had failed to reach the criterion were automatically assigned to the other learning technique. Following 24 sessions of the learning treatment received in stage 2, the SOM was again administered and the results communicated to M.P.F., again following a brief interview. At this point J.F.O. informed M.P.F. whether or not the treatment received in stage 2 was the last to be received by the patient or whether, in the event of stage 2 not achieving success, he was to be given a further period of treatment. If the patient had received one of the two learning treatments in stage 1, but had failed to achieve the criterion of success, he was reassigned to the other learning technique for stage 2, following which his treatment terminated irrespective of the change in SOM scores obtained. However, if the patient had received psychotherapy in stage 1, and had failed to reach the required post-treatment criterion, had been reassigned to one of the two learning techniques for stage 2 and had still failed to reach the criterion, he was then automatically reassigned to the other learning technique for stage 3. Should the latter prove to be the case, M.P.F. informed the patient that further treatment was to be received and arrangements were made for doing so. M.P.F. did not know which of the learning techniques had been received in stage 2. This was also true of stage 3, during which patients who had originally had psychotherapy in stage 1 and a learning technique in stage 2 were treated by the other learning technique. However, M.P.F. could deduce that patients still in treatment by stage 3 had been treated by psychotherapy in stage 1. At the conclusion of stage 3, patients who had passed this far were again interviewed by M.P.F. and their current sexual behaviour and interests noted. They again completed the SOM questionnaire, and were informed that their treatment was now completed.

In summary, some patients received 24 sessions of treatment, attaining the criterion of improvement at the end of stage 1, some had 48 sessions of treatment, and some had 72 sessions of treatment. The reason for allowing all patients who had failed to respond to one method of treatment, the opportunity of receiving another method, rather than allowing a lengthy follow-up period, was that we were trying to combine the requirements of a scientifically acceptable trial with a reasonable standard of ethical professional behaviour. It will be seen, when the results of the trial are discussed later in this chapter, that the second objective somewhat conflicted with the aims of the first.

All patients attended for follow-up 2 weeks, 4 weeks, 6 weeks, and 12 weeks after the conclusion of their treatment. A longer interview than usual was administered, sometimes by M.P.F. alone, sometimes by M.J.M. alone, and sometimes by both together, at the 12-week follow-up. The patients continued to be followed up, even after the 12-week major assessment, until the closing date of the trial. The longest period of follow-up by interview was 58 weeks and the shortest 12 weeks. It was felt that 12 weeks was a sufficiently long period of minimum follow-up, as it seemed likely that if relapse was going to occur it would do so within this period. If patients showed evidence of relapse following initial improvement, as indicated by the return of their SOM scores to the pre-treatment levels, they were given AA treatment in the flexible manner made possible by the new system. This was necessary for two patients—one who received CC and improved sufficiently after the initial 24 sessions of treatment to be considered successful, and another patient who made a similarly successful response to his initial 24 sessions (12 hours) of psychotherapy.

The plan of the trial, showing stages 1, 2, and 3, and the follow-up, is shown in Fig. 5.3.

DESCRIPTIVE DATA ON THE TRIAL PATIENTS

1. SOCIAL AND PSYCHIATRIC FACTORS

Twenty-eight of the 30 patients in the trial were male homosexuals and 2 were female homosexuals (one was randomly assigned to AA and the other to CC). The data on these 2 patients will be presented as part of the total body of data except when strictly relevant.

Table 5.3 shows the ages of the patients when first referred. It will be seen that, in general, the sample of patients is rather younger than those treated in the series, all but 5 being under 30. There were no marked systematic differences in age range between the 3 groups. Only

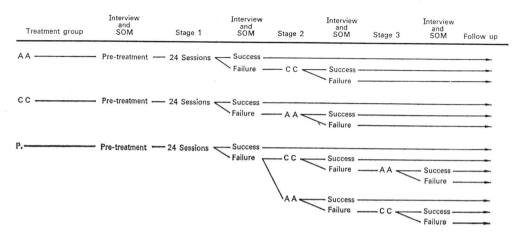

Fig. 5.3. Schematic stage-by-stage diagram of the sequence of events in the controlled trial of homosexuality by AA, CC, and P.

2 of the patients in the trial were married—1 in the AA group and 1 in the P group. The married AA patient had 2 children and the married P patient had 1 child.

Table 5.4 shows the extent to which patients came from a home "broken" before the age of 16. As in the case of the series patients, the majority of those in the trial came from a home which had survived intact until they had reached the age of 16. There were no marked differences in the nature of the home background between the 3 groups of patients.

Table 5.5 refers to the incidence of mental ill health in the family of the patient. While this was present in only 1 of the CC patients and 2 of the P patients, no fewer than 6 of the AA patients had a family history of mental ill health. However, the comparison between the groups failed to reach an acceptable level of statistical significance.

One-third of the total sample had passed an examination to enter a secondary grammar school; this approximated to the proportion in the series described in Chapter 3 and is, again, somewhat higher than would be expected in the general population. There were no marked differences in educational level between the 3 groups, nor were there differences between the groups in the proportions of the various religious categories which comprised them.

TABLE 5.3. AGE ON FIRST REFERRAL

Age range in years	AA[a]	CC	P	Total
15–20	3	4	2	9
21–25	4	1	3	8
26–30	3	3	2	8
31–35	0	1	3	4
36–40	0	1	0	1
Total	10	10	10	30

[a]Throughout, AA = patients initially assigned to anticipatory avoidance treatment, CC those assigned to classical conditioning treatment, and P those assigned to treatment by psychotherapy.

TABLE 5.4. OCCURRENCE OF A "BROKEN" HOME PRIOR TO THE AGE OF 16

Age range	AA	CC	P	Total
0–5	2	1	1	4
6–10	0	2	0	2
11–15	2	2	1	5
Never	6	5	8	19
Total	10	10	10	30

TABLE 5.5. MENTAL ILLNESS IN THE FAMILY

Mental illness	AA	CC	P	Total
Present	6	1	2	9
Absent	4	9	8	21
Total	10	10	10	30

The reasons for appearing for treatment are shown in Table 5.6. The most marked difference is that none of the AA patients appeared on an order of the court as against 2 in each of the other 2 groups. In addition, 5 of the AA patients were originally referred for psychiatric illness as against 2 in each of the other 2 groups. In all, 9 patients appeared originally for a psychiatric illness, the proportion of the total sample being greater than in the case of the series patients. The number appearing entirely of their own accord was roughly the same in all three groups.

The motivation for treatment is shown in Table 5.7 and it can be seen that this was high in 9 out of 10 patients in each group.

Table 5.8 shows the number of homosexual offences on which patients had been charged and found guilty. Whereas none of the patients in the AA group had been so charged, two each in the CC and P groups had had one offence, and 2 in the CC and 1 in the P group had had two or more offences. Table 5.9 shows the number of non-homosexual offences on which patients had been charged and found guilty. Once again, none of those in the AA group fell

TABLE 5.6. REASONS FOR APPEARING FOR TREATMENT

Reason	AA	CC	P	Total
[a]On an order of the court	0	2	2	4
Originally referred for psychiatric illness	5	2	2	9
Entirely of own accord	5	6	6	17
Total	10	10	10	30

[a]Or as a sequel to a court appearance (not an order).

TABLE 5.7. MOTIVATION FOR TREATMENT

Level	AA	CC	P	Total
Equivocal	1	1	1	3
Strong	9	9	9	27
Total	10	10	10	30

TABLE 5.8. HOMOSEXUAL OFFENCES: CHARGED AND FOUND GUILTY

No. of offences	AA	CC	P	Total
0	10	6	7	23
1	0	2	2	4
2	0	2	1	3
Total	10	10	10	30

in this category as against 3 in the CC and 1 in the P groups. There was, therefore, a tendency for a history of court appearances both for homosexual and non-homosexual offences to be found somewhat more frequently in the CC and P groups than in the AA groups. However, these differences did not reach an acceptable level of statistical significance.

Table 5.10 shows the psychiatric history of the groups prior to their appearance for treatment. Because several patients displayed more than one type of psychiatric disturbance, the numbers under each heading, when added up, sometimes exceeded 10. On the basis of a simple count, it seems that the P group had the greater incidence of past psychiatric disturbance, the AA group the next, and the CC group, the least. For all 3 groups, the majority of patients showed one or other of the several psychiatric abnormalities listed. Table 5.11 shows the psychiatric status on presentation for treatment.

It will be recalled that under the criteria for inclusion in the trial, patients suffering from a psychosis, alcoholism, brain damage, etc., were excluded. Table 5.11, therefore, shows the proportion of the only other psychiatric abnormality which was acceptable, namely personality disorder (Schneider's classification, 1959). It can be seen that whereas 7 of the AA group were displaying a personality disorder on presentation, 6 of those in the CC group and only 4 in the P group were doing so. Although the original decision was to exclude all personality disorders other than those of the self-insecure type, it became clear during the

TABLE 5.9. NON-HOMOSEXUAL OFFENCES: CHARGED AND FOUND GUILTY

No. of offences	AA	CC	P	Total
0	10	7	9	26
1	0	3	1	4
Total	10	10	10	30

TABLE 5.10. PSYCHIATRIC HISTORY PRIOR TO APPEARING FOR TREATMENT[a]

	AA	CC	P	Total
Acute psychogenic reactions:				
re homosexuality	5	3	5	13
re other than homosexuality	2	1	3	6
Endogenous depression	1	1	1	3
Abnormal psychogenic development	5	4	8	17

[a]In several instances patients experienced more than one of the several disorders.

TABLE 5.11. PSYCHIATRIC STATUS ON PRESENTATION

Status	AA	CC	P	Total
Personality disorder	7	6	4	17
No personality disorder	3	4	6	13
Total	10	10	10	30

course of interviews subsequent to the initial interview that 2 of the patients were displaying other types of personality disorder. One of those in the AA group had a labile personality disorder, and one in the P group had an attention-seeking disorder.

Finally, 5 of the patients in the AA group were under current psychiatric therapy as compared to none of those in the CC group and two in the P group. (AA versus CC and P combined gave a χ^2 of 3.93, $p < 0.05$.) The implication of the above data on psychiatric variables is that the patients in the AA group were somewhat more disturbed than those in the other 2 groups. This was particularly true in the sense that from whatever past psychiatric disturbances the patients had suffered, those in the AA group were suffering to a more marked extent than those in the other 2 groups at the time when they appeared for treatment. This is shown most clearly by the last finding presented above, namely the numbers of those under current therapy. Such therapy usually took the form of drugs for states of anxiety, and in some cases supportive psychotherapy. The data on personality, as clinically assessed, are completed in Table 5.12, which shows the personality abnormalities elicited on presentation for treatment; that is, those features of personality which, whilst standing out markedly from the general pattern of personality traits, fell short of being describable as a disorder. Psychometric data on personality are given in detail in Chapter 7. Table 5.12 consists of all the personality abnormalities elicited; in several instances, patients displayed more than one abnormality of personality so that the group totals in 2 cases exceed 10. Whenever a patient displayed a personality disorder of a particular type, this automatically excluded him from displaying abnormality of that particular type—a disorder being, of course, a more marked deviation on the same parameter.* The only marked difference between the groups was that 7 of the P group displayed self-insecure abnormalities—that is, all the psychotherapy patients not displaying a self-insecure disorder showed a self-insecure abnormality. It was found in previous work (MacCulloch and Feldman, 1967b) that self-insecure personality features had a favourable prognosis for treatment, as compared to other personality

TABLE 5.12. PERSONALITY ABNORMALITIES ELICITED ON PRESENTATION FOR TREATMENT[a]

Abnormality	AA	CC	P	Total
Self-insecure	3	3	7	13
Attention seeking	0	3	3	6
Labile	3	3	1	7
Explosive	0	2	0	2
Depressive	3	1	1	5
Fanatic	0	0	1	1
Weak willed	1	1	2	4
Total	10	13	15	38

[a]In several instances the patient displayed more than one abnormality of personality.

abnormalities or disorders. The fact that the P group, therefore, contained a larger number of patients with self-insecure abnormalities, was no indication of a less favourable prognosis for treatment in that group. It is, however, noteworthy that whereas 3 patients in each of the CC and P groups displayed attention-seeking abnormalities, none of those in the AA group did so. There are other minor differences in the incidence of personality abnormalities in the 3 groups, but these are not worthy of detailed comment. Overall, it can be stated that the patients who presented for treatment were, as a whole, somewhat disturbed in personality, and had been so disturbed for fairly long periods of time prior to presentation for treatment. There is considerable evidence, as in the case of the series patients, that the individuals who seek help are those who are suffering, either because of their personality structure in general, or because of their response to being homosexual.

2. SEXUAL PRACTICES

Data on the sexual practices of the patients and the lengths of time for which these had been engaged in are now presented. Table 5.13 shows the age of first masturbation of the patients in the 3 groups, and it can be seen that the age range is fairly wide, varying from 10 to over 16, and that 3 of the patients (1 in AA and 2 in CC) had not yet commenced masturbation at the time when they appeared for treatment. This did not prevent an intense phantasy life concerning their own sex, although not leading to orgasm. Two of the 3 non-masturbating patients were female homosexuals, only 1 of the 28 male patients in the series not having yet begun to masturbate by the time he appeared for treatment. There are

*A more satisfactory procedure than the arbitrary division into abnormality or disorder is to assign a scale score—see Chapter 7—between 0 and 5.

no marked differences between the groups in onset of masturbation, although there is a slight tendency for the P patients to have begun somewhat earlier. There thus appears to be no major difference in the rate of biological maturation between the groups. This factor, which possibly is related to the strength of acquisition of the homosexual habit, is further discussed in Chapter 8.

TABLE 5.13. AGE OF ONSET OF MASTURBATION

Age	AA	CC	P	Total
10	1	0	1	2
11	0	1	2	3
12	3	2	3	8
13	4	2	1	7
14	0	2	2	4
15	0	0	1	1
16	1	1	0	2
Nil	1	2	0	3
Total	10	10	10	30

The years of duration of the main homosexual practice are shown in Table 5.14. There is a slight tendency for the P group patients to have been practising for a longer period of time than the AA group patients, with the CC group falling between. There is a marked difference between the patients in the series and those in the trial in respect of the duration of the main homosexual practice, no fewer than 8 of the patients in the trial having engaged in their main homosexual practice for less than a year. This reflects the fact that the average age of the patients in the trial was rather lower than that of those in the series.

TABLE 5.14. DURATION IN YEARS OF MAIN HOMOSEXUAL PRACTICE

Years	AA	CC	P	Total
Less than 1	4	1	3	8
1–2	2	3	1	6
3–4	1	4	0	5
5–6	1	2	2	5
6 or more	2	0	4	6
Total	10	10	10	30

Table 5.15 shows the homosexual practices on presentation. This table, as in the case of similar data on the series patients, is organized in such a way as to show the patients who were engaging in more than one type of practice on presentation. No fewer than 16 of the 30 trial patients were using phantasy only on presentation, although many of these patients had engaged in an overt homosexual practice in the past. However, the decision to seek help seems to have led many voluntarily to abandon overt homosexual practice for a short period of time at any rate. They then restricted their homosexual life to phantasy, the latter not being as subject to voluntary control as is overt behaviour. Seven of these 16 had engaged in overt homosexual behaviour at sometime in the past, the break-down in groups

TABLE 5.15. HOMOSEXUAL PRACTICES ON PRESENTATION

Practice	AA	CC	P	Total
Phantasy only	7	4	5	16
Mutual masturbation (MM) only	0	1	2	3
Anal intercourse (AI) only	0	0	0	0
MM and AI	1	5	0	6
Fellatio (F) only	0	0	0	0
MM, AI, and F	2	0	3	5
Total	10	10	10	30

being 3 in the AA group, 2 in the CC group, and 2 in the P group. This may be compared to the situation in the series patients, of whom 8 out of the 43 were engaging in phantasy only on presentation for treatment, whereas only 2 had never engaged in overt homosexual behaviour at any time in the past. This serves to indicate the importance of taking a full history of sexual behaviour throughout the patient's life, since reliance on the nature of the behaviour immediately on presentation for treatment is misleading in indicating the extent of the homosexual habit. There is a strong suggestion that overt homosexual behaviour was somewhat more frequent in the CC and P groups than in the AA group at the time of presentation. No fewer than 5 of the CC group were practising both mutual masturbation and anal intercourse on presentation for treatment, and a further patient was practising mutual masturbation only. Five of the P group were practising either mutual masturbation only, or all three of the major varieties of homosexual behaviour. The difference between the groups is brought out more clearly in Table 5.16, which shows the major homosexual practice on presentation. It can be seen that for 5 of the CC patients the major homosexual practice was anal intercourse, whereas this was true for only 1 of the AA groups; by contrast, 2 of the AA patients and 3 of the P patients had fellatio as their major homosexual practice, whilst none of those in the CC group did so. We had no basis for predicting response to treatment from the last type of homosexual practice; none of those who formed the series of patients had fellatio as their major homosexual practice. Table 5.17 presents data on the number of homosexual affairs in which the trial patients had participated. It can be seen that the majority—19 out of 30—had had no homosexual affairs, i.e. a sexual and emotional relationship with another male, exceeding 1 month in duration. Of those who had had affairs, only 1 was in the AA group, whereas there were 4 in the CC group and 6 in the P group. There was no indication in the data on the series patients that the number of homosexual affairs was a prognostic sign (of either success or failure in response to treatment)

TABLE 5.16. MAJOR PREFERRED HOMOSEXUAL PRACTICE ON PRESENTATION

Practice	AA	CC	P	Total
Strong phantasy only	7	4	5	16
MM	0	1	2	3
AI	1	5	0	6
F	2	0	3	5
Total	10	10	10	30

TABLE 5.17. NUMBER OF HOMOSEXUAL AFFAIRS

Number	AA	CC	P	Total
0	9	6	4	19
1	0	0	1	1
2	0	3	2	5
3 or more	1	1	3	5
Total	10	10	10	30

independent of other prognostic factors such as a previous history of heterosexual interest, nature of personality disorder, etc. The fact that there was an increased incidence of homosexual affairs in the CC and P groups, could not, therefore, be taken as a negative prognostic factor for the members of these groups. On the contrary, it might be that the *lack* of homosexual affairs among the AA patients could be taken in conjunction with their increased incidence of personality disorder and of being under psychiatric care at the time of presentation for treatment, to indicate that the AA patients were rather less capable of forming stable relationships with another human being, and hence as a negative prognostic sign. The most conservative way to interpret the data in Table 5.17 is probably that the AA patients were on average, rather more immature in social development, as well as somewhat less stable in personality and psychiatric state than the patients in the other 2 groups.

There are also some data on the extent to which our patients were mixing in the homosexual sub-culture. These somewhat parallel the data on homosexual affairs, although not completely so. Eleven of the 30 patients were mixing in the homosexual sub-culture—3 in each of the AA and P groups, 5 in the CC group. It is perhaps noteworthy that although only 1 of the AA patients had had a homosexual affair, 3 were mixing in the homosexual sub-culture; this is perhaps a further indication of the personality difficulties suffered by at least some of our AA patients.

We next turn to sexual interest in the opposite sex, and Table 5.18 shows the interest which the patient reported himself as having between the ages of 6 and 10. There was a rather greater tendency for such interest to be noticed by the AA patients than in the CC patients. Table 5.19 shows the extent to which heterosexual interest developed between the ages of 11 and 15, and it can be seen that whereas the majority of the patients in the AA and CC groups (7 in the former and 6 in the latter) had acquired such an interest by the age of 15, only 4 of those in the P group had done so.

Table 5.20 shows overt heterosexual behaviour between the age of 11 and 15 in the sense of whether this was present or absent. It can be seen that it was present in the majority of the AA and CC groups, but in only 4 of the P group.

TABLE 5.18. HETEROSEXUAL INTEREST BETWEEN 6 AND 10

Interest	AA	CC	P	Total
Present	5	2	3	10
Absent	5	8	7	20
Total	10	10	10	30

TABLE 5.19. HETEROSEXUAL INTEREST BETWEEN 11 and 15

Interest	AA	CC	P	Total
Present	7	6	4	17
Absent	3	4	6	13
Total	10	10	10	30

TABLE 5.20. OVERT HETEROSEXUAL BEHAVIOUR BETWEEN 11 and 15

Behaviour	AA	CC	P	Total
Present	7	7	3	17
Absent	3	3	7	13
Total	10	10	10	30

TABLE 5.21. NATURE OF OVERT HETEROSEXUAL BEHAVIOUR BETWEEN 11 AND 15

Behaviour	AA	CC	P	Total
Dating and kissing (even once)	5	5	1	11
Petting (even once)	1	2	1	4
Sexual intercourse (even once)	1	0	1	2
Nil	3	3	7	13
Total	10	10	10	30

Table 5.21 shows the type of overt heterosexual behaviour between the ages of 11 and 15. In the great majority of cases it was confined to dating and kissing. This is not dissimilar to the figures for an unselected sample of young people reported by Schofield (1965a). Table 5.22 shows whether or not heterosexual behaviour, of any nature, was present from the age of 16 to the time of presentation for treatment. Heterosexual behaviour was present in 22 out of the 30 patients and in almost equal numbers of the patients in the 3 groups. That is, although several of the patients in the P group did not begin their heterosexual behaviour as early as did the majority of patients in the other 2 groups, eventually they did display both interest and overt behaviour. However, as was pointed out in Chapter 3 with reference to the married homosexuals in the series, the occurrence of overt behaviour does not necessarily indicate true heterosexual arousal, perhaps being displayed only to observe social conventions.

TABLE 5.22. OVERT HETEROSEXUAL BEHAVIOUR FROM THE AGE OF 16 TO PRESENTATION FOR TREATMENT

Behaviour	AA	CC	P	Total
Present	7	7	8	22
Absent	3	3	2	8
Total	10	10	10	30

Two of the 8 P patients who had displayed heterosexual behaviour felt no satisfaction or pleasure as a result of their behaviour. One had engaged in heterosexual intercourse with his wife, but had always used homosexual phantasy in order to obtain an erection.

Table 5.23 shows the type of the overt heterosexual behaviour from the age of 16 to presentation for treatment. Many of the patients showed a normal course of development, being more advanced in their heterosexual behaviour after 15 than between the ages of 11 and 15. No fewer than 10 of the total 30 trial patients had experienced heterosexual intercourse at least once between the age of 16 and presentation for treatment. Only 8 of the total series had experienced no overt heterosexual behaviour prior to presentation.

TABLE 5.23. NATURE OF OVERT HETEROSEXUAL BEHAVIOUR FROM THE AGE OF 16 TO PRESENTATION FOR TREATMENT

Behaviour	AA	CC	P	Total
Dating and kissing (even once)	1	2	2	5
Petting (even once)	3	2	2	7
Sexual intercourse (even once)	3	3	4[a]	10
Nil	3	3	2	8
Total	10	10	10	30

[a]One patient had occasional sexual intercourse with his wife, without pleasure, and requiring homosexual phantasy.

Table 5.24 shows the major heterosexual practice on presentation. It must be re-emphasized that 4 of those patients who appear in the "nil" category had either engaged in overt heterosexual behaviour with enjoyment or experienced heterosexual arousal at some stage during their past histories. One of these 4 patients was in the AA group, 1 in the CC group, and 2 in the P group. The patient in the P group listed under the category of "sexual intercourse" was the same patient referred to in the footnote to Table 5.23.

Table 5.25 shows the major masturbatory phantasy in the 3 groups. No marked differences were found except that, as mentioned earlier, 3 of the patients were not yet masturbating on presentation for treatment, 2 of these being the 2 female homosexual patients in the trial.

TABLE 5.24. MAJOR HETEROSEXUAL PRACTICE ON PRESENTATION FOR TREATMENT

Practice	AA	CC	P	Total
Weak phantasy	2	0	0	2
Strong phantasy	3	1	1	5
Dating	1	1	0	2
Kissing	0	3	2	5
Petting	1	0	1	2
Sexual intercourse	0	1	1	2
Nil	3	4	5	12
Total	10	10	10	30

The only male patient who was not masturbating on presentation for treatment had begun to do so by the time his treatment actually started. (A number of the patients had to wait for some time between their initial interview and the time when their treatment began, the maximum waiting period being 4 months.) There were no major differences between the groups in the nature of the masturbatory phantasy.

TABLE 5.25. MAJOR MASTURBATORY PHANTASY ON PRESENTATION FOR TREATMENT

Phantasy	AA	CC	P	Total
Boys under 16 only	1	0	0	1
Boys under 16 and men	1	1	0	2
Men only	4	5	6	15
Men and women	3	2	4	9
Nil	1	2	0	3
Total	10	10	10	30

TABLE 5.26. PRE-TREATMENT KINSEY RATINGS

KR	AA	CC	P	Total
3	2	3	1	6
4	3	0	3	6
5	3	4	0	7
6	2	3	6	11
Total	10	10	10	30

The data on sexual practices for the 3 years prior to presentation for treatment are summed up in the pre-treatment Kinsey ratings, which are shown in Table 5.26. It can be seen that 6 of the 30 patients were rated as Kinsey 3, 6 as Kinsey 4, 7 as Kinsey 5, and 11 as Kinsey 6. It was pointed out in Chapter 3 that a major prognostic factor of response to treatment was not so much the pre-treatment Kinsey rating as the presence or absence of pre-treatment heterosexual interest and pleasurable behaviour. Although 6 of the P group had a Kinsey rating of 6, 2 of these did have pre-treatment heterosexual interest and pleasurable practice. Neither of the 2 AA patients with a Kinsey rating of 6, and none of the 3 CC patients with a Kinsey rating of 6, had pre-treatment heterosexual interest or practice. The Kinsey rating data can, therefore, be rearranged such that 8 of the AA group, 7 of the CC group, and 6 of the P group had a pre-treatment history of heterosexual interest and behaviour. This must be borne in mind when the treatment data are analysed, as will be seen later in this chapter.

Finally, Table 5.27 shows the extent to which the patients had had recourse to homosexual prostitution, either as client or prostitute. Only 4 of them had done so—3 as client and 1 (once) as prostitute. This factor was not expected to be a major one and may be compared for interest with the series of patients of whom a larger proportion had participated in homosexual prostitution. It probably reflects the fact that the series patients were on average older than those in the trial.

TABLE 5.27. HOMOSEXUAL PROSTITUTION

Nature of prostitution	AA	CC	P	Total
As client	1	2	0	3
As prostitute	1	0	0	1
Neither	8	8	10	26
Total	10	10	10	30

THE RESULTS OF TREATMENT: SOM SCORES

The most important prognostic sign to emerge from the analysis of the series of patients, described in Chapter 3, was the presence of a pre-treatment history of heterosexual interest and practice accompanied by satisfaction. In describing the results of the trial we shall anticipate the discussion of the importance of pre-treatment heterosexual history (see Chapter 8), by dividing the patients in the trial into two types—*primary* and *secondary* homosexuals. The primary homosexual is characterized by an absence of pre-treatment heterosexual interest and practice, accompanied by satisfaction. The secondary homosexual has experienced satisfactory heterosexual behaviour at sometime in his history, however remote in time from his appearing for treatment. The probably crucial importance of the primary–secondary dichotomy was not fully appreciated at the beginning of the trial, so that the random assignation of patients to treatment techniques was made without reference to membership of one or other of the proposed types. By chance, therefore, the numbers of primary homosexuals were not the same in the 3 treatment groups, there being 2 in the AA group, 3 in the CC group, and 4 in the P group. The detailed data on the pre-treatment heterosexual practice or lack of it, of the patients in the trial, were given earlier in this chapter.

At the beginning of the trial it had been intended to compare the response to the 3 techniques of treatment by changes in scores on the homosexual measure of the SOM questionnaire. Accordingly, the differences between the pre- and post-treatment scores of the 3 groups of patients were submitted to analysis of variance. The means and standard deviations of the data are shown in Table 5.28, both for the 3 groups of patients and, within each group, for the primary and secondary homosexuals.

TABLE 5.28. MEAN DIFFERENCES BETWEEN PRE- AND POST-TREATMENT SOM SCORES IN THE CONTROLLED TRIAL OF AA, CC, AND P

Treatment	Homosexual type	No.	Measure					
			Homosexual		Heterosexual		Combined	
			Mean	SD	Mean	SD	Mean	SD
AA	Primary	2	0	0	1.0	1.41	1.0	1.41
	Secondary	8	13.0	6.0	11.0	6.0	24.0	5.92
CC	Primary	3	4.33	9.23	2.66	4.03	7.0	14.17
	Secondary	7	21.0	17.11	8.71	10.44	29.71	24.17
P	Primary	4	2.50	2.64	7.00	9.41	9.50	7.68
	Secondary	6	9.83	12.28	8.00	4.69	17.83	4.28

It can be seen from Table 5.28 that in all 3 treatment groups, the primary homosexuals showed a smaller change after treatment than did the secondary homosexuals on both homosexual and heterosexual scores. The analyses of variance of these scores are shown in Table 5.29. None of the F ratios are significant either for the homosexual difference scores, the heterosexual difference scores, or the combined difference scores (i.e. homosexual difference plus heterosexual difference), with the exception of the primary versus secondary homosexual variable (shown in the analysis tables as Patient Type). This variable reaches the 5% level of significance for the homosexual difference scores, almost achieves the 5% level for the heterosexual difference scores, and is significant at beyond the 1% level for the combined difference scores. That is, irrespective of the treatment technique used, the secondary homosexuals showed a significantly better response to treatment than the primary homosexuals as measured by the difference between pre- and post-treatment SOM scores.

TABLE 5.29. ANALYSES OF VARIANCE OF THE DIFFERENCES BETWEEN PRE- AND POST-TREATMENT SOM SCORES IN THE CONTROLLED TRIAL OF AA, CC, AND P

(a) Homosexual differences scores

Source	df	SS	VE	F	P
Treatment (T)	2	53.59	26.80	<1	N.S.
SS(AA + CC)vP	1	15.56	15.56	<1	N.S.
SS AA vCC	1	38.03	38.03	1.226	N.S.
Hom. Type (HT)	1	228.17	228.17	7.36	0.05
T × HT	2	22.21	11.10	<1	N.S.
SS HT × [(AA + CC)vP]	1	18.75	18.75	<1	N.S.
SS HT × (AAvCC)	1	3.36	3.36	<1	N.S.
Within S's	24	744.41	31.02		

(b) Heterosexual differences scores

Source	df	SS	VE	F	P
T	2	3.75	1.87	<1	N.S.
SS(AA + CC)vP	1	3.65	3.65	<1	N.S.
SS AA vCC	1	0.10	0.10	<1	N.S.
HT	1	48.44	48.44	3.49	N.S.
T × HT	2	20.35	10.17	<1	N.S.
SS HT × [(AA + CC)vP]	1	16.45	16.45	1.18	N.S.
SS HT × (AAvCC)	1	3.90	3.90	<1	N.S.
Within S's	24	333.45	13.89		N.S.

(c) Combined difference scores

Source	df	SS	VE	F	P
T	2	48.84	24.42	<1	N.S.
SS (AA + CC)vP	1	20.14	20.14	<1	N.S.
SS AA vCC	1	28.70	28.70	<1	N.S.
HT	1	595.96	595.96	11.78	0.01
T × HT	2	35.31	67.65	<1	N.S.
SS HT × [(AA + CC)vP]	1	35.18	35.18	<1	N.S.
SS HT × (AA vCC)	1	0.13	0.13	<1	N.S.
Within S's	24	1214.59	50.61		

The analysis of variance apparently shows no difference in response to the three types of treatment. However, as can be seen from Table 5.29, the between-subjects sum of squares is unusually large for all three sections of the table, and this implies that the variance is very far from meeting the assumption of relative homogeneity, which is mandatory for the use of the analysis of variance technique. That is, we were analysing data which included both patients who had responded successfully to treatment and those who had failed to respond to treatment. Some of the difference scores were, therefore, very large (the maximum possible difference score for both the hom. and het. scales was 42, and the maximum for the combined scale 84) and some very small. Patients were thus arranged over a very wide scatter of scores on distributions which tended to be bi-modal. The highest combined difference score was 61 and the lowest −1. The variance was so large that it was likely to be swamping any differences between the groups in response to treatment. It was so large as to reduce to somewhat below a significance level of 5%, the clearly large difference on heterosexual difference scores between the primary and secondary homosexuals.

It was decided to turn to a simpler method of analysing the results of the trial by dividing patients into success or failure according to whether or not they had achieved the criterion of a 12-point improvement (i.e. decrease) on the homosexual score from immediately *pre*-treatment to immediately *post*-treatment the first 24 sessions. Table 5.30 shows the outcome of treatment of the 3 groups of patients, each group being divided into primary and secondary homosexuals. Only 1 of the 9 primary homosexuals made a satisfactory response to treatment immediately after 24 sessions as compared to 13 of the 21 secondary homosexuals. The association (by χ^2) between a successful response to treatment and being a secondary homosexual, *irrespective of treatment*, was significant at well beyond the 5% level. The next stage was to make a comparison of the response to treatment of the secondary homosexuals between each pair of treatments. Six of the 8 secondary homosexuals treated by AA achieved

TABLE 5.30. THE RESULTS OF THE TRIAL. ATTAINMENT OF THE CRITERION OF A 12-POINT IMPROVEMENT ON THE SOM HOMOSEXUAL MEASURE

(a) Primary homosexuals

Treatment group	Success	Failure	Total
AA	0	2	2
CC	1	2	3
P	0	4	4
Total	1	8	9

(b) Secondary homosexuals

Treatment group	Success	Failure	Total
AA	6	2	8
CC	5	2[a]	7
P	2	4	6
Total	13	8	21

[a]Includes patient no. 2.

the criterion of a 12-point improvement on homosexual scores compared to 5 of the 7 secondary homosexuals treated by CC, the difference being non-significant. Two of the 6 secondary homosexuals treated by P achieved the criterion. While this was a poorer outcome than those achieved with the other two treatment techniques, neither was significantly superior to psychotherapy by statistical test. Finally, we compared the psychotherapy group to the two learning groups combined, again using the data shown in Table 5.30. Eleven of the 15 secondary homosexuals who had received either AA or CC as their first treatment reached the criterion, compared to 2 of the 6 psychotherapy patients. The association between receiving a learning technique of treatment and achieving the criterion failed to reach even the 10% level of significance (which is not normally regarded as impressive proof of the strength of an association). However, *both* the psychotherapy patients failed to maintain their improvement; trial patient no. 20 undoubtedly relapsed, and the other patient failed to return for further interviews. In accordance with our usual practice (see Chapter 3), he was also considered to have relapsed. The difference between the combined learning groups and the psychotherapy group now becomes very large indeed in that there was only one relapse (trial patient no. 2) among the 11 secondary homosexuals treated by avoidance learning techniques as compared with *both* of the successful psychotherapy patients. We consider this to represent clear evidence of the superior efficacy of an avoidance learning technique over psychotherapy in the treatment of secondary homosexuals.

The 4 secondary homosexuals (6 minus 2) who were unimproved after 24 sessions of psychotherapy were randomly reassigned to one of the two learning techniques and 3 of these made a successful response to treatment, achieving the criterion of a 12-point improvement on the SOM homosexual score. Two were treated by CC and the other by AA. The fourth of this group of patients failed to respond to either learning technique. The 4 secondary homosexuals who failed to respond to either AA or CC as their first technique of treatment (see Table 5.30) were assigned to the other of the 2 learning techniques, but 2 of the 4 failed to receive the treatment to which they had been re-assigned. One (trial patient no. 15) left the district and the other failed to re-attend, although he was still physically able to do so. This last patient (no. 24) was a very severely disturbed individual with a marked history of personality disorder, and it was probably a mistake to have accepted him for treatment. One secondary homosexual, who had originally been treated by AA, proceeded to CC and made a successful response. The other patient who had failed with CC moved to AA but did not make a successful response. Hence, by the time that all patients who were secondary homosexuals had had the opportunity to be treated by one or both of the two learning techniques, either initially or following psychotherapy, all but 4 of the 21 secondary homosexuals had achieved the criterion for a successful response. Two of these 4 had not taken the opportunity to move to the other learning technique, having failed with the first.

As stated above, 8 of the 9 primary homosexuals failed to respond to their first technique of treatment. Six of these 8 then proceeded to an alternate method of treatment, but 5 of the 6 failed with all other techniques with which they were treated, the exception being trial patient no. 11, who failed to respond to P but did respond to AA. However, he relapsed during follow-up. One of the primary homosexuals (trial patient no. 7), having failed to respond to AA did not proceed to CC, as should have occurred, but instead described himself as being unable to find time for further treatment. However, he did return to interview, of his own accord, nearly a year after treatment, and, on the questionnaire measures as well as on interview, was found to be very much improved. He is, therefore, listed as a success at latest follow-up.

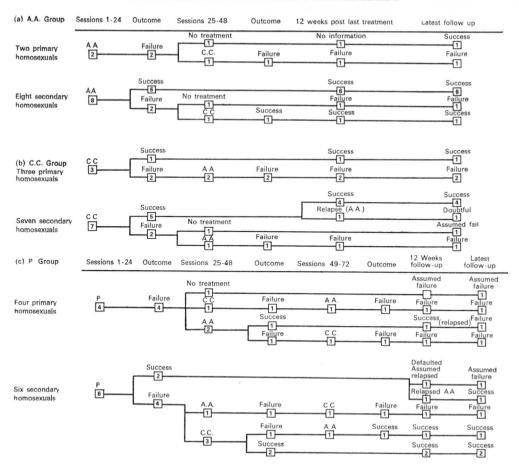

Fig. 5.4. Detailed chart of patient progress through treatment and follow-up.

To sum up; 17 out of 21 secondary homosexuals and 2 out of 9 primary homosexuals improved (i.e. achieved the criterion of a 12-point decrease on the SOM homosexual measure) at some stage from the beginning of the trial to the end of stage 3. Hence, 19 homosexual patients can be said to have responded successfully at the end of their last stage of treatment.

In order to increase the ease of following the somewhat complex nature of the results of the trial, Fig. 5.3 shows the flow of patients through initial and subsequent treatments and the extent to which they achieved the criterion for success at each stage up to the latest follow-up. Section (a) of Fig. 5.4 shows the history of the 10 patients originally assigned to AA, section (b) that of those assigned to CC, and section (c) refers to the P group of patients.

The change in SOM homosexual score is measured from immediately pre-treatment to immediately post-treatment. The term "failure" means that the criterion of a 12-point improvement had not been achieved by the *end* of the treatment stage in question, counting from immediately prior to the first treatment received. One or two patients improved by a few points, but by less than 12 during one technique of treatment, and were then assigned to another, following which they had improved by 12 points or more as compared with the position prior to the *first* treatment. Success was arbitrarily attributed to the treatment *immediately* preceding the *overall* improvement of 12 points or more. The term "relapse" refers to a return to the original, or near to the original SOM homosexual score. In all 3 cases of *known* relapse, the decline in SOM score was accompanied by a return to strong homosexual phantasy and usually overt homosexual practice.

The mean length of follow-up was 46.2 weeks, with a standard deviation of 19.7 weeks. The majority of patients were followed up for at least 6 months or more. At the latest follow-up, 15 patients (1 primary and 14 secondaries) out of the 19 who responded successfully immediately following treatment, had maintained an improvement of at least 12 points on the SOM homosexual score in the period between the end of the final treatment and the latest follow-up. Three of the 4 patients who relapsed were secondary homosexuals. The first (trial patient no. 20) had made a successful response to psychotherapy; he then relapsed and received a relatively brief period of treatment by AA, following which he immediately improved—an improvement which was maintained over the period of follow-up (6 months following his AA treatment). Another trial patient (no. 14) had made a similar improvement after 24 sessions of psychotherapy, had then failed to return for any follow-up interviews, and was assumed to have relapsed. It may be assumed with some confidence that he would have responded successfully, given the opportunity, to either AA or CC. The third of the relapsed secondary homosexual patients (trial patient no. 2) made an initially successful response to CC, then relapsed, and was treated by AA. He again improved, but again relapsed. As can be seen from the graph of his SOM data (see Appendix A) this patient's response has fluctuated wildly throughout the period from the beginning of treatment to the latest follow-up, and it has been decided to label him as neither improved nor unimproved, but to describe his outcome as "doubtful". The last of the 4 mentioned above (trial patient no. 11) was a primary homosexual who relapsed following a successful response to AA, which in turn had followed an unsuccessful response to P. Finally, one trial patient (no. 7)—a primary homosexual—appeared to make a spontaneous improvement without any further treatment, after his initial failure to respond to AA.

As only 2 of the psychotherapy patients originally improved, and as both of these either relapsed or defaulted, the remainder of the data will be concerned only with the 27 patients who either had AA or CC initially, or crossed over to one or other of them following a failure with psychotherapy. (The third of the remaining 3 patients, i.e. other than the 27, was another psychotherapy patient (trial patient no. 21) who failed in response to psychotherapy. He also failed to return for further treatment. As he was a primary homosexual, it is unlikely that either learning technique would have been successful.)

RESULTS OF TREATMENT: SEXUAL PRACTICES

Table 5.31 shows the major homosexual practice at latest follow-up of the 27 patients referred to above. Column (a) shows those patients who had either AA or CC with no cross-over; column (b) shows those who did cross over, in terms of the *last* treatment received; and column (c) the total of columns (a) and (b).

It can be seen that 7 of the 8 patients who had AA only were engaging in no homosexual practice at follow-up compared with 5 of the 7 who had CC only. By contrast, of the 6 cross-over patients who received AA as their last treatment, only 1 was not engaging in homosexual practices at the latest follow-up; 3 of the 6 whose last treatment was CC were

TABLE 5.31. MAJOR HOMOSEXUAL PRACTICE AT LATEST FOLLOW-UP
(a) No cross over. (b) Cross over: practice as a function of the *last* treatment. (c) (a) plus (b)

Practice	AA			CC			Total		
	(a)	(b)	(c)	(a)	(b)	(c)	(a)	(b)	(c)
Strong phantasy	1	5	6	2	2	4	3	7	10
MM	0	0	0	0	0	0	0	0	0
AI	0	0	0	0	1	1	0	1	1
Nil	7	1	8	5	3	8	12	4	16
Total	8	6	14	7	6	13	15	12	27

similarly engaging in homosexual practice at the latest follow-up. That is, 5 of the 6 who had crossed over to AA (4 primary, 1 secondary) were *at least*, using strong phantasy, and 3 out of the 6 who crossed over to CC (2 primary, 1 secondary) were behaving similarly. But the majority of those who did cross over were primary homosexuals, and it is clear that the two learning techniques were making little further impact on them after one had failed to do so. A change in homosexual attitude, as indexed by the attainment of the SOM criterion of success, generalized to real life behaviour, and this change in behaviour was maintained over the follow-up period in the majority of patients. No fewer than 12 of the 15 patients who received AA or CC only were neither engaging in homosexual practice nor using homosexual phantasy at the latest follow-up. By contrast, only 4 of the 12 patients who crossed over to one of the two learning techniques were neither engaging in homosexual practice nor using homosexual phantasy at follow-up. Three of these 4 patients had crossed over to AA or CC from psychotherapy, and hence were receiving a learning technique for the first time.

TABLE 5.32. MAJOR HETEROSEXUAL PRACTICE AT LATEST FOLLOW-UP
(a) No cross over. (b) Cross over: practice in terms of last treatment. (c) (a) plus (b)

Practice	AA			CC			Total		
	(a)	(b)	(c)	(a)	(b)	(c)	(a)	(b)	(c)
Strong phantasy	1	0	1	1	1	2	2	1	3
Dating	1	1	2	1	1	2	2	2	4
Kissing	1	0	1	2	1	3	3	1	4
Petting	2	0	2	3	1	4	5	1	6
Sexual intercourse	3	1	4	0	0	0	3	1	4
Nil	0	4	4	0	2	2	0	6	6
Total	8	6	14	7	6	13	15	12	27

Turning to the major heterosexual practice at latest follow-up, a rather similar picture emerges (Table 5.32). All 15 of those who received AA or CC only were displaying heterosexual practice of some kind, even if this was only strong phantasy, at the latest follow-up. By contrast, only 4 of those who crossed over were engaging in heterosexual practice or using heterosexual phantasy at latest follow-up. Once again, 3 of these 4 were secondary homosexuals who had failed to respond to psychotherapy.

TABLE 5.33. KINSEY RATINGS AT LATEST FOLLOW-UP

(a) No cross over. (b) Cross over: KR in terms of *last* treatment. (c) (a) plus (b)

KR	AA			CC			Total		
	(a)	(b)	(c)	(a)	(b)	(c)	(a)	(b)	(c)
0	6	1	7	4	1	5	10	2	12
1	1	0	1	1	1	2	2	1	3
2	0	0	0	0	1	1	0	1	1
			Success						
3	1	1	2	2	0	2	3	1	4[a]
4	0	0	0	0	1	1	0	1	1
5	0	0	0	0	0	0	0	0	0
6	0	4	4	0	2	2	0	6	6
			Failure						
Total	8	6	14	7	6	13	15	12	27

[a]Includes patient no. 2, who has fluctuated wildly during the follow-up period.

The data on sexual practices at the latest follow-up are combined into Kinsey ratings in Table 3.53, which is laid out in the same way as the previous 2 tables. Twelve of the 27 patients were rated as Kinsey 0, 3 as Kinsey 1, and 1 as Kinsey 2. These 16 patients form the group who are considered successful. The patient rated Kinsey 2 is considered to fall within the improved group, partly because his pre-treatment Kinsey rating was 6, and partly because his post-treatment Kinsey rating of 2 is a rather conservative one. (He was not engaging in homosexual practice or using homosexual phantasy, but did experience occasional mild interest in directly observed males.) One of the 3 patients not included in the group of 27, with whom the last 3 tables have been concerned, was trial patient no. 20, and, as mentioned above, he relapsed following psychotherapy but improved after a number of sessions of AA. He remained improved at latest follow-up to the extent of being assigned a Kinsey rating of 0. Trial patient no. 20 was a secondary homosexual and had a good prognosis for treatment by a learning technique, as had trial patient no. 14, the second of the 3 patients omitted from the last 3 tables. Patient no. 14 defaulted from follow-up interviews, following a successful response to psychotherapy, and the last of the 3 was trial patient no. 21, a primary homosexual who was also referred to above. Hence, of the 21 secondary homosexuals, 20 were treated by a learning technique, 19 as part of the trial, and 1 subsequently to it. Fifteen of these secondary homosexuals were improved at latest follow-up, and the 5 who were not were suffering from personality disorders describable as severe—a point amplified in Chapter 7.

One of these 5 trial patients, no. 15, may be considered to have made a partial improvement in that his score on the SOM heterosexual measure did improve from 30 before treatment to 48 immediately after treatment although there was a fall to 42 at the latest follow-up. Neither he nor patient no. 24, who failed to respond to CC initially, availed themselves of the opportunity to switch to the other learning technique. Only 2 of the primary homosexuals were improved at follow-up, giving a total of 17 out of 30 improved at the latest follow-up. If we add to this total of 17, trial patient no. 14, who defaulted after psychotherapy and whom we assumed would have responded well to a learning technique, then we have a probable total of 18 out of 30 improved. The percentage rate of 60% is very similar to the success rate obtained in the series of 43 described in Chapter 3.

CONCLUSIONS

1. In terms both of changes in SOM scores and in sexual practices there was no difference in degree of success between the two avoidance learning techniques—anticipatory avoidance and classical conditioning.

2. Hence, in the form in which it was used in this trial, AA learning has failed to show a superiority to CC, and this will be discussed further in Chapter 8. Perhaps it would be more precise to state the CC was not found to be *inferior* to AA in the treatment of *secondary* homosexuals.

3. Both learning techniques were superior to psychotherapy in effecting changes in the sexual attitudes of secondary homosexuals, particularly as both the psychotherapy patients who initially improved can be considered to have relapsed later.

4. *Irrespective* of learning technique, the response to treatment of secondary homosexuals was very much better than that of primary homosexuals. This confirms the major finding from the series of homosexual patients reported in Chapter 3, namely that homosexual patients with no prior pleasurable heterosexual experience have a poor prognosis irrespective of their motivation for treatment.

5. Despite the generally poor prognosis for the primary homosexuals, 2 of the 9 who formed this group were improved at latest follow-up, both following exposure to only one learning technique. One of these 2 patients had appeared to fail immediately following treatment. At the latest follow-up, neither of these 2 individuals was yet engaging in overt heterosexual practices, although both were mixing socially with females to the extent of dancing and dating. This is a similar finding to the one reported for the series of patients described in Chapter 3. (It will be recalled that none of the 3 primary homosexuals in the series, who were improved at follow-up, were engaging in overt heterosexual practice at that time.)

6. Despite the attempts to exclude patients with the type of personality disorder which was found in the series to have a poor prognosis, 5 of the secondary homosexuals nevertheless failed to make a satisfactory response to either learning technique. All 5 displayed a very marked and severe disorder of personality. This aspect of the trial is discussed in more detail in Chapter 7.

CHAPTER 6

BEHAVIOURAL AND PHYSIOLOGICAL MEASURES WITHIN TREATMENT

I. AVOIDANCE LATENCY RESPONSES

During the early part of the treatment of the series of 43 patients, techniques were developed to measure the temporal sequence of the treatment events. These were the time of onset and offset of the stimulus picture, the time of onset and offset of the patient's avoidance responses, and the time of onset and offset of the unconditional stimulus (UCS shock). The apparatus which was developed to take these measurements consisted of a series of water-containing pressure bulbs attached to the appropriate switches which transmitted pressure changes via hydraulic tubes to a pen recorder. The stimulus presentation switches and the avoidance switch were so arranged that when they were manipulated the hydraulic recording system was activated; in this way recordings were obtained from which were constructed avoidance response latency curves.

Because it has been our policy continuously to refine both the learning paradigm and the technology concomitantly, the hydraulic recording system was extant only for a short period of time, during which we were able to obtain and analyse avoidance latency responses on series patients nos. 2, 3, 11, and 13.

METHOD

Figure 6.1 shows a sample of the kymograph recording obtained. Track 4 at 1A shows the presentation of the male slide, track 3 at point 2A shows the patient's response to remove that slide. The distance between the onset of 1A and the onset of 2A was measured in millimetres and the results were converted to seconds (paper speed 15 mm/sec). These measurements were taken throughout each session of treatment, and the graphs of avoidance response latencies for each of the 4 patients are presented below; full case histories for these patients are given in Appendix A.

It will be seen from Fig. 6.2 that the patient very quickly acquired the avoidance habit, and, in fact, only once during session 1 did he fail to avoid and so received a shock. There were fluctuations in his response latencies during this first session, with most of them falling above 3 seconds, indicating that the slide did hold some degree of attraction for him. During session 2, there was a steep decline in the attractiveness of this slide, as is shown by the very short latencies. The same pattern is also shown in the succeeding 4 sessions. In fact a change in session 5 from the fourth to the fifth slide in the hierarchy produced no increase in response latencies.

It will be seen, from the results for the response latency series for series patient no. 3,

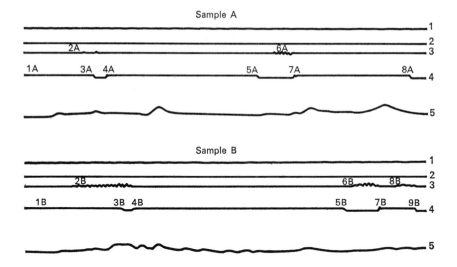

FIG. 6.1. Samples of kymograph recording during treatment. *Sample A:* 1A = male slide (CS). 2A = avoidance response (CR1). 3A = operator terminates 1A. 4A = operator presents female relief slide (CS2). 5A = operator terminates female relief slide (CS2). 6A = subject makes multiple requests (CR2) for return of CS2. 7A = operator represents CS2. 8A = operator terminates CS2. *Sample B:* 1B = operator presents CS1. 2B = subject avoids but the offset of CS1 is delayed. 3B = operator terminates CS1. 4B = operator presents CS2. 5B = operator terminates CS2. 6B = subject requests return of CS2 which is denied. 7B = operator presents CS1 which is very rapidly avoided = 8B and reinforced = 9B.

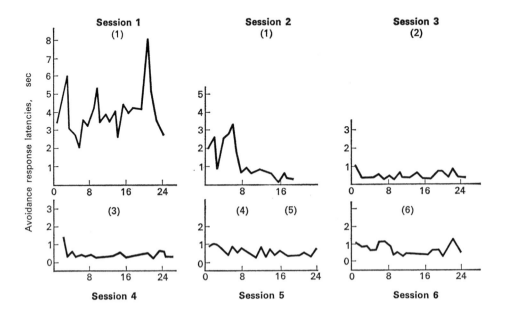

FIG. 6.2. Trial by trial avoidance latencies over 6 sessions for series patient no. 2.

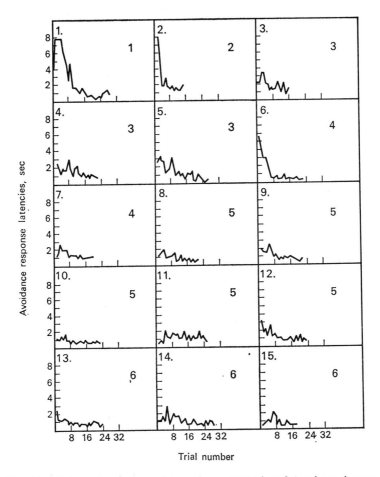

FIG. 6.3. Trial by trial avoidance latencies over 15 sessions for series patient no. 3.

which are set out in Fig. 6.3, that his response to treatment was steady and progressive. Early in the first 2 sessions there were a number of trials on which he failed to avoid at all and therefore received shocks. During the remainder of these 2 sessions his response latencies steadily shortened. It is noteworthy that at the beginning of session 2, when he went on to the next slide in the hierarchy, his response latency immediately increased as compared with the end of the first session, thereafter again declining. His latencies during sessions 3, 4, and 5, when he was on the third slide, were quite short and showed little variation. At the beginning of session 6 he moved on to the fourth slide and the latency was again very much longer, steadily declining thereafter. There was no such increase in response latency between the fourth and fifth slides nor between the fifth and sixth, and it will be seen that in the last few sessions he displayed a long series of short latency responses indicating little or no interest in slides which had previously been markedly attractive to him.

The response latency data for series patient no. 11 are shown in Fig. 6.4. It is immediately clear that there were considerable fluctuations in the first few sessions, although towards the end of the 11 sessions of treatment which he received he displayed a fairly protracted run of

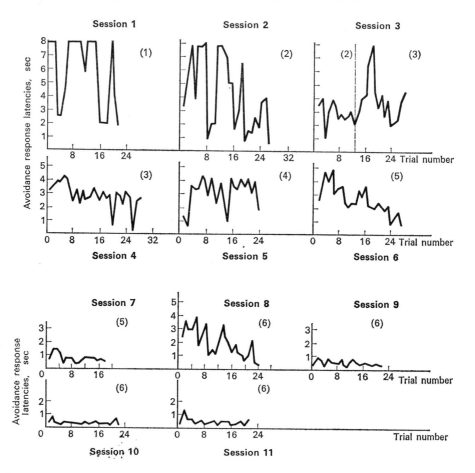

FIG. 6.4. Trial by trial avoidance latencies over 11 sessions for series patient no. 11.

short latency responses. The sharp increase in session 3, associated with the change from the second to the third slide, is also of interest.

The response latencies for series patient no. 13 (Fig. 6.5) are quite interesting. Firstly, his responses during session 1 are rather too good to be true in that he made a large number of short latency responses despite not having received a single shock. During session 2, in which the second slide was used, the result was exactly opposite in that he made no avoidance responses at all. However, sessions 3, 4, and 5 show him returning to his earlier pattern of a large number of short latency responses. Session 6 again demonstrates increasing response latency following the introduction of a more attractive slide; this is followed by a decline. Finally, in session 8 there were again almost no avoidance responses, and the patient then said that his behaviour during this session represented his true feelings. He stated that if he were being honest he would never switch off without the shock. It was felt at this point that the treatment was unlikely to succeed and, therefore, it was terminated.

These figures show that there is a tendency for the patients to show increasing shortness of response latencies as treatment proceeds. We might expect that patients who are exposed to

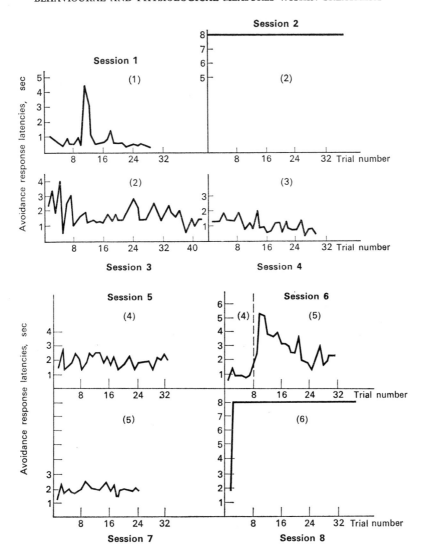

Fig. 6.5. Trial by trial avoidance latencies over 8 sessions for series patient no. 13.

anticipatory avoidance would eventually learn that there was an 8-second interval between the stimulus and the shock and respond to this by waiting for 7½ seconds before switching off once they had learned that there was no simple relationship between their responses and what actually happened: in fact none of the patients did this; either they found the slide so attractive that they were prepared to leave it on until the shock occurred, or they switched it off at varying intervals of time within the 8-second period. Although series patient no. 2 had had no actual homosexual experience apart from being sexually assaulted in adolescence, there was a clear relationship between his loss of homosexual interest over the course of treatment and after treatment and his quick acquisition of the avoidance habit. Series patient no. 3 also displayed a clear relationship between steady improvement in the avoidance learning situation within treatment, unmarked by fluctuations in avoidance latency responses, and a good response to treatment.

On the other hand, series patient no. 11 showed a very marked inconsistency of his avoidance latency responses, and the early improvement in his homosexual scores relapsed. The fourth patient, series no. 13, fluctuated most violently of all, and throughout the last session of treatment he displayed virtually no avoidance responses; it seems possible that in the early sessions he was not responding "naturally". There was, therefore, clear evidence that 2 patients did learn to avoid and did display progressively shorter response latencies. The next problem was whether or not this within treatment behaviour was going to generalize to the real life situation. In patients nos. 2 and 3 this did undoubtedly occur. Patient no. 11 showed some generalization to real life situation, but then appears to have relapsed.

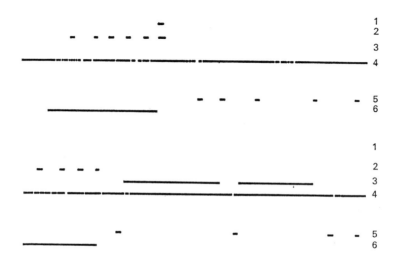

FIG. 6.6. Two sample tracings obtained from a 6-channel electromagnetic event recorder. (In sample 1 channel 3 is void. In sample 2 channel 1 is void.) *Key:* 1 = UCS. 2 = CR1 (avoidance response). 3 = CS2 (female slide). 4 = respiration (no. of blips = respiratory excursion). 5 = CR2 female request switching. 6 = CS1 (male slide).

Patient no. 13 showed no change. Turner and Solomon (1962) concluded that a considerable degree of fluctuation, between avoidance and escape responses, was a bad predictor for the adequate learning of an avoidance response. Similarly, these preliminary data suggested that a high degree of variation in response latency with a large number of escape responses also predicts to a poor outcome.

During the modification of the treatment paradigm, the stimulus projection and event logging apparatus was rebuilt (see Chapter 5).

We continued to record avoidance latency data on paper moving at 1.5 cm/sec; in this instance using electromagnetically operated fibre-write pens. A sample of the tracing is shown in Fig. 6.6, which shows an NR trial followed by a D trial. In both instances there is female request switching following the cessation of the CS1.

The output from the electromagnetic recorder was made compatible with an 8-channel electroencephalography (EEG) machine, so that avoidance latencies, pulse, respiration, and electromyography (EMG) could be recorded on one chart. This technique is described in detail in MacCulloch and Atkinson (1968). Figure 6.7 shows the form of that tracing and clearly illustrates the increased rate of avoidance responding, which occurred in D and NR trials as treatment proceeded.

The measurement of individual avoidance latencies entails a considerable amount of detailed tedious work, and an automatic avoidance latency write-out was designed and constructed. This produced histograms of the avoidance latency responses at the time of treatment. Briefly, it consisted of a pen-carrying trolley which was set in motion to draw a line at the precise time of onset of the CS. The pen was made to retract from the writing surface at the moment of the first avoidance response. The machine was constructed so that the occurrence of the UCS could also be recorded and the pen-carrying trolley automatically re-set itself between trials; all that was required of the operator was to move the writing surface to the left a set distance. In this way the machine drew a histogram which indicated the relative avoidance latency times for each trial.

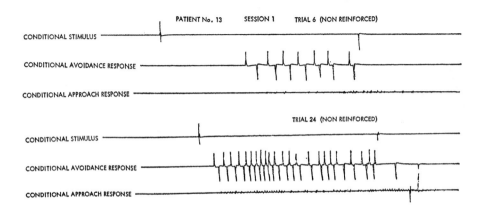

FIG. 6.7. A sample tracing from an 8-channel EEG machine, adapted to record CS1, CR1, and CR2.

The machine was set to record on cards as many treatment sessions as possible of the patients undergoing anticipatory avoidance (AA) treatment in the controlled trial. In some cases, for technical reasons, the machine failed to record, so that a small proportion of the AA data is missing. On the other hand, although only 10 patients were initially randomly assigned to the AA group, there are AA latency data available on 14 patients; the additional recordings being made on a number of patients who crossed over from other treatments (see Chapter 5).

The construction "work up" of this machine carried out on a small number of patients prior to the beginning of the controlled trial, suggested aspects of avoidance response data which might have prognostic implications. Accordingly, two categories of factors were proposed, positive and negative.

POSITIVE PROGNOSTIC FACTORS

(A) Learning curves in which 6 or more of the last 12 avoidance response latencies were less than 2 seconds in duration.

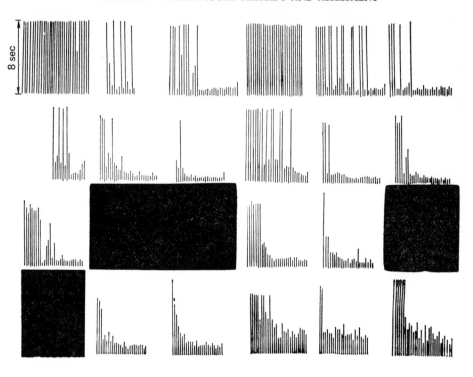

FIG. 6.8. Automatically recorded avoidance latencies for sessions 1–13, 16–17, 20-24. The CS (the male slide) was changed every 3 sessions. There was a tendency for a greater proportion of longer latencies in sessions 1, 4, 7, and 10 compared with sessions 3, 6, 9, and 12.

(B) Learning curves in which 2 of the last 3 avoidance latencies of the session were shorter than 2 out of the first 3 latencies in the session. Examples illustrating these 2 types of prognostic factor are shown in Fig. 6.8. Examples of factor A are seen in sessions 8 and 9, and an example of factor B is shown in session 3.

NEGATIVE PROGNOSTIC FACTORS

(A) Learning curves in which more than 6 of the last 12 avoidance latencies exceeded 4 seconds.

(B) Histograms which showed avoidance latencies, in the second half of the session, whose time varied irregularly in such a way that the short latencies were 4 seconds shorter than the long ones, and in which there was a strong tendency for the short and long latencies to alternate.

(C) Avoidance latency curves in which 4 of the last 12 latencies showed consecutively increasing values. An example of negative prognostic factor A is shown in Fig. 6.9, session 3, one of factor B in session 5 and one of factor C in session 15. It was further postulated that where a patient showed a high number of sessions containing positive prognostic factors, his degree of success after treatment as judged by the change in SOM score would be higher than that of a patient who only showed a small number of sessions containing positive prognostic

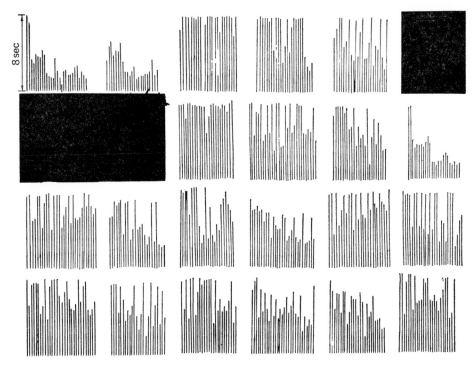

FIG. 6.9. Automatically recorded avoidance latencies recorded for sessions 1–5, 9–24. Compare with Fig. 6.8 the relative lack of contrast between sessions 1 and 3, 6 and 8, 9 and 11, etc.

curves. Similarly, where a patient produced a high number of sessions whose avoidance latency curves contained a high proportion of negative prognostic factors, he would do worse than a patient whose session by session curves contained a low number of negative prognostic factors; further, it was expected that the factors would tend to be mutually exclusive.

METHOD OF ANALYSIS

Apart from sessions in which there was an apparatus failure of avoidance latency write-out, there were avoidance latencies for 24 sessions on each of 14 patients.

Previous experience on series patients nos. 2, 3, 11, and 13 and an inspection of mechanically produced avoidance latency curves from non-trial patients suggested that where prognostic factors were going to emerge, they did so in early sessions. It was therefore decided to take sessions 1–6 for detailed analysis of the 14 patients in this trial. Should the factors outlined prove predictive, it would then in future be possible to predict outcome following 24 or more sessions from the inspection of the avoidance latency histograms of the first 6 treatment sessions, thereby providing a further means of economizing on therapeutic time and enabling us to increase efficiency.

The cards containing the avoidance latencies for each of 24 sessions of the 14 patients were put in sequence of 6 columns and 4 rows and photographed; the photographs were then examined blind by one of us (M.J.M.), and the time scale for the avoidance latencies was derived from the longest trials, e.g. the longest avoidance latencies were 8 seconds. Individual avoidance latencies were measured as a proportion of that length, so that it was possible to carry out the counts for obtaining positive and negative prognostic factors. Variations in avoidance latency length in relation to negative prognostic factor C were derived from direct visual inspection—in practice it proved relatively easy to decide whether consecutive lines differed in length. The histograms for each of the first 6 sessions were examined and scores for each factor for each patient were prepared. For example, the number of sessions out of the first 6 which showed positive prognostic factor A was divided by 6.

Product moment correlations between positive and negative factors and the changes which occurred in SOM scores over the period pre-treatment to 3 months post-treatment were calculated for trial patients, nos. 1–4, 7–8, 11–12, 13, 16–18, 24, and 28 and the results are shown in Table 6.1.

TABLE 6.1. AVOIDANCE RESPONSE LATENCIES IN 14 PATIENTS TREATED BY AA LEARNING

Correlation between positive and negative factors and changes in SOM scores between pre-treatment and 3 months' post-treatment.

	Correlation	p
1. Positive factors correlated with:		
(a) Change in homosexual score	+0.322	0.1
(b) Change in heterosexual score	+0.356	0.1
2. Negative factors correlated with:		
(a) Change in homosexual score	−0.5708	0.05
(b) Change in heterosexual score	−0.4995	<0.1 >0.05
3. Positive factors correlated with negative factors	−0.2327	N.S.

Positive and negative factors were negatively correlated, $p = -0.2327$ (NS) confirming our prediction that these two factors are not significantly correlated, and therefore can be considered separately. Table 6.1 shows that the positive factors correlated positively with both homosexual and heterosexual SOM scores, both falling just short of an acceptable level of statistical significance. However, the negative prognostic factors correlated negatively and significantly with change in homosexual ($p = < 0.05$) and heterosexual scores ($p = < 0.1 > 0.05$). This means that as the negative factors' scores increased the change in SOM scores in response to treatment decreased.

DISCUSSION

The ability to predict from objective within treatment behaviour to probable success or failure in response to treatment is of obvious importance. In some cases the warning signal will be a high preponderance of long avoidance latencies without any asymptotic curve, in others a gross irregularity of the avoidance latencies with some reversed learning curves. Where early trials in early sessions show medium avoidance latencies and few escape trials, it is reasonable to infer that these patients are performing under a high level of anxiety which initially causes them to avoid shock without first having gone through a number of escape trials. Since each patient is carefully instructed to leave the slide on for as long as it was attractive, this pattern of response indicates that the patients had not been following instructions. The therapist ought to use a lower level of shock as well as reassuring the patient.

The avoidance latency curves may also be taken to indicate the need, or otherwise, for further avoidance conditioning with the slide in use.

In several instances in the controlled trial, patients were moved on to the next slide in their hierarchy before they had achieved consistently short avoidance latencies. This was necessitated by the design of the trial (see Chapter 5). In normal treatment practice, as opposed to a controlled trial situation, patients should not move up their slide hierarchy until they are showing consistently short avoidance latencies. If the avoidance latency scores on the first 6 sessions show high negative factor scores, action on the part of the therapist is indicated. This might take the form of changing some aspect of the technique such as reducing the level of shock, as mentioned above, or substituting a less attractive slide. Alternatively, further diagnostic interviewing might be in order to re-assess the patient's suitability for treatment. Finally, a preponderance of negative factors should at least suggest to the therapist that a larger number of treatment sessions than usual might be necessary and should prepare him for the necessity of giving frequent booster sessions in the post-treatment period.

II. OBSERVATIONS ON TOTAL BODY MOVEMENT DURING CONDITIONING

During the early part of AA aversion therapy it was noticed that patients tended to display patterns of movement which appeared to have a degree of consistency. At the time these original observations were made the patients were sitting on a bent-wood chair which tended to squeak when movements took place; it was observed that some patients "froze" when the CS1 was presented, and later became increasingly restless as the advent of the UCS approached during D 7.5 and NR trials.

During our modification of the original AA learning paradigm we altered our projecting system so that patients lay on a bed; the bed was sprung ballistically, and a suitably sensitive inertial switch was designed in order to record bed and, hence, patient movements. The output from the total body movement inertial switch was fed to one pen unit in the 10-channel marker. The relays which formed the basis of this system required 9–10 volts sustained for several milliseconds in order to mark with the pen. The current in these pen-activating coils was measured by the EEG machine whose sensitivity was far greater than that of the relay. This resulted in 2 recordings, one on the high-gain amplifier which contained a large number of strokes per second (it appeared that the high-gain amplifier was picking up the change in charge which was occurring when the disc of the inertial switch was swinging free, without actually making electrical contact with the centre part of the switch) and one on the pen relay unit which only recorded when the switch made firm metallic contact. There was thus an electromechanical constant in the pen relay circuit which reduced the sensitivity of this system compared with that of the high-gain amplifier.

It appeared to be most useful to measure the output of the pen relay system because the high-gain amplifier did not distinguish clearly between swings of the switch and contacts.

The data from the ballistic bed were contaminated by the switching behaviour of the patient and by the muscular responses evoked by the shock. It was not possible, therefore, accurately to measure the output of this device during the time that the first (male—CS1) or second (female—CS2) conditional stimuli were on. These conditions did not apply in a very small number of trials, where switching behaviour was not occurring within 15 seconds of the presentation of the CS1 slide. In this situation it was possible to gain an impression of the effect of the CS1 on the patient's general body movement. In some cases the patient was moving slightly and the CS1 produced an inhibition of movement or "freezing" which occurred after the onset of the stimulus. In general CS1 presentation trials were contaminated by the patients' avoidance responses.

Figure 6.10 shows trial 24 of session 24 for trial patient no. 4 (success) in which the patient's pre-CS1 movement count is slightly increased by the CS onset, and then abolished by the continued CS1 exposure, uncomplicated by an avoidance response. The same record shows that movement reappears as the shock becomes more certain, peaks as shock is administered, and, following a further post-UCS freeze, returns to the pre-CS1 level.

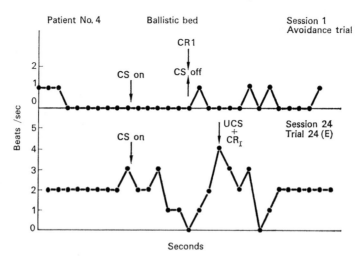

FIG. 6.10. Ballistic bed count means during sessions 1 and 24 for trial patient no. **4.**

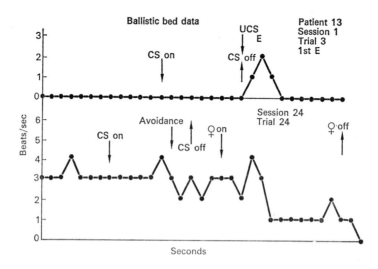

FIG. 6.11. Ballistic bed count means during sessions 1 and 24 for trial patient no. 13.

The same patient's early movement pattern (session 1 pre-programme, CS1 presentation, escape response) does not show the same level of pre-CS1 movement (see upper part of Fig. 6.10) and the freeze response is absent.

The upper part of Fig. 6.11 compares closely with Fig. 6.10, however; trial 24, session 24, in trial patient 13 (failure) shows a high pre-CS1 level of activity with only a very minimal transient increase in movement rate before the avoidance at 6 seconds. The second operant response (CR2) produced a momentary increase in movement followed by a marked reduction in movement during the exposure of the female slide (CS2).

Figures 6.10 and 6.11 both show an increase of pre-CS movement occurring over the interval between session 1 and session 24. The successfully treated patient (no. 4) shows a freezing response which was not seen in patient no. 13.

The inter-trial periods were mainly contaminated by attempts to switch on the female slide. The records of each session were therefore samples by counting the output for two 20-second epochs before the onset of trial 1 for each session. This provided two measures of body movement for each session of treatment. The 24 treatment sessions were divided into sixths and the mean rates of movement for each consecutive batch of 4 samples were calculated, e.g.:

20-second epoch	1	
20-second epoch	2	mean for session 1
20-second epoch	1	
20-second epoch	2	mean for session 2
20-second epoch	1	
20-second epoch	2	mean for session 3
20-second epoch	1	
20-second epoch	2	mean for session 4

Mean

The data (14 cases) were examined to see if there was a trend which differentiated the success group from the failure group (where success was defined as a reduction in 12 points on the SOM homosexual scores). The results are presented in Fig. 6.12, which shows bed counts for the success and failure groups.

The mean duration of follow-up in success and failure groups did not differ significantly.

The graph indicates that the 2 groups differ slightly; the bed count rate for the success group slightly exceeds that for the failure group during the first half of treatment.   Table 6.2 presents the results of a success vs. failure analysis both for pre/post-treatment score changes and pre-follow-up changes.

Over the first three-sixths the bed count for success and failure groups differ at the 5% level of significance when the outcome is assessed as a drop in 12 points on the SOM homosexual score at the final follow-up. Immediately post-treatment, the group constitution is such that the difference is predictive at the 10% level of confidence; this implies that a number of subjects whose treatment bed count scores are high do not show an immediate post-treatment success but continue, over time, to lower their male scores. High bed movement count during the first half of treatment has a tendency to be predictive of later improvement. The overall increase in body movement between the beginning and end of treatment,

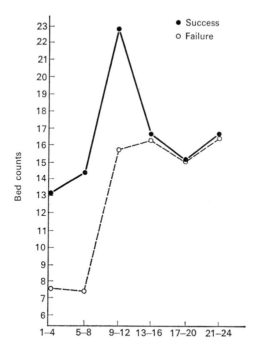

FIG. 6.12. Ballistic bed count means for trial patients (success versus failure) in sessions 1–4, 5–8, 9–12, 13–16, 17–20, and 21–24.

TABLE 6.2. MEAN TOTAL BODY MOVEMENT COUNTS. SESSIONS 1–12 vs. 13–24

Group	Portion of treatment	t	p
Success vs. Failure (pre/FU)	1st half	2.197	0.05
Success vs. Failure (pre/post)	1st half	1.7	0.1
Success vs. Failure (pre/FU)	2nd half	1.148	0.25
Success vs. Failure (pre/post)	2nd half	1	NS
Success (pre/FU)	1st half vs. 2nd half	1	NS
Success (pre/post)	1st half vs. 2nd half	1	NS
Failure (pre/FU)	1st half vs. 2nd half	1.01	NS
Failure (pre/post)	1st half vs. 2nd half	1	NS

irrespective of outcome, showed a trend at the 10% level of confidence. The authors do not feel that total body movement responses are easy to measure in that they are too readily contaminated by the effects of coughing, deep respiration, and operant responses; nonetheless, one trend emerged; pre-CS total body movement tended to increase as conditioning proceeded; the level of movement, pre-CS onset, was high during the first 12 sessions in patients who successfully conditioned, as judged by final follow-up homosexual scores. It would seem most reasonable to conclude that this raised level of movement is a reflection of a high level of anxiety in this group of patients; the hypothesis would fit in with our findings on pre-CS pulse-rate findings (see section V of this chapter). We have measured electromyographic responses taken from the right forearm during conditioning, and these results suggest that further research in this area be directed to levels of muscle activity by direct electromyographic techniques rather than further measurements of total body movement. Electromyograph data would be best managed by electronic integration techniques to provide accurate quantitative between-patient comparisons of muscle tension of subjects undergoing classical and AA aversive conditioning.

III. ELECTROMYOGRAPHIC RESPONSES

A high-gain amplifier (portable 8-channel EEG machine) was used on the first and twenty-fourth sessions with all patients who had AA conditioning. This machine was connected to give a measure of muscle activity by taking an electromyogram via two surface electrodes attached to the flexor aspect of the middle of the right forearm. We recorded muscle potentials which appeared to indicate general muscle-tone levels, and bursts of spikes which occurred in relation to switching behaviour in the right hand (see Fig. 6.13 for example). In the treatment by AA, the patient lay with the fingers of the right hand on the knob of his avoidance switch. He was instructed to leave the homosexual slide on so long as it was attractive and then attempt to switch it off. On delay trials he was instructed to keep trying the switch until he was successful. When the homosexual slide was removed from the screen, the patient was able to request the appearance of a female slide by operating a second switch. His operant behaviour consisted of removing the male slide (CS1) by operating switch 1 (CR1), and then pressing switch 2 (CR2), which was separated from switch 1 by 5 cm.

RESULTS

The EMG channel showed without exception bursts of spike potentials which temporally coincided with coarse finger movement in the act of making the first and second conditioned responses. However, in the later trials of sessions 1 and 24 it was noted that there were bursts of spike potentials in the periods between the onset of the homosexual slide, and the onset of these muscle potentials which were coincident with the avoidance switching (CR1) response. These early spike potentials appeared to indicate a preliminary tightening of the muscles in the forearm which clearly occurred before coarse finger movement.

Figure 6.13 shows 8-channel traces for trials 1, 12, and 24 of session 1 for trial patient no. 4 (successful outcome); and traces for trials 1, 3, and 23 for session 1 for trial patient no. 13 (unsuccessful outcome).

The traces for trial 1, patient no. 4 (channel 6), show an EMG burst coincident with the CR1 (channel 2). Corresponding EMG bursts in trials 12 and 24 clearly antecede the CR1 responses.

This anticipatory EMG is not shown by trial patient no. 13 and it is of interest that session 1, trial 1, showed a short avoidance latency. It is of further interest to note that the unsuccessful patient showed no galvanic skin responses (channel 5 baseline) and fewer changes in total body movement (channel 4).

The time between the onset of the conditional stimulus and the onset of the first muscle spikes was measured, as was the time between the onset of the muscle spikes and the onset of

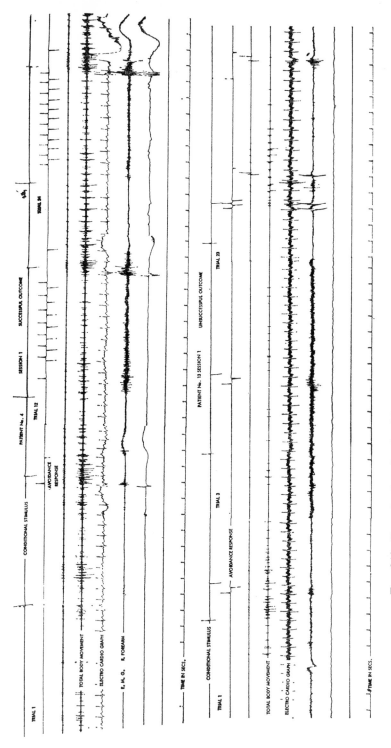

FIG. 6.13. Records of session 1, trials 1, 12, and 24 for trial patient no. 4 (successful) and session 1, trials 1, 3, and 23 for trial patient no. 13 (unsuccessful).

the switching response. It was then possible to construct two learning curves for each patient: the first was the conventional learning curve of the latencies of the avoidance response indicated by switch operation: the second from the muscle avoidance latencies indicated by the time from the slide onset to the first muscle spikes (EMG latencies). Figure 6.14 shows avoidance latency and EMG latency curves for trial patients nos. 4 and 11, both taken from treatment session 1.

In the curves for patient 4, it will be seen that the EMG and avoidance latencies temporally coincide on trials 1–7. These are termed synchronous latencies. On trials 8, 9, and 10 there is a temporal separation in that the EMG latency precedes the avoidance latency by 0.3 seconds approximately. These are termed non-synchronous latencies. On trial 11 and thereafter the EMG latencies are short, e.g. 0.25 seconds, and precede the coarse operant response by 0.5–1 second.

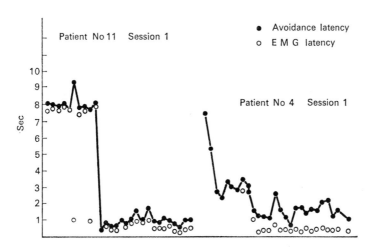

FIG. 6.14. Electromyograph and avoidance latencies for trial patients nos. 4 and 11.

The curves for trial patient no. 11 differ quite strikingly in that there is no EMG/operant latency coincidence in any of the first 11 trials, all of which were escape trials. The avoidance latency jumps to 0.5 seconds on trial 12 and thereafter the EMG/operant separation does not generally exceed 0.3–0.5 seconds. Full data were only available for a small number of cases, and so the percentage of trials on which the EMG and avoidance latencies were synchronous for sessions 1 and 24 were calculated and the percentage of trials per session on which there was a change from synchronous to non-synchronous latencies between sessions 1 and 24, was compared between failure and success groups. Success was defined as a drop of 12 or more points on the SOM scale over the period of treatment.

Table 6.3 summarizes the findings and suggests that failure group patients tend both to have a lower initial percentage of synchronous latencies and in session 24 retain a higher percentage of synchronicities. The success group commence session 1 with a higher number of synchronous responses which are totally absent by session 24. Statistical analysis of the percentage of change of synchronicity from session 1 to session 24 indicated that the groups differed on this measure at the 5% level ($t = 2.21$). A possible explanation of these findings is as follows.

TABLE 6.3. COMPARISON OF SUCCESS AND FAILURE PATIENTS IN THE CHANGE BETWEEN SESSIONS 1 AND 24 IN THE PERCENTAGE OF TRIALS ON WHICH THE ELECTROMYOGRAPHIC RESPONSE AND THE AVOIDANCE RESPONSE OCCUR SIMULTANEOUSLY

Latencies	Success patients (3)		Failure patients (2)	
	Session 1	Session 24	Session 1	Session 24
Synchronous response (%)	44.07	0	22.87	15.9
Non-synchronous response, i.e. anticipatory EMG (%)	55.93	100	77.13	84.1
Change S1–S24 (%)	44.07		7.03	
Success vs. Failure	$t = 2.2$　($p < 0.05$)			

In session 1, conditioning of the anticipatory EMG has not yet occurred. Early non-synchronous, i.e. anticipatory, EMG responses indicate conscious eagerness to avoid shock as often as possible rather than the desire to persist in leaving the slide on for as long as it is attractive. The less well-motivated patient is likely to display this response more frequently than the patient with good motivation for treatment. By session 24 *no* shocks are received, i.e. all patients are on programme 4 (see Chapter 5). Non-synchronous EMG's indicate conditioned muscle anticipation for the coarse response of switching off, successful patients show these to a more marked degree than do unsuccessful ones as would be expected on theoretical grounds.

The greater capacity of the successful group to become conditioned is reflected in both the coarse movement avoidance latencies and this anticipatory EMG response.

IV. MEASUREMENTS OF RESPIRATION CHANGE DURING AVERSIVE CONDITIONING

Deane (1964) investigated human heart rate response to experimentally induced anxiety and was able to show that the cardiac rate changes were not substantially affected by respiration rate, phase, or depth.

We therefore measured pulse rate both in our series and trial patients without controlling for respiration: however, a crude pneumatic respiratory cuff was developed which produced a trace where amplitude reflected respiratory cage excursion.

This apparatus proved unreliable, and it was not possible to obtain regular recordings of respiration. The traces that were obtained could not easily be replicated because of the variability in the gas pressure in the cuff–diaphragm system.

In spite of these difficulties a number of interesting—albeit isolated—observations were made. Figure 6.15 shows a reproduction of four portions of recordings obtained from trial patient no. 3 in session 17. Section A shows a well-established repetitive avoidance response CR1 to the CS1 which was presented in the context of a 4.5-second delay trial. The ballistic bed output at that point is clearly contaminated by the CR1 and respiration is inhibited for 8 seconds. At the point when the (CR2) request for the appearance of the female is granted, i.e. the female slide (CS2) is projected, respiration is recommenced at double the pre-CS1 onset rate. The respiration trace shows a pulse artefact during the apnoea which is caused by abdominal aortic pulsations being recorded by the thoracic pneumatic cuff, which, in this case, overlapped the upper abdomen.

It is of further interest to note that the initial effect of the appearance of the CS2 was to reduce total body movement (see ballistic bed channel). Section B of Fig. 6.15 shows more complex respiration changes, once again the CS1 (D trial) produced a marked apnoea and small inspiration at its offset. The first CR2 response was immediately followed by a deep inspiration and although respiration was then re-established at a high rate, i.e. 30 per min, the amplitude was much reduced compared to the pre-CS1 onset level.

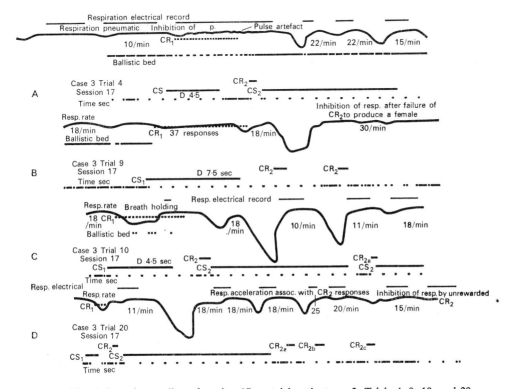

FIG. 6.15. 6-channel recording of session 17 on trial patient no. 3. Trials 4, 9, 10, and 20. Downward deflection represents inspiration.

Section C shows trial 10 and largely replicates section A in that CS1 induced apnoea appears followed by an inspiration coinciding with the first CR2. The appearance of the CS2 is associated with large amplitude respirations of diminished rate.

Section D shows trial 20 in which the CR2a was not rewarded, that is after the first reward female was removed the patient was not able to successfully recall the female slide.

The CS1 induced apnoea is not seen in this instance because the trial was of the R type and of short duration. The onset of the first CS2 produced a deep inspiration gasp followed by an acceleration of rate which coincided with unsuccessful CR2 response, i.e. CR2a, b, and c. At the point where CR2c occurred, the respiratory trace is characterized by an inhibition of amplitude and the beginning of a rate deceleration.

It is therefore possible to discern patterns of respiratory behaviour occurring in this successfully treated patient:

(I) A high level of anxiety engendered by the very threatening situation of a long D trial results in respiratory inhibition.

(II) Moderately raised levels of anxiety may result in tachypnoea (raised respiratory rate) and reduced tidal volume (reduced trace amplitude).

(III) Reduction of anxiety either resulting from (a) the decision to make a CS1-postponing CR1 response, (b) making the response, or (c) receiving the CS2, may result in an inspiratory gasp.

We were able to contrast the results outlined in Fig. 6.15 with those found in trial patient no. 19 (failure) (Fig. 6.16), which shows trial 7 of session 32 (i.e. session 8 of AA following 24 sessions of unsuccessful CC). The respiratory trace shows virtually no change in rate and a minimal change in amplitude. It is of interest to note that even in the eighth session of AA treatment the avoidance latency was 7 seconds, indicating a poor response to treatment.

It became apparent that there were meaningful respiratory changes to be seen in patients

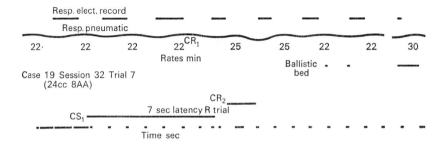

FIG. 6.16. Respiratory trace in trial case 19, trial 7 of session 32.

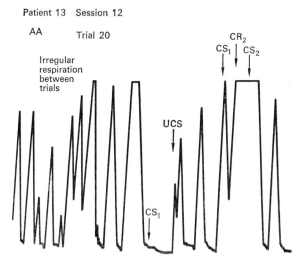

FIG. 6.17. A tracing obtained using the respiratory thoracic switch, which shows the inhibiting effect of the CS1, a gasp produced by the UCS, and an apnoea produced by CS2.

undergoing aversive conditioning which appeared to be broadly in line with those changes described as part of the "orienting" reflex (Pavlov, 1927). We therefore began to develop a system for measuring and displaying respiratory rate. This consisted of a pen of the *xy* plotter type which was constructed to change its direction of constant movement in the vertical plane every time a respiratory cycle was completed. Although this device was still in the experimental stage at the completion of the trial, it seems likely that such a system, recording on a slowly moving paper, would produce a pen trace whose width was proportional to the respiratory rate (Fig. 6.17).

This type of display would enable the significance of respiratory rate changes in response to stimuli readily to be appreciated because it compresses the length of the recording and renders changes in rate readily apparent.

V. PULSE-RATE CHANGES DURING ADVERSIVE CONDITIONNIG

1. SERIES PATIENTS

Such was the sensitivity of our hydraulic stimulus response measuring system that we found it possible to produce a modification which would hydraulically record pressure changes occurring in the radial artery and so provide a record of pulse rate. Details of the apparatus used in this technique are provided in MacCulloch *et al.* (1965).

Different authors have used different methods to quantify and classify pulse-rate responses. In a detailed study on autonomic response specificity, Lacey *et al.* (1953) were able to demonstrate the principle of relative response specificity, finding that individuals tended to respond with an idiosyncratic pattern of autonomic activation in which maximum activation occurred in the same physiological measure irrespective of the stress and that the pattern was reproducible from stress to stress. The tendency to show response specificity was more marked for autonomic tension than for autonomic lability. Some individuals responded with a given hierarchy of autonomic activation whatever the stress; others showed greater fluctuation from stress to stress although they tended to exhibit one pattern more frequently than another; yet other individuals randomly exhibit one pattern and then another. The quantitative difference between the degrees of activation of the different physiological measures fluctuated quite considerably. Lacey and Smith (1954) constructed autonomic lability scores in an experiment in which they measured the effect of a word signal which had become conditioned to a painful stimulus; in these experiments they sampled the six fastest heart beats in a 15-second period preceding the onset of their stimulus word, and during a 15-second period of stimulus pairings. A reliability study showed that their sampling technique was highly satisfactory. They pointed out that reactivity of heart rate was a characteristic of the individual, and that numerical changes in heart rate depended on pulse rate base level. In addition, they found that following a number of pairings of words and painful stimuli the subject displayed an autonomic response to the word alone. In a later study, Lacey *et al.* (1955), using similar techniques for measuring and calculating pulse scores, concluded that situational anxiety could readily be induced by a conditioning process at an unconscious level: further, the situational anxiety generalized to other stimuli present in the situation. The chronic anxiety level of the individual might have been a factor in the ease with which the individual patient acquired the generalized anxiety response.

When heart-rate changes have been studied in relation to an electrical aversive stimulus, the results have been conflicting; some studies have reported cardiac acceleration and other deceleration in the interval between warning signal and shock. Notterman *et al.* (1952) noted cardiac deceleration as the predominant response in a 6-second interval between warning signal and shock (Lacey and Smith, 1954). On the other hand, Zeaman and Wegner (1957) reported both factors occurring in different subjects and suggested that differing breathing patterns might be related to these dual cardiac effects. The results of Deane and Zeaman (1958) have effectively rejected this suggestion, and in a further study Deane and Zeaman (1958) sought to elucidate the controlling mechanism of cardiac acceleration and deceleration. (They plotted beat-by-beat rates, averaging 5 runs in each case, and analysed the mean rates during a set period of time prior to the onset of the anxiety-provoking stimulus.) They found "when the subject expected a noxious stimulus of unknown strength, a state of anxiety with its associated response of cardiac acceleration is aroused a relatively long time before the stimulus is expected". After the subjects had been shocked and were in the position to assess when the next shock would appear, they showed a cardiac deceleration response. Deane and Zeaman (1958) concluded that the shock was responsible for the acquisition of the cardiac deceleration response. The acceleration response following shock instruction was stable; that recorded in subjects who had received shocks was less marked than those who remained unshocked. Instructions about when to expect the shock were more effective in producing a cardiac deceleration than was actually getting the shock. They speculate that the two cardiac effects are unlearned responses associated with anxiety and fear, and they conclude "it is apparently the case that even experiencing the noxious stimulus as relatively mild is not sufficient to abolish the fear response at the expected locus of the stimulus". Jenks and Deane (1963) investigated the effects of a loud tone on cardiac rate using numbers to signal the occurrence of the tone; their results tended to support the hypothesis that when a subject expects to receive a noxious stimulus, a state of anxiety with the associated response of cardiac acceleration is aroused and that, in addition, if the subject expects the noxious stimulus at a *particular* instance in time, a cardiac decelerative response is produced immediately prior to and during the time the stimulus is expected.

Pulse-rate changes to a previously neutral conditional stimulus have been studied by Black (1959) in the *anticipatory avoidance* situation using dogs as his subjects. We were interested both in measuring displayed pulse-rate changes in our homosexual patients following the presentation of the conditional stimuli as conditioning proceeded, and also in the predictive value for post-treatment behaviour of such (presumably conditioned) cardiac changes. Black had found the gradual emergence of a conditioned cardiac response following several pairings of sound and shock of the following form: "whilst the dog was avoiding regularly the cardiac rate began to rise from its base level just before the occurrence of the conditional stimulus (presumably due to stimulus cues) and continued to rise several seconds after the avoidance response had been made, it then subsided and fell below its pre-stimulus level finally returning to the pre-stimulus level." Black found a correlation between the occurrence of a cardiac change of the type described and successful avoidance learning; if there was no cardiac elevation to the conditional stimulus alone the subject failed to avoid. Eighty per cent of his dogs showed cardiac conditioning, and the slowest avoidance learners were those who showed no cardiac conditioning.

Method

The first series of measurements were made on series patients nos. 2 and 13 (see Appendix A1). Both patients were seated in the chair and used their right hands to make operant responses. The pulse capsule was attached to the left hand which was itself supported on the padded left-hand arm of the chair. On occasions it was necessary lightly to bandage the patient's left arm to the chair on a pad in order sufficiently to restrict the random movements which tended to occur during the time in which the patients were making repetitive avoidance responses with their right hand. The amount of artefact was insufficient to vitiate the measurements of the pulse rates during conditional stimulus exposure. We recorded pulse rate during sessions 1, 3, and 5 for series patient no. 2, and sessions 1, 3, and 7 for series patient no. 13. The distances between adjacent pulse beats were then measured by means of a pair of specially constructed perspex calipers. The distance between the two pulse beats was magnified 15 times and the scale of the calipers presented the result in rate per minute. Pulse rates were consistently measured to 3% accuracy. The data for series patients nos. 2 and 13, together with control data, are presented in Figs. 6.18 and 6.19.

Results

For each patient there are 5 columns of graphs and each column consists of 4 rows. All 4 rows of column 1 consist of the same sample of the patient's resting pulse rate during session 1. This sample was selected at random from his pulse-rate record during 2 minutes following the first 5 minutes of this session. That is, after he had settled down and adapted to the situation but before treatment actually started. All 4 rows of column 5 consist of the same sample of the patient's pulse rate in session 1 during the showing of a male slide which he had described as attractive and before any introduction of shock. The 2 outer columns are available for comparison purposes with the 3 inner columns. These comprise randomly chosen data taken respectively from the first session of treatment, a session in the middle of treatment, and a session near the end of treatment. As is indicated on the graph, the first row of these 3 middle columns consists of reinforced trials. The next row consists of delay trials in which the delay time was $4\frac{1}{2}$ seconds, the third row of delay trials in which the delay was 6 seconds and the fourth row of delay trials in which the delay time was $7\frac{1}{2}$ seconds. For each graph the first dotted line indicates slide onset and the second, slide offset. We present pulse rates for each successive beat, and in all instances pulse rates are shown for the 10 beats immediately preceding stimulus onset and the 10 beats immediately following stimulus offset, as well as for beats during stimulus presentation.

The pulse rate data for series patient no. 2 (Fig. 6.18) indicate the following:

(a) There is very little pulse rate change in session 1 (before any introduction of shock) to the attractive male slide (column 5).

(b) On the reinforced trials, there is a gradual change from session 1 to session 5, so that by session 5 the pulse-rate changes described by Black (1959), details of which were given earlier, are clearly present. That is, an up-swing which then declines when the CS is removed.

(c) Turning to the $4\frac{1}{2}$-second delay trials, there is little change in session 1, but in sessions 3 and 5 there is a clear up-swing. The down-swing on this occasion occurs very soon after the removal of the slide.

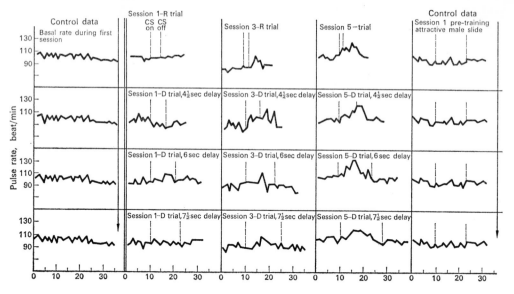

FIG. 6.18. Pulse rate changes by series patient no. 2.

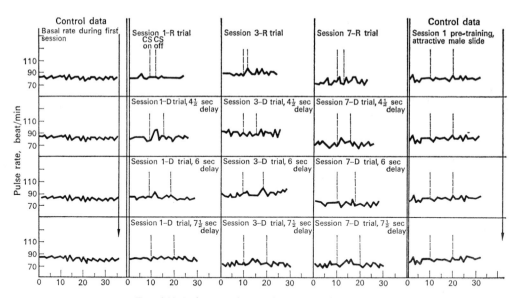

FIG. 6.19. Pulse rate changes by series patient no. 13.

(d) There is, again, very little change in session 1 for the 6-second delay trial, but by session 5 there is an up-swing followed by a down-swing which is, in fact, completed before the slide is removed.

(e) Finally, there is no effect in session 1 for the $7\frac{1}{2}$-second delay trial, but a clear-cut effect by session 5. That is, an up-swing following CS onset and a down-swing which is completed before the removal of the CS.

Series patient no. 13. By way of contrast, there are no changes worth commenting on for this patient throughout all the sessions and for any of the different reinforcement conditions (Fig. 6.19). Clearly, there has been no cardiac response conditioned in this patient which is remotely comparable to that brought about in series patient no. 2.

The data on series patient no. 13 show no change throughout. That is, there is very little variation from the basal rate for any type of learning trial in any session. In view of his poor avoidance learning, this is of course not surprising. It will be recalled that Black (1959) found that those subjects who displayed little or no cardiac elevation to the CS were also those who failed to avoid.

The pulse-rate changes of series patient no. 2 are quite different. He displays a steadily greater increase in cardiac elevation, associated with CS onset, throughout the sessions. These swings are so great, being of the order of 20 beats/minute or more, particularly by the time session 5 has been reached, and occur within such a small space of time, that they are very unlikely to be artefacts. Certainly, if one looks at the basal rate and male stimulus data for session 1 (Fig. 6.18, columns 1 and 5 respectively), there is no comparable swing in either situation.

In each treatment session there were about 25 trials, one-third of which involved the patient receiving a brief shock which ceased as the picture was removed. By session 3, series patient no. 2 had developed a mild cardiac response to the male picture on non-shock trials, which is clearly marked by session 5. This was not present either prior to treatment or early in treatment (session 1), and it may therefore be regarded as a CR. The general shape of this response is the same, irrespective of the type of trial. However, the time relationships between CS onset and offset and cardiac elevation and return, do differ according to the type of trial. Whereas for the reinforced trials the time relationship is very similar to that described by Black (1959), that for the delay trials is rather different. This difference is greatest for the 6- and 7½-second delay trials. For these trials the cardiac elevation and decline in sessions 3 and 5 is actually completed before the CS has been finally removed. This result is in accord with Deane's finding that "When a subject expects a noxious stimulus of unknown strength, a state of anxiety with its associated response of cardiac acceleration is aroused, and, in addition, if the subject expects the noxious stimulus at a particular instance of time, the state of fear with its associated response of cardiac deceleration is aroused, immediately prior to and during the time the stimulus is expected" (Deane, 1961).

We can therefore account for our data as follows. The patient *may* receive a shock on all trials. Hence he will show cardiac acceleration on all trials. However, he is not certain that he will receive a shock because he has learnt that on most occasions he will succeed in removing the picture before the shock is due. That is, there is a possibility that shock may be avoidable, so that deceleration—associated with anticipation of shock—does not inevitably occur prior to CS offset. Assuming that we have reached the stage at which the patient is attempting to avoid within 2–3 seconds of CS onset, and, re-membering that the interval before shock occurrence is 8 seconds after onset, the argument proceeds as follows. On a reinforced (R) trial, the first avoidance response is reinforced, that is the picture is removed, indicating that shock has been success-fully avoided. In this case deceleration takes place only after CS removal, and it can be seen as a simple return to the basal level of cardiac rate. On delay trials, the patient's initial avoidance response is not reinforced. The longer the delay to which he is subjected, the more likely it is that he will receive a shock. The deceleration response is, therefore, displayed on delay trials and the extent to which it is completed prior to CS offset is a func-tion of the length of the delay, as can be seen in Fig. 6.18. On the 4½-second delay trials, deceleration coincides with CS offset, while on the 6- and 7½-second delay trials, it precedes CS offset. It may be that this cardiac deceleration serves some biological function such as enabling the organism to "set itself" to receive the shock. Whatever the explanation, the effect is clear-cut and appears similar to that described by Deane. It is of interest that Deane (1964) demonstrated that the cardiac changes which he obtained were not due to respiratory changes associated with CS onset, so that this explanation for our findings is ruled out.

The lack of cardiac conditioning shown by series patient no. 13 may be due to a variety of reasons. In the first instance he had a very low neuroticism score on the Eysenck personality inventory (Eysenck and Eysenck, 1964) as compared with series patient no. 2, who had a higher than average score. Secondly, he was undoubtedly poorly motivated for treatment. Thirdly, the habit strength of his homosexual interest, because of the extent and frequency of his practice, was very much greater than that of series patient no. 2. Finally, as Lacey and Lacey (1958) have pointed out, autonomic responses may be rather specific, so that using cardiac responsiveness as our only indicant may not have been sufficient. Whatever the precise explanation, it is quite clear that whereas series patient no. 2 showed successful avoidance learning, pronounced cardiac elevation and a good post-treatment response, series patient no. 13 showed poor avoidance learning, no cardiac elevation, and a poor post-treatment response.

2. TRIAL PATIENTS

Method

Our apparatus was, to say the least, make-shift and not entirely reliable; further, it suffered from the very marked disadvantage that the hydraulic pressure line which was used to conduct pulse pressure changes had to be no longer than 1 metre because pressure changes were dissipated by the conducting fluid viscosity. We were therefore in the rather unsatisfactory position of having a recording machine almost within touching distance of the patient's left hand, and as it was necessary from time to time to adjust the pens in relation to position and ink flow, etc., there was an unsatisfactory congruence of patient and therapist.

Several attempts were made to construct an electromechanical wrist capsule which could be used to drive an electromechanical pen-marker. These attempts were not successful, and the problem of recording was finally solved by a portable EEG machine which was made available to us from the Department of Electroencephalography. We designed and built a modified system for presenting stimuli and recording their occurrence *pari passu* with the preparation of the second learning paradigm; these advances in technique were jointly used in the controlled trial described in Chapter 5. The output from the 10-channel electromagnetic recorder (MacCulloch and Atkinson, 1968) was modified to be electrically compatible with the 6 free channels of the portable EEG machine. We used the EEG to record cardiograph (i.e. pulse rate), and right forearm EMG electromyograph. We were therefore able to produce all the behavioural and physiological data on one record.

Shortly after the commencement of the controlled trial we were in a position to record pulse-rate changes using the newly developed apparatus. Previous measurements of heart rate under this conditioning situation had indicated the responses were very complex: theoretical considerations suggested that highly aroused patients should condition more readily than poorly aroused ones. Such a concept poses the problem of general cardiovascular autonomic control. We thought it possible that patients might differ in their arousal response to the beginning of the conditioning: and that they might differ in the rate of extinction of arousal over the 24 conditioning sessions.

In the absence of an integrating cardiotachograph, pulse rates were measured by the calipers previously described. An analysis of every pulse beat for every trial of sessions 1–24 was thought to be too large an undertaking and the data were sampled to answer the following specific questions:

(A) What were the relationships between (1) pre-CS-onset rates, and (2) rate modulation, conditioning and outcome?

(B) What were the cardiac rate responses in relation to pre-,intra- and post-conditioning trials: and if consistent trends emerged, were they related to outcome?

In order to answer question A it was decided to sample the periods of time before CS exposure in trials 1–5 and 19–24 of sessions 1 and 24. The inter-beat interval was measured and expressed as rates per minutes for the 3 beats before the onset of the CS. This procedure gave two measures of pulse rate immediately prior to the CS onset, which were then compared to provide a figure for pre-CS onset pulse rate variation. These data are set out in Table 6.4.

Results

A. I. Mean pulse rates compared within and between sessions

The mean pulse rates of the first 5 trials and the last 5 trials for sessions 1 and 24 were calculated for 16 subjects (5 classically and 11 avoidance conditioned patients). Table 6.4 presents the means of the pulse rates immediately prior to the first 5 and the last 5 trials in sessions 1 and 24 for each patient.

It will be noted that in some instances data are available for one session and not for the other; it was nevertheless still possible to include incomplete data in some computations.

TABLE 6.4. MEAN PRE-CS ONSET RATES

Treatment, i.e. AA or CC	Case number	Session 1		Session 24	
		Trials 1–5 Rate mean (beats/min)	Trials 19–24 Rate mean (beats/min)	Trials 1–5 Rate mean (beats/min)	Trials 19–24 Rate mean (beats/min)
AA	10	83.7	79.4	101.3	99.3
AA	13	101.4	100.9	101.8	97.5
AA	4	94.5	82.7	85.1	81.5
AA	26	not available		108.2	93.8
AA	28	96.2	94.6	83.5	82.6
AA	8	79.0	74.2	not available	
AA	7	75.4	67.8	72.0	72.9
AA	11	77.4	73.6	not available	
AA	16	109.6	106	99.1	96.6
AA	12	103.7	99.1	not available	
AA	15	not available		77.9	72.6
CC	1	76.7	72.8	76.2	71.8
CC	5	102.8	100	113.3	108.0
CC	23	97.4	88.4	111.6	97.8
CC	29	98.5	93.2	97.8	92.9
CC	6	105.6	105.2	not available	

Figure 6.20 shows the mean pulse rates for trials 1–5 and 19–24 for sessions 1 and 24, dichotomized by outcome into success and failure groups. Patients were judged to be successful if their male SOM scores fell 12 points between immediately pre- to immediately post-treatment. It will be seen from Fig. 6.20 that the success group had a higher pulse rate for the first 5 trials of session 1 than did the failure group; and that this initial rate did not fall markedly. The failure group's initial rate was lower than the corresponding value in the success group but not greatly so. Thereafter the values in the failure group steadily fell. A statistical analysis of the differences in pulse rate means between the success and failure groups, irrespective of treatment type, is given in Table 6.5.

The values show a between-groups trend from non-significance at the beginning of session 1 to $p = 0.05$ at the end of session 24; the overall difference being highly significant ($p = 0.001$). It is reasonable to deduce that the patients who conditioned most successfully had a somewhat higher initial level of arousal as indicated by pulse rate with little fall in rate by the end of treatment. The failure group was both initially less highly aroused, and in addition

TABLE 6.5. A COMPARISON OF MEAN PRE-CS ONSET PULSE RATES FOR SUCCESS AND FAILURE GROUPS

Session	Trial	Success $n = 6$	Failure $n = 3$	t	p
1	1–5	97.75	90.7	0.944	NS
1	19–24	91.67	87.767	1.260	0.25
24	1–5	101.367	85.767	2.863	0.05
24	19–24	96.017	84.333	2.670	0.05
Overall				6.489	0.001

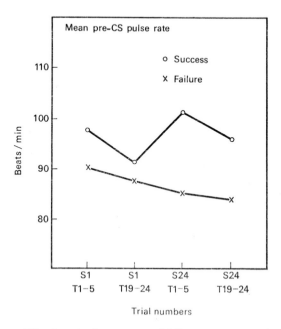

FIG. 6.20. Mean pre-CS pulse rates for success and failure groups on session 1, trials 1–5 and 19–24, and session 24, trials 1–5 and 19–24.

their pulse rates steadily fell during further treatment. An intra-group analysis of rate decrement of the 2 groups was made comparing session 1 (trials 1–5) scores with session 24 (trials 19–24) scores. Although the rates in the failure group progressively fell, the difference did not achieve significance. When the overall mean of rates of classically conditioned patients was compared with the overall mean of the anticipatory conditioned patients, *irrespective of outcome*, they did not differ.

A.II. Pre-trial pulse-rate variations

TABLE 6.6. PULSE-RATE DATA

Treatment, i.e. AA or CC	Case number	Mean pre-CS onset pulse-rate variability			
		Session 1		Session 24	
		Trials 1–5 Mean of (CS1)–(CS2) (beats/min)	Trials 19–24 Mean of (CS1)–(CS2) (beats/min)	Trials 1–5 Mean of (CS1)–(CS2) (beats/min)	Trials 19–24 Mean of (CS1)–(CS2) (beats/min)
AA	10	1.8	1.6	6.8	4.2
AA	13	0.8	0.6	0	1.2
AA	4	2.2	1.4	1.4	1.4
AA	26	not available		0	2.8
AA	28	2.4	0	1.2	1.0
AA	8	1.0	1.6	not available	
AA	7	2.8	2.4	2.8	4.6
AA	11	0	0.8		
AA	16	1.6	2.4	2.2	2.6
AA	12	2.5	4.2	not available	
AA	15	not available		1.8	2.5
CC	1	1.0	0.8	2.0	3.2
CC	5	0.4	1.6	1.0	0
CC	23	0	0.4	0	0.4
CC	29	0.2	1.8	0.4	1.4
CC	6	4.0	1.2	not available	

Table 6.6 shows for each patient the mean pulse-rate difference between the 2 beats immediately before the CS onset for the first 5 and last 5 trials of sessions 1 and 24. Figure 6.21 shows the values plotted for success outcome versus failure irrespective of treatment type. The mean values for session 1 (trials 19–24) differed significantly (see Fig. 6.21: $t = 2.652$; $p = 0.05$). The overall groups differ at the 10% level ($t = 2.151$; $p = 0.1$). There is therefore at least some difference in the pre-CS onset rate variability although no great weight can be placed on this for two reasons. Firstly, the numbers are small, and, secondly, data are not available for sessions 2 through 23. The variability of rate for 2 beats prior to the CS onset was next examined in relation to type of treatment, irrespective of outcome (Table 6.7 presents the statistical findings). It was found that the variability in AA patients exceeded that in CC patients at the start of treatment (session 1), but that there was no difference at the end of treatment (session 24).

We tentatively advance two postulates: (I) The autonomic control of pulse differed in the success and failure groups in that the former were more prone to sustained anxiety in an

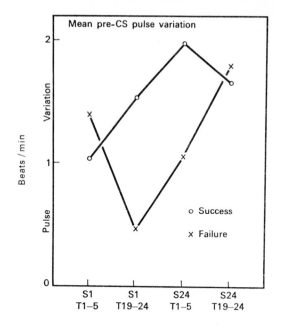

Fig. 6.21. Mean pulse-rate difference between the two beats prior to the CS1 onset for session 1, trials 1–5 and 19–24, and session 24, trials 1–5 and 19–24.

TABLE 6.7. PULSE-RATE VARIABILITY OVER 2 BEATS PRIOR TO CS ONSET

Session	Trial	Variability means			
		CC	AA	t	p
1	1–5	0.4	1.7	5.678	0.001
1	19–24	1.15	1.2	1.2998	0.25
24	1–5	0.85	2.3	1	NS
24	19–24	1.25	2.1	1	NS
Overall		0.9125	1.84	2.392	0.05

aversion situation; (II) AA conditioning reduced pulse-rate modulation more than did CC conditioning, probably because it induced and maintained a higher level of arousal. This latter suggestion is in keeping with theoretical expectations concerning the anxiety-producing properties of all the features of the AA paradigm.

B. Pulse-rate responses to conditional stimuli

Continuous pulse-rate recordings were taken throughout the first and last treatment sessions, i.e. 1 and 24. In session 1 the patient was allowed 5 minutes to settle after the pulse and EMG electrodes were attached to him, and a record of his pulse was taken before the shock electrodes were fastened on to his leg. We then presented him with a non-hierarchy male slide rated by him as equivalent to the first male slide in the treatment hierarchy, without attaching the electrodes through which the unconditional stimulus was to be administered. The CS1 time was 8 seconds. We were thus measuring the effect on cardiac rate of presenting the stimulus equivalent of the first homosexual stimulus in a situation in which the patient knew he could not receive a shock. These CS presentation trials have been called "pre S1 electrodes off".

Treatment then proceeded through to session 24. At the conclusion of the last trial (no. 24), the patient's electrodes were removed and a further period of 5 minutes was allowed to elapse. The patient was then re-presented with the non-hierarchy male slide whilst the pulse rate was continuously monitored.

From these data it was hoped to confirm the hypothesis that successfully conditioned patients displayed a conditioned cardiac response both to the in-treatment CS trials and to the post-session 24 trial after the removal of the electrodes.

It might have proved possible to pick out trials during the sessions in which the patients did display a cardiac rate change corresponding to those changes seen in series patients nos. 2 and 11. But it was felt that this procedure might not be representative of the true state of affairs and also would almost certainly be contaminated by the autonomic concomitants of requesting and watching relief slides, much of which occurred immediately before the onset of the conditional stimulus of the following trial.

It was therefore decided to sample the pulse rates for 13 beats before the onset of the CS1 during the CS exposure, and for 13 beats after the CS offset in the following trials: Pre-session 1 (electrodes off); session 1, trials 1 and 24; session 24, trials 1 and 24, and post-session 24 (electrodes off).

Table 6.8 shows the amount of data available, dichotomized for treatment type. The CS exposure time was too short during classical conditioning to provide data.

The data were recorded on specially prepared sheets. Graphs of pulse rates in relation to CS exposure are presented at the end of each trial case summary where the data were available.

On inspection several features of the individual graphs are noticeable. One of the most striking is that in some patients there is a cardiac acceleration occurring just before or after the onset of the conditional stimulus, before the patient has undergone shock trials. This is seen in trial patients nos. 23, 26, 15, 4, 7, 16, 28, 13, and 11, who also show a cardiac acceleration and/or deceleration on trial 24 and post-trial 24, of session 24. Trial patient no. 12

TABLE 6.8. DATA AVAILABLE ON PULSE CHANGES IN RELATION TO CS
PRESENTATION

Trial type		Treatment type		
		CC	AA	Total
Pre-session 1	Electrodes off	4	9	13
Session 1	T1	0	10	10
	T24	0	2	2
Session 24	T1	0	7	7
	T24	0	3	3
Post-session 24	Electrodes off	3	6	9

showed a pre-treatment acceleration which was not seen on the post-treatment trial. In addition, a further 2 trial patients, nos. 1 and 5, show an acquired cardiac acceleration on trial 24 or, on the post-treatment trial, of session 24. It is possible to explain the first finding by considering the pre-treatment programming of the patient. The patients had had a shock threshold experiment performed on them prior to the onset of the first session. Therefore, in the context of the total situation the first CS, even though the electrodes were not connected, might be expected to generate anxiety, and hence a cardiac acceleration.

A fourth finding is that a number of patients showed minimal pulse variation and lability either during the period of exposure to the conditional stimulus or immediately after it, e.g. trial patients nos. 13, 10, 4, 12, even though in some cases their initial pulse rates were high. Conversely, some of the patients showed great lability of the pulse before and after the conditional stimulus without, however, showing any marked conditioned cardiac acceleration or deceleration after 24 sessions of treatment. It must be inferred that the patients differ markedly in their autonomic cardiac control in this situation. In some, cardiac rate is poorly damped, in others overdamped. This conclusion is further strengthened by the appearance of marked swings in pulse rate following the offset of the conditional stimulus in a number of patients who show a clear cardiac acceleration and/or deceleration during the time of exposure to the conditional stimulus. A statistical analysis of the data quantitatively described above was clearly necessary.

The amounts of acceleration, deceleration and pulse variability *during CS exposure* were measured using the following definitions:

Acceleration: the highest rate attained, minus the rate at CS onset.
Deceleration: the rate at CS onset, minus the lowest rate attained.
Variation: the total sum of the rate changes sequentially calculated, starting from the CS onset to the CS offset.

The mean acceleration, deceleration, and variation figures for the following stimulus situations were calculated for patients for whom data were available. Pre-treatment CS1 exposure, session 1, trials 1 and 24, session 24, trials 1 and 24 and post-treatment CS exposure. The results were dichotomized into success and failure. (The former was a drop of 12 points on the SOM homosexual measure between pre- and post-treatment scores.)

The results of the findings in relation to acceleration and deceleration are shown in Figs. 6.22 and 6.23.

The hypothesis that the success and failure groups differed in autonomic vascular control parameters was supported by the findings that the groups were distinguished by the amount of cardiac acceleration which occurred in response to CS1 exposure.

Overall, the success group showed a tendency to greater degrees of acceleration, an exception being session 1 (session 1, trial 24). The groups did not differ in degree of deceleration.

The degree of variability in pulse rate during CS exposure was measured, and Fig. 6.24 shows that the successful group of patients displayed an increasing variability of pulse rate as treatment proceeded, whereas the failure group initially tend to decrease their degree of pulse variability.

At the post-treatment test the variability in the failure group is slightly lower than that at the pre-treatment test.

When the means for pulse variability of each sample were statistically compared, the success and failure groups differed only in the overall comparison, the separate measures failing to reach acceptable levels of significance although the direction of the differences was

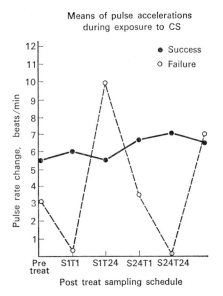

FIG. 6.22. Means of pulse accelerations during exposure to CS1 in session 1, trials 1 and 24, and session 24, trials 1 and 24.

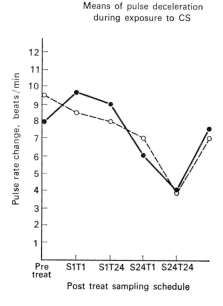

FIG. 6.23. Means of pulse deceleration during exposure to CS1 in session 1, trials 1 and 24, and session 24, trials 1 and 24.

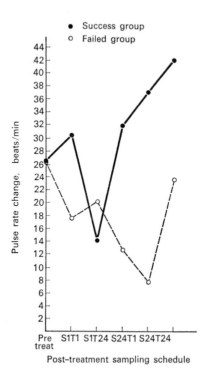

Means of pulse rate changes
during exposure to CS

• Success group
○ Failed group

FIG. 6.24. Means of pulse rate changes during exposure to CS1 in session 1, trials 1 and 24, and session 24, trials 1 and 24.

the same throughout (except in session 1, trial 24). Table 6.9 presents the differences between success and failure groups over the period of treatment for pulse rate variability during CS exposure.

These findings clearly indicate a trend; a process (aversive conditioning) is occurring which increasingly differentiates the two potential success and failure groups. The pre-treatment variability was strikingly similar in the 2 groups, but by session 24, trial 24, the difference had achieved the 10% level of significance.

The amount of available pulse data for the pre- and post-treatment responses (i.e. electrodes not worn in both cases) was insufficient for separate statistical comparison.

TABLE 6.9. PULSE-RATE VARIABILITY DURING CS EXPOSURE SUCCESS VERSUS FAILURE

Session	Trial	Means			
		Success	Failure	t	p
1	1	30.4	17.5	0.080	NS
24	1	31.8	12.5	1.182	0.25
24	24	37.0	7.5	6.881	0.1
Overall (includes S1 T24, pre- and post-)		30.8	17.8	2.907	0.02

DISCUSSION

The findings on pulse-rate change in relation to treatment are complex, and the lack of more extensive and more complete data is a handicap in drawing firm conclusions. However, several points clearly emerge: successfully conditioned patients (as defined by SOM change pre- to post-treatment) differed significantly from failed patients, when the pre-CS rates were sampled twice in each of sessions 1 and 24 ($p = 0.001$). The success (S) group started session 1 with a higher pre-CS onset pulse rate than did the failure (F) group, the rate dropped during session 1 but was higher at the start of session 24. In contrast the failure group show a steady decline in rate both within and between sessions. Although the groups were heterogeneous for treatment type, i.e. CC and AA, both treatments involved a method of producing anxiety; it may tentatively be concluded that the patients in the 2 groups, S and F, differed in their arousability to aversive conditioning. This in turn affected the ease of acquisition of conditioned emotional responses, and hence of a conditioned avoidance response to homosexual slides. That the distinction is between the patients, irrespective of method of treatment, is supported by the finding that the mean intra session *pulse rates* did not differ when the CC group was compared to the AA group, irrespective of outcome. When the data on mean pre-CS onset pulse rates in AA patients are re-analysed in terms of primary and secondary homosexual type (see Chapter 5) versus outcome, a rather striking trend is revealed. Figure 6.25 shows the mean rates for the first and last 5 trials of sessions 1 and 24, dichotomized into success and failure groups.

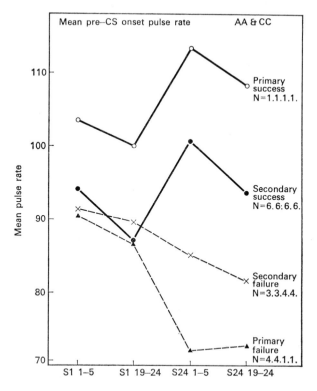

FIG. 6.25. Mean pre-CS1 onset pulse rate for primary and secondary homosexuals, treated by AA, and dichotomized by outcome. Data are shown for session 1, trials 1–5 and 19–24, and for session 24, trials 1–5 and 19–24.

Each outcome group is further divided into primary and secondary homosexuals.

The mean rates in session 1 for the secondary homosexuals and the primary homosexual failures are all similar and show a decrease in pulse rate from early (trials 1–5) to late (trials 19–24) trials. In session 24 the 4 groups behave in strikingly dissimilar ways: the successful groups, that is both primary and secondary homosexuals, steeply increased their mean pulse rates during the early trials of session 24 by comparable amounts, and then both values fall by the later trials of that session.

By contrast the failure groups' rates fall, in the case of the secondary homosexuals, at a steady rate. Although the fall in the primary homosexual is very marked, it only represents one case.

The numbers in these groups do not permit statistical analysis in relation to homosexual type; nevertheless, the graph serves to indicate three things: firstly, the positive relationship between pulse rate and score change is upheld, and, secondly, secondary failures show a trend towards having the lower pulse rates. Thirdly, it is very interesting to see that the only successful primary homosexual displayed a very high pulse rate in excess of the upper value of the range for successful secondary homosexuals.

However, a difference in the effect of AA as compared to CC is clearly reflected in the pre-CS onset *variability* figures. These show that AA conditioning results in a greater pulse-rate demodulation than CC in the two beats immediately prior to the CS onset. This effect was maximal at the beginning of session 1; by way of contrast, the difference in variability when the patients were dichotomized according to outcome is most marked at the end of session 1 and the beginning of session 24. In summary it would seem that there are two factors operating:

(1) Comparing treatment types: AA reduces pulse-rate modulation, the effect being maximal at the start of treatment.

(2) Comparing treatment outcome: in the success group the demodulation occurs maximally between session 1, trial 24, and session 24, trial 1, and precedes that in the failure group, although in the absence of data on sessions 2–23, it is not possible to be sure of this phenomenon.

It is probable that demodulation is related both to innate autonomic parameters of cardiac output control which are themselves subservient to a higher influence and to the ambient anxiety level at the time under consideration; the latter is in itself dependent on the aversive technique used. Demodulation occurs earlier in treatment in AA than in CC, and early demodulation is a favourable prognostic sign for treatment success. There is a suggestion, therefore, in this aspect of the pulse data, that AA might be a more effective treatment technique than CC. In this present study the cardiac accelerative and decelerative responses to impending shock occurred to a marked extent although less so than to the actual receipt of shock. Nevertheless, these two opposing heart-rate responses during experimentally induced anxiety are clearly not specific to the occurrence of shock. The Jenks and Deane study and that of Lacey and Smith (1954) are relevant to the cardiac acceleratory and deceleratory responses which we have now more reliably recorded. It appears that the sounds produced by the slide projecting apparatus and other aspects of the stimulus situation have (by generalization) acquired the signal properties of anxiety-evoking stimuli. It is this phenomenon that has tended to confuse our results. Autonomic responses occurring to signal stimuli other than the CS itself, reduced the degree of change due to CS onset and clearly indicate the desirability of sound-proofed and separate accommodation for patients, apparatus, and operators. Lacey *et al.* (1953) found that autonomic specificity for tension is more marked than for lability, and this suggests that a study of the type which we have undertaken would expect to derive its most clear-cut results from measures of autonomic tension. Our highly significant finding that the mean pre-CS onset pulse rates most clearly differentiate success and failure patients is in agreement with this prediction. A further reason for the unsatisfactory nature of our data was the lack of appropriate apparatus for data collection and analysis. The most satisfactory technique of recording and data manipulation would be that of computed average transients (CAT). The various effects of pre-programming and type of stimulus on the pulse responses in different individuals could be readily partialled out. We feel that individual differences in autonomic nervous systems, and hence responses to learning situations, have been partly responsible for differences in response to treatment. It may be that autonomic responsiveness outside the treatment situation is particularly important once the conditioned autonomic response has been acquired, a possibility discussed in detail in Chapter 8. Be that as it may, studies of the autonomic concomitants of the classical and AA learning situations should assist the development of more powerful learning paradigms, possibly including the use of drugs. Such learning models will be expected to increase the *rate* of successful response to treatment in patients who now respond relatively slowly, despite being highly motivated, free from personality disorders, and who have a pre-treatment history of heterosexual interest and practice.

GENERAL DISCUSSION

The changes which we have reported in the electromyograph data, total body movement and pulse-rate data during aversive conditioning might reasonably be subsumed under the heading of the investigatory reflex or orientation reaction (Pavlov, 1927). "It is this reflex which brings about the immediate response in man and animals to the slightest change to the world around them, so that they immediately orientate their appropriate receptor organs in accordance with the perceptible quality in the agent bringing about the change and making a full investigation of it." The orientation reaction is made up of a number of components which have been analysed by, amongst others, Robinson and Grant (1947), and Dykman *et al.* (1959). Berlyne (1960) has summarized the main changes, which include:

(1) changes in skeletal muscles which direct sense organs;
(2) changes in general skeletal musculature:
    (a) *ongoing actions are temporarily arrested* (see freezing response in ballistic bed and respiration data);
    (b) general muscle tonus rises as indicated by an increase in electrical activity of muscle (EMG);
(3) vegetative changes:
    (a) sweat gland activity in the palms of hands increases (see GSR responses in the normal volunteers, Appendix B);
    (b) tachycardia and bradycardia.

"The orientation reaction is a complex response comprising many orientating responses, all serving to increase the animal's preparedness for any ensuing environmental change" (Lader and Wing, 1966).

Clearly, our results show that those patients whose vegetative nervous systems and striated muscular systems markedly responded to the alerting conditional stimuli were showing in this situation a set of more adaptive responses than are their less responsive fellows; it would appear that the differences in responses to aversive learning and the generalization to real life situation between these 2 groups appear to stem from these differing capacities for performing the orientation reactions.

Those patients who have readily reorientated their sexual interest may be assumed to have done so in part for the same reason that they readily acquired homosexual responses in the first place. It would seem highly likely that the capacity for the orientation reaction and for avoidance learning is inherited, although different components of the orientating reflex will hold differing levels of significance between individuals. A number of genetic studies on autonomic measures are available which tend to support this view.

Carmena (1934) found a great similarity of PGR response in 26 of 36 MZ twin pairs, but in only one of 16 DZ pairs. Moderate response similarity was seen in 5 MZ and 3 DZ pairs. In 1944, Jost and Sontag investigated pulse rate, GSR, respiration, and blood pressure on 16 MZ twins, 54 non-twin sibling pairs, and 1009 pairs of unrelated children. The MZ pairs were most similar, the unrelated pairs were least similar, and the sibling pairs showed intermediate similarities.

Eysenck (1956) measured pre- and post-exercise pulse rates as part of a larger study on 26 MZ and 26 DZ twin pairs. These pulse variables were the most strongly influenced by genetic factors, MZ pairs being more alike than DZ pairs.

Similarly, in another twin study, Vandenberg et al. (1965) confirmed that respiration and pulse-rate changes in response to a set of 5 stimuli were significantly affected by genetic factors. It would seem to us, therefore, that further replicatory studies of the type that we have described, with the genetic component held constant, i.e. twin studies, would be of the utmost value in the further elucidation of the role played by physiological variations in the acquisition of learned behavioural patterns.

CHAPTER 7

THE ASSESSMENT OF PERSONALITY AND ITS INFLUENCE ON THE OUTCOME OF TREATMENT

J. F. ORFORD

THE treatment of any psychiatric or psychological disorder is likely to be improved by an attempt at assessing the personalities of those patients undergoing treatment. This improvement may occur in one or more of at least three ways. Firstly, a knowledge of the personalities of patients who present with this disorder may enable us to provide a more adequate description of the disorder itself than had previously been possible, and this in turn should lead to greater insight into the nature, and possibly the aetiology, of the disorder. Secondly, by relating personality to the outcome of treatment, a more precise prognosis can be made. Treatment facilities may be more economically used by confining them to patients of good prognosis; at the same time, active experimentation may be pursued with new forms of treatment for the remaining patients who are known to respond badly to existing treatment methods. Thirdly, a knowledge of the prognostic significance of different personality types may give some clue as to the actual processes involved in the treatment given and hence may offer good grounds for improvements in treatment methods.

Despite these obvious possible benefits of personality assessment in the treatment setting, little attempt has been made previously to assess systematically the personalities of those undergoing treatment for homosexuality. In particular, this author is unaware of any previous attempt to relate personality, as assessed by a standard questionnaire or objective test, to the outcome of such treatment, although assessments of this sort have been made of groups of homosexuals not under treatment (e.g. Grygier, 1957; Cattell and Morony, 1962; Kenyon, 1968; Oliver and Mosher, 1968) and relatively unsystematic clinical assessments of the personalities of homosexuals under treatment have also been made (e.g. Curran and Parr, 1957; Scott, 1964; Patterson Brown, 1964). Of the several authors who have reported treatment of homosexuality by various forms of aversion therapy (see Chapter 1), none has discussed the relationship of personality to the outcome of treatment. The only previous report of this nature is that of MacCulloch and Feldman (1967), in which they demonstrated the predictive validity of personality variables, assessed by clinical interview, for the first 32 homosexual patients treated by the AA method. Their results will be referred to again later in this chapter.

TWO METHODS FOR ASSESSING PERSONALITY

The personalities of all patients whose treatment has been described in earlier chapters of this book were assessed in two very different ways which are representative of the two main methods of personality evaluation in current use in psychiatry and clinical psychology. The first, which might be called the clinical method, makes use of a clinical psychiatric interview on the basis of which the interviewer classifies the patient's personality according to some recognized nomenclature. Within the limits of the interviewer's training and the specification of different personality categories provided by the particular nomenclature used, the interviewer is free to conduct the course of the interview in whatever way he chooses in order to arrive at an assessment of the patient's personality. The second, which might be called the questionnaire method, simply requires that the patient give a forced-choice answer to a large number of questions presented to him in a standard form. There should be no subjective element in the scoring. The latter method should have all the advantages of freedom from interviewer or rater-bias, high reliability, and the provision of norms, against which to compare the results of any particular patient or group of patients. The former method allows flexibility to the interviewer and hence the possibility of overcoming the various response sets which tend to interfere with questionnaire assessment such as the social desirability response set. In addition, the former method often tends to be more clinically relevant in practice. At the present time, the two methods probably complement one another, both being necessary for adequate personality description.

A DESCRIPTIVE STUDY

THE CLINICAL METHOD

The system of classification used to make clinical assessments of patients whose treatment is reported upon in this book is that described by Schneider (1959). Schneider describes 10 features of personality, each of which he considers are possessed to some degree by all individuals. In respect of each feature, the individual is classified as normal, abnormal (i.e. possessing this feature to an abnormally high degree), or disordered. Schneider's formal definition of personality abnormality is: "A variation upon an accepted yet broadly conceived range of average personality." Of personality disorder, or as he prefers to call it "psychopathic personality", Schneider says: "The group contains abnormal personalities who either suffer personally because of their own abnormalities, or make the community suffer because of it." The normal, the abnormal, and the disordered are thus to be thought of as ranged along a continuum, the differences between the three being quantitative. The exact division between abnormality and disorder is somewhat arbitrary, but important conceptually; whereas the patient with personality abnormality can adjust both to himself and to society, the patient with the disordered personality is constantly running into difficulties from his personal symptoms or legal censure from his social environment.

The 66 homosexual patients who received treatment (36 in the series and 30 in the trial) were classified according to Schneider's (1959) system of personality. The result is shown in Table 7.1. The classification was normally made by one of the authors (M.J.M.), a psychiatrist, when the patient was interviewed prior to the commencement of treatment, although in a few cases the final assessment of personality was made when fresh information became available at a subsequent interview.

As abnormalities and disorders of the self-insecure type are more common in this sample than those of all other types combined, the classifications made are tabulated somewhat differently in Table 7.2. Here the number of patients is shown with abnormalities and dis-

TABLE 7.1. THE CLINICAL ASSESSMENTS OF THE PERSONALITIES OF 66 HOMOSEXUAL PATIENTS

	Series (n = 36)			Trial (n = 30)		
	No abnormality	Abnormality not amounting to disorder	Disorder	No abnormality	Abnormality not amounting to disorder	Disorder
Self-insecure	2	19	15	2	13	15
Attention-seeking	27	4	5	23	6	1
Labile	31	4	1	22	7	1
Weak-willed	30	5	1	26	4	0
Asthenic	35	0	1	30	0	0
Explosive	36	0	0	28	2	0
Cold affectionless	35	1	0	30	0	0
Depressive	35	1	0	25	5	0
Hyperthymic	35	1	0	30	0	0
Fanatic	36	0	0	26	4	0

orders of the self-insecure type, with and without abnormalities or disorders of any other type. This method of tabulation anticipates a discussion, later on in this chapter, of the different prognostic significance of self-insecure and "other" abnormalities or disorders reported by MacCulloch and Feldman (1967) for 32 of the patients in the preliminary series, and partially confirmed for the 30 trial patients.

The difference which is apparent between the personalities, as clinically assessed, of patients in the trial and those in the preliminary series, is due to the variation in selection procedure mentioned in Chapter 3. For the trial an attempt was made (as a result of experience with the preliminary series of patients) to confine treatment to patients free from a personality disorder or abnormality other than one of a self-insecure variety. As the figures in Tables 7.1 and 7.2 show, this attempt was largely successful, but failed in a few instances due to the final assessment being known only after a patient had been accepted for treatment.

The personality abnormality—whether amounting to a disorder or not—most commonly found in this sample, is, therefore, that of the self-insecure type. This was so even before selection for the trial on the grounds of personality was attempted. Unfortunately, no

TABLE 7.2. CLINICAL PERSONALITY CLASSIFICATIONS OF 66 HOMOSEXUAL PATIENTS IN TERMS OF SELF-INSECURE AND "OTHER" ABNORMALITIES AND DISORDERS

	Series	Trial
Self-insecure abnormality only	7	6
Self-insecure disorder only	7	5
Self-insecure abnormality plus "other" abnormality	7	7
Self-insecure abnormality plus "other" disorder	5	0
Self-insecure disorder plus "other" abnormality	5	10
Self-insecure disorder plus "other" disorder	3	1
"Other" disorder without self-insecure abnormality or disorder	1	1
Schizophrenic defect state	1	0
Normal	0	0
Total	36	30

information on the incidence of this or other abnormalities in the general or psychiatric populations exists in a form which would make possible a comparison with the results for this sample. Nonetheless, the figures strongly suggest that persons with a homosexual condition who approach psychiatric services for help are very likely to possess a self-insecure personality to an unusually high degree. As described by Schneider, the self-insecure personality consists of two overlapping sub-types—the sensitives and the anankasts. Sensitives are described as: "those who show a conscious retention of affect-laden complexes together with much intra-psychic activity and a small capacity for discharge." Increased impressionability, reduced power for active expression, pent-up working over of experience, chronic self-uncertainty, and self-blame are frequent attributes. Schneider himself points out that in this group conflicts over sexuality are frequent. The ethical development of the sensitive stands in sharp contrast to the frequently abnormal quality and quantity of sexual drive. "Extravagant sexual phantasies, frequently of perverse character, lodge in their minds like foreign bodies." Anankasts, or obsessive or compulsive personalities, are outwardly pedantic, correct, scrupulous, and yet inwardly exceedingly insecure. They are prone to compulsive ideas, thoughts, and rituals. The self-insecure group as a whole is characterized by high standards with inner feelings of anxiety, guilt, inadequacy, and inferiority.

THE QUESTIONNAIRE METHOD: (i) THE EPI (EYSENCK PERSONALITY INVENTORY)

The same patients completed forms A and B of the EPI before the commencement of their treatment. Both the EPI and its progenitor, the Maudsley personality inventory (MPI), are designed to measure what their authors (Eysenck, 1959; Eysenck and Eysenck, 1964) consider to be the two major dimensions of personality—namely extraversion–introversion (E) and neuroticism–stability (N)—the inventories, especially the EPI, having been designed so that scores on these 2 scales should be independent of one another. In addition, a smaller number of items in the EPI constitutes a "lie scale" (L), partly designed to detect individuals attempting to "fake good". The authors of the EPI recommend that the E and N scores of individuals who obtain L scores of 10 or more should be "regarded with considerable scepticism". Only 1 out of 67 patients in this sample obtained such a score.

There is, indeed, a considerable amount of evidence, both from the work of the authors of the EPI and from the work of others (Eysenck, 1960; Cattell and Scheier, 1961) to support the claim that E and N are two of the most important dimensions of personality, capable between them of accounting for more of the variation in individual personality than any other combination of two factors. Furthermore, the measurement of E and N is particularly relevant in the context of treatment based on conditioning techniques. Both high introversion (Franks, 1956) and high neuroticism (Spence, 1964) have been suggested as leading to better conditioning under certain circumstances, although evidence for and against both propositions has from time to time been presented (Eysenck, 1965a).

In Table 7.3 are shown the means and standard deviations of scores on the 3 scales obtained from the 30 homosexual patients in the trial and from 37 of those in the series, in both cases prior to treatment. The results from these 2 samples are shown separately in the first 2 columns of the table. As t tests revealed that the 2 samples were not significantly different on any of the 3 scales, they were combined, as shown in the third column of the same table. In the fourth and fifth columns are the results for E and N from a normal standardization sample of 2000 men and women and a sample of 108 psychiatric patients with a diagnosis

TABLE 7.3. A COMPARISON OF THE EPI SCORES OF HOMOSEXUALS, NORMALS, AND ANXIETY NEUROTICS

		Homosexuals			Normals	Anxiety neurotics
		Series	Trial	Total		
N	Mean	28.54	29.60	29.31	19.59***	32.29*
	SD	10.15	9.09	8.78	9.03	9.97
E	Mean	23.51	23.43	23.48	26.22**	20.70*
	SD	7.70	8.52	8.00	7.77	7.70
L	Mean	4.50	4.00	4.27		
	SD	2.28	2.45	2.43		
Age	Mean		24.12		27.45	35.05
	SD		5.57		12.00	10.92
Total no.		37	30	67	2000	108
No. of males			28		1097	59

Asterisks indicate mean scores which are significantly different from those of the total homosexual group (column 3). $*p < 0.05$, $**p < 0.01$, $***p < 0.001$.

of anxiety neurosis (Eysenck and Eysenck, 1964). It is apparent that the total homosexual group differs from the normal group in the same direction, but to a lesser degree, as does the group of anxiety neurotics, by being more neurotic and less extraverted than the normals. On both E and N, the homosexual sample lies between the normal and the anxiety neurotic samples; calculations of the standard errors of the differences between the mean scores revealed that these differences are statistically significant in all cases.

THE QUESTIONNAIRE METHOD: (ii) THE 16PF (SIXTEEN PERSONALITY FACTOR QUESTIONNAIRE)

The 30 patients who took part in the controlled trial were, in addition, given form A of the 16PF (Cattell and Stice, 1957) to supplement the information already provided by the EPI. Although this involved only a slightly larger number of questionnaire items than are involved in the two forms of the EPI (187 as opposed to 114 in the EPI), 16 scores can be derived from the 16PF, as against only 3 from the EPI. This is largely the result of different methods of rotation of factors being used during the factor analyses involved in the development of the 2 tests (Adcock, 1965).

The 16 scores are not necessarily meant to be independent of one another, significant correlations usually being found between certain of the scores and certain others. The number of factors can, therefore, be reduced by a second-order factor analysis, and when this is done, 2 of the 4 major second-order factors which usually result (anxiety and invia) bear much similarity to the E and N factors of the EPI, although the agreement may not always be perfect (Hundleby and Connor, 1968). The 16PF was given in this instance in the hope that it might provide a more precise description of personality and hence offer greater opportunities for successful prediction of treatment outcome.

Technical labels and brief descriptions of the 16 personality factors are given in Fig. 7.1, along with a graphic presentation of the means and standard deviations of the 16 score distributions obtained from the sample of 30 homosexuals. The scores shown in the figure are "sten" scores, that is, raw scores converted in such a way that the distribution of converted

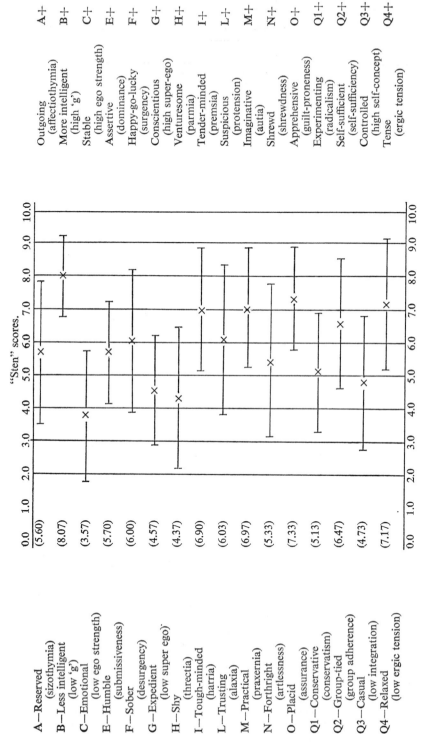

FIG. 7.1. The 16PF scores of 30 homosexual (trial) patients. Crosses indicate mean scores. Horizontal bars extend for a distance equivalent to one standard deviation on either side of the mean.

scores obtained from a sample of the normal American population, on which the test was standardized, has, for each of the 16 scales, a mean of 5.5 and a standard deviation of 2.0.

Table 7.4 shows the means scores obtained from 8 other samples, with which it is instructive to compare the homosexual sample. Columns 1 and 2 deal with 2 samples of Australian homosexuals (Cattell and Morony, 1962), the first being 100 male prisoners convicted of one or more homosexual acts, the second 33 uncharged male homosexuals obtained "through social worker contacts and discrete infiltration of the communication channels of homosexuals". It is not clear from Cattell and Morony's report how many of this latter group were, or had at any time been, under treatment for their homosexuality. To this author's knowledge these are the only previously published results of applying the 16PF to groups of homosexuals. The results given in columns 3–7 were all presented by McAllister (1968), the normal group largely consisting of medical, nursing, and other professional staff and students, and members of the 4 abnormal groups all having been under psychiatric treatment in the north-east region of Scotland at some time between 1963 and 1966. By "personality disorder" is meant a diagnosis of psychopathy or pathological personality; by "neurosis" a diagnosis of anxiety neurosis, hysteria, neurotic depressive states, or obsessional neurosis; by "integrated psychosis" manic-depressive illness, paranoia or paranoid states; and by "nonintegrated psychosis", schizophrenia. In the last column are the scores of 38 alcoholics who had been referred to an alcoholism clinic, again in Scotland (Walton, 1968).

The method used here to compare each of these profiles with the profile obtained from the sample of 30 homosexuals was simply that of ranking for each sample separately the 16 mean scores from highest to lowest and comparing each of the rank orders so obtained with that obtained in the same way from the homosexual sample by means of the Spearman rank order correlation coefficient (ρ). This statistic is, in some ways, less accurate for comparing profiles than the profile similarity coefficient favoured by some (e.g. Cattell and Morony, 1962; McAllister, 1968) as it takes no account of differences in overall level or scatter of means scores. But in view of the fact that the samples reviewed here are not matched with the homosexual sample with which they are being compared, even on such basic variables as age and sex, an approximate comparison was felt to be sufficient. For this purpose ρ seems ideally suited.

In the course of calculating the values of ρ it became apparent that in several cases differences between samples in mean scores on scale B (intelligence) contributed disproportionately to the final result. This was particularly so by virtue of the fact that the 30 homosexual trial patients were highly intelligent as a group (as assessed by this scale). For this reason, the rank order correlation coefficients were recalculated, eliminating from consideration mean scores on that one scale. This course of action could be criticized on the grounds that to eliminate one scale arbitrarily is to prejudice the results unfairly. Alternatively, it could be argued that the Cattell system of personality assessment is unusual in considering intelligence a proper subject for a personality questionnaire and that it would, therefore, be unfortunate if differences between samples in terms of intelligence were allowed to interfere with a proper comparison in terms of personality. As opinions differ on this point, both the coefficients based on all 16 scales and those based on 15 (with B eliminated) are given at the bottom of Table 7.4.

From Table 7.4 it can be seen that the homosexual profile is positively correlated with the profiles of all other abnormal samples apart from that of the "personality disorders", with which it has a correlation of approximately zero. With the normal sample it has a negative correlation, which becomes significant only when mean scores on the B scale are eliminated.

TABLE 7.4. A COMPARISON OF THE MEAN 16PF SCORES OF HOMOSEXUALS, NORMAL CONTROLS, AND VARIOUS ABNORMAL GROUPS

	1 Convicted Australian homosexuals	2 Unconvicted Australian homosexuals	3 Normals	4 Pers. disorders	5 Neurotics	6 Integrated psychotics	7 Non-integrated psychotics	8 Alcoholics
Total no.	100	33	100	100	100	70	30	38
Males	100	33	46	63	41	27	16	NR
Mean age	30	NR	36.7	29.6	42.3	49.2	32.6	NR
A	6.2	7.6	5.2	6.3	5.4	5.2	4.1	5.5
B	3.6	5.9	6.7	5.7	5.3	4.1	3.9	5.4
C	2.7	2.2	6.3	5.2	4.4	4.3	4.1	4.3
E	4.8	5.5	5.4	6.7	4.7	5.2	4.7	6.8
F	4.7	5.2	6.1	7.2	4.6	4.2	4.2	4.4
G	3.5	3.8	6.5	4.1	4.2	5.4	4.8	4.7
H	4.2	8.5	6.2	6.3	6.1	5.9	5.6	4.5
I	7.4	8.3	4.9	4.1	5.7	6.8	6.1	5.4
L	7.3	7.4	4.7	5.9	5.1	6.4	6.3	5.8
M	7.5	8.2	5.2	5.3	6.2	6.7	7.1	6.6
N	5.3	5.3	6.3	7.4	4.8	6.2	4.4	7.0
O	8.1	7.2	5.1	5.3	7.3	7.5	7.2	6.4
Q1	5.8	6.9	4.8	5.2	4.9	5.6	4.7	6.6
Q2	6.5	6.9	5.7	5.9	4.3	6.1	6.4	6.2
Q3	4.8	4.9	6.1	4.5	4.2	5.3	5.8	3.9
Q4	7.6	6.7	5.1	6.2	6.9	6.3	7.3	7.6
Correlation (ρ) with British homosexual (trial) profile	+0.65*	+0.34	−0.24	+0.06	+0.57*	+0.38	+0.40	+0.44
Same—eliminating B	+0.88**	+0.43	−0.66*	+0.08	+0.60*	+0.67*	+0.70*	+0.54

*$p < 0.05$. **$p < 0.01$. NR = not reported.

Before the elimination of the B scale, the highest correlation, apart from that with the convicted Australian homosexuals, is with the Scottish group of psychiatric patients, each of whom had been diagnosed as suffering from a form of neurosis. However, with the elimination of the B scale, the correlations with the two psychotic groups become significant in addition and, in fact, now exceed in size the correlation with the neurotic group.

THE RELATIONSHIPS BETWEEN THE PERSONALITY MEASURES

The first set of relationships is shown in Table 7.5. It can be seen that the correlations, both within and between the EPI and the 16PF, are in line with expectations. In addition, the significant correlations of the EPI lie (L) scale with 16PF O − (placid) and Q3 + (controlled) demonstrate that it has a potential validity in addition to its intended usefulness for screening out unreliable respondents.

Perhaps the most intriguing part of Table 7.5 lies in the 2 columns at the far right, which illustrate the relationships between the clinical assessment and the questionnaire assessments. For the purposes of calculating these correlations, the ratings of clinical personality were scaled in the following way:

On the basis of the personality assessment provided by the psychiatrist (M.J.M.) all patients were assigned a value on each of 2 scales; a self-insecure disorder scale (S) and an "Other disorder" scale (O), on the grounds that types other than self-insecure were relatively infrequent, so that any attempt to scale each type separately would result in a markedly non-normal distribution of scale values. In addition, the different prognostic significance of self-insecure and other types had already been demonstrated for the preliminary series of patients (MacCulloch and Feldman, 1967b). The values assigned on both scales were: 5, severe or marked disorder; 4, disorder; 3, marked abnormality; 2, abnormality; 1, mild abnormality; 0, normal. In the case of the O-scale, the most severe category mentioned with respect to *any* feature of personality other than the self-insecure determined the value assigned.

It is important in interpreting the pattern of intercorrelations shown in Table 7.5 to bear in mind that each clinical scale is being compared with 19 questionnaire scales and that one correlation, significant at a probability of 0.05, is therefore to be expected by chance alone. The actual figures do not depart greatly from this chance expectation, and there is, therefore, no reason to assume that the correlations, significant in this sample, would be replicated for any further sample. This disappointing result might be due to the unreliability of the clinical ratings or to the failure of the questionnaire techniques to determine those personality characteristics of most clinical relevance. However, it seems most likely to be due to the factorial complexity of the concept of the self-insecure personality in the one case and to lack of sufficient variance in the O-scale scores in the other.

Nonetheless, it is interesting to note that the significant correlations found in this sample suggest that those of self-insecure personality are shy and do not lie, whilst those with other types of abnormality or disorder are more intelligent than others. It is difficult to offer a ready explanation of the latter finding, which may be no more than a chance peculiarity of the present sample. However, it is plausible that those of self-insecure personality should tend to an abnormal degree of shyness and that they should have a propensity for exaggerating their faults rather than for distorting the truth about them.

TABLE 7.5. CORRELATIONS BETWEEN THE VARIOUS PERSONALITY MEASURES USED FOR THE 30 HOMOSEXUAL TRIAL PATIENTS

| | EPI | | | 16PF | | | | | | | | | | | | | | | | Clinical | |
	E	N	L	A	B	C	E	F	G	H	I	L	M	N	O	Q1	Q2	Q3	Q4	S	O
E		−34	−08	2	−19	32	05	61*	01	42*	−16	20	−02	08	−06	−21	−39*	−09	−18	−31	06
N			−18	06	10	−48*	16	−05	−09	−11	22	27	07	−03	58*	31	38*	−46*	55*	24	11
L				21	31	12	19	00	02	23	07	−16	−01	−11	−50*	17	−32	46*	−08	−46*	33
A					08	12	−12	10	18	40*	00	07	25	−27	11	−15	−44*	−04	13	−16	26
B						−19	33	−01	−21	−10	28	01	23	−06	−20	27	09	−25	19	05	43*
C							17	13	24	37*	−08	−20	−25	30	−45*	−01	−44*	31	−75*	−06	−16
E								40*	−29	28	29	36*	34	11	−16	31	01	24	26	06	27
F									−32	46*	−04	54*	16	07	09	02	−42*	−29	−18	−16	07
G										18	−46*	−38*	−26	28	08	14	−24	57*	−30	−04	15
H											01	−04	−15	10	−19	−03	−50*	15	−43*	−36*	07
I												−16	26	−39*	00	−08	25	−45*	22	00	04
L													12	−05	−47*	01	−13	−43*	17	13	17
M														−01	−07	30	30	−14	13	−16	10
N															−12	11	−04	19	−46*	09	−13
O																−10	06	−53*	50*	28	08
Q1																	22	05	−08	−03	16
Q2																		−23	30	12	−21
Q3																			−46*	−31	−04
Q4																				07	20
S																					−17
O																					

*Indicates correlations significant at the 0.05 level or beyond.

SYNTHESIS AND DISCUSSION

In comparing the mean 16PF profile of the 30 homosexuals with the profiles of other groups, the highest degree of association was found to be with the sample of convicted Australian homosexuals despite the cultural differences between the 2 samples. This supports Cattell and Morony's (1962) conclusion that it is possible to talk of a homosexual profile. However, this conclusion needs some qualification in view of the substantially lower correlation between the British homosexual profile and that of the Australian *uncharged* homosexuals. It seems likely that it is those homosexuals who are not sufficiently well-adjusted either to keep clear of the law or to avoid seeking psychiatric help who may have in common certain features of personality—features which may not necessarily be shared by better-adjusted homosexuals. This would tend to support Schofield's (1965b) conclusion, based on lengthy interviews with 150 homosexuals (a third of whom were in prison, a third under treatment, and a third who had experienced neither conviction nor treatment for homosexuality) that it is dangerous to generalize from findings obtained from homosexuals in trouble to those who have never been in trouble. Finally, it should always be kept in mind that a group mean profile is merely an average, from which the profiles of all individual members of the group will deviate to a greater or lesser extent.

In what way does the average homosexual patient's personality differ from the normal? Examination of the mean 16PF scores in Table 7.4 shows that the British homosexuals differ by at least 1.0 sten score from both the 100 Scottish normals whose scores are shown in the table and the American normal standardization population (i.e. from 5.5 sten) on the following scales: B, O, Q4, M, and I—on all of which the homosexuals score more highly than the normal groups—and C and H, on which they score lower. They are thus to be seen as more *intelligent, emotional, apprehensive, tense, imaginative, tender-minded,* and *shy* than most normal people.

Three of these scales (C minus, O, and Q4) are amongst those usually found to "load" on the 16PF second-order factor of anxiety. These results are thus very much in line with the finding that the neuroticism (N) score of the EPI is significantly higher than normal for this sample. Interestingly enough, Kenyon (1968) has also found EPI N scores to be significantly higher than normal in an entirely female group of 123 homosexuals who were not under treatment. The 16PF profile of our homosexual sample is rather similar to that of the neurotic group in Table 7.4. This finding is very similar to that of Cattell and Morony (1962) who found that their combined group of 133 homosexuals gave a profile closely related to a comparison profile obtained from neurotic patients. They pick out for special mention the fact that emotionality or ego weakness (C minus) was even greater for the homosexuals than for the neurotics. (This was true also when our homosexual patient group was compared with the Scottish neurotic group.) On the grounds that low C has been found to be the most consistent sign of psychopathology, either psychotic or neurotic, Cattell and Morony argue that homosexuality may be " . . . based on a weakness of personality structure more generic than, and perhaps prior to, that developing in neurosis".

The clinical assessments of personality are consistent with the questionnaire findings in demonstrating a high degree of personality abnormality in our group of patients. Approximately half the group were thought to have a disorder of personality in addition to their homosexuality. However, it is important to point out that "personality disorder" in terminology other than that of Schneider, such as was presumably being used, for example, in diagnosing the patients who form the comparison group shown in column 4 of Table 7.4, is usually a more restricted concept, bearing a closest relationship, perhaps, to Schneider's cold affectionless type of disorder. Most of the remainder of the group were thought to have a personality abnormality. Amongst both disorders and abnormalities, those of the self-insecure type predominated. A recent factor analytic study by Brooks (1969) has shown the concept of the self-insecure personality to be separable into at least 4 elements—vulnerable, doubting, thorough, and paranoid—of which all but the third are related to neuroticism as measured by the EPI and the 16PF second-order factor anxiety. The existence of this third factor may well be responsible for the absence of significant correlations in the last 2 columns of Table 7.5.

In Eysenckian terminology, the group as a whole is "dysthymic" or *introverted* neurotic, as are groups of patients diagnosed as anxiety neurotics. The low H score (indicating shyness) on the 16PF is consistent with this, as H minus loads highly on the 16PF second-order invia (or introversion) factor. However, on other scales which also load highly on that factor, such as A, E, and F, the homosexual group tends, but not significantly, to greater extraversion than normals. It seems that the single extraversion–introversion score of the EPI may obscure a more complex underlying pattern.

It would seem likely, *a priori*, that a self-insecure personality disorder or abnormality would be found mostly in persons of introverted temperament and, indeed, the findings here support this notion with the clinical S-scale (self-insecurity) correlating significantly with H minus. Whether a similar correlation would be found in a normal (i.e. heterosexual) sample cannot, of course, be answered from the data presented here.

There are certain features of the homosexual patients 16PF profile which are apparently shared by psychotic patients. This is, of course, by no means the same as saying that the group displays psychotic features. The diagnosis of a psychotic illness depends on the presence or absence of specific symptoms; the absence of such symptoms does not rule out the possibility of similarities in personality with patients who do show them. It is, however, a somewhat unexpected finding that the homosexual and psychotic profiles should bear such a similarity, particularly as the ability of the 16PF to distinguish psychotics from other groups, such as neurotics and normals, is often cited as a reason for its use in research with clinical groups (e.g. McAllister, 1968; Walton, 1968). Nonetheless, Oliver and Mosher (1968) have also commented on the similarity between the personalities of psychotics and those of a group of homosexual reformatory inmates on the basis of their use of another personality questionnaire, namely the MMPI (Minnesota multiphasic personality inventory).

A close inspection of the figures in Fig. 7.1 and Table 7.4 shows that the similarity of the psychotics and homosexuals lies in the high imaginativeness of the homosexuals and both groups of psychotics (M) and the high tender-mindedness (I) of the homosexuals and the group of integrated psychotics. Other similarities, such as high emotionality (C minus) and apprehensiveness (O) are shared also with the neurotic group. Cattell (1965) has stated that this label—"tender-mindedness"—may be misleading as "... the central feature of the I plus pattern is a certain imaginative escapism or even an undisciplined mind...". He believes there is evidence that it arises from parental over-protection or indulgence, is related to creativity, and is significantly higher in females than in males. Concerning imaginativeness, Cattell *et al.* (1968) have recently reported that M is one of the less conforming of the 16PF scales, being factorially less pure than most of the others. Its fascination lies in its emergence from factor analytic personality research, "... as something never previously seen by the clinical eye .... The nearest clinical concept to M is autistic tendency

. . . . It is, however, not the withdrawing autism of some schizophrenic expressions, but an autism of strong subjectivity of emotions and high pressure of inner cognitive activity. It is significantly associated with both creativity and accident-proneness, as well as with 'bohemian' social adjustments." It is tempting to try to see elements of the self-insecure personality in these descriptions, but as Table 7.5 shows, there is no statistically significant association between clinical ratings of self-insecurity and either the M or the I scales of the 16PF although, as previously mentioned, the factorial impurity of the self-insecure concept may obscure a real relationship here.

The results presented here give no support to another conclusion of Cattell and Morony's (1962), namely that homosexuals tend to be lower than anxiety neurotic patients on ". . . the main persuaders to general morality of behaviour—the superego factor G, and the guilt proneness (or apprehensiveness) factor O", although they certainly score lower than normals on the former scale. There is some support, however, for a further conclusion of the same authors, that homosexuals have a tendency to greater radicalism (Q1) than anxiety neurotics, this again being a feature seemingly shared with psychotics. Finally, it is difficult to know how the present results could be used either to support or to refute Grygier's (1957) suggestion that homosexuals are high on "narcissism".

SUMMARY

1. The mean 16PF profile of the present group of 30 homosexual patients is strikingly similar in shape to that of a group of convicted Australian homosexuals reported by Cattell and Morony (1962).

2. The different methods of personality measurement used here are in broad agreement that a greater degree of personality abnormality is to be found in this group of homosexuals than is to be found in the normal population. In several respects, the abnormality is of a type shared by groups of anxiety neurotics.

3. In addition, the group manifests high imaginativeness, tender-mindedness, and radicalism on the 16PF—features shared by groups of patients diagnosed as psychotic.

PREDICTION OF TREATMENT OUTCOME

The remainder of this chapter will be devoted to the question of whether personality assessment aids in the prediction of treatment outcome. As this question has been dealt with for the preliminary series of patients in a previous report (MacCulloch and Feldman, 1967b), their findings will be summarized first. This will be followed by a lengthier discussion of the results from the 30 patients who took part in the controlled trial.

PREDICTION FOR 32 PATIENTS IN THE PRELIMINARY SERIES

MacCulloch and Feldman were able to show that personality, as clinically assessed, was significantly related to the outcome of treatment as determined by changes in scores on the SOM described in Chapter 4. Tables 10 and 11 from their original report are reproduced here as Tables 7.6 and 7.7. From these it can be seen that having a disorder of personality of an attention-seeking or weak-willed type carries a poor prognosis for both a reduction in homosexual orientation and an increase in heterosexual orientation. The 29 patients contributing to these figures were from a sample of 32 consecutively treated patients, 1 of whom had a normal personality, 1 a schizophrenic defect state and the third a hyperthymic personality abnormality. The group comparisons made in the 2 tables are between mean post-treatment SOM scores corrected for age. (Before this correction was made, age was found to be significantly related to treatment outcome, the younger patients faring better, and an analysis of variance had shown that group C patients were significantly older than the members of the other 2 groups.)

TABLE 7.6. A COMPARISON OF THE IMMEDIATE POST-TREATMENT SOM HOMOSEXUAL SCORES (CORRECTED FOR AGE) OF 29 MALE HOMOSEXUAL (SERIES) PATIENTS IN THREE CLINICAL PERSONALITY GROUPS

		No.	Mean	SD	Comparison	t	p
A.	Self-insecure disorders	13	23.92	10.98	A vs. B	1.83	0.10
B.	Self-insecure abnormalities	9	16.44	6.31	A vs. C	1.09	NS
C.	Other disorders (attention-seeking or weak-willed)	7	30.57	15.01	B vs. C	2.41	0.05

(This table appears as Table 10 in the report by MacCulloch and Feldman (1967b).)

TABLE 7.7. A COMPARISON OF THE IMMEDIATE POST-TREATMENT SOM HETEROSEXUAL SCORES (CORRECTED FOR AGE) OF 29 MALE HOMOSEXUAL (SERIES) PATIENTS IN THREE CLINICAL PERSONALITY GROUPS

		No.	Mean	SD	Comparison	t	p
A.	Self-insecure disorders	13	42.46	3.79	A vs. B	1.10	NS
B.	Self-insecure abnormalities	9	44.66	5.66	A vs. C	2.27	0.05
C.	Other disorders (attention-seeking or weak-willed)	7	31.14	6.03	B vs. C	2.23	0.05

(This table appears as Table 11 in the report by MacCulloch and Feldman (1967b).)

PREDICTION FOR 30 PATIENTS IN THE CONTROLLED TRIAL

The various relationships between personality and treatment outcome for the trial patients are shown in Table 7.8 in the form of product moment correlations between personality scale scores and post-treatment SOM scores. In columns 1–6 are shown the correlations between personality and SOM scores, assessed immediately after treatment of a particular type. Columns 7 and 8 give the correlations with sexual orientation at the completion of all treatment (i.e. when a patient had either successfully fulfilled the 12-point homosexual score reduction criterion or had experienced a full course of both types of aversion treatment—see Chapter 5). Finally, columns 9 and 10 give correlations with SOM scores at the latest follow-up. (See Chapter 5 for details on the length of follow-up. For 3 of the patients, who failed to return for follow-up, the scores are those at the completion of the treatment to which they were first assigned.)

TABLE 7.8. CORRELATIONS BETWEEN PERSONALITY MEASUREMENT AND POST-TREATMENT SOM SCORES FOR 30 HOMOSEXUAL (TRIAL) PATIENTS

		Immediate after treatment of a particular type						Last treatment		At latest follow-up	
		AA (n = 20)		CC (n = 19)		Psychotherapy (n = 10)		(n = 30)		(n = 30)**	
		Hom. 1	Het. 2	Hom. 3	Het. 4	Hom. 5	Het. 6	Hom. 7	Het. 8	Hom. 9	Het. 10
EPI	E	−19	00	−31	+12	−55	−09	−25	−11	−26	+08
	N	+54*	−30	+23	+20	−04	+32	+24	+13	+26	+02
	L	−11	−04	−16	−16	−04	71*	−07	−22	+04	−19
16PF	A	+15	−38	−14	+19	+13	+22	−03	−07	+01	−14
	B	+13	+53*	+07	+09	+67*	−29	24	+31	+09	+20
	C	−39	+39	−33	−05	−58	−00	−37	+12	−42*	+23
	E	−18	+63*	+25	+07	−29	−44	+02	+27	−05	+16
	F	−19	+34	−43	+03	−46	−21	−29	+07	−10	−01
	G	+05	−52*	+20	−51*	+04	−16	+19	−51*	+04	−22
	H	−31	+13	−23	−08	−12	−43	−26	−07	−13	−19
	I	−17	+24	−08	+35	+47	−42	−07	+28	+01	+21
	L	+23	+09	−17	+26	−36	+58	−13	+20	−07	+13
	M	−05	+24	−01	+33	−10	−61	+17	−06	−08	+14
	N	+01	+22	+12	−38	−37	+09	+21	−04	−01	−02
	O	+24	−60*	+06	+18	−08	+57	+05	−08	+17	−15
	Q1	+02	+39	+21	−06	−57	−58	+14	−01	−03	+15
	Q2	+06	+43	+56*	+15	+36	+28	+33	+36*	+01	+31
	Q3	−28	−24	−07	−39	+04	−50	−12	−34	−12	−15
	Q4	+51*	−66*	+14	+20	+39	+23	+22	−08	+38*	−16
Clini-	S	+43*	+15	+33	−16	+20	+85*	+36*	+36*	+14	+08
cal	O	+14	−27	+21	−03	+19	−47	+21	−28	+39*	−05

The correlations shown in the table are partial correlations, pretreatment SOM scores having been partialled out.

Those correlations high enough to be significant at $p < 0.05$ are marked with an asterisk.

**Three patients defaulted after their first treatment; the calculations have used their "end of first treatment score" as their "follow-up score".

The odd-numbered columns of Table 7.8 show correlations with post-treatment SOM *homosexual* scores (positive SOM homosexual scores indicating positive attraction and are therefore unfavourable) with, in each case, pre-treatment SOM homosexual scores partialled out. Partial correlations were calculated because of the invariably positive and sometimes substantial correlations, between pre- and post-treatment orientation scores. In the even-numbered columns of the same table are correlations with post-treatment SOM *heterosexual* scores (positive SOM heterosexual scores being favourable) with, in each case, pre-treatment heterosexual SOM scores partialled out.

(a) *Predicting outcome for all 30 patients at the end of all treatment and at follow-up*

Considering first the results shown in columns 7–10 of Table 7.8, that is those in which all 30 trial patients are involved, it can be seen that the number of significant correlations is not greatly in excess of the number to be expected by chance. However, three of the significant correlations involve the two clinical ratings which can stand as a separate technique on their

own. At the completion of treatment, clinical S-scale scores (extent of self-insecure personality abnormality) were positively correlated with both SOM homo- and heterosexual scores
indicating that those patients of greater self-insecurity tended to respond to treatment with a
greater *increase* in heterosexual orientation but a smaller *decrease* in homosexual orientation,
relative to other patients.

Both the 16PF C and G scales have near zero correlations with the clinical S scale, and
therefore contribute independently to the prediction of outcome at the end of treatment.
The more emotional (C minus) have made least progress in terms of reduction in homosexual
orientation and the more conscientious (G plus) have made least progress in terms of increase
in heterosexual orientation. The significant correlation with Q2 is partly a result of its correlation with G, and when the latter scale is partialled out the correlation between Q2 and
outcome ceases to be significant.

At latest follow-up, C scale scores (emotionality) provide, if anything, a slightly better
prediction, and the Q4 (tension) correlation has become significant, although this does not
provide an altogether independent source of prediction, as C and Q4 are highly correlated
in this sample (see Table 7.5) as in most others on whom the 16PF has been used.

Neither conscientiousness (G), nor any of the other personality measures used, provide a
significant prediction of heterosexual orientation at latest follow-up.

The degree of clinically assessed self-insecurity has also, by the time of the latest follow-up,
ceased to give a significant prediction, but the clinical O scale (extent of personality abnormalities of types other than the self-insecure) does add significantly to the prediction of
homosexual orientation at latest follow-up, which is already partly provided by the C and
Q4 scales of the 16PF. (The correlation between 16PF C and clinical O for this sample was
−0.16.) The greater the degree of personality abnormalities of "other" types (mainly
attention-seeking, labile, and weak-willed—see Table 7.1), the smaller the reduction in
homosexual orientation which was apparent at follow-up.

(b) Predicting outcome immediately after treatments of different types

The significant predictions are shown in columns 1–6 of Table 7.8. The numbers of
patients contributing to the results in different columns vary because patients who were
unsuccessful under the treatment to which they were first randomly assigned were allowed
to cross over to an alternative (aversion only) treatment. (For the design of the trial, see
Chapter 5.) Of the 30 patients who took part in the trial, 20 experienced AA at some time
(10 as their first or only treatment and a further 10 as a treatment at some stage subsequent to
their first); 18 experienced CC (10 as their first or only treatment and a further 8 subsequently), and 10 experienced psychotherapy (all as their first or only treatment).

The pattern of significant correlations obtained from the group of 10 patients who were
assigned to psychotherapy for their first treatment (columns 5 and 6) looks quite different
from those obtained from patients who at any time had received AA or CC (columns 1–4).
Immediately after psychotherapy, the more self-insecure patients (clinical S scale) are
achieving a more satisfactory heterosexual orientation than others, and the size of this
correlation (+0.85) is significantly higher than the equivalent correlations for AA or CC
(+0.15 and −0.16 respectively). The significant negative correlation with the EPI lie scale
score for the psychotherapy group is almost entirely due to the high correlation of this scale
with the clinical S scale for this group of patients. The third significant correlation for the
group, namely that between the 16PF B scale and homosexual orientation, although high, is
not significantly higher than the correlations for the other 2 groups (+0.13 and +0.07).

Comparing the figures in columns 1 and 2 with those in columns 3 and 4, the similarity of the correlations between post-treatment heterosexual orientation and conscientiousness (16PF G scale) is worthy of note. The most obvious difference between the two groups lies in the apparently much greater importance of differences in neuroticism, apprehensiveness, tension, and self-insecurity for treatment by AA than for treatment by CC. The negative correlations between apprehensiveness and tension and heterosexual orientation in the former group are both significantly higher than the equivalent correlations in the CC group, but the other significant correlations in columns 1 and 2 are insignificantly higher than their equivalents in columns 3 and 4.*

DISCUSSION

Self-insecurity and the Results at the End of Treatment

An interesting finding is the association between the degree of self-insecurity and *both* homo- and heterosexual orientation at the completion of all treatment. This suggests that a certain group of patients, particularly those clinically considered to have a personality disorder of the self-insecure type, are reacting to treatment by increasing their heterosexual orientation more than most, whilst at the same time reducing their homosexual orientation less than most. That such a response to treatment occurs at all is interesting, and that to some extent it can be predicted on personality grounds is important. It can be seen from Tables 7.6 and 7.7 that this result was hinted at also by the results from the preliminary series of patients reported by MacCulloch and Feldman (1967b); group A patients (self-insecure disorders) were doing as well at the end of treatment as group B patients (self-insecure abnormalities) in terms of heterosexual orientation, but not significantly better than group C patients (other disorders) in terms of homosexual orientation.

Conscientiousness and Change in Heterosexual Orientation

That greater conscientiousness, or superego strength, should make it more difficult to bring about an increase in heterosexual orientation during the course of treatment, particularly when treatment is by one or other of the aversion techniques, may be an important indication that the method used to increase heterosexual orientation (see Chapters 2 and 3) may not have been suitable for all patients and that alternative methods should be tried out. Alternatively, the fault may lie not in the method but in the inability of the more conscientious (or, in view of the low mean score of this group on the G scale, it might be more appropriate to say the less expedient) person to respond to any inducement to heterosexual arousal in the treatment situation. A further possible explanation is that the more expedient may manifest an unrealistic "flight into health".

*The test used to compare the sizes of correlations from different groups, namely a comparison of the difference in size of the Fisher's Z transformations of the two correlations with the standard error of this difference, may be more conservative than necessary, as its legitimate use is confined to circumstances in which groups are independent, having no subjects in common. This condition was not fully met by these data.

Ego-strength and Results at Follow-up

The most significant predictor of outcome at the time of the follow-up for the group as a whole was the 16PF stability–emotionality (or ego-strength–ego-weakness) scale C—a scale that has already been mentioned in connection with the description of the group in terms of personality earlier in this chapter. In a discussion of the prognostic factors in the treatment of homosexuality by psychotherapy, Ovesey and Willard (1965) list ego-strength, defining it in rather general terms as " . . . the capacity for successful psychologic adaptation". They consider it to be an important prognostic factor for all groups of psychiatric patients. Eber (1966) found the C scale of the 16PF predictive of successful follow-up adjustment in a group of clients of vocational rehabilitative services. Barron's success (1953) in predicting the response to psychotherapy of psychiatric patients, using an ego-strength scale of his own design, is well known although there is little, other than the name, to suggest that his scale necessarily measures the same variable as the 16PF ego-strength scale. Whether high ego-strength indicates a willingness on the part of the patient to make efforts on his own to consolidate the improvement brought about by treatment (Gelder, 1968b), or whether low ego-strength confers vulnerability to stressful events occurring during the course of, or after, treatment, can only be guessed at at the present time. In view of the low mean C score of the entire group of homosexuals, those with the lowest C scale scores on this in the group must have exceptionally low scores, and it is therefore not at all surprising that emotionality or ego-weakness of this degree should interfere with a successful long-term response to treatment.

Clinical Personality Assessment and Results at Follow-up

An extra source of prediction of outcome at follow-up is provided by the clinical O scale. This confirms MacCulloch and Feldman's (1967b) finding that disorders of personality of Schneiderian types, other than the self-insecure, are prognostic of an unfavourable outcome. In order to determine the exact degree to which the clinical personality assessment added predictive accuracy to that provided by questionnaire methods, the clinical O scale and the 16PF C scale were combined as the two independent variables in a multiple regression equation, with homosexual orientation scale score at follow-up as the dependent variable. The result was a multiple correlation coefficient of 0.60, with partial regression coefficients of -3.80 for C and $+3.84$ for O. The considerable improvement in ability to predict treatment outcome brought about by combining these 2 scales illustrates the complementary nature of clinical and questionnaire assessments of personality.

The EPI and the Prediction of Treatment Outcome

The choice of the EPI as a means of assessing personality for this group of patients was partly dictated by theoretical predictions concerning the relationship of introversion and anxiety to ease of conditioning. The results presented in Table 7.8 include only one significant prediction of treatment outcome by EPI scale scores, namely a significant positive correlation between neuroticism (N) score and homosexual orientation immediately after treatment by

AA. This result is, in fact, opposite to that predicted by the theory relating anxiety to ease of acquisition of an avoidance response (Spence, 1964).

The relationship between E and N scores and the results of treatment at follow-up are shown in a different way in Table 7.9. It can be seen that, as far as E is concerned, the only difference which approaches significance suggests that patients in the "recovered" group are more extraverted—not less—as would have been predicted by the Eysenckian theory relating extraversion with relatively low conditionability than those in the "not improved" group. However, this alternative manner of presenting the results has established a significant effect due to N score, namely that the "recovered" patients are, as a group, less neurotic than the "not improved" patients. This result, again opposite to that theoretically predicted,

TABLE 7.9. EPI EXTRAVERSION AND NEUROTICISM SCORES OF 27 HOMOSEXUAL (TRIAL) PATIENTS WHO RECEIVED AVERSION THERAPY AND WHO WERE RECOVERED, IMPROVED, OR NOT IMPROVED AT FOLLOW-UP

	Extraversion		Neuroticism	
	Mean	SD	Mean	SD
A. "Recovered" (a reduction of 26 points or more in homosexual orientation) ($n = 11$)	25.55	10.02	26.09	7.00
B. "Improved" (a reduction of between 10 and 25 points) ($n = 5$)	18.60	6.37	30.60	14.01
C. "Not improved" (a reduction of less than 10 points) ($n = 11$)	21.45	6.05	33.18	6.16
Comparisons A vs. B	$t = 0.73$ NS		$t = 0.43$ NS	
A vs. C	$t = 1.11$ NS		$t = 2.39$ sig. (0.05)	
B vs. C	$t = 0.45$ NS		$t = 0.26$ NS	

can probably be explained by saying that as the group is high on neuroticism as a whole, they should, therefore, all be expected to condition well (Morgenstern *et al.*, 1965). However, patients high on N might be expected to respond less well to treatment by virtue of the association between neuroticism and low ego-strength. There may be additional reasons why patients high on N might respond badly to treatment by AA, and these will be discussed below.

Predicting the Response to Different Treatments

The rather varying pattern of significant correlations found among columns 1–6 of Table 7.8 tempts the conclusion that the three varieties of treatment are successful with patients of different personality types and may, therefore, operate via quite different processes. However, it is important to point out that the numbers of patients involved are small and hence a comparison of correlations between columns of Table 7.8 (i.e. between treatments) yields very few significant differences. Nonetheless, some of the variations are large and, if they were to be confirmed in the course of further research, could be important both in determining the suitability of different types of treatment for different types of patient and in illuminating the processes involved in the different forms of treatment.

Self-insecurity and Psychotherapy

Despite the small numbers, there is a strong suggestion that whilst patients with higher degrees of self-insecurity are no more or less likely than others to increase their heterosexual orientation in the course of treatment by AA or CC; however, when treatment is by psychotherapy, they seem to be at an advantage in this respect. This would clearly be a very important fact* if it were to be replicated.

Neuroticism and AA

Differences in levels of anxiety or neuroticism seem to be of greatest importance in predicting the immediate response to aversion therapy of the AA type. With that type of treatment, those patients who have the highest levels of anxiety or neuroticism make the worst immediate response to treatment both in terms of a reduction in homosexual orientation and an increase in heterosexual orientation. This conclusion is of great importance, as it suggests that particular aspects of personality may be important for one of the two forms of aversion therapy but not for the other, and also because it probably could have been predicted on theoretical grounds as follows. The AA patient is required to make operant responses in accordance with his own feelings; cognitive decision processes are involved, and the task for the patient is a much more complex one than for the CC patient. Research has tended to show that in simple, uncomplicated learning situations such as CC procedures involve, high-anxiety subjects are, if anything, at an advantage (Kimble, 1964)—a result in line with theories postulating anxiety as a source of drive strength (e.g. Taylor, 1956)—whereas in more complex learning situations they are at a disadvantage. Moreover, in AA the patient has some control over his own receipt of noxious stimulation—a situation known to be more stressful than the receipt of noxious stimulation over which the subject has no control (Jones *et al.*, 1960). Furthermore, it has recently been shown by Lovibond (1969) that a regular, anticipated series of electric shocks, administered in much the same way as shocks were administered in the course of the CC type of treatment, are felt by the subject to be less noxious than shocks administered in an irregular series, as in the AA type of treatment. For all these reasons, therefore, the latter type of treatment may well have been too stressful for high-anxiety patients.

These results for the AA group are consistent with previously published reports of behaviour therapy used for the treatment of other disorders. Morgenstern *et al.* (1965) found that transvestites scoring highly on the N scale of the Maudsley personality inventory did less well than others, under a form of aversion therapy which was designed to correspond to the CC paradigm, but which in fact involved the patient in complex (cross-dressing) activity. Response to this form of treatment correlated positively with a laboratory test of operant conditioning and not with a test of CC, leading the authors to suppose that an operant conditioning process was in fact involved. Beech (1960), as a result of treating writer's cramp with avoidance conditioning, concludes that high patient anxiety should suggest an alternative choice of treatment. In addition, Gelder (1968b) reports finding that high levels of anxiety interfere with the response of phobic patients to a quite different form of behaviour therapy—desensitization.

*It will be recalled (Chapter 5) that both patients relapsed who initially responded to psychotherapy.

Predicting Treatment Outcome from a Combination of Personality and Previous Heterosexual Interest

It was stated in Chapters 3 and 5 that a factor of great predictive importance had been found to be a previous history of pleasurable heterosexual behaviour at any time in the past. Patients lacking such a previous history (termed primary homosexuals) had a very much poorer prognosis than those who were able to report some previous pleasurable heterosexual behaviour (termed secondary homosexuals).

The value of personality as a predictor of treatment outcome can only really be judged in comparison with the predictive usefulness of this classification of patients into primary and secondary types. In saying that patients with a certain type of personality respond badly to treatment, it is possible that we are just saying in another way that primary homosexuals respond badly. The correlations between personality and homosexual orientation scores at follow-up, which are shown in column 9 of Table 7.8, are partial correlations, but only the effect of pre-treatment *homosexual* orientation score has been partialled out. When, in addition, the effect of pre-treatment *heterosexual* orientation score is partialled out, the correlation between follow-up homosexual orientation and the clinical O scale is in fact increased slightly, whilst the correlation with ego-strength or emotionality (16PF C scale), although reduced slightly, is still just significant. This shows that, in the prediction of homosexual orientation at follow-up, pre-treatment heterosexual orientation scores and personality evaluation provide supplementary information to a certain degree. But it must be realized that heterosexual orientation immediately before the commencement of treatment may not be precisely the same thing as the presence or absence of pleasurable heterosexual interest at any time in the past.

The interdependence of personality and the primary–secondary patient classification in predicting outcome is demonstrated in Table 7.10, in which patients have been classified into one of three outcome groups, on the basis of the reduction in homosexual orientation score between pre-treatment and follow-up. The combined ego-weakness–personality-disorder score has been calculated for each patient by subtracting the clinical O scale score from the ego-strength score. This particular combined personality score was chosen on the grounds that the 16PF C scale and the clinical O scale provided the two major personality predictors of follow-up homosexual orientation. When they were combined in a multiple regression equation (see above), the partial regression coefficients applied to the two scores to give the best prediction were nearly identical in size, but of opposite signs. Table 7.10 shows strikingly the predictive significance of *both* this combined personality score *and* the primary–secondary classification of the homosexual disorder. In addition, there is a strong suggestion of a relationship between the two, with none of the 8 primary homosexuals in the group having a combined personality score higher than 4.

Simplifying the picture given by Table 7.10 still further by dichotomizing the combined personality scores into those of 2 or above ("good" personality) and those below 2 ("poor" personality) and dichotomizing reduction of homosexual orientation measured by the SOM into those with a reduction of at least 10 scale-points ("successes") and those with a smaller reduction ("failures"), it is possible to arrive at the success rates of the 4 types of patient determined by this double dichotomy. These are shown in Table 7.11. Here is a demonstration of the value of supplementing historical information provided by the patient about his previous heterosexual interest, with information about his personality, gathered at the time

TABLE 7.10. CHANGE IN SOM HOMOSEXUAL SCORES FROM PRE-TREATMENT TO FOLLOW-UP AS A FUNCTION OF PERSONALITY AND SCORES FROM HOMOSEXUAL "TYPE"

Reduction in SOM homosexual score	16PF C scale score *minus* clinical O scale score		
	8, 7, 6, 5	4, 3, 2	1, 0, −1, −2, −3
More than 25 points	4	7(1)	0
10–25 points	3	1(1)	1
Less than 10 points	0	5(4)	6(2)

The figures in brackets indicate the number of patients in each cell diagnosed as "primary homosexuals" (i.e. without previous heterosexual interest).

TABLE 7.11. THE SUCCESS RATES OF FOUR "TYPES" OF HOMOSEXUAL PATIENT FOUND AMONGST THE 27 TRIAL PATIENTS WHO WERE TREATED BY AVOIDANCE LEARNING

Personality	Previous pleasurable heterosexual behaviour	
	No ("primary")	Yes ("secondary")
"Good"	2/6 successes	14/14 successes
"Poor"	0/2 successes	0/5 successes

of his presentation for treatment. A combination of previous heterosexual interest (secondary homosexuality) and "good" personality, as here defined, ensures success (14 successful out of 14), as defined by a reduction of at least 10 points on the homosexual orientation scale between the beginning of treatment and the time of follow-up. Even with previous heterosexual interest, a "poor" personality is an unfavourable prognostic sign (zero successes out of 5), although a "good" personality seems to confer some advantage in primary patients (2 successes out of 6). Finally, success is unlikely when both prognostic signs are unfavourable (zero successes out of 2). Table 7.12 shows that almost as good a prediction of treatment outcome can be made, using a combination of personality and SOM heterosexual scores immediately prior to treatment. The latter provides a readily ascertainable measure of heterosexual attitude at the beginning of treatment, and may be generalized to other samples of patients.

TABLE 7.12. THE SUCCESS RATES OF THE FOUR "TYPES" OF HOMOSEXUAL PATIENT GENERATED BY COMBINING PERSONALITY AND PRE-TREATMENT HETEROSEXUAL SCORES

Personality	Pre-treatment SOM heterosexual score	
	Less than 20	20 or more
"Good"	3/6 successes	13/14 successes
"Poor"	0/4 successes	0/3 successes

CONCLUSIONS

1. A systematic assessment of the personalities of homosexual patients prior to treatment made a significant addition to the ability to predict the outcome of treatment.

2. In predicting outcome at follow-up, the combination of clinical and questionnaire assessment of personality and SOM heterosexual pre-treatment score was more effective than either personality or SOM measures used alone. A very high degree of predictive accuracy appears obtainable. A psychometric equivalent of the clinical O scale must be sought, and, together with the 16PF C scale and the SOM, used to cross-validate the present findings in another group of homosexual patients.

3. Clinically, the greater the degree of personality abnormality of any of the types described by Schneider (1959), other than the self-insecure type, the greater was the likelihood of a poor outcome (in terms of reduction in homosexual orientation) at follow-up. This was so both for the preliminary series of patients (MacCulloch and Feldman, 1967b) and for those who took part in the trial, the two sets of results being analysed separately.

4. Of the questionnaire scales used, the C (ego-strength–ego-weakness or stability–emotionality) scale of the 16PF afforded the best prediction of outcome at follow-up. A poor outcome was more likely the lower the score on that scale. This result is consistent with both a description of the supposed construct underlying the scale and with previous research findings.

5. The use of the EPI failed to confirm hypotheses concerning the relationship between personality and conditioning. There was a non-significant tendency for extraversion to relate positively to favourable outcome after aversion therapy, and a significant tendency for neuroticism to relate negatively to the same thing. This latter finding is, however, consistent with the findings of at least one predictive study of aversion therapy for a sexual disorder (Morgenstern et al., 1965).

6. The greater the degree of conscientiousness in a patient, as assessed by the G scale of the 16PF, the less likely was there to be an increase in heterosexual orientation during the course of treatment, particularly when treatment was a form of aversion therapy.

7. Personality indications for a certain type of treatment were found. In particular, a high degree of anxiety or neuroticism predicted a poor response to aversion therapy of the AA type. No such prediction held for either aversion therapy of the CC type or for psychotherapy.

8. The degree of personality abnormality of Schneider's self-insecure type was significantly positively related to increases in heterosexual orientation during the course of psychotherapy (i.e. the greater the degree of abnormality, the more favourable the immediate result). No similar relationship held for either type of aversion therapy.

CHAPTER 8

CONCLUSIONS AND SPECULATIONS

M. P. Feldman, M. J. MacCulloch, and J. F. Orford

I. THE SERIES OF 43 AND THE CONTROLLED TRIAL: SUMMARY AND DISCUSSION

A. THE SERIES

The total group of 43 was an unselected series of all the patients who attended between June 1963 and July 1965 with a complaint concerning their homosexual behaviour. This complaint was either independent of psychiatric symptomatology, in the context of such symptoms, or in the context of a court appearance for behaviour of a homosexual nature. Because this series was unselected, with the exception of patients who refused the offer of treatment, it can be taken to be a representative sample of the homosexuals who present for treatment at general hospitals, so that the results of the series can be generalized at least to general hospitals throughout Britain.

Treatment by AA learning was successful in nearly 60% of the cases after a follow-up of at least a year. Success was defined as a cessation of homosexual behaviour, the use of no more than occasional and mild homosexual phantasy and equally occasional mild homosexual interest in directly observed males, together with at least strong heterosexual phantasy and in the majority of cases overt heterosexual behaviour. The dependent measures used to ascertain change, or lack of it, were a structured clinical interview, and the SOM questionnaire. In addition, within-treatment measures were taken of the latencies of avoidance responses and changes in pulse rate to the male slides which were used as conditioned stimuli. There was a marked tendency for all the measures to cohere in indicating change or lack of change.

The most clear-cut favourable prognostic sign was a pre-treatment history of pleasurable heterosexual behaviour. The next most favourable sign was the absence of a disorder of personality of the weak-willed or attention-seeking type (using the classification of Schneider, 1959).

B. THE TRIAL

The comparative degree of success of the series prompted a controlled trial of AA learning, CC, and psychotherapy. The use of CC was intended to control for the possibility that a classical (Pavlovian) explanation could partially account for the comparative degree of success obtained with the series of patients.* Psychotherapy was intended to control for the

---

*This possibility was raised by Dr. J. Rachman in a personal communication and is discussed at length in a recent book (Rachman and Teasdale, 1969).

possible contribution to success of a positive relationship between therapist and patient. Five potential patients were excluded from the trial on various grounds; patients with no prior pleasurable heterosexual history were not excluded, as the major importance of this variable was not then appreciated. The outcome of the trial, after a follow-up of at least 3 months, and averaging 44 weeks, was that AA and CC were equally successful with patients with a prior pleasurable heterosexual history, and both were more successful with such patients than was psychotherapy. All 3 treatments were largely unsuccessful with patients with no prior pleasurable heterosexual history. Severe personality disorder was associated with failure to respond to treatment, irrespective of prior heterosexual history.

C. THE PREDICTION OF RESPONSE TO TREATMENT

Because lack of prior pleasurable heterosexual experience (termed "primary", as opposed to "secondary" homosexuality) emerged as the major prognostic sign in both series and trial patients, the 2 groups were combined and a further analysis was carried out. In order that all patients were strictly comparable, both in terms of relative similarity of treatment (AA and CC are regarded as similar for the present purpose and are subsumed under the heading of "avoidance learning" techniques) and of *known* outcome, several patients were omitted from these analyses as follows. Seven series patients (who failed to complete treatment) and the 3 trial patients (who did not receive a full course of avoidance learning) were all omitted, leaving 63 (73−10) in all. The association between primary homosexuality and unsuccessful outcome at latest follow-up was significant, by the χ^2 test, at beyond the 0.1 % level (Table 8.1).

TABLE 8.1. THE ASSOCIATION BETWEEN HOMOSEXUAL TYPE (PRIMARY OR SECONDARY) AND SUCCESS AT LATEST FOLLOW-UP IN RESPONSE TO AVOIDANCE LEARNING. SERIES AND TRIAL PATIENTS ARE COMBINED

	Primary	Secondary	Total
Success	5	36	41
Failure	12	10	22
Total	17	46	63

$\chi^2 = 12.21$. $p = < 0.001$.

In order to reduce the dependence of the therapist on retrospective evidence when making his prognosis, the next stage was to compare the pre- and post-treatment SOM scores of the primary and secondary homosexuals; the results of the comparison are shown in Table 8.2.

The groups differ significantly, at the pre-treatment stage on both SOM homosexual and heterosexual measures; however, the latter difference is much greater (15 points as against 4 points), with correspondingly less overlap between the groups. The post-treatment differences are both very large and highly significant. It can be concluded that pre-treatment SOM heterosexual scores relate reasonably closely to the assignation by clinical interview to primary and secondary homosexuality, and this may serve as a major predictor of treatment success. In order to test this directly, the pre-treatment SOM heterosexual scores of the

TABLE 8.2. PRE-TREATMENT AND LATEST FOLLOW-UP SOM HOMOSEXUAL AND HETEROSEXUAL SCORES OF 63 HOMOSEXUAL PATIENTS TREATED BY AVOIDANCE LEARNING. SCORES ARE SHOWN BY HOMOSEXUAL TYPE

		Homosexual measure		Heterosexual measure	
		Primary	Secondary	Primary	Secondary
(a)	*Pre-treatment*				
	No.	17	46	17	46
	Mean	45.89	41.85	15.94	31.5
	t Primary vs. secondary	3.59		6.01	
	p	<0.001		<0.001	
(b)	*Post-treatment*				
	No.	17	46	17	46
	Mean	40.17	20.54	20.33	43.24
	t Primary vs. secondary	5.40		7.19	
	p	<0.001		<0.001	

TABLE 8.3. PRE-TREATMENT AND LATEST FOLLOW-UP SOM HOMOSEXUAL AND HETEROSEXUAL SCORES OF 63 PATIENTS CLINICALLY ASSESSED AS SUCCESSFUL OR UNSUCCESSFUL AT LATEST FOLLOW-UP

		Homosexual measure		Heterosexual measure	
		Success	Failure	Success	Failure
(a)	*Pre-treatment*				
	No.	41	22	41	22
	Mean	41.90	44.77	30.31	22.81
	t success vs. failure	2.15		2.64	
	p	<0.05		<0.02	
(b)	*Post-treatment*				
	No.	41	22	41	22
	Mean	16.78	42.36	43.85	26.68
	t success vs. failure	11.08		5.52	
	p	<0.001		<0.001	

successful and unsuccessful patients were compared, and the results are shown in Table 8.3. This confirms the considerably greater predictive power of the pre-treatment heterosexual score (7.5 points of difference in mean score, against 2.8 points of difference for pre-treatment homosexual score). However, the prediction is far from perfect, and the next stage was to combine the separate predictive powers of pre-treatment personality measures and pre-treatment SOM heterosexual scores, an approach adopted in the last section of Chapter 7, and shown as Table 7.12 of that chapter. Unfortunately, we did not administer the 16PF to the series patients, so that the number of patients available for the combined SOM/personality predictive exercise is restricted to those taking part in the trial. Moreover, we need a measure of personality more reproducible than the O scale, the data for which are obtained by clinical interview. It is possible that detailed exploration of 16PF scores by profile analysis will produce a profile closely related to O scale scores; alternatively, the possibility that the psychopathic deviate and hysteria scales of the Minnesota multiphasic personality inventory (MMPI) may be related to O scale scores, has a reasonable face validity. A study to explore such possibilities will be started shortly.

TABLE 8.4. THE SUCCESS RATES OF THE FOUR "TYPES" OF HOMO-
SEXUAL PATIENT GENERATED BY COMBINING PERSONALITY AND
PRE-TREATMENT HETEROSEXUAL SCORES

Personality	Pre-treatment SOM heterosexual score	
	Less than 20	20 or more
"Good"	3/6 successes	13/14 successes
"Poor"	0/4 successes	0/3 successes

Returning to Table 7.12 as it stands (here reproduced, for convenience, as Table 8.4), it can be seen that the use of a triple "sieve" to select patients would vastly increase the effective use of therapist time in treatment by avoidance learning. The 3 stages of the "sieve" are as follows. Firstly, exclude all patients with a "poor" personality. This would exclude 7 patients, all of whom failed to respond (an eighth patient, who failed with P and then defaulted, had both a "poor" personality and failed the other 2 "sieves", see below). The second "sieve", a pre-treatment SOM heterosexual score of 20 or more, would eliminate a further 6 patients, of whom more shortly. Of the remaining 14 patients, 13 made a successful response, the four-teenth being a primary homosexual with a pre-treatment SOM heterosexual score of 22. The primary–secondary dichotomy supplies the third "sieve". Three of the 6 patients in the quadrant "good" personality but pre-treatment heterosexual score of below 20, failed to respond; all 3 were primary homosexuals. Of the remaining 3 successful patients, 2 were secondary homosexuals, both having a pre-treatment SOM heterosexual score of just below 20. The remaining successful patient, no. 7, is the puzzling exception, previously referred to in Chapter 5.

The application of the successive "sieves" to the 27* patients treated by AA or CC would have resulted in the treatment of 16 patients, all of whom were successful; of the 11 patients who would not have been treated, only 1 was successful. The suggested "sieving" is thus as follows:

(a) Treat those of "good" personality (the urgent need to make this criterion more objective has been referred to above) *and* a pre-treatment SOM heterosexual score of 20 or more (13 patients).

(b) *Re* "sieve", by homosexual type, those with a "good" personality, but a pre-treatment SOM heterosexual score of less than 20, reinstating as suitable for treatment the secondary homosexuals (3 patients).

It is important to add a note of caution; not only is there a necessity to objectify the O scale score, but the entire set of "sieves" must be cross-validated on a separate sample of patients.

Thus far we have been concerned with pre-treatment criteria for predicting the successful response to treatment by *either* AA or CC (as used in the trial) in order to maximize the efficacy of treatment by restricting it to those likely to succeed. In the next section we shall attempt to provide reasons for regarding either AA or CC as the treatment of choice for

*Two of the 3 patients not treated by AA or CC in the trial, were both of "good" personality, and had a pre-treatment SOM heterosexual score of over 20. Both would have been likely to respond either to CC or AA; one definitely relapsed following P, the other defaulted and is presumed to have relapsed.

patients of good prognosis, in terms of which of the two avoidance learning techniques is likely to be most economical of therapist time. That is, we shall discuss the use of within-treatment measures in maximizing the *efficiency* of the treatment of patients for whom a successful outcome has been predicted.

D. CC VERSUS AA

The outcome of the comparison of the two avoidance learning techniques was that both were relatively unsuccessful with primary homosexuals, but relatively (and equally) success-ful with secondary homosexuals. The first finding was predictable from the series of patients reported in Chapter 3 and will be further discussed in section II of this chapter. The second was contrary to expectation. AA learning was selected as the method of choice for the aver-sion therapy of homosexuality (Feldman, 1966) because it was more resistant to extinction than CC (Solomon and Brush, 1956). Both AA and CC failed with secondary homosexuals who scored beyond the cut-off point of 2, on the combined measure of clinical O scale, and 16PF C scale scores (see Chapter 7). There are two major questions to answer. Firstly, why did CC succeed as well as AA with secondary homosexuals of "good" personality? Secondly, why did they fair equally badly with secondary homosexuals of "poor" personality? In discussing these two questions (consideration of the second of which is deferred until section III of this chapter), it must be borne in mind that we are dealing with small numbers of patients. Only 5 secondary homosexuals who were treated by AA or CC or both, failed to respond to treatment; 3 had both AA and CC, 1 AA only, and 1 CC only.

Concerning the first question, it is clear that for secondary homosexuals of "good" person-ality, *either* the view of Solomon and Brush (1956), that avoidance learning by CC leads to rapid extinction, is incorrect, *or* that certain elements of both of the conditioning techniques used in the trial conferred an increased resistance to extinction. At least one of these elements was present in both AA and CC as follows.

On a proportion of trials, AA patients were shocked, irrespective of their instrumental avoidance behaviour; these non-reinforced (NR) trials may also be termed unavoidable shock trials with a warning period (CS–UCS interval) of 8 seconds. All the CC trials involved unavoidable shock, the shock following 2 seconds after the onset of the CS (homosexual slide). The differences between unavoidable shock in AA and CC are, firstly, the length of the warning period (8 seconds against 2 seconds) and, secondly, the provision of a response switch in AA. The homosexual slide left the screen in both AA and CC contiguously with shock cessation. In AA it did so in temporal association with the patient's action in pressing the switch and hence, seemingly, under his control. The removal of the homosexual slide in CC, whilst also in temporal association with shock cessation, was entirely under the control of the therapist. The crucial difference between AA and CC, namely the *locus* of control of slide removal and appearance, does not appear to be a *necessary* condition for successful response to treatment in secondary homosexuals. However, this statement only holds for CC and AA as used in the trial, that is both included the provision of an alternative sexual response. We have not obtained data for treatment which has dispensed with either the use of heterosexual slides (i.e. homosexual slide and shock alone) or homosexual slides (i.e. desensitization to heterosexual slides alone).* Without such data it is difficult to separate out the relative importance for response to treatment of decrease in homosexual approach and decrease in heterosexual avoidance. Both CC and AA involve a temporal association

*See p. 161 for a recently completed study by Dr. J. H. J. Bancroft.

between relief of anxiety (following the removal of the homosexual slide) and the appearance of the heterosexual slide. In AA the appearance of the latter is under the control of the patient, and in CC under that of the therapist. Our belief is that homosexual behaviour involves both approach to males and avoidance of females. It seems likely that for secondary homosexuals, both reduction of homosexual arousal and reduction of *fear* of heterosexual stimuli are necessary elements for successful treatment. The generalization from animal work which led Solomon and Brush (1956) to consider avoidance learning by CC to be poorly resistant to extinction, did not include the provision of an alternative response as a means of satisfying the relevant drive state of the organism (usually hunger or thirst). It may be that CC is effective in leading to avoidance behaviour which is resistant to extinction so long as an alternative sexual outlet is provided in the same learning context. We are arguing that the association between heterosexual slide and relief of anxiety, common to both CC and AA, had imposed a common factor on the two techniques. By enabling an alternative outlet for the patient's sexual drive, the use of heterosexual slides may be masking a real difference between AA and CC in resistance to extinction.

To complicate the matter, even if heterosexual slides were *not* used, there might still be no difference between AA and CC in outcome. This would be because both techniques, by reducing the strength of approach to homosexual stimuli, might block one outlet, thus easing the use of the alternative sexual outlet, even *without* the direct use in treatment of heterosexual stimuli. To put the matter in another way—with the habit strengths of both homosexual and heterosexual responses low (following the reduction of homosexual habit strength by avoidance learning)—heterosexual habit strength may be just sufficiently the greater of the two for overt heterosexual behaviour to occur. Assuming that such real-life experiences have successful outcomes, and are thus positively reinforced, a favourable cycle of events may occur leading to the progressive incrementation of heterosexual habit strength. In our view this is somewhat unlikely. There is evidence, both clinical and from questionnaires (see section II of this chapter), that the relative lack of heterosexual behaviour in secondary homosexuals is associated with a positive fear of sexual contact with females, leading to an avoidance of potential heterosexual contacts. Because of this, treatment should also include desensitization of heterosexual avoidance. It may even be that such desensitization alone would be sufficient, and that no direct attempt to reduce the strength of homosexual approach behaviour would be necessary. A study to test this possibility has recently been completed at the Institute of Psychiatry, London, by Bancroft (personal communication, 1969).* Whatever the result of studies concerning the possibility of using either homosexual or heterosexual stimuli alone in treatment, a conclusion can be drawn concerning the use of heterosexual stimuli, *in addition* to homosexual stimuli; the ability of the patient to control his degree of exposure to heterosexual stimuli (AA) is not a *necessary* element for therapeutic success.

* Desensitization was carried out in the standard manner. The aversion technique involved the administration of an electric shock when the patient displayed a penile volume change to male slides (measured by a plethysmograph) of more than a predetermined amount. This technique is rather different from both AA and CC and is more akin to punishment learning. Very briefly, the result was "very little to choose between them with a slight edge to desensitization" (Bancroft). In more detail: "aversion worked better with those generally less anxious before treatment . . . desensitization better in those with clearly defined heterosexual anxiety and also higher general anxiety." Both AA and CC, as used in this book, could be construed as *combining* aversion to homosexual stimuli with reduction of anxiety to heterosexual stimuli—through association with "anxiety relief". Bancroft did not include in his experimental design a third group treated by *both* aversion and desensitization. Moreover, Bancroft himself assessed the patients before and after treatment and served as the therapist for both treatments.

Before concluding that the relatively complicated apparatus which is needed for AA can be abandoned, and that the simpler CC technique is all that is required, we must consider certain arguments in favour of the use of AA. These are twofold. Firstly, avoidance response latencies provide a constant flow of information on the rate of response to treatment; secondly, in the trial described in Chapter 5, AA was not used in the most flexible manner possible. (By comparison, it is difficult to see how CC could have been used more efficiently.) Evidence was given in Chapter 6 for the predictive usefulness of response latency data for the outcome of treatment. Such data were not used in the trial to match the slide in use with the point reached in treatment because of the necessity for a rigorous similarity between patients and treatments. The AA technique provides the therapist with constant information on the degree of attraction that the patient feels for each successive slide, so that the therapist knows when to change the slide, to alter the order of the slide, to increase shock strength, etc. All this information potentially increases the *efficiency* of treatment. For instance, it may be that the degree of attitude change obtained after 24 sessions of treatment could have been reached by 20 sessions or less, enabling treatment to cease at the earlier point; little feedback other than SOM scores is available to the therapist using CC, and the too frequent use of this measure might lead only to stereotyped and hence less reliable responses. The increased efficiency of treatment in AA, because of the constant feedback of information, enables the saving of both patient time (and hence the time away from work) and therapist time (and hence a greater number of patients treatable in any given unit of time).

From the data reported in Chapter 6, AA seemed to lead to a greater level of autonomic activity than CC (as evidenced by the heart-rate measures) with a higher level of heart rate being associated with successful response. It is difficult to relate this to the finding (reported in Chapter 7) that high levels of questionnaire-measured anxiety seemed to reduce response to AA but not to CC, indicating a possible restriction on the use of AA. However, questionnaire-measured anxiety (a self-report based on introspection) may not be the same as physiologically measured reactivity (heart rate as an indicant of "anxiety") because of individual differences in the self-perception of autonomic reactivity (Mandler and Kremen, 1958). Leaving aside such individual differences in self-perception of autonomic functioning, the level of physiological reactivity is probably dependent on the level of shock used as well as the precise "mix" of the learning variables (delayed or immediate reinforcement, length of delay, etc.). It should be possible, again because of the potential flexibility of the AA technique, deliberately to produce the optimal level of anxiety for rapid avoidance learning. It is less easy to do so in the CC situation, although it would be possible systematically to vary the length of exposure to the homosexual slide before shock onset (the expectation would be that the longer the delay, up to an optimal length of delay, the greater the anxiety). However, the fact that shock is used on every trial in CC makes the monitoring of autonomic measures very difficult. The vital information for the systematic matching to individual patients of learning variables such as length of exposure to homosexual slide prior to shock onset is, therefore, not available.

There is clear evidence from the trial that the provision for the patient of operant response manipulanda was not a necessary requirement for therapeutic *success*. However, we conclude by arguing that the additional information provided by operant responses, together with the more ready manipulation of anxiety (as indicated by autonomic measures) are strong arguments for preferring AA to CC, as both sources of information are likely to increase the *efficiency* if not the *efficacy* of treatment.

Recently, the treatment has been completed by Mrs. Valerie Mellor of an unselected series of 30 homosexual patients in the same hospital in which we carried out our work, using the same apparatus (Mellor, personal communication, 1969). She used AA flexibly, continually matching the slide to the patient's operant behaviour, and the first reports are most satisfactory.

An additional argument for preferring AA to CC concerns the use of electrical aversive stimulation. CC demands the use of shock on every trial; AA does not, and on ethical grounds it is desirable that the therapist uses the minimum shock necessary for successful outcome.

Finally, it may be desirable to use neither AA nor CC exclusively, but a combination of both. Banks *et al.* (1966) reported that a discriminated instrumental avoidance response was established only in those of their animal (monkey) subjects who manifested a discriminated cardiac response prior to the acquisition of the motor response. The detailed results were not entirely consistent with a two-process theory of learning, e.g. (Solomon and Wynne, 1954) in which the associative conditioning of emotional responses is assumed to precede and provide the motivation for the learning of instrumental avoidance responses. However, the Banks *et al.* study provides sufficient support for the following suggestion. It may be that the most efficient treatment procedure would be for the first few trials with each successive homosexual slide to consist of CC in order rapidly to establish the conditioned anxiety response to the slide, and then to manipulate and strengthen this by a longer series of AA trials (reinforced and delayed, randomly interspersed). The sequence of CC trials followed by AA trials would be repeated for each homosexual slide in a hierarchy in turn. The decision when to proceed to the next slide would be based on avoidance response latencies and physiological data, monitored during AA trials.

On a more fundamental level, the elegant and crucial experiments (with rats) of Neale Miller and his colleagues (e.g. Miller, 1969) have provided powerful evidence that instrumental learning can produce changes in many autonomic variables (once thought modifiable solely by CC techniques, and then only to a limited and uncertain degree). Such changes cannot be accounted for in "classical" terms, having been shown to be relatively long lasting (up to at least 3 months), and to be produced most effectively by the gradual shaping of relatively small changes of, for example, heart rate, the final level being very different from the initial one. Shapiro *et al.* (1969) has shown that changes in blood-pressure level may be produced instrumentally in human subjects. It is particularly interesting that Shapiro's subjects were rewarded for blood-pressure changes by slides showing *Playboy* nudes! Miller's work suggests, firstly, the artificiality of the traditional distinction between classical and instrumental learning, and, secondly, the great range of visceral responses modifiable by instrumental techniques. The implications for the therapy, not only of sexual deviations but of a very wide range of problems, are enormous.

E. AVOIDANCE LEARNING VERSUS PSYCHOTHERAPY

The final major conclusion from the trial was that while the two learning techniques did not differ from each other in effectiveness, both were superior to psychotherapy. It might be argued by proponents of psychotherapy that neither the time allowed for psychotherapy nor the psychotherapist himself (M.J.M.) were optimal. In answer to the first argument we would point out the importance of making maximum use of both the time and of the skilled personnel available for treatment. In the present state of staffing in the National Health

Service, 12 hours is probably *more* psychotherapy than is received by the majority of homo-sexual patients treated by this method. It seems mandatory, both on economic and on ethical grounds, to use a treatment which will enable the greatest number of patients to be treated successfully in any given unit of time. Even assuming equal success for psychotherapy in an equal unit of time (and this assumption does not hold in practice), a further economic argument becomes relevant. Learning techniques may be automated so that they require little more than general supervision by a junior psychologist or even by a suitably trained nurse. We have given a description elsewhere of such an automated apparatus (MacCulloch *et al.*, 1970a) which recently has been developed. By contrast, psychotherapy requires the skilled and *relatively* costly time of an experienced psychiatrist (and hence one of at least senior registrar grade). This leads us to the second possible criticism made by the proponents of psychotherapy, namely the possible lack of expertise of M.J.M. The most relevant answer to this is that if M.J.M. was insufficiently expert in psychotherapy, despite holding an appointment as a consultant psychiatrist, then this would be equally true of the vast majority of National Health Service psychiatrists. Hence, the level of success achieved in the trial by psychotherapy would potentially have been exceeded only by a handful of trained psychoanalysts, all located in London, and all of whom would insist on a period of treatment well in excess of 12 hours. It will be recalled that the psychoanalytically treated patients described in Chapter 1 received treatment lasting in most cases more than 150 hours (see Bieber *et al.*, 1963, who achieved the highest rate of success, 27%, in any reported psycho-analytical series). Our conclusion is that psychotherapy/psychoanalysis, even under optimal conditions, is both less effective than avoidance learning techniques and immensely more time consuming. The latter fact effectively restricts the number of patients to whom psycho-therapy can be offered, even apart from the scarcity of "qualified" personnel.

A final argument of relevance to the avoidance learning–psychotherapy discussion is the ethical undesirability of treatment which involves inflicting on patients electric shocks—albeit from low-voltage batteries. Two points may be made in reply. Firstly, the patients are the best judges as to what is more bearable—the considerable distress which many feel as a consequence of their homosexual orientation or a relatively short period of weeks during which they are in receipt of a number of electrical shocks over a total of about 12 hours. The fact that 63 patients completed their course of treatment as opposed to only 7 who did not, is perhaps the best evidence for this first point. Legal pressure cannot be adduced as a reason for continuing treatment—the majority of the 7 series patients who *failed* to complete treatment presented in connection with a court appearance. The second point arises from the therapist's ability to predict the probability of success—an ability vastly enhanced by the research reported in this book. Certainly, there is no point in bombarding with shocks a patient who has a poor prognosis. If the data in section I.C of this chapter are (when repli-cated) systematically applied, there would be no need to do so. Nor is there any need for the level of shock to exceed the bare minimum required for avoidance; not only is this distaste-ful on ethical grounds, it is also counter-productive, as witness the high patient drop-out rate reported by Schmidt *et al.*, 1965 (see Chapter 1).

Future research may even demonstrate that desensitization to anxiety-evoking hetero-sexual stimuli is more important than the evocation of anxiety to homosexual stimuli. Pending such research, the present evidence concerning treatment efficacy is such that we feel the retention of avoidance techniques to be well justified for the present.

It has been reported previously (Feldman, 1966) and is worth repeating here, that none of our patients treated by avoidance learning have received treatment in addition to avoidance learning other than adjuvant drug therapy and supportive psychotherapy of a superficial kind. No patient received drug therapy as the sole or even major portion of his treatment. No patient, with the exception of the psychotherapy group in the trial, received psychotherapy as the sole or even major portion of his treatment. Nevertheless, it would be quite incorrect to deny that a relationship developed between the patient and the aversion therapist, even in the rigidly controlled regime of the trial. Patients receiving either AA or CC were not encouraged to discuss their problems with J.F.O. (As far as possible he actively *dis*couraged this.) However, it would have been quite unreal for him to maintain a stony silence, so that a little conversation did take place, although this was kept as neutral as possible. A somewhat more liberal attitude was possible in the AA treatment of patients in the series, and matters raised by patients during treatment were briefly discussed, though neither at length nor in the sense of exploration or explanation. Perhaps more important is the fact that towards the end of the treatment of the patients in the series, and during the follow-up interviews of both series and trial patients, their verbal reports of progress were solicited. These reports were never taken at face value, but were carefully probed. If the patient's reports of success survived our attempts to disprove them (made with particular force if there was a discrepancy between a verbal statement of progress and an SOM score indicating lack of progress), then *he was reinforced with praise and encouragement* to further efforts. We cannot agree with Wolpe (1962) that in behaviour therapy the relationship between therapist and patient is totally irrelevant. As Wilson *et al.* (1968) have pointed out, "behaviour therapy, derived as it is from behaviour-theory principles, offers potentially fruitful leads to attaining a clearer understanding of the critical variables involved. The relationship, operationally defined in social reinforcement terms and conceived of as an integral aspect of more basic social behaviour–influence methods, is systematically used to achieve well defined pre-determined therapeutic goals." It seems likely that the increasing sophistication of attitude change techniques (Goldstein *et al.*, 1966) will increasingly operate to reduce the present gap between psychotherapy and behaviour therapy.

F. HETEROSEXUAL SOCIAL BEHAVIOUR AND THE SOCIAL SETTING

We have concentrated on homosexual object choice and overt homosexual behaviour as the problems to be modified by treatment, and the success of treatment has been judged in terms of significant changes in these two areas of functioning. In doing so, we have followed the practice of therapists as widely divergent in theoretical allegiance as Freund (1960), who used chemical aversion, and Bieber *et al.* (1963), who used psychoanalysis. A major current trend in sexological research is that exemplified by Masters and Johnson (1966) who concentrated entirely on anatomically and physiologically defined aspects of sexual behaviour. However, we have become increasingly aware of the great importance of the social preliminaries of sexual behaviour (Feldman, 1968). Patients frequently asked for advice on verbal and non-verbal social skill techniques in the heterosexual situation. In effect, they were attempting to telescope into a few weeks, or months, the process of heterosexual social skills learning which probably takes many years normally, through adolescence and early adulthood. In the absence of systematic data on human heterosexual social behaviour, which could have been used to design a training programme to carry on from the aversion therapy proper, we were able to supply only very general elementary and unsystematic advice together with praise for successful progress, as mentioned above. In addition to the value for treatment purposes of such a body of knowledge, systematic data on heterosexual social skills would have been useful in designing measures of therapeutic success to supplement verbal report, SOM scores, etc.* Future research on the therapy of sexual deviations would derive great benefit from a close aquaintance with future developments in research in social skills and non-verbal communication (see Argyle and Kendon, 1965, and Sebeok and Hayes, 1964, for the current state of knowledge). Errors in the social preliminaries of sexual encounters are likely both to reduce the probability of a successful encounter, and to restore the anxiety concerning heterosexual behaviour which treatment has attempted to reduce.

There is a further aspect of the social context of the patient which is of relevance to the successful outcome of treatment. We noticed this particularly clearly in a small series of patients showing sexual deviations other than homosexuality, such as transvestism and fetishism (Feldman *et al.*, 1968). It seemed that therapeutic success was related not only to the use of a sound treatment technique and to personality factors, but also to the social setting of the patient. This last point is exemplified by 2 transvestite patients, both married, one of whom was an undoubted success despite a rather unfavourable personality structure, the other a partial success at best, despite an apparently more promising personality. The successful patient's wife was most supportive, and was a willing partner both socially and sexually. The wife of the partially successful patient was supportive in neither area of his functioning. It is likely that some of the success we have obtained has been aided by the availability to patients whose attitudes and desires have changed of the means of putting into practice their newly restored heterosexual desires. The most readily accessible and probably supportive sexual partners have been wives, fiancées, or existing girl friends. The post-treatment period is much more difficult for those patients who have not been participating in such relationships before treatment started. (Even for those who have, the relationship pre-treatment has been much less than satisfactory—by definition, otherwise treatment would not have been sought.) The post-treatment social task has been more difficult for the older (over 40) unmarried patients than for those still in their 20's or early 30's, both because of the greater lapse of time since their adolescent and early adult heterosexual experiences, and the relatively lesser availability of female partners. Post-treatment relapse may be due to factors other than the simple failure to resist extinction of responses acquired in treatment, and in assessing the probability of a successful response, the total social setting of the patient should be taken into account as well as the personality and heterosexual sexual interest factors emphasized earlier in this section. We suggest that future therapists devote more attention to social context factors than we have. It is hoped that they will be aided in doing so by future advances in research into heterosexual social behaviour.

II. PREDISPOSITION, INCUBATION, AND COGNITIVE DISSONANCE

A. FACTORS PREDISPOSING TO HOMOSEXUAL BEHAVIOUR†

1. *Genetic Influences*

Ideally, in order to separate out genetic from environmental influences on the developing phenotype, the requirement is for studies of animals under controlled environments and

---

*We are indebted for this suggestion, to one of our Birmingham postgraduate students, Mr. M. J. Dickerson.

†The discussion of "predisposing factors" which follows is far from exhaustive; it serves only to indicate some of the current major lines of research.

prescribed mating, using the refined techniques of analysis developed by Jinks, Broadhurst, and their colleagues, e.g. Jinks and Fulker (1970). No such studies have been carried out in the field of sexual object choice in animals, let alone in man. Clinical evidence has been largely contributed by Kallman (1952), who studied 40 monozygotic twin pairs and 40 dizygotic twin pairs, where one member of each pair was known to be homosexual. A very significantly higher rate of concordance for sexual choice was found in the monozygotic than in the dizygotic twins. However, Kallman's conclusion was far from exclusively genetic in emphasis. "On the whole adaptational equilibrium between the potentialities of organic sex differentiation and consequent patterns of psycho-sexual behaviour, seems to be so labile that the attainment of the maturational balance may be disarranged at different developmental stages by a variety of disturbing mechanisms".

MacCulloch *et al.* (1970b) have reviewed several papers, all citing instances of non-concordance for sexual orientation in undoubtedly monozygotic twin pairs, and also describe, in detail, the failure to respond to AA treatment of a highly motivated monozygotic twin whose co-twin was totally heterosexual (see Appendix A, trial patient no. 17). The difficulty in accounting for the total discordance between trial patient no. 17 and his co-twin, raised the logical possibility of other explanations than that of genetic predisposition to a specific direction of sexual orientation.

2. *Foetal Prenatal Circulating Steroids*

Many authors have sought to prove hormonal deviation in homosexuals, e.g. Appel (1937), Bauer (1940), Foss (1951), Glass *et al.* (1940), and Kinsey (1941). This work is inconclusive in the human adult. However, a large number of studies are now available on the effects of the varying amounts and kinds of gonadal hormones present in the newborn lower mammal. Early work concerned itself with the transplantation of gonads. More recent work has involved either prenatal or post-natal injections of hormones. The effects of the former have been reviewed by Young *et al.* (1964). Pfeiffer (1936) transplanted the gonads of newborn male rats to litter-mate females and vice versa. He concluded that all rats are physiologically female at birth but are capable of differentiation into males if testes are present. Levine and Mullins (1964), Whalen and Nadler (1963), Harris and Levine (1965), and Whalen (1969) showed that injection of oestrogen into intact newborn male rats did disturb male reproductive function in contrast to the findings of Pfeiffer (1936), whose transplantation of ovaries into the newborn intact male produced no observable effect. It may well be that transplanted ovaries do not produce significant levels of oestrogen in the transplantee. Later work by Wilson *et al.* (1940) produced a loss of spontaneous mating behaviour in female rats who had been post-natally injected with testosterone 3 times per week from day 1 after birth to 4 weeks. There was also acyclicity, sterility, and a lack of behavioural response to exogenous oestrogen in the mature animal. These data have been confirmed by the reports of Harris and Levine (1965), Barraclough (1961), and Segal and Johnson (1959), whose work indicates that post-natal administration of androgen during critical periods markedly and irreversibly affects subsequent reproductive behavioural functions. Injections when the rat is more than a week old were ineffective. Male rats, given oestrogen in infancy, showed such marked defects in sexual behaviour as excessive aberrant mounting, rarely achieved intromission, and failure to ejaculate.

Castration of the newborn male rat also markedly affects sexual behaviour. Adult males castrated in early infancy exhibited complete female sexual behaviour if they were given injections of oestrogen and progesterone. By contrast, males castrated in adulthood showed no such behaviour after these procedures. It has been suggested (Young *et al.*, 1964; Harris and Levine, 1965), that gonadal hormones exert a dual influence on the central nervous system, organizational during development, and excitatory or activational in the adult. Their studies showed that the presence of either androgen or oestrogen in the newborn rat causes the sexually undifferentiated brain to be organized so that the acyclic male pattern of hormone release occurs in the adult. In the absence of gonadal hormones, the basic female (cyclic) hormone-release pattern becomes established, and these patterns of hormone release are part of a "hormonostat", whereby the concentration of sex steroids circulating acts as a "feedback" to influence the central nervous system which, in turn, controls the rate of steroid production, or release, or both. It has been shown that the aberrant neuro-endocrine function and behaviour in the adult given hormones in infancy is not due to a hormone deficit present in adulthood. It seems likely that these procedures alter the sensitivity of the controlling brain mechanisms, and it can be seen that experimental procedures must be carried out during a certain period of the animal's development.

In work on monkeys, Young *et al.* (1964) produced female pseudo-hermaphrodites by injecting testosterone into the mother during pregnancy, and they later showed that the behaviour of the pseudo-hermaphrodite offspring became much more similar in type to that of a normal male monkey and clearly different from that of a female control. The concept of specifically susceptible areas in the developing brain in relation to circulating sex hormones is further supported by the work reported by Pfaff (1965) on the uptake of radioactive C^{14} diethyl stilboestrol di-butyrate by the cells in the dentate gyrus in rats (Altman and Dass, 1964).

Work by Fisher (1956) showed that, using an implantation technique, it was possible to produce exaggerated male mating response in rats by introducing testosterone into the lateral pre-optic areas in the brain. That sexual behaviour is controlled by specific *loci* in the brain has been shown by Maclean and Ploog (1962) who have carried out extensive studies on the cerebral representation of penile erection in the squirrel monkey. These authors have been able to map out areas in the limbic system and its projection pathways to the thalamus, hypothalamus, and the papez circuits, which, when stimulated, produced penile erection. Similar work on the cerebral representation of genital display centres has been described by Maurus (1964). It is clear that adult sexual behaviour and sex associated behaviour in mammals depend on a neurophysiological substrate, and it may be that some neuronal circuits are composed of cells which have a specific affinity for sex hormones. These loci may well turn out to be the centres which govern sexual behaviour, possibly under the influence of feedback hormones or stimulation from higher centres.

A good deal of the animal literature has been summarized by Neumann and Elgar (1966), who have adduced convincing evidence to back up their statement that the target organ in relation to circulating sex steroids is not the pituitary but the hypothalamus. They have shown that anti-androgenically active steroid effectively inhibits the differentiation of the pituitary diencephalic system only during a critical phase of receptivity in the rat. Further, they have also shown that feminized genotypically male rats will show female phenotypic sexual behaviour. Whilst it is incumbent upon us to be extremely cautious in our extrapolation of data obtained on lower mammals to supposed function in man, nevertheless, when the dichotomy between primary and secondary homosexuals that we have described is considered, the implications are clear. It seems entirely possible that there are "male and female" areas in the human foetal brain which are critically susceptible to circulating levels of male and female hormones. It may well be that the levels of circulating sex steroids in the unborn foetus are influenced by placental activity, and it is even possible that the circulations of 2 monozygotic twins are affected differentially in this respect.

If the human foetal brain is preconditioned by circulating sex steroids, then one possible mechanism for the development of primary homosexuality is available; the argument for this is outlined in Section III of this chapter.

3. *Sex-typed Behaviour: Peer and Parental Reinforcement; Modelling and Vicarious Reinforcement*

Money and Hampson (1957) have provided impressive evidence of the powerful reinforcing effects of parental responses on the sex-typed behaviours of the developing infant. Sex-typed behaviours can be defined as behaviours which typically elicit different rewards for one sex than for the other. Money and his colleagues studied children whose originally assigned gender was either incorrect or ambiguous. They concluded that gender role was entirely the result of a learning process which was independent of chromosomes or hormonally determined sex; that is, the gender role adopted was that which had been assigned by the parents and consistently reinforced. The critical period for the establishment of gender role was 18 months to 3 years. It is tempting to link up the several aspects of trial patient no. 17 which are puzzling: preference for female companions in early childhood, his lack of aggression, and the occurrence of homosexual behaviour as his initial and sole sexual outlet—all as resulting from consistent and early parental reinforcement for sex-typed behaviours appropriate to the female rather than the male child. However, the previously discussed predisposing factor of differences in pre-natal circulating steroids between him and his co-twin might equally or entirely be implicated, and only speculation is possible on the basis of retrospective histories.

There is ample evidence for the importance of modelling and vicarious (i.e. self-provided) reinforcement in the acquisition of behaviour in social situations (Bandura and Walters, 1963). The model may be either the parents of either sex, or another child, who may be a sibling of either sex, or simply a friend. The extent to which the model is imitated depends on many factors, such as observed similarity between model and imitator, the receipt of reinforcement for imitation, the occurrence of vicarious self-reinforcement, and the appropriateness of such reinforcement to the needs of the imitator. In the quite separate field of juvenile delinquency the acquisition of anti-social attitudes through physical contiguity with the members of the criminal subculture forms the basis of the influential association theory of crime (Sutherland, 1955). Membership of a single-sex subculture such as a boarding school, the norm in which was homosexual behaviour, would provide a similarly powerful environment for the acquisition of homosexual behaviour. Unfortunately, there is very little evidence for or against the hypothesized increase in homosexual behaviour in such single-sex environments. Schofield (1965a), as a minor aspect of his excellent survey of the heterosexual behaviour of adolescents, asked his subjects questions concerning their homosexual experiences. A very much higher proportion of those educated in single-sex boarding schools reported such experiences than did those educated at day schools, either co-educational or single sex. However, Schofield did not question his subjects concerning their *present* preferred orientation, and, in any event, the sample went up to the age of 19 years only, so that the persistence of the effect of school experiences is unknown. West (1968) has cited anecdotal evidence of the acquisition of homosexual behaviour by previously heterosexual males incarcerated in prisons or prisoner of war camps. He suggests that the post-confinement persistence of such homosexual behaviour is dependent on whether it afforded a sexual outlet only, or was also associated with emotional gratification.

4. Specific Learning Experiences, Both Positive and Negative

It has been strongly argued by McGuire et al. (1965) that the nature of the first sexual experience, followed by orgasm, is crucial for the establishment of the direction of sexual orientation, and they cite several case studies in support of this theory. It is particularly relevant to our emphasis on the importance of incubation of behavioural experiences (see later in this section), that McGuire et al. also emphasized that the deviant behaviour is maintained by the phantasy of the behaviour becoming a cue for sexual response (such as masturbation). Further anecotdal evidence in support of this approach is provided by a striking case report by Gebhard (1965). It may be that learning involving only a single trial, or a few trials, does occur in at least some individuals, and it may further be that such brief learning is the more likely to be crucial in determining the direction of sexual orientation if it occurs at a particular, and hence critical, stage of development. The stage at which secondary sexual characteristics are developed would be an obvious candidate for such a critical period.

The data of Kinsey et al. (1947) seemed to suggest that the onset of sexual behaviour, of any nature, occurred earlier in their homosexual than in their heterosexual subjects, and it is plausible that the younger the subject the more likely he would be to associate with peers of his own rather than the opposite sex. Hence, children who attain puberty earlier than the average may be considered more "at risk" than those attaining puberty at an age when cross-sex social mixing has already begun. Those educated at single-sex boarding schools until well past the age by which all adolescents have attained puberty would all be "at risk" as compared with day-school attenders. As the evidence is anecdotal at the present time, it is particularly appropriate to include the possibility of the crucial importance of the initial or early sexual learning trial being homosexual in nature under the heading of "speculations".

The above has been concerned with positive reward conditioning to homosexual stimuli as a major explanation of homosexual orientation. Another possibility is the occurrence of unpleasant heterosexual experiences which have led to heterosexual avoidance, and by implication, homosexual approach being more acceptable.

In Chapter 1, the psychoanalytical emphasis on this point was mentioned, together with the explicit therapeutic attempts of some psychoanalysts, notably Ovesey et al. (1963), to increase the attempts of their patients to approach females. Similarly, Stevenson and Wolpe (1960) stressed the desensitization of heterosexual avoidance in their patients treated by reciprocal inhibition. Bieber et al. (1963) concluded that heterosexual fear was one of the main elements in homosexuality. A questionnaire study of homosexual and heterosexual attitudes in homosexual and heterosexual males was reported by Ramsey and Van Velzen (1968). They found highly significant differences between the groups, with homosexuals reporting more dislike of intimate heterosexual situations. No data were reported by Ramsey and Van Velzen on the occurrence of unpleasant heterosexual experiences which might provide the basis for adult heterosexual avoidance behaviour.

B. A THEORY OF INCUBATION OF BEHAVIOURAL EXPERIENCES THROUGH COGNITIVE REHEARSAL

As well as presenting this theory in brief outline, as it might operate in general, we shall also discuss possible individual differences in the incubation of behavioural experiences.

Eysenck (1968) has presented a theory of incubation of anxiety/fear responses which restricts the concept of incubation to "an increment in CR (conditioned response) over a period of time when the CS (conditioned stimulus) is applied once or a number of times, but without reinforcement". (It is tempting to construe the behaviour of the volunteer students (see Appendix B) as suggestive evidence in human subjects of this "Napalkov" phenomenon (Eysenck, 1967).) By defining the term "incubation" in this way, Eysenck indicates that he is not talking about it in connection with the consolidation of the memory trace over relatively short periods of several hours by the transference of the memory trace from short- into long-term storage forms. By contrast, the studies discussed by Eysenck concern increments in CR "over weeks or even years". Eysenck's basic notion is that while the presentation of a CS unaccompanied by a UCS always provokes a decrement in CR strength, it also provokes an increment in CR strength. "The observed CR is the resultant of two opposing tendencies; extinction will be observed if the decrementing tendencies are greater than the incrementing ones, while *incubation* will be observed if the incrementing tendencies are greater than the decrementing ones."

Through its association with the UCS such as shock, CS, the reinforced stimulus has come to signal pain—termed by Eysenck the nocive response. Next, through the intermediacy of the UCS, the CS has become associated with the NRs (nocive responses) and signals their arrival to the organism. The crucial point is that "CS, though unaccompanied by UCS or UCR is accompanied by CR. . . . A partial NR. Its presence would theoretically lead to a strengthening of the CR/NR bond . . . and hence some form of incubation." Eysenck suggests that "conditioning sets in motion a positive feedback cycle in which the CR provides reinforcement for the presentation of a CS unaccompanied by a UCS". Further, Eysenck states: "it is not the CR itself which acts as a reinforcer, but rather the response produced stimuli; not the autonomic, hormonal and muscular reaction of cells, but rather the experience of fear/anxiety based on them". Fear so generated is itself a painful event, and the stimuli associated with it by CC come to evoke more fear, thus producing a positive feedback. Eysenck does not specify the "certain circumstances under which the extinction process may be weaker than CS/NR reinforcement process and observable incubation will result", except to give as an example the instances in which the UCS is exceptionally strong. This is possibly because he remains rigorously within the confines of Hullian learning theory, which restricts itself to events occurring *during training*, and not to the possibly much more important events *following* training (i.e. the 23 hours of each 24 when the patient is not in contact with the therapist in the treatment situation). However, Eysenck shows his awareness of possible mechanisms which might mediate between training and real life, e.g. "the theory . . . is probably deficient in not taking explicitly into account Pavlov's 'second signalling system'."

Eysenck makes the point even clearer by referring to the work of Schachter and his colleagues, e.g. Schachter and Singer (1962), in emphasizing the importance of cognitive factors in the interpretation of emotionally arousing situations. He also mentions the reports, such as that of Lang and Lazowick (1963), which have described long-delayed cognitive and autonomic effects of desensitization therapy, as well as the immediate behavioural effects. Eysenck opens a bridge between his classical Hullian account and more recent cognitive approaches as follows: "NRs are strictly speaking response produced stimuli; cognitive type theories are based on the stimulus properties of these responses". A further brief excursion by Eysenck into a cognitive approach speculates on the possibility of incubation phenomenon in appetitive conditioning. This is as far as he goes, and the rest of the paper is a series of brief and incompletely worked-out examples of several applications of his theory of incubation to the genesis and treatment of neurotic disorders.

We propose to develop a theory of incubation which involves both the CC approach of Eysenck as well as cognitive elements. The former type of approach uses data gathered from animal experiments, the latter from human subjects. Hence they are not really in opposition, rather in juxtaposition. The elements of the learning situation: UCS, CS, CR, etc., are present in both the laboratory training of animals and the therapy of humans. Where humans differ crucially is in the use of language as an internal signalling system, so that the verbal and visual representations of situations are "carried away" by the subject from the situation to serve as the essential elements of the feedback cycle to which Eysenck refers. Such extra-training cognitive rehearsal through verbal, visual, or other sensory symbols, may or may not occur in animals; everyday observation suggest that it most certainly does occur in human beings. Hence, any theory of incubation in humans must include not only the nature and intensity of the stimuli and responses in the learning situation *per se*, but also the possibilities for cognitive rehearsal *between* learning trials, perhaps at a considerable physical distance from the learning situation. Such an approach vastly increases the power of an incubation type of theory. In speculating on the circumstances in which incubation may be stronger than extinction, Eysenck mentions only one, namely the occurrence of an exceptionally strong UCS. Including the role of cognitive rehearsal *following* learning allows other possibilities such as an encounter with stimuli which lie on the gradient of generalization from the laboratory CS, e.g. males, visually encountered in the street, who are similar to those appearing on the slides used in treatment, chance remarks by workmates, etc. Perhaps most important are learned or unlearned *habits* of rumination over the events of the day and the re-creation of the emotional associations experienced in the learning situation. This enables the elaboration of the complex of attitudes, verbal labels, and associated emotions, set in train by the recollection of the learning situation. We suggest that such cognitive rehearsal serves as a powerful source of learning, *unprogrammed* and *uncontrolled* by the experimenter or therapist. Moreover, cognitive rehearsal is unlikely to occur to the same degree in all persons, even following exposure to identical learning situations. Individual differences in cognitive rehearsal habits are likely to occur (it is surprising that Eysenck made no reference to such a possibility), and the proposal of such individual differences is a major element of our approach to incubation. A further major element is to emphasize the importance of incubation both for approach *and* avoidance learning. Where positive, appetitively satisfying consequences have followed the occurrence of stimulus–response sequences in training, the cognitive rehearsal of the sequence of events will increase the probability of the response being evoked the next time the stimulus is encountered in training. Moreover, and even more important, the "aspiration level" of the subject may be raised— that is, he may elaborate in thought the pleasant consequences which occurred in training. Indeed, Eysenck (1968) in his paper on incubation makes brief reference to Mowrer's concept of "hope" (1956) in the context of appetitive conditioning.

Cognitive rehearsal will be important also for avoidance learning, although at first sight it might appear that the cognitive evocation of a fear-producing CR, not followed by a painful consequence in reality, would lead to extinction. It might indeed do so, perhaps partly as a function of the intensity of the reality encountered UCS, e.g. (shock), and partly as a function of individual differences in the intensity of autonomic responses to the cognitively occurring stimuli. Relatively low levels of UCS and a relatively low tendency for frequent and intense recall would both favour extinction through cognitive rehearsal. Relatively high levels would favour incubation. The importance of such individual differences in rehearsal habits will be enlarged in more detail later. A further source of incubation of the habit of avoidance, following avoidance training, is the provision in training of an alternative to the punished response. For example, in the AA technique the patient may request a female slide; this postpones the anxiety-evoking male slide. The cognitive re-creation of this cycle of events will strengthen *both* avoidance and approach responses as follows: the random appearance in consciousness of an attractive male stimulus will evoke the anxiety conditioned in training; the lack of punishment during cognitive rehearsal might normally extinguish this anxiety; however, in addition, the provision in training of the alternative response of female approach enables the avoidance of anxiety imagery with the associated relief of unpleasantness learned in training, and possibly also the occurrence of gratifying sensations. Hence both male avoidance and female approach will be strengthened.

In proposing a set of postulates to describe how increments occur in the habit strength of behavioural responses in the interval between exposure to externally occurring stimuli and the re-exposure to such stimuli, we will make use of the concept of a "model" as the internal representation of external events. This is similar to Bartlett's (1932) conception of "schemata" and to Hebb's "conceptual nervous system" (1955). The "model" has an electrochemical basis, as have all "mental" events.

Postulate One

A sequence of stimulus–response and reinforcement, occurring in laboratory or therapy training or other real life situations, is internalized through the process of attaching a verbal visual "label" or "engram". This is what we mean by a "model". The response originally evoked may have both motor and autonomic components, and both components will be represented in the neuronal model of the behaviour sequence.

Postulate Two

The internal representation of the responses originally evoked by an external stimulus can be produced as part of the internal model of the original external stimulus. That is, the entire behavioural sequence becomes internalized.

From time to time, and particularly in the period immediately prior to sleep, persons rehearse events of the immediate past, more time being devoted to those events of greater significance for the life of the individual. Sexual behaviour is an obvious example of such significant events.

Postulate Three

There are three aspects of the internalized sequence in which individuals differ. Firstly, the ability of the subject to convert the external behavioural sequence into an internal model, i.e. the ability to label both the motor and the autonomic components of a response. Secondly, the degree to which some internal system amplifies the external stimulus, so that one individual may "augment" and another may "reduce" stimuli of equal intensity (see Silverman, 1968, for a similar concept in relation to neutral, content-free stimuli; our present discussion relates to stimuli with emotional, pleasant–unpleasant connotations). Finally, the frequency of cognitive rehearsal of the internal models of behavioural sequences.

The first variable is reminiscent of Schachter's explanation of psychopathy as an inability to label internal autonomic reactions (Schachter and Lattané, 1964). The second and third are rather more relevant to our present purpose. They concern the difference between individuals in the increment of habit strength accruing to a response through cognitive rehearsal, indexed as an increase in the intensity or speed of the response on the next exposure of the person to the external stimulus. Persons may be high "incubators" either because of a relatively high augmentation of external stimuli or because of the frequency of cognitive rehearsal, or both. Tentatively, we would identify such individuals with Schneider's (1959) "sensitives" or Eysenck's "neurotic introverts". It might be that individuals differ not only in the degree to which they label, augment, and rehearse their behaviour sequences, but also according to whether these are pleasant or unpleasant. Sensitives or neurotic introverts might "incubate" the latter, but not the former, and at this point reference may be made to Byrne's concept of repression–sensitization (RS; Byrne, 1964). This refers to the habitual use of repressing or sensitizing defences against anxiety, repressors dealing with anxiety by denial and sensitisors by heightening. An interesting study by Merbaum and Kazaoka (1967) found that questionnaire-defined sensitisors reported negative emotions more frequently than repressors, but positive emotions less frequently. It was further shown that these differences extended also to the subject's awareness of his own overtly expressed emotions. Correlational studies, reported by Byrne (1964), suggest that the R end of the RS dimension is identifiable with high extroversion and high neuroticism (EN) and the S end with eN, supporting our hypothesis of *differential* incubation according to the nature of the experience, i.e. anxiety neurotics (sensitives) incubate and recall unpleasant events more than pleasant, hysterics (attention-seeking personalities), pleasant ones more than unpleasant ones. Further support for the identifiability of our hypothesized high incubators with those clinically describable as anxious is provided by a study by Desiderato and Wasserman (1967). They trained subjects verbally to label a visual stimulus and then tested them, either immediately or after a delay, for generalization of the verbal response. Half the subjects within each period of delay received their initial training under aversive conditions—an intensive white noise—and the other half under non-aversive conditions. Each subgroup was further subdivided into high and low anxious (A) subjects—as measured by extreme scores on a forced choice version of the manifest anxiety scale (Taylor, 1953). Gradients of higher elevation, indicating greater generalization, were produced both by aversive training and by the high A subjects; if the latter were tested *after a delay*, more generalization was observed. The opposite was found for the low A subjects. A similar study relating the generalization of positive reinforcement both to the Eysenckian dimensions, and to personality classified according to Schneider's scheme, would be most valuable.

Postulate Four

The hypothesized individual differences vary randomly throughout the population and are largely, or entirely, genetically determined. Hence, identical twins would be expected to "incubate" to the same degree and would therefore show a high inter-correlation for a variety of behavioural measures in the increase in response following a period away from the training situation. This would, of course, be testable in an experiment of the Desiderato and Wasserman type. The empirical evidence for this postulate is sparse, as most studies of twins have used psychometric measures of complex variables, such as intelligence, whereas we are concerned with more simple variables, such as approach–avoidance learning. However, suggestive support for Postulate Four is provided by Lader and Wing's review (1966) of inter-twin correlations for autonomic measures. These were significantly higher in identical twins than in non-identical twins; it is highly unlikely that learning has played a part in such similarity, hence, at least the autonomic components of the total response pattern seem likely to be genetically determined.

To repeat our postulates, they may be summed up as follows. Persons differ in the frequency and intensity of the cognitive rehearsal of their behavioural experiences, that is they differ in the extent to which an increment of strength is added by incubation to the habit acquired during training. It is possible for persons displaying disorders of personality that there is a negative correlation between the frequency and intensity of the incubation of pleasant and unpleasant events, with self-insecure (sensitive and anankastic) disorders being low for the former type of event and high for the latter, the opposite being true for attention-seeking disorders. These individual differences are largely genetically determined. Hence "learning" *between* environmental events is at least as important as learning by direct exposure to external stimuli.

C. COGNITIVE DISSONANCE THEORY

The theory of cognitive dissonance, advanced by Festinger (1957), has had a wide influence in experimental social psychology, e.g. Brehm and Cohen (1962). The studies to which it has led have been carried out in laboratory settings and field studies are rare, i.e. studies in which dissonance has occurred as a result of real life experiences rather than by experimental manipulation. As we are concerned with a rather powerful pattern of real life behaviour, occurring over long periods of time, the results of laboratory studies in which relatively mild degrees of dissonance were achieved over the period of the experiment only, are not very relevant, and we shall refer largely to Festinger's original theory as an important source of theoretical ideas. The relevance of these to the problem of the acquisition of homosexual behaviour, the decision to seek treatment, and the response to treatment, will be spelled out in the next section; the purpose of the present section is briefly to outline Festinger's theory, and we shall quote directly from his 1957 text.

Dissonance refers to the existence of *non-fitting relations* between cognitions, where cognition means "any knowledge, opinions or belief about the environment, about oneself or about one's behaviour. Cognitive dissonance can be seen as an antecedent condition which leads to activity oriented towards dissonance reduction, just as hunger leads to activity oriented towards hunger reduction." Festinger's two basic hypotheses are as follows:

"(1) The existence of dissonance, being psychologically uncomfortable, will activate the person to try to reduce the dissonance and achieve consonance. (2) When dissonance is present, in addition to trying to reduce it, the person will actively avoid situations and information which would be likely to increase the dissonance."

Festinger states further. "The reality which impinges on a person will exert pressures in the direction of bringing the appropriate cognitive elements into correspondence with reality."

Another statement of relevance to the theme of this chapter is as follows: "If two elements are dissonant with one another, the magnitude of the dissonance will be a function of the importance of the elements."

Dissonance between relevant elements (i.e. those which have importance and meaning for the life of the person concerned) will lead to pressure to reduce or eliminate that dissonance.

Cognitive and behavioural elements may be highly resistant to change. For instance, the change may be painful or involve loss, the present behaviour may be otherwise satisfying, or making the change may simply not be possible due to the lack of voluntary control both of behaviour, and of the associated emotional reactions. Finally, Festinger discusses the avoidance of an increase in dissonance as a major human motive, which enforces a high degree of selectivity in the seeking of social support and new information. Moreover, the fear of dissonance may lead to a reluctance to commit oneself behaviourally because of the irreversibility of many actions (e.g. certain surgical operations).

Dissonance is argued by Festinger to be the inevitable consequence of a *decision* to embark on a particular course of action which is different from the present behaviour. The magnitude of the post-decision dissonance is dependent on the importance of the decision, the relative attractiveness of the unchosen alternative to the chosen one, and the degree of overlap of cognitive elements corresponding to the alternatives. Once post-decision dissonance exists, the methods of reducing it include *increasing* the relative attractiveness of the chosen alternative, *decreasing* the relative attractiveness of the unchosen alternative, establishing cognitive overlap, or possibly revoking the decision psychologically (e.g. to anticipate the next section, leaving treatment before it is completed). The reader may already have translated dissonance theory, as outlined above, into the present context; a systematic attempt to do so follows, together with the relevance of our theory of incubation. We shall consider in turn the acquisition and maintenance of homosexual behaviour, the motivation for treatment, and the response to treatment, in each case as related to the 2 hypothesized types— primary and secondary homosexuality.

III. PREDISPOSING FACTORS, INCUBATION, AND COGNITIVE DISSONANCE APPLIED TO PRIMARY AND SECONDARY HOMOSEXUALITY

A. ACQUISITION OF HOMOSEXUAL ATTITUDES AND BEHAVIOUR

1. *Primary Homosexuals*

We consider that primary homosexuals differ from secondary homosexuals in that their developing brains have been preconditioned, prior to birth, by an imbalance of sex steroid, derived either from maternal or placental sources (see Section II. A.2 for a full résumé of this topic). It is unlikely that the sex steroids affecting the brain of the developing foetus are either in perfect balance, leading to a sexually normal person, or in total imbalance, inevitably leading to primary homosexuality. A continuous variation in the degree of balance of prenatal sex steroids seems more likely, so that the probability of the infant developing post-natally a total pattern of behaviours, inappropriate to the morphological sex, increases the greater the degree of imbalance. We mean by the total behaviour pattern a constellation (e.g. in the morphologically male child) of low aggression, interpersonal deference, preference for female children as friends and for "feminine" toys, the converse pattern being regarded as inappropriate for morphologically female children. Once again we consider such behaviour patterns as not being all or none, but as lying on a continuum, from what may be termed for convenience as "highly masculine" to "highly feminine". The extent to which pre-natal hormonal influences are reflected in the behaviour pattern of the developing infant will be a function of the type of reinforcement, positive or negative, and the intensity and frequency of reinforcement, provided by the parents for the display of sex appropriate or inappropriate behaviours. For example, a male child behaving in the manner of trial patient no. 17 who is consistently and positively reinforced for such behaviours would be more likely to develop and strengthen these than one who is punished. We consider that a child displaying a behaviour pattern inappropriate to his morphological sex would have an increased probability of developing another form of inappropriate behaviour, namely emotional and sexual attachments to a person of the same sex. Once such homosexual behaviour has occurred, there is a raised probability that it will continue to do so. Two specific predictions follow from the above argument—one testable retrospectively, the other prospectively. The former is that interviews of adult primary homosexuals will reveal childhood behaviour patterns similar to that of trial patient no. 17; that is, a behaviour pattern inappropriate to the morphological sex as compared *both* to adult secondary homosexuals and adult heterosexuals. The latter prediction would be of a positive correlation between the pre-natal sex steroids to which the developing foetus is exposed and post-natal behaviour patterns. Unfortunately, even with the most modern hormone assay techniques available, it is very difficult to measure the levels of circulating foetal steroids. However, it is possible (personal communication from Dr. B. Rudd, Biochemist, Institute of Child Health, University of Birmingham) to measure circulating maternal androgen and oestrogen during all stages of pregnancy. We would then study a cohort of children produced by such pregnancies and investigate their rate and direction of acquisition of sex-typed behaviour patterns post-natally. The success of such a study would depend on the assumption that levels of sex steroids in the foetal circulation are a relatively precise reflection of circulating maternal sex steroids; or, if the placenta is the relevant site of steroid source, that its output is also reflected in the maternal circulation.

The expectation that adult primary homosexuality would be associated with sex-inappropriate childhood behaviour raises the question of the relationship between primary homosexuality, trans-sexualism (we consider trans-sexuals as homosexuals by definition), and transvestism, occurring in homosexuals. In our view, these three types of sexual deviation are probably closely related, a view supported in a recent major review by Kockott (1970). The problem is to explain why only a minority of primary homosexuals (who are then termed trans-sexuals) not only display sex inappropriate behaviour, but in *addition* wish to change their bodily appearance so that morphology and behaviour will be consistent. No obvious answer suggests itself at present, but we feel the above constellation of primary homosexuality, trans-sexualism, and homosexual transvestism to be of heuristic value. The major importance for our present purpose is to emphasize our view that primary homosexuals are more similar to trans-sexuals than they are to secondary homosexuals.

A final implication of the complex interrelationship between pre-natal hormonal levels, parental reinforcement, and early sexual experience is that some individuals, relatively predisposed through hormonal influences to primary homosexuality, might be less strongly "typed" than others, so that it is difficult in adulthood to assign them clearly to one of the two types of homosexuality. Conceivably, it is such individuals who provide the rare instances of successfully treated "primary" homosexuals. This question cannot be answered without prospective studies of the kind outlined above. At the moment it is convenient to adopt a dual typology of homosexuality.

2. *Secondary Homosexuals*

We now invoke the theory of cognitive dissonance to account for the acquisition of homosexual behaviour in secondary homosexuals. Such individuals will show a relatively normal development of mild to increasingly strong heterosexual interest until the early to middle teens. It is likely during this period that there will be both sexual encounters with other school boys without any great degree of emotional content, as well as the early beginnings of sexual encounters with females. At this point we suggest the occurrence of an unsuccessful heterosexual encounter or series of unsuccessful encounters, resulting in the individual becoming anxious and uncertain about his ability to cope successfully with females. Such unpleasant heterosexual experiences will be rehearsed and "incubated" by some young men more than others. When anxiety becomes attached to approach behaviour to females, a dissonance is set up between the attitudinal desire for heterosexual sex and the overt avoidance of this behaviour. (The desire to avoid further unpleasant experiences leads to the avoidance of heterosexual stimuli.) Such a dissonance between positive attitudes and negative behaviour may be reduced, as Festinger has suggested, by either changing the attitude or changing the behaviour. Because approach behaviour to females is now associated with anxiety and fear, it may be easier to change the attitude than to change the behaviour. Hence the dissonance is resolved by a change in the evaluation of heterosexual behaviour so that such behaviour now becomes derogated.

At the same time there is a similar shift in the attitude to males. Previously, there has been no dissonance between attitudes to homosexual behaviour and the behaviour itself, with both a derogation of the behaviour and a relative avoidance, certainly of attaching *emotional* significance to casual schoolboy encounters. However, if the attitude to females now changes, consequent upon heterosexual failure, it may be that the individual will seek a sexual outlet through a channel which has not previously been associated with anxiety and failure, namely a homosexual one. If this now leads to consequences which are enjoyable, there will be a dissonance between the behaviour of approaching homosexual stimuli and the previously held derogatory attitude towards such behaviour. This dissonance can be reduced by changing either the attitude or the behaviour. In the latter case, the individual will be left with no sexual outlet as he has begun to avoid approach behaviour to females. Hence it may be easier for him to change his attitude to homosexual behaviour by no longer regarding it as unpleasant or unacceptable. We are postulating a double reduction of cognitive dissonance, so that *at the same time* the attitude to females becomes less favourable and the attitude to homosexual behaviour becomes more favourable. It will be recalled that Ramsey and Van

Velzen (1968) have reported considerably more anxiety about heterosexual experiences in homosexuals than in heterosexuals. We would predict that this anxiety is much more likely to be found amongst secondary homosexuals than primary homosexuals and in younger rather than older secondary homosexuals. We make the latter statement because, while the younger secondary homosexuals are still working through the lengthy process of reduction of cognitive dissonance, the older ones may have reached the stage where they are relatively neutral towards females rather than actively fearful of them. We would also predict an absence of heterosexual experiences, by definition, in the past histories of primary homosexuals. Such experiences will be found in the past histories of secondary homosexuals, and will have been associated with unpleasant consequences. Unpleasant outcomes of attempts at heterosexual experiences are likely to happen to many young people in our society, and in order to explain why only a proportion of these become secondary homosexuals we again utilize our notion of incubation through cognitive rehearsal. That is, those young people who *both* experience unpleasant consequences of attempts at heterosexual behaviour and have a relatively high tendency to rehearse and incubate *unpleasant* experiences, are more likely to turn to homosexual behaviour, providing also that there are opportunities for such behaviour. This analysis will not apply in exactly the same way to all secondary homosexuals. Experiences are not divisible precisely into "pleasant" or "unpleasant", but will lie on a dimension of emotional tone which is continuously graded. For a person with a relatively high tendency to incubate unpleasant experiences, a relatively minor heterosexual failure may be sufficient to lead to heterosexual avoidance. At the other end of the scale would be a person with a relatively low tendency to incubate unpleasant experiences who would require a much greater amount of failure before reducing heterosexual approach behaviour. The degree of pleasantness of early homosexual experiences would also vary, as will the tendency to incubate pleasant experiences, and hence increase the habit strength of homosexual approach. A final variable, which is likely to be relevant, is the normative evaluation of overt heterosexual behaviour in the immediate environment of the developing adolescent and the extent to which he is influenced by such norms. Other things being equal—such as the tendency to incubate—an adolescent living in an environment with strong barriers against overt heterosexual behaviour—for instance certain religious subcultures—would be more likely to avoid heterosexual attempts following failure than one living in a subculture with no barriers against overt heterosexual behaviour. The secondary homosexual who is fearful of females may confine his heterosexual contacts largely to females who appear unlikely to make sexual advances towards him (e.g. those much older than himself). A more pathological alternative would be occasionally to seek out the company of females who are *likely* to make sexual advances towards him; such predatory behaviour would increase his sexual fear of females, confirm his belief that they are harmful, and provide additional evidence of the need for avoidance of heterosexual behaviour. Hence, heterosexual avoidance is not evidence of a fault in himself but becomes a sensible thing to do. We would, therefore, predict that a study of the cognitive structure of homosexuals, for instance by the repertory grid method pioneered by Kelly (1955), would reveal relatively neutral heterosexual attitudes in primary homosexuals, but strong attitudes of fear and aversion in secondary homosexuals, particularly in the younger ones.

It is not to be expected that the avoidance of heterosexual behaviour will be total, that the verbal representations of such behaviour will consist solely of "fear" words, or that there will be a clear division, without overlap, between secondary homosexuals and non-homosexual heterosexuals, with heterosexual avoidance being high in the former but non-existent in the latter. Not all secondary homosexuals will show heterosexual avoidance to all females; avoidance behaviour and/or attitudes indicating aversion will be unlikely to be shown to females unless these are behaving in such a way as to indicate sexual designs on the subject. It would be expected, apparently paradoxically, that relatively heterophobic males would be particularly at ease in the company of *non*-sexually threatening females, such as those a considerable number of years older in age than themselves, as mentioned above.

It is likely that there will be a triple interaction between the standing of the subject on a trait which we term "heterophobia" (in which individuals will differ according to the interaction between genetic and neo-natally determined predispositions, and their total reinforcement history), the nature of the current heterosexual stimulus (how sexually possible—in terms of age, social class, etc., and how attractive), and the nature of the situation (the presence of other persons, appropriateness of the setting for sexual behaviour, etc.). Endler and Hunt (1966) have argued strongly for such a triple interaction view of personality and have presented evidence for the view that personality differences may best be understood in terms of the "kinds of responses individuals make, with what intensity, in various kinds of situations". Very little experimental work has been carried out on the perceptions held by one sex of the other. The few existing studies are summarized in Eleanor Maccoby's admirable compilation of studies on sex differences (Maccoby, 1967).*

It is difficult to know the extent to which writers and novelists concerned with such themes have been influenced by psychoanalytical theory and to what extent by the culturally known facts of homosexual attitudes. Techniques are becoming available which will make possible the objective experimental study of heterosexual attitudes in both male and female homosexuals and non-homosexual controls. In studying such social preliminaries of sexual behaviour, it is important that the measuring devices be as unobtrusive as possible. MacCulloch *et al.* (1969) have described a subject-sensitive floor area which automatically records the positions of 2 people on the floor and as they move about its surface. The data are automatically recorded, and no intervention of the human observer is necessary. There is evidence (Sommer, 1967) that preferred distance apart is an important indicant of the attitudes held by people about each other, and it would be expected that the more "heterophobic" the individual, the further apart would be his preferred distance from an individual of the opposite sex who is displaying a sexual interest in him. It would be readily possible to manipulate many aspects of the heterosexual stimulus person, using the preferred distance of the subject as the dependent variable. Recordings of such autonomic variables as heart rate, respiration, and skin potential could readily be made, preferably telemetrically, so as to eliminate the constraint of wires leading from the subject to the recording apparatus, and to enable them to be completely ambulant. The above suggestions bring the study of heterophobia, or heterosexual avoidance behaviour, as it may more precisely be termed, into line with the study of avoidance behaviour in general, and enable it to be subjected to the same theoretical and experimental analyses (e.g. Miller, 1959).

B. MOTIVATION FOR TREATMENT

1. *Primary Homosexuals*

We postulate that one of the main factors causing both types of homosexuals voluntarily to seek treatment is the existence of a dissonance between their homosexual behaviour and

*In contrast, of course, a large number of novels and plays have as their theme the destructive effects of the female on the male, examples being the works of Somerset Maugham and Edward Allbee.

the heterosexual behaviour which they would like to be able to display. In the case of the primary homosexuals, who have no past memories of the latter on which to draw, the dissonance is between their behaviour and the attitude of society towards such behaviour. This dissonance is likely to be resolved by many primary homosexuals by seeking the exclusive company of other homosexuals—in the homosexual subculture or by simply ignoring the opinion of society. Primary homosexuals who seek treatment will be those who (a) find it distasteful to identify themselves as homosexuals by mixing in the homosexual subculture, and/or (b) are strongly motivated to behave like other people in their society. It is likely that such primary homosexuals seeking treatment will be more sensitive, in the Schneiderian sense, than those not seeking treatment. It is also likely that they will be strongly influenced by prevailing social norms towards leading a family life (e.g. trial patient no. 17).

2. Secondary Homosexuals

The secondary homosexual's most usual motivation for seeking treatment voluntarily will arise out of the dissonance between his current, homosexually orientated, behaviour and his previous response, which may still persist to some extent, of being aroused by heterosexual stimuli. This is likely to be more marked amongst younger, than older, secondary homosexuals because the younger persons are nearer in time to their experiences of heterosexual behaviour. Dissonance theory would predict that the more behaviour can be said to have been voluntary, the greater the degree of cognitive dissonance, and, therefore, the greater the motivation toward *attitude change*. This theory would predict, e.g. that if a person of predominantly homosexual orientation were to commit him or herself to behaviour incompatible or at variance with this orientation, then a decrease in homosexual orientation, presumably including effective components of this orientation, should occur. Carlin and Armstrong (1968) have suggested, in the context of an anti-smoking conditioning procedure for volunteer subjects, that a change in the expected direction following such a procedure should largely be attributed to the dissonance induced in the person by his voluntarily committing himself to the procedure which involves receiving repeatedly an unpleasant aversive stimulus, and which he knows to be aimed at altering his attitudes towards something which previously had pleasurable associations for him. If there is truth in the theory of cognitive dissonance (and there is an increasing amount of experimental evidence to support this), then it could be argued that the voluntary commitment of a homosexual patient to one or other of the conditioning procedures described in earlier chapters is in itself a powerful source of attitude change. Brief acquaintance with the procedure leaves the patient in no doubt that it represents a direct assault upon his homosexual orientation, involving as it does the repeated association of pictorial representations of stimuli associated with previous sexual gratification and aversive electric shocks. If the patient's self-concept included thinking of himself in any way as a homosexual now and in the future, this must be difficult to maintain in the face of his commitment to continue with such a programme. The same cannot be said to anything like the same extent of psychotherapy, involving as it clearly does psychic self-exploration, which most patients must have experienced to some extent previously, and which, therefore, carries only a possible (though by no means a certain) pay-off, in the form of decreased homosexual orientation. The notion of commitment to treatment will be returned to in the next section, when we discuss the reasons for the differential response to treatment of the 2 types of homosexual.

C. RESPONSE TO TREATMENT

1. *The Different Outcomes of Primary Homosexuals and Secondary Homosexuals of "Good" Personality*

We have to account for the general failure to respond to treatment of primary homosexuals and the equally general tendency to respond to treatment of secondary homosexuals. We begin by returning once more to the theory of cognitive dissonance. The AA technique might be thought to be especially effective in arousing dissonance, as it requires the patient repeatedly to make operant responses, the effect of which is to terminate the exposure of a homosexual stimulus or to initiate the exposure of a heterosexual stimulus. However, if dissonance reduction is at all operative in producing successful results of treatment, the lack of any substantial difference in outcome in those patients receiving the two conditioning techniques suggests the possibility that this second element of dissonance induction, involved in conditioning, is relatively unimportant in comparison with the effect of *commitment to treatment*.

The operation of a process of attitude change brought about by dissonance induction, as described above, may not be incompatible with the simultaneous operation of a conditioning process. Indeed, the simultaneous operation of these two processes may be the most effective means of bringing about change, as they may be thought of as operating upon different components of the attitude which is the object of the attempt at modification. However, the assumption that a conditioning process is not the only one at work will explain a number of facts which are difficult to explain by means of conditioning alone. Firstly, it is a clinical impression that when change occurs it does so very rapidly after the commencement of treatment, perhaps within the first two or three treatment sessions. Secondly, in nearly all cases in which change did occur, changes in attractiveness of stimuli, as reported by the patient, generalized completely from those stimuli used in the course of treatment to those stimuli of equal initial attractiveness which were shown to the patient before and after treatment, but were not experienced by the patient in the course of treatment. Such a rapid response to treatment, with such total generalization of its effect, is difficult to explain by conditioning principles alone, and even more surprising to some conditioning theorists (e.g. Rachman and Teasdale, 1969) is the degree of generalization observed between changes that occur within the treatment situation and analogous changes that occur outside treatment. (A more detailed attempt to explain the generalization between the treatment and the real life situations is given below.) Such facts might partially be explained on the grounds that the modification of the effective component of an attitude would, according to the principles of consistency of attitude organization, bring about similar changes in cognitive components, but all the facts prove to be most easily explained by the postulation of a process which operates directly upon cognitive components. Perhaps the fact most readily accounted for by such an explanation is the lack of any observable difference between the effects of the two conditioning procedures used here, despite their differences in design.

The relationship of theories of attitude change to aversive conditioning techniques becomes more clear when it is recalled that one of the methods postulated by Festinger (1957) for reducing post-decision dissonance was to increase the relative attractiveness of the chosen alternative (and by implication *reduce* the relative attractiveness of the rejected alternative). While we can reduce the relative attractiveness of the rejected alternative, i.e. attach anxiety to homosexual stimuli, we are not, in either of the two aversion techniques described in this book, doing anything *positively* to increase the attractiveness of the heterosexual stimuli. By reducing the anxiety previously attached to heterosexual stimuli, however, the dormant heterosexual approach behaviour may be restored in secondary homosexuals. No such restoration is possible for primary homosexuals. That is, for them, neither the commitment to treatment nor the reduction in the tendency to find males attractive, is sufficient for a successful response where this is defined as an increase in heterosexual interest and overt behaviour. We can explain this failure more clearly by making an analogy with a very different area of learning, namely the "Crespi effect" (Crespi, 1942). This refers to an experiment in which rats were divided into groups, one group learning to run a runway to a small reward, the other performing the same response for a large reward. The speed of running of the large-reward group was very much faster than that of the small-reward group. The next stage was to reverse the amounts of reinforcement so that the small-reward group now had a large reward, and *vice versa*. The effect was that the group which had previously had the small reward now increased its speed of running to a point approximating that of the previous large-reward group. Conversely, the group which at first had a large reward reduced its speed of running, when shifted to a small reward, to a rate even below that previously shown by the small-reward group. The analogy between this study, and the response to treatment of the secondary homosexuals, is that aversion therapy (whether AA or CC) reverses the relative amounts of reward attached to the two types of sexual stimuli. Whereas female stimuli were previously either neutral or associated with anxiety, they now become associated with relief from anxiety. Conversely, the male stimuli which were previously rewarding, now become associated with anxiety. Because the previous habit strength of approach to females has been zero for the primary homosexuals, there is nothing to restore or increase. All we can do is to suppress, for perhaps a short period of time, approach behaviour to males. In the absence of any possible alternative outlet, this suppression is likely to extinguish fairly quickly. Hence the failure to respond to treatment of primary homosexuals. An urgent research task is the development of a technique to incorporate heterosexual approach responses into the behavioural repertoire of the primary homosexual.

A method of even further improving the rate of reacquisition of heterosexual approach behaviour in secondary homosexuals in general might be the use of the false feedback technique of Valins (1966a). He was able to demonstrate that the false feedback to subjects of increased heart rate increased the degree to which they avoided previously aversive stimuli —in this case, grass snakes. Valins (1967) showed that the effects of such false feedback were more marked in subjects whom he classified on a questionnaire, originally devised by Lykken (1957), as emotional, as opposed to unemotional. It is tempting to equate Valins's emotional subjects with our notion of high "incubators" because of a further study by Valins (1967). He had his subjects look at slides of heterosexual stimuli; some weeks later he had the same subjects return and by a subterfuge asked them to nominate those slides which had been found to be most attractive. It appeared that the subjects who had had a false feedback (apparently increased heart rate to a rate perceived as fast) while they were looking at the slides of the females on the first occasion, showed a greater increase in the ratings of attractiveness of the slides on the second occasion than those who had not been given such a false feedback. Moreover, the effect was more marked amongst those subjects who were rated as emotional on the basis of their questionnaire responses than those rated unemotional. If we can equate Valins's "emotional" subjects with our "high incubators", then we have at least some incidental evidence that the effect of the passage of a period of time on such individuals is to increase their rating. i.e. their felt degree of attractiveness, of heterosexual slides. The implication from Valins's work for the treatment of secondary homosexuals would be that the therapist might falsify the information on heart rates obtained from subjects in treatment and feedback such false information—that is of an increased arousal response to heterosexual slides. The expectation would be that such a false feedback would further increase the rate of favourable change of attitude to heterosexual stimuli.

False feedback may profitably be combined with the autonomic "shaping" technique suggested by Neale Miller's recent work—see section I.D of this chapter—to increase still further the rate of change.

2. *Secondary Homosexuals of "Poor" Personality*

The suggestions made in section III.C.1 may make it somewhat easier to explain the personality correlates of change discussed in Chapter 7. Whereas the personality correlates which would be expected if conditioning were the only process operating were only slightly, if at all, confirmed, other significant personality correlates were established. It could be argued that patients of "poor" personality (as defined in Chapter 7), lacking the resources of personality necessary for a commitment to a procedure which would deny them a source of immediate gratification in the interests of a satisfactory adjustment in the long term, avoided—in one way or another—a total commitment to their treatment. There are, presumably, many ways, by rationalization or denial for example, in which a patient may avoid a total commitment to a treatment regime, whilst at the same time going through the necessary motions. One patient, for example, who was of "poor" personality (as defined) and who failed to respond to treatment, went through his treatment whilst several times denying that the homosexual slides were of any sexual interest to him. One possible construction which could be placed upon this, though not the only one, is that this patient, by denying the appropriateness of the treatment, enabled himself to avoid a total commitment to treatment.

The clear implication is that even the most sophisticated variations in learning technique may be relatively unimportant for such patients, and even irrelevant to the problem of overcoming unfavourable features of personality. The response to treatment depends not only on events within treatment but also on the interaction such events have with what occurs outside treatment. One such extra-treatment variable might be the frequency and intensity of cognitive rehearsal of responses learned during treatment. If future research shows both that such rehearsal is an important element in successful treatment, so that failure in secondary homosexuals is associated with relatively infrequent or weak rehearsal, and also that "poor" personality individuals are low in frequency and intensity of rehearsal, then a possible partial remedy suggest itself. This is to artificially supplement for the secondary homosexuals of "poor" personality the opportunities for attaching verbal labels to the responses acquired in treatment. A simple example would be for the therapist to record the patient's verbal responses to the homosexual slides to which anxiety has become attached. The next stage would be to play back the recording to the patient in the hope that this would encourage the habit of rehearsal. Another useful consequence might be that the commitment of the patient to treatment (as discussed above) would be more completely established. (The suggestion of playing back to the patient his verbal behaviour within-treatment is rather different from the method used by several therapists (e.g. James, 1962), who required their patients to listen to tape recordings of the *therapist* describing homosexual behaviour in unfavourable terms.) Similarly, favourable statements made by the patient concerning heterosexual behaviour could be recorded and played back to him. The possibility that patients of "poor" personality are low on the incubation of unpleasant events, such as the experience of anxiety to homosexual slides, can be readily tested. The method would be to study the amount of increase in avoidance responding (latency or frequency) following an interval after a training session.

D. FROM TREATMENT TO REAL LIFE

Rachman and Teasdale (1969) have drawn attention to the problem of bridging the gap between button pressing in the treatment situation and the performance of the appropriate approach and avoidance responses in real-life situations. Their doubts are summed up as follows: "The surprising thing about aversion therapy is not that its effects are uncertain but that it works at all". At the beginning of our research we were equally uncertain concerning the probability of response generalization between the treatment room and the real-life situation, and hence of the likely success of treatment. That the treatment did succeed with the majority of secondary homosexuals is made clear in Chapters 3 and 5. This is indicative of the fact that response generalization *must* have occurred, and the problem is to explain *how* it has done so. Reference has been made above to the way in which the theory of cognitive dissonance may contribute to this explanation. In addition, remarks made by patients during follow-up interviews suggested two further possible mechanisms. Firstly, many patients reported that they had found themselves looking at male passers-by in the street, and then involuntarily looking away, experiencing a feeling of relief as they did so. Conversely, they reported looking at females for longer periods than prior to treatment, experiencing a feeling of pleasure. Secondly, patients made it clear that they reflected both upon their experiences in treatment and their changes in response outside treatment. Once the patient has learned to press a switch to remove a male slide in treatment, this provides a response which can generalize from this situation to looking away from a male encountered in the street. (Instead of the usual stimulus being removed, he removes himself from the visual stimulus—the outcome is the same.) In a similar manner, the response of continuing to look at a female in treatment is one which is akin to the real-life response. If the consequences of these two visual responses in real life are pleasurable, they will be reinforced with an increasing probability of occurrence. From visual responses it is a relatively simple step physically to avoid the company of homosexuals and physically to seek that of members of the opposite sex. If appropriately reinforced at each stage, the latter approach responses then move further and further along the response chain leading to overt heterosexual activities. The crucial link between the treatment room and real life would be provided both by the *relative* similarity between avoidance by button pressing (to remove a visually presented slide) and avoidance by looking away from a male visually encountered in the street, and the *precise* similarity between the autonomic consequences (relief from anxiety) of the two responses.

Cognitive rehearsal, accompanied by the autonomic changes associated with stimuli encountered both in treatment and in real life, may increase very greatly the habit strength of the behavioural responses originally learned in treatment, and hence the probability of occurrence of the next response in the chain—the visual behaviour in the real-life situation.

Hence, we are postulating that the first link in the chain is the response acquired in treatment, and the next, the cognitive rehearsal of such a response. This is followed by visual behaviour in real life, and in turn this is succeeded by further cognitive rehearsal of the visual behaviour. The sequence continues in this way, with real-life behaviour being continually strengthened by rehearsal.

Finally, the difficulties reported by Rachman and Teasdale (1969) in being able to understand the success of AA treatment may have been lessened, if instead of requiring the patient to press a button to remove a slide from the screen, we had set up a situation such that a head movement operated a switch which removed a slide from the screen. There would then be an exactly parallel situation between the response acquired in treatment and the response performed in the street. Recently, a former colleague has devised a mercury switch which transmits to the recording device the avoidance response made when the patient looks away from the slide, and also causes the slide to leave the screen.*

IV. A SPECULATION ON FEMALE HOMOSEXUALITY

Finally, we shall discuss some possible differences between male and female homosexuality. Firstly, a number of recent reports (Bene, 1965a, b; Kenyon, 1968) have suggested that the relationship in childhood between the female child and the father is particularly important, perhaps even more so than between the male child and the mother. Both Bene and Kenyon report a significant increase in unsatisfactory relationships between their female homosexual samples and their fathers as compared to male homosexuals in the case of Bene, and to female heterosexual controls in the case of Kenyon. This is a most interesting area of research, and certainly one which will repay further investigation. It would be particularly profitable to carry out such a study among a cohort of children produced by mothers whose foetal circulating sex steroids have been assayed during pregnancy (a research design suggested in Section II of this chapter). Other studies on developing infants which are desirable, and which may usefully be mentioned at this point, are as follows:

(1) An analysis of the relationship between child-rearing practices and the development of sexual object choices.
(2) A longitudinal study of the relationship between the friendship choices made by children and the development of their sexual object choices.
(3) A longitudinal study of the relationship between the developing self-concepts of children, their role-taking behaviour, and their eventual sexual object choices.

It is clear that there will be a very large number of variables operating, and a multi-factorial design is the only one that is satisfactory.

To return to the problem of the female homosexual, our impression from the relatively small number of female homosexuals whom we have interviewed is that their heterosexual attitudes are rather more complex than are those of male homosexuals. For instance, whereas male homosexuals tend to report relatively uncomplicated attitudes of fear and avoidance, female homosexuals sometimes report, in addition, a degree of aggression and contempt. It may be, if these impressions are confirmed by a more detailed study, that such a difference between male and female homosexuals is related to the possible differences in the sexual roles of the two sexes. In order to avoid female contacts, all that male homosexuals

*Personal communication by Mrs. Valerie Mellor, 1969.

have to do is not approach females (although this may be complicated in the case of particularly attractive male homosexuals who are actively sought after by females, and those male homosexuals who seek confirmation of their fear of females by deliberately approaching those who are likely to make powerful sexual demands on them). On the other hand, females have positively to avoid males who have made approaches towards them. One way in which females might deal with such approach behaviour is to respond aggressively. If such aggressive behaviour leads to the male no longer pursuing his attentions, then it will serve to reduce the anxiety consequent on the approach behaviour of the male. Such anxiety reduction would reinforce the heterosexual aggression of the lesbian, thereby increasing the probability of her responding to further male approaches in an aggressive manner. Like other anxiety-reducing mechanisms, this is initially successful but finally maladaptive in that it has the long-term effect of decreasing the probability of successful heterosexual adaptation (aggression by females may provoke anxiety in males if the female is attractive and reciprocal aggression if she is not). In either event, the consequence will be a reduced probability of males displaying a sexual interest in the female homosexual concerned.

If this analysis of female homosexuality is correct, several predictions follow. Firstly, the cognitive structure of female homosexuals (and there may be a division between primary and secondary female homosexuals, although the numbers we have seen are far too small for us to draw such conclusions from our own study) may be rather different from that of male homosexuals. The secondary female homosexuals would show attitudes of contempt and frank derogation of males, as well as attitudes of fear and anxiety. Secondly, the use of behavioural measures of aggression with various subgroups would demonstrate a greater degree of overt aggression in female homosexuals towards males perceived to be both heterosexual and sexually responsive to the subject, than in female heterosexuals. Several behavioural techniques suggest themselves as suitable for such a study. Amongst them is the technique used by Epstein and Taylor (1967) whereby a subject participates in a rigged reaction time test with another subject, the "winner" being able to inflict an "electric shock" on the loser. A further possible technique would be that used by Milgram (1963) in which a "teacher" monitors the performance of another subject on a learning task. The consequence of errors is that the "teacher" inflicts on the "learner" an apparent, but in fact faked, series of electric shocks of increasing strength. Indeed, realistic behavioural measures, both of heterosexual avoidance and aggression, are generally to be preferred to cognitive measures, which may be open to dissimulation or faking.

V. CONCLUDING REMARKS

We close this last chapter of the book with a brief re-statement of the major findings.

We have divided male homosexuals into two types—primary and secondary—according to the occurrence (secondary type) or lack of occurrence (primary type) of pleasurable heterosexual behaviour in the life histories. The primary type does not respond to aversion therapy; the secondary type does respond except where the personality of the patient is unfavourable. The response to treatment, as measured by a variety of techniques, is relatively independent of the type of avoidance learning used. The combination of sexual attitude scores, personality measures, and homosexual type predicts the outcome of treatment to a high degree of accuracy; cross-validation of these predictors is urgently needed.

Finally, we have put forward several speculative theories to account for the development of the two proposed types of homosexual, the reasons why some homosexuals seek treatment, and the differential response to treatment of the two types. In outlining these theories, we have drawn on concepts from several areas of behavioural research in the hope of accounting for sexual behaviour within general theories of behaviour, and so reducing the present relative scientific isolation of the sexologist.

We have probably left more questions than answers; it is our hope that the questions will stimulate well-directed and carefully controlled research not only into homosexuality but into all aspects of sexual behaviour in general.

APPENDIX A

CASE HISTORIES

1. THE SERIES

The 14 case histories which follow have been selected to illustrate both the range of patients treated (primary/secondary types, personality disorder, and nature of disorder, etc.) and the varied outcomes of treatment.

Sexual Orientation Method (SOM) data are presented for every case except series case no. 41.

SERIES CASE 1

Case 1 presented for treatment of homosexuality in February 1963 when he was 22. He was a practising homosexual and stated his wish to be "normal and have children", a desire largely motivated by a loyal girl friend. His homosexuality was entirely unknown to his relatives and fellow employees, and this dual existence had begun to pall.

Sexual History

The patient acquired his knowledge of sexual matters such as pregnancy and contraception at the age of 14 from his class mates.

He was shown how to masturbate by a school friend at 14 years, and he indulged in mutual masturbation, accompanied at first by feelings of guilt, which later resolved. He continued the practice regularly until he was 15 years old when he changed schools and lacked further opportunity. At the age of 16 he became conscious of his sexual attraction to other males and began, on occasion, to linger in men's lavatories without, at first, any mishap. When he was 18 he met another homosexual, aged 30, in a public bar, and at the other's instigation they had mutual masturbation. The patient enjoyed this event, and from then on believed himself to be a homosexual. There were five similar incidents during the next few months. When he was 19 he was introduced to buggery to partners whom he had met in a homosexual public house. He took the active part and had an "affair" lasting 2 months.

From this time onwards he became a regularly practising homosexual, and indulged in active and passive sodomy, fellatio, body kissing, and intra-crural techniques, all with pleasure and satisfaction.

Towards the end of his 21st year he formed an emotional homosexual alliance which lasted 2 months, the termination of which by the partner caused the patient a great deal of regret and unhappiness.

His heterosexual interests and activities have been limited. He was first sexually attracted to a girl at 15, and at 18 had two girl friends, although failing to experience any sexual excitement. At this stage he indulged over a period of 3 months in oral kissing which he found to be pleasant but not erotic. Since the age of 18 he has been out with three other girls, but has only kissed them in a desultory fashion and without much interest.

In September 1962 he met a girl 2 years older than himself and began to form a non-erotic emotional attachment to her. However, 3 weeks prior to seeking treatment he attempted to break off the relationship because of lack of sexual interest in the girl, explaining to her that he was a homosexual. She pressed him to maintain the relationship and persuaded him to see his GP who referred him for treatment.

Personal History

His early life and upbringing had been entirely normal. He was the elder of two boys in a well-knit Methodist family, with both parents still living. His father did not take a great deal of interest in either boy during their early years. However, it can be said that he has no particular antipathy to either parent, nor are there any unusually strong emotional ties between the patient and any other member of his family. There was no other known case of homosexuality in the family and no mental illness.

The patient passed five O-levels and was employed as a librarian.

Clinical Findings

On examination the patient was a fair-haired, blue-eyed man, nearly 6 ft tall, of athletic build. There were no abnormal findings in any system. The genitals were entirely normal, the body hair was sparse but masculine in distribution. Mentally he was rather anxious at the earlier interviews. There was no depression of mood, and at no time was thought disorder or passivity experience elicited. He had a well-balanced mature manner, being rather slow and deliberate in speech. He never made statements of which he was not sure, and his ideas and outlook always appeared well thought out.

He was able to derive erotic excitement from thinking about males, and observing them, buttocks being thought especially exciting. He was excited by photographs and drawings of males and male cinema stars, particularly those with bright eyes, smooth complexions, and a slim, boyish build. The only stimulating auto-erotic situation was to see himself naked in a mirror, and this only excited him occasionally. In the heterosexual field, thinking of and seeing girls had no effect on him, but physical contact, such as dancing, was beginning to interest him when he presented.

His usual source of homosexual partner was introduced by personal friends, occasionally augmented by "pick-ups" in homosexual pubs and public lavatories. Sexual relations usually took place in the patient's or the partner's places of residence.

Treatment

Progress under treatment, which occupied 28 sessions, each of 20 minutes, over 2 weeks and which was on an in-patient basis, was steady. The patient reported a continuing decrease in the attractiveness of each male photograph in turn and a continuing increase in the attractiveness of each female photograph.

He reported a decrease in his homosexual phantasy life, and the attractiveness of males observed in the ward. The nursing staff reported an increasing display of overt affection between the patient and his visiting girl friend. At the conclusion of treatment they left together for a holiday, and on return the patient reported mutually satisfactory intercourse with some slight remaining, although easily controlled, interest in men.

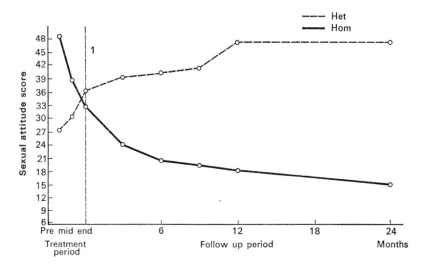

FIG. A1. Series case 1. SOM data.

Follow-up

Follow-up data by interview existed for 2 years and there was no further homosexual problem. He became engaged and later in 1964 married. He said "I can now look forward to living normally and having a home life and children—a year ago this seemed less and less likely. I feel that progress is being more than maintained."

The patient wrote in 3 years after follow-up to report that all was well sexually and socially; in addition, his career progress had improved.

SERIES CASE 2

Case 2 was a 34-year-old piano teacher who sought treatment of his own accord. He complained of anxiety and inability to concentrate on his work at a boys' school, caused by the development of a strong emotional feeling towards one particular pupil, together with sexual interest in other male pupils.

Sexual History

Sex was a taboo subject in the home. At 15 he was attacked and masturbated by a man; he was terrified and reported no pleasure in this event. In a play at school he first noted an interest in female clothes, and later in life he consistently enjoyed looking at female clothes when he went window shopping with his mother. At the age of 16 he began to find male ankles sexually attractive, and 12 years before he was seen he began to feel that boys at school were attractive: he eventually realized the significance of these feelings and, knowing that an overt homosexual response would probably mean dismissal, he became extremely tense and anxious and finally sought psychiatric help. At this time he was able to gain sexual pleasure from observing himself nude, as well as from watching and thinking about the boys at school. He did not, however, engage in active sexual practices of any kind.

Personal History

He was the only child of a rigid, poorly functioning marriage. He described his father as being "completely in the background". His mother kept him close to her physically and emotionally, insisting on choosing his clothes and friends. He was treated as a minor even at 30 years of age. He said of his parents: "They should never have married because their interests are totally dissimilar, and they made fun of me as a child."

Personality

On examination he was a reticent, insecure person with a markedly anankastic personality. He was of high intelligence, and apart from an asthenic habitus, the falsetto pitch of his voice was the only point of note. There was no evidence of a depressive illness.

Treatment

He was given anticipatory avoidance therapy.

Follow-up

Within 10 days of treatment he reported that his homosexual thoughts and urges were much less powerful and fairly easily controlled. He resumed teaching, and a reduction in the level of his anxiety was noted. He was closely followed as an out-patient, and speech therapy was given to help him pitch his voice lower. A month after discharge he complained of headache and tension, and it was found that he was overworking (giving extra music lessons), and he was advised to cut down on his work. Three months after discharge he was beginning to find girls interesting and to have no anxiety at school. He was beginning to go out socially in mixed groups, but complained of episodes of depression. Twelve months after treatment he reported no attraction to schoolboys, and he had just returned from holiday abroad in which he had made a fairly close heterosexual friendship without, however, any overt sexual activity. He felt himself to be much more interested in females than males, and he was free from depression and other psychiatric symptoms. He remained in *statu quo* for a further 2 years, but his SOM scores at follow-up 3 years post-treatment in retrospect indicated that his orientation was drifting back to being homosexual. This point was not realized at the time, and 4 years after treatment the patient reappeared complaining of mild anxiety. He had just returned from a holiday abroad with a male homosexual who was keen to carry on the relationship which had progressed as far as mutual masturbation on four occasions in a hotel bedroom. He reported that his home life was slightly improved and that his heterosexual social life was as desultory as before. The prospect of a continuing overt homosexual relationship did not occasion his alarm, and he did not report any increase in attraction to male pupils. The possibility of further aversion therapy was rejected mainly because of the patient's poor motivation.

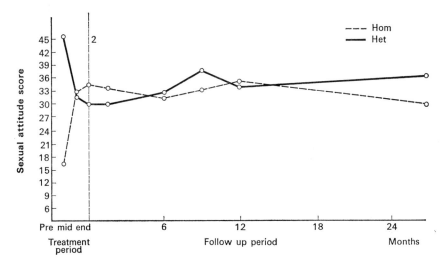

FIG. A2. Series case 2. SOM data.

Discussion

It cannot be denied that this patient was helped through a difficult period in which he suffered uncontrollable pederastic thoughts. It is, however, tempting in retrospect to label his personality weak-willed. He would not engage in heterosexual behaviour even when the opportunity presented itself; later he arranged a holiday with a male whom he knew to be homosexual. This behaviour could simply be dismissed as evidence of his poor motivation, but his expressed wish to become heterosexual, together with his regular visits to the clinic over 3 years, support the hypothesis of weak-willed personality disorder. The SOM data gave an indication of the ultimate outcome as early as 6 months post-treatment.

SERIES CASE 3

Case 3 was a 40-year-old semi-skilled operator referred via the courts, having received 2 years' probation and a £50 fine for a homosexual offence involving a 19-year-old boy.

Sexual History

His first sexual experience, namely mutual masturbation, occurred at the age of 10. His refusal of homosexual approaches at the age of 16 and 19 was caused by shyness and fear of the consequences rather than lack of interest. At the age of 24 he commenced homosexual activity which took place in cinemas and public lavatories. His usual form of activity was mutual masturbation, and he frequently paid his partners small sums of money. He commenced active anal intercourse with the 19-year-old boy who figured in his eventual court appearance, several months before he appeared in court. This was one of the few instances in which the patient was able to feel some degree of emotional attachment to his partner. The patient had never displayed any heterosexual interest, phantasy, or behaviour.

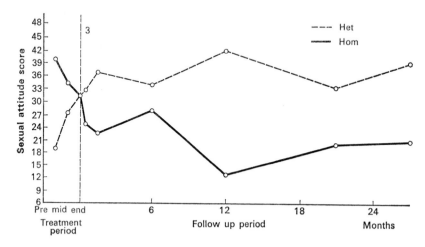

Fig. A3. Series case 3. SOM data.

Personal History

The patient's father drank heavily and beat his mother, and at the age of 14 the patient and his mother went to live with his elder married sister. The patient's father visited the mother for sexual intercourse, and the patient found these visits sexually exciting, wishing to take his mother's place. There was no previous medical or psychiatric history of note.

Personality

The patient was clinically assessed as obsessional with marked sensitive traits. He found social relationships of any kind extremely taxing for his reserved nature, and prior to treatment expressed sensitive ideas of reference.

Family History

There was no known family history of psychiatric illness or homosexuality.

Treatment

He responded well to anticipatory avoidance treatment and this good response has generalized to his external behaviour.

Follow-up

On discharge he described only slight homosexual phantasy and interest, and slight heterosexual phantasy and interest. In the 2 years of follow-up since discharge he displayed no homosexual behaviour, and his interest and phantasy have diminished almost to extinction. He became interested in looking at females, and he used them instead of males in his masturbatory phantasies. He had begun taking ballroom dancing lessons with a view to attending public dances, and he found social mixing a great deal easier than previously; there was a marked increase in his confidence and ease of manner.

SERIES CASE 4

Case 4 was a 24-year-old assembly worker who was referred by his GP because his wife had discovered that he was a practising homosexual.

Sexual History

He was buggered at the age of 7 by a man whom he estimated to be aged 40. He was afraid and hated it. At 11 years he was introduced to mutual masturbation by school friends and practised this twice weekly, principally with two boys, for the following 4 years. When he was 15 he was asked to perform mutual masturbation with a 28-year-old man in a public convenience. This was his first experience of homosexuality apart from school, and he enjoyed it. He continued to meet the same man at the latter's home in order to practise buggery and naked petting, which continued for 2 years. The patient finally broke the arrangement because he "got frightened because the man was married".

At 19 he had a homosexual relationship with a 22-year-old soldier which lasted 6 months. The predominant activity was buggery in which the active and passive roles alternated.

In the 5 years preceding referral he continued to pick up men on a casual basis and took them home to perform homosexual acts. His wife was employed as a nurse on permanent nights. His auto-masturbatory phantasy was bisexual.

At 12 he became interested in a girl whom he met several times a week for 3 months; they kissed with enjoyment. Later the same year he acquired another "girl friend" with whom he kissed and petted for a period of 2 months.

Eighteen months later he performed sexual intercourse with a 14-year-old girl with enjoyment. At 17 he attempted sexual intercourse but was unable to come to orgasm.

At 18 he met his wife, and later at 21 the relationship progressed to the stage at which full sexual intercourse was undertaken once a week. His wife became pregnant and they married shortly afterwards. The marital relationship was satisfactory; intercourse continued at the rate of twice per week, mainly regulated by his wife's off-duty.

Personal History

He was the eldest of four boys; there was considerable parental marital disharmony arising partly from the father's heavy drinking and from the mother's "meanness".

The patient could not remember his parents ever demonstrating affection, and of his mother he said: "I would not ask her for *anything*, I was never allowed out." He was an average pupil at school, left at 15, and went down the pit. He was forced to give up mining because of severe anxiety in relation to being underground. He tried nursing for 6 months and was later called up for Army service in the medical corps. On demobilization he worked in an electrical components factory.

Personality

From childhood the patient remembers the sense of resentment engendered by his father's loss of self-control in drink. He disliked his nearest sib, E, 6 years his junior, and his relationship with his mother was cool and distant. His intelligence was average (100 WAIS). The predominant personality trait was insecurity, characterized by some obsessionality and sensitivity. He tended to become depressed by his homosexual problem.

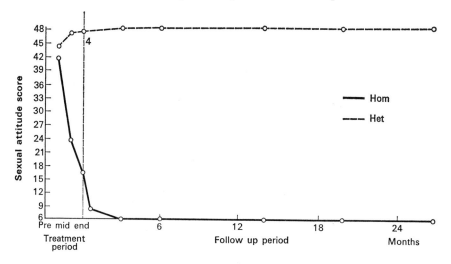

FIG. A4. Series case 4. SOM data.

Treatment

He was admitted for 2 weeks for anticipatory avoidance treatment. After 10 sessions of treatment he found that his interest in men was much reduced. "I don't dwell on it, but I am worried about my will power" (particularly when his wife was out at night). Before treatment he had frequently to resort to homosexual phantasy to bring himself to orgasm during sexual intercourse with his wife. This problem disappeared with treatment, and was accompanied by an overt and increasing interest in other females. Further treatment was prescribed.

Follow-up

Eight months after treatment he had a fresh job, his wife had had a second child, and he was less prone to depression. His sexual intercourse with his wife was more satisfactory, but he was still prone to obsessional doubt over his homosexuality. "I wonder if it [homosexual sex] would be the same now or changed."

Twenty-two months after treatment the position was maintained; he said: "I feel different —I am pleased with myself." He appeared more confident in manner and admitted that at first heterosexual relationships had been a strain for him, a problem which was no longer present. His progress continued unchanged to final follow-up at 27 months.

SERIES CASE 9

Case 9, a 26-year-old architect, sought treatment 2 weeks after a conviction for gross indecency. The actual offence was fellatio involving two other men in a public convenience.

Sexual History

His childhood was uneventful; his parents always stressed that sex was nasty. When he was 12 he was introduced to mutual masturbation at school. He continued this practice as well as auto-masturbation with homosexual phantasy. When he was 17 he was groped by a clothing shop assistant (during a fitting) and they performed fellatio. This experience seemed to be important, and he said: "It satisfied something in me." Following this his auto-masturbatory phantasy was homosexual.

He went to university at 18 and went about with one or two girls. The one girl he did like strongly rejected his sexual advances. After university (where there was an absence of homosexual practice) he went to another large city to start his working career. He became very lonely and became aware of the homosexual life there. He commenced mutual masturbation in lavatories, later went to homosexual pubs, and from there to the homes of his homosexual pick-ups. He felt a need for an emotional relationship but was loath to enter one because of the jealousy and bickering that he knew would ensue. He felt that women were much more difficult to approach than men, and he had very little heterosexual experience beyond kissing.

Personality

When he was first seen he was very anxious, a little depressed, and very resentful towards the Police. He did not really feel he could say goodbye to an exciting way of life, i.e. homosexuality, especially as he could not be given any guarantee that heterosexual relationship could either be achieved or be satisfactory. He had marked anankastic personality features, and there was an immature flavour to the way in which he approached the problem of retaining or relinquishing homosexuality.

Treatment

He was given a course of anticipatory avoidance therapy with some improvement, but continued to have sporadic homosexual practice. After 10 sessions he refused one homosexual pick-up, and had taken out a girl, the first for 3 years. As treatment continued he asked for the female slides back more often.

Follow-up

One month after treatment he was still looking at men, for whom he felt quite strongly. "I feel I ought to change (from homosexuality) but I don't really want to." He was asked to decide for himself and return in 2 weeks.

Six weeks later he reported a little homosexual practice, and he was continuing his relationship with his girl friend.

Three months later still, he met another girl whom he was instantly attracted to and noted a lessening interest in his current homosexual affair.

Four months later he had stopped visiting the homosexual coteries (pubs) and he had become emotionally involved with the girl mentioned above. He was very tense and anxious

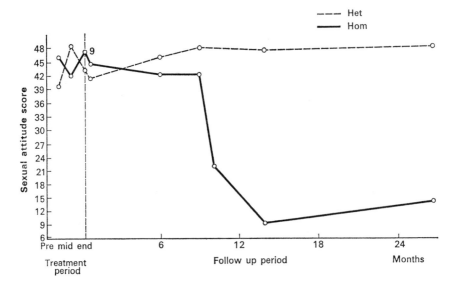

FIG. A5. Series case 9. SOM data.

about the homosexual/heterosexual conflict. Chlordiazepoxide 10 mg t.d.s. was prescribed and a further course of anticipatory avoidance therapy was suggested; he agreed.

A month after the start of the second course, in which his girl friend's photograph was used as the relief stimulus, he reported great improvement. He had stopped his sexual homosexual relationship although he still occasionally met his last homosexual affair.

He was advised to tell his girl friend about his conviction. Their relationship was improving and they were practising kissing and petting. They went on holiday together and had sexual intercourse. "I had always felt before that women wouldn't be as good as men." They became engaged shortly afterwards and decided not to have further sexual intercourse but petting to climax. The patient found this somewhat anxiety producing, for, as he said, "We don't get much time together on our own". He reported that his fiancée was interested in mutual masturbation several times a week, but he sometimes was not and he did not always have an orgasm. This made him depressed and anxious. Aspects of his anankastic personality were revealed when he recounted in detail their saving for a house which was bought and meticulously furnished well before the wedding.

Seventeen months after completion of the second course of treatment he was happily married and settled. Sexual intercourse with his wife was satisfactory. He had no homosexual problem: "You can sit in front of somebody (a man) in the train who is eyeing me up and I'm not excited." He had not had homosexual phantasy for 8 months.

Comment

This patient had been very active homosexually both in phantasy and behaviour; he had also been heterophobic. The change in orientation after a second course of anticipatory avoidance therapy was as dramatic as it was unexpected; successful heterosexual approach behaviour was probably a crucial precursor to aversion therapy.

SERIES CASE 11

Case 11 was a 34-year-old newspaper worker who presented for treatment following a conviction for importuning, stating that he felt guilty after homosexual activity.

Sexual History

His homosexual behaviour started at the age of 16 with mutual masturbation, and over several years later extended to anal intercourse. On one occasion he had formed a slight emotional attachment to his partner, but for the most part he only went with the same person once, feeling guilty and unhappy afterwards. He had had two girl friends before the age of 26 but no intercourse with females apart from joining group sexual activity at the age of 16 which he did not enjoy. Since the age of 26 he had had no girl friends.

Personal History

The patient's father had died when he was 10, but his home life appeared happy. He found it necessary to drink heavily to maintain social adjustment in the face of his guilt and anxiety about homosexuality. The patient was brought up in a strongly Catholic environment which stressed sex as undesirable, and he found mixing with females very difficult.

Personality

He presented with a mild acute anxiety reaction and was fearful that his family would find out his sexual activities. He showed features of self-insecure and weak-willed personality disorders.

Treatment

The patient's anxiety diminished during the course of anticipatory avoidance treatment; and following treatment he began visiting dance halls and seeking female company.

Follow-up

He was heterosexually aroused on a number of occasions, and he reported his attraction to men to be waning. However, several weeks post-treatment he reported that his homosexual interests were beginning to return. Three months after treatment he failed to attend for follow-up despite several reminders, and it was thus presumed that he had again become a practising homosexual.

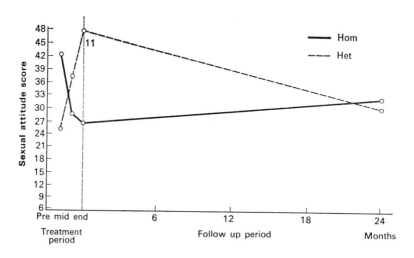

FIG. A6. Series case 11. SOM data.

Discussion

From the avoidance latency data it is immediately clear that there was considerable fluctuation in the first few sessions, although towards the end of the 11 sessions of treatment which he received, he displayed a fairly protracted run of short latency responses. The sharp increase in session 3 associated with the change from the second to the third slide is also of interest.

The patient spontaneously reappeared 24 months post-treatment, the purpose of his visit remained obscure, he was once more practising homosexual acts and he had undergone an attention-seeking psychogenic development. He was boasting about his homosexuality and a recent leg fracture.

SERIES CASE 13

Case 13 was a 47-year-old wages clerk referred by the courts after being charged with having intercourse with a minor.

Sexual History

He was a life-long homosexual with no heterosexual interest or experience of any kind.

He had had a number of "affairs" in which he was emotionally involved and had lived with several partners. The history is taken verbatim from a tape recording which he made prior to his suicide attempt which failed because of lack of money in the gas meter.

Life History

"I was born of humble parents in N, during the 1914–18 war. I did not know my father until the age of about 3 or 4, that was when he first returned from the forces. I don't think on looking back that I have ever had really fond affection for him. He always appeared to me as a rather indifferent type of person, very fond of drink, which I don't condemn him for, but less fond of work, which I do. We were a happy family in many ways, my aunt, my mother—whom I idolized, my two brothers—one born after me and an older brother E, whom I always had very strong affection for, and an older sister O, fair, good-looking, kind, and I always wanted to be in her company; I feel so sad that I have let her down. Now I come to E, she was my other sister, she was somewhat sterner—she was a brunette, but she was a lovely girl, and I know that she thought a lot of me. I can remember the time when E, who can't then have been very old, used to ask me to go to the little shop at the top of the steps to buy things for her; she would also take me on visits to the night school, and I was introduced to her teachers, who made a great fuss of me. I always enjoyed those journeys. Later she went to work, she worked for . . . chocolate and cracker people; she would tell me of her duties, and sometimes she gave me little trinkets. I used to take messages for her, and I really enjoyed doing all these things. Now, there was another great person in my life. That was A, who was O's boy friend. I can never remember a time when we were without A. He did everything for us. He used to take me out, show me the theatre, of which I was very fond, even at an early age. He used to show me the box office, take me behind the scenes, introduce me to the manager, a Shakespearian actor, of great charm and personality. And with this kind of life I grew up. E, my other brother, was just going out to work, and worked very hard indeed, as he has always done. He has been a credit to himself and to the family. He and his friends used to take me out. I can remember a lot of them, a policeman, a coal merchant. We went to football matches, and some of them took me to billiard games. I arrived at the age of 8 years old, and we moved to one of the new council houses in N. It was a great thing to have a house where everybody could have a bedroom, and with a garden. Things were much better. I was never what you would call very well. I had to go to a school which was known as the open-air school. I attended a hospital in N, a nasal clinic, and I think I am right in saying that since the age of 5 years old I have undergone 10 nasal operations. I still get severe trouble with my nose, and also with my sinuses. Well that was that. We went along in our way. Father was never in regular employment. There was always trouble at home because he did not pull his weight. He never agreed with my mother. She was always asking for money which was not forthcoming. It was rather a rough time. E was one of the mainstays of the family. O eventually got married to A. They lived in . . . Street, later moving to a little house in . . . Street where my dear nephew B was born. His name then was N; it was about 1930, and we thought the world of him, at least I know that we still do. E married F. She was lucky, well I shouldn't say lucky, since they saved money, and managed to put a small deposit down, and buy a bungalow. I used to go and visit them and baby sit. Those were my happiest days when I was doing something for my family. They had two charming children, first M and the second M. They are still charming. I can only say I loved them both, and how sorry I am to have let them down. Then life proceeded. I went to work. I did not like it very much. I was working in a factory. I was an apprentice pattern cutter. That was the work I was doing until I took up shop work and became a shop assistant, until, as a result of some misdemeanour, I left, and I joined the army. In 1938 I joined the Royal Army Medical Corps as a private. I worked very hard, one had to work very hard in those days. I think the first payment was 14s. of which 4s. was stopped, and 10s. given to a soldier. Those were happy days. And then in 1939, as you know, war broke out. I was first made a lance-corporal. I was then sent to the Army School at . . . and from then on I graduated and became an instructor. I was a corporal, and I stayed at the Boys Barracks and Training Centre of the Medical Corps until about 1941, when I was transferred to N, when I eventually became in charge of the Reception Centre in 1943. I was demobbed out of the army in 1943. I then went to live with A's in-laws in H. I got employment with D, a gear manufacturing company. I was there for about a year, and was then transferred to. . . . I worked there quite happily until the war ended. Then I managed to get a job at . . . the Office Equipment Company, and I represented them until roughly 1947.

"This you must remember, is only a brief résumé of my life. I do remember I was homosexual, of course, in those days, and one could only lead a very tiresome, lonely life. I did make friends, and I would mention one friend in particular. This was the manager of a theatre. I know that I cannot incriminate him in any way because he is dead now, but we did have quite nice times together. After leaving my job with the Office Equipment Company, I joined the Eastern Electricity Board. Before I left, I went to a pub in N, which was run by a very strange character, known as B. Now B kept this garrison as a club. He would not let anyone else join because there was a shortage of beer and spirits in those days, and his argument was that if people did not support him when there was plenty, why should he look after them when there was a shortage. Now there was one gentleman who used this pub regularly. His name was F. We got on very well together and became inseparable, and I think I would be right if I say that I knew F (Swiss as we used to call him) for 15 years. Now I can put a lot on to this. We had wonderful times in N together, with such people as T, and we played cards together. I wish it could be possible to meet some of these people again, because I know they would understand something of my sorrow. While we were in N, things went along smoothly. It was F, Swiss, and I, and we more or less lived for one another. I looked for no other outlet. I know people condemned it, but then people don't know everything. Eventually Swiss had trouble with his sister—I don't blame her in any way, I think he must have been something of a trouble to her, but they decided that they must sell out, and he would take his share of the business and she would have hers. This occurred in 1951, as Swiss left for Australia. He left me on my own, and I am not much good at this, as you will see when you listen to the rest of the recording. He went away. He wrote me letters. I am very careless about letters. I leave them lying about, not believing that other people would read other people's letters, as I myself would never do so. But seemingly this is not so.

"Well, I was living with my dear mother. We moved to W Rd. and we were very happy. We had a little dog called Sally, whom I loved very much, and also a cat called Mickey. We had some wonderful times. E and E would come up on Sundays. So would E and F, M and M, O and A, D and her husband, my aunt and uncle. F (or Swiss) was away, and I used to go to the club. I used to drink, and then think about trying to get a passage to Australia. This was forthcoming, but nevertheless the trip to Australia never did materialize.

"I left the Electricity Board, and I am sorry to tell you, I ran away to Dublin. I spent 6 months there, 6 very unhappy months, apart from the time I spent with a person I worked for, Rev. R, of course I can only say he was a Christian and I enjoyed every moment I was there. I left Dublin in September. It is funny but September, you will find, plays a great part in my life. It will probably play a part in my death. I left Dublin, after telephoning F from there to say I would meet him in London, when he came off the boat. I did so. We went to stay at a hotel. I was not well at this time. We stayed at this hotel in R. Square (the same one as O stayed with her husband when in London) for about a week. We scanned the papers, and eventually we found a flat in Maida Vale. We lived there for about 6 months. During this time I was not working, and S's money was running out, so I had to get a job, and I asked him to get one also. It was very difficult. Eventually I did get a job with the Naafi, and I stayed there for about 6 months until I came back to London on S's request, because he could not stand being on his own and being in lodgings. When I came back I got another job at S and W. That was in 1952. I went there as invoice clerk. I think, my wages to start with were around £7 10s. 0d. a week. This was a meagre wage, and in the meantime S had obtained employment in a school shop in C and he was earning a round wage of £10 a week. So we put this money together and we got a small flat in N Lane. We did not stay there long, and moved to another flat soon after, in C Road. After about a year we heard of a flat that was going from some friends of ours, dear old JK, her son-in-law kept a hotel and had a flat in S Road, which he offered us, at, I think, about £4 a week. We were delighted to take this residence, and we lived there well up to 1960. During this time S changed his job—I was still at S and W—and he worked for the Civil Service, to be precise the Ministry of Civil Aviation. Now they were very good to him, but his health all the time was failing. When he came back from Australia he came back at a time when there was much smog in London, and he contracted asthma. He had to give up smoking, and he was off work for very long periods. I nursed him, looked after him, and he was always in and out of hospital. Finally, I took him to hospital in 1960, and this time he never came out of hospital; he had cancer of the lung and after 6 months he died. I had to tell him this in the August, and it is a very sorry thing to have to tell a person of whom one is very fond, that there is no hope for him. He eventually died after being transferred back to N, in September. Again this month crops up. Previous to that in the July of the same year, my father died, and I am very sorry to say that on 30 September, which was my mother's birthday, she was taken ill on the eve of her birthday, I was summoned by telephone on the following day. I travelled down to N and on the Sunday, that was Sunday evening, or early Monday morning, I stayed with her; we were on our own, with the exception of Mrs. S, a dear old lady who stayed to keep us company. She passed away on the early Monday morning. So in that year I lost my father, whom I had grown more fond of, I lost my greatest and dearest friend, Swiss, and I lost the best friend anyone could have, my mother.

"Well, I had changed jobs, and moved to another firm. A good friend was responsible for getting me the new job. I started with them at about £15 a week as a salesman. I did very various jobs for them. I worked in the West End, I was transferred to C. I could have had the C shop as manager but I refused. I volunteered to go up to M, and eventually in May 1961, I came up to M, and was assistant manager until 1962, when through no fault of my own, a cheque, which we were not supposed to take, bounced to the value of £62. I covered up for the manager, who was a married man with three children, and he asked me if it would be all right if we could pay the money in so that we would not be found out. A friend of mine lent me £30—that was JH, and he is a friend, and I paid him back a pound a week. and I think I owe him a balance of £7. But so far I have not received the other £23 from Mr. . . ., but that is just by the way. So I was suspended last year, 1962, and took another job. That again was in September. I was lucky enough to gain employment by the International Computers and Tabulators, and was in this job as their wages clerk. Now I have been very happy there, and I must say they treated me very well indeed, and of the manager, Mr. T, I can say nothing but praise. He has been most understanding, and has given me every assistance. As a matter of fact he has put me in line for a much better job, and a job that I feel sure I could have done, had it not been for the following event.

"This took place on Saturday, 17 August, when I met a boy, brought him back to my flat, and we had sexual relations. He again returned on the Sunday. He enjoyed it, and so did I. Like me he was homosexual, and we could have been, if it had been possible, quite good friends, but there was a great difference in our age, and I was entirely to blame. When I got away to L I was thinking about him and I wrote him a letter, not because I knew I was not going to see him again, but just like one would write a letter to someone, one loves. This letter was intercepted, taken to the police. His father, quite naturally, was perturbed, and a case is being brought against me, gross indecency, under Section I of the Sexual Offences Act, and I am now on remand."

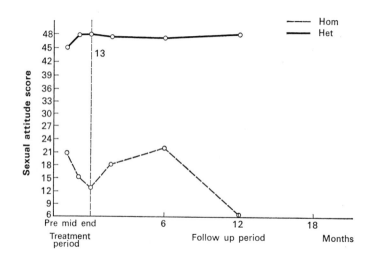

Fig. A7. Series case 13. SOM data.

Personality

He was somewhat obsessional in personality and had strong attention-seeking traits. He made a frankly attention-seeking suicidal attempt the day before admission to hospital. He was a man of practised charm who would undertake any course of behaviour which was to his advantage.

Treatment

Treatment had no effect on his interests, and during its course he attempted to make an assignation with another homosexual in-patient (case no. 11) who refused his offer. On discharge, he was placed on a weekly injection of oestrogen and claimed as a result of this to have little libido. However, there was evidence from attitude scale measurements that this was unlikely to be true, quite apart from his known ability to present a smooth and deceptive front.

Follow-up

He was last seen 12 months post-treatment at which time he remained unchanged.

Discussion

The response latencies for this patient* are quite interesting. Firstly, his responses during session 1 are rather too good to be true in that he made a large number of short latency responses despite not having experienced a single shock. During session 2, in which the second slide was used, the result was exactly opposite in that he made no avoidance responses at all. However, sessions 3, 4, and 5 show him returning to his earlier pattern of a large number of short latency responses. Session 6 again demonstrates increasing response latency following the introduction of a more attractive slide; this is followed by a decline. Finally, in session 8 there were again almost no avoidance responses, and the patient then said that his behaviour during this session represented his true feelings. He stated that if he were being honest he would never switch off without the shock. It was felt at this point that the treatment was unlikely to succeed and, therefore, it was terminated.

SERIES CASE 17

Case 17 was urgently admitted under Section 29 of the Mental Health Act to a neighbouring mental hospital at the age of 25 years. He was thought to be suffering from schizophrenia; after treatment with stelazine his symptoms resolved and he was transferred for treatment of his homosexuality. He started his story as follows: "I thought there was a plot."

He had been alone on a youth hostelling holiday in the Lake District. One night as he was dozing off to sleep he heard whispering which said "meet me tomorrow". He was sharing a room with a group of men whom he thought to be homosexual. A voice said "he's not innocent". The patient was unable to pin-point the speakers, and he developed the strong feeling that he was being provoked. Next day he moved to another hostel, only to be followed there by the same group of people; he witnessed one male of 40 trying to sexually seduce two youths. He thought that this was done to provoke him into revealing his homosexual leanings.

He talked to the man and felt that the latter seemed to know "too much about me". He began to feel there was a plot against him—the boys were sent to spy on him to get him to join the coterie. He became panicky and depressed. It *seemed* that the boys could read his thoughts; he took a train back to his digs and even there whispers continued in his bedroom; the voices were inside his head, accusing him of homosexuality. He thought the landlady had a microphone hidden in the light fitting. In great distress he consulted a minister who arranged for his urgent admission to hospital. At no time had he experienced first-rank

*See Fig. 6.5, p. 99.

symptoms of schizophrenia. He had felt mildly depressed before his holiday, and the total content of his experiences and thoughts was readily explained in terms of his sensitive personality abnormality and his sexual history.

Sexual History

He discovered self-masturbation at 11 and felt guilty afterwards. He first became sexually aware of girls at 12, and he held hands in the cinema; he felt indifferent to this experience.

Again at 18 he desultorily associated with three girls and kissed them with very little interest. At 19 he took a girl out for 4–5 months, kissing and holding hands.

From 13 he had thought about men and thought that if he had been approached by one he would have responded easily. He continued to admire handsome men. At 19 he was approached by a 23-year-old man. They went to bed naked and kissed passionately. He fell in "love", and they practised naked petting for several months until the "affair" broke up.

One year later he practised masturbation at a Baptist college and fell in love with another man at 23. He was introduced to fellatio and began to frequent homosexual coteries where he diligently sought the "perfect affair" by embarking on a series of affairs involving partners whom he described as "butch". His main practice was fellatio and active buggery with heavy emphasis on kissing and nudity. He never had "casual" sex after 19 years of age, and displayed a great deal of ambivalence to his sexual behaviour, having hoped at one period to enter the ministry.

Personal History

He was an only child. His father died in the Second World War, he remembered little of his childhood, attained five O-levels at school, and after attending a Baptist college for 3 years, became a librarian at 23.

Personality

On examination his dress and manner were "camp". His verbal manner was obsessional, slow-studied, and unenthusiastic. No symptoms or signs of psychosis could be elicited, and there was no family history of such. He had consulted a psychiatrist about his homosexuality 5 years previously but had been told that no help was available. He said that he wanted to become heterosexual, but his real motivation was thought to be poor.

Treatment

He was accepted for a trial of anticipatory avoidance as an in-patient.

Follow-up

After 20 sessions he had a fairly strong interest in girls and his homosexual interest had diminished.

After a further 10 treatments he was discharged from the ward. One week later he was feeling slightly depressed, although he was free from homosexual phantasy during masturbation. He still looked at males in the street and "weighed them up". He was advised to look away from men and to make a practice of looking at all girls, interesting himself in as many facets as possible, e.g. fashion styles, clothes, faces, figures, etc. He decided to take dancing lessons, but it was still felt that he had low general drive and poor motivation to give up homosexuality. One month post-treatment he had been to a homosexual pub and had gone back to a friend's flat. The usual advances were made to him and he "found it hard to kiss him, I had active intercourse, I found it revolting—I was much slower to orgasm than before.

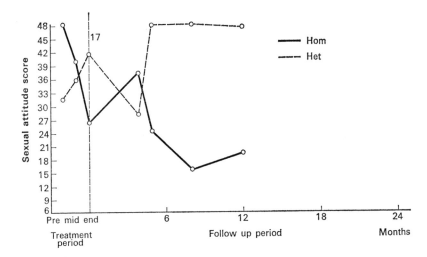

Fig. A8. Series case 17. SOM data.

I would have preferred it to have been a girl." He was pleased with this change. At his next visit, 5 weeks post-treatment, he described a friendship with a 41-year-old widow whom he thought was attracted to him. He became anxious about the relationship, and one night in bed he heard a whispered voice saying "she wants to marry you". On further questioning this turned out to be an inner voice. For months, post-treatment, he had visited a homosexual club and performed buggery after 4 pints of beer. He claimed to feel nauseated by his partner's expression of love. He was sharing a flat with another male who formed the content of his auto-masturbatory phantasy.

Further booster sessions of anticipatory avoidance were suggested and accepted.

Sixteen months after the initial treatment he had a girl friend whom he had been dating for a month: he was holding hands and kissing. On a weekend that she was away, he revisited a homosexual haunt and felt "really out of it . . . nothing happened".

He was subject to mood swings from euthymia to depression; often becoming depressed when he was lonely or bored. It was at these times that the patient felt the urge to go to homosexual coteries.

In depressed moods he heard voices particularly when an attractive male guest was present in the hostel where he was staying.

The patient reappeared some months after final follow-up in order to state that he had finally "found himself". Over the previous 4 months he had not made or received any homosexual advances until 4 weeks prior to interview. He met a man, a fellow guest, at a wedding; at first he refused the man's advances, but after receiving several letters decided that he had fallen "in love". He said, "This is the first time I've been able to justify it" (homosexual sex). He had been on holiday with his partner and practised masturbation and buggery.

SERIES CASE 21

Case 21 was a 19-year-old university student who sought help directly. "I have lesbian tendencies involving one girl for the past 18 months. Men give me feelings of revulsion and yet I enjoy conquering them sexually. I feel the need to be liked, admired and found attractive by everyone . . . female and male."

Sexual History

At 8 she slept at weekends at the house of a girl friend and they played at "sex games", kissing and caressing. At 12–14 she repeated the same games of playing at being man and wife. S took the role of the man although she had phantasy of being made pregnant herself. At 15 she slept with a 13-year-old Austrian girl on an exchange scheme, they kissed and caressed. At 17 she met P (case no. 34) at a party. The patient was drunk, she put P to bed and got into bed with her; they made "love" (mutual masturbation) right through the night. Later, they attempted not to see each other, but S's parents found out and she was sent on a holiday.

They corresponded, declaring "undying love". They spent a holiday together a year later, making love nightly by mutual masturbation in which they hurt each other deliberately in order to heighten orgasm.

She then met a boy friend who persuaded her to seek psychiatric help.

She recalled flirting with boys from the age of 7; commenced kissing boys at 12, petting at 14, and had her first experience of intercourse at 16 with one boy over a period of 18 months. She then had sexual intercourse with a succession of boys—without achieving orgasm. "The affairs I have with men make me hate myself and leave me with disgust for both them and myself."

Personal History

Her birth and early milestones were normal. She remembers marked tantrums resisting conformity, always tending to be excitable. She describes her parents as follows: "My mother is a very forceful character—giving a semblance of benevolence to everyone, she is basically selfish and always makes a martyr of herself. I was made the centre of attention, her inconsistency to me has confused me and made me very insecure. She wants to use me to satisfy her own inadequacies. I am quite sure deep down she hates me. My father is rather weak, he always needs to depend on someone. He has always given me the impression that his own sex life has been very dreary—he often discusses his sex life with me."

Personality

She had a self-insecure and attention-seeking personality abnormality, the former being the most prominent.

Treatment

She was given anticipatory avoidance and advised to disassociate herself from her lesbian partner who in fact presented for treatment several months later. She made steady progress in becoming sexually averse to females, including her former sexual partner.

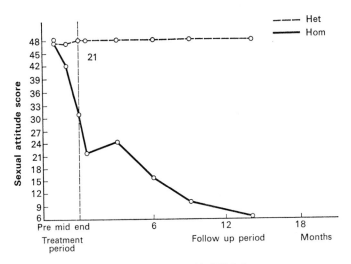

FIG. A9. Series case 21. SOM data.

Follow-up

At follow-up sessions her relationship with her parents was worked through, and her attitude to men and heterosexual sex reappraised. She continued to be somewhat impressionable, and received several "love" letters from her former partner at times when the latter was particularly stressed.

Seven months after treatment she became pregnant and a therapeutic abortion was undertaken upon the recommendation of a consultant psychiatrist. The pregnancy and termination formed a key experience for her, and subsequently she appeared much more mature and stable. She settled down with one steady boy friend and took her degree 31 months after treatment, as well as keeping up her interest in amateur music. At her last follow-up she reported an absence of lesbian interest, thought, and behaviour. She was experiencing a normal heterosexual life, and at 35 months post-treatment she was reported, by hearsay, to be happily married.

SERIES CASE 22

Case 22 was a 20-year-old grocery salesman who was referred by another psychiatrist with complaints of homosexual practices.

Sexual History

He discovered masturbation at 8, and later witnessed mutual masturbation at school but did not join in because he thought it was "wrong".

At 15 he saw an adult's penis for the first time. The man displayed his erect penis in a public convenience and attempted anal intercourse with the patient in a cubicle. The attempt was unsuccessful because it was painful and the patient was frightened. However, from then on he thought of the erect penis continually, and returned to the lavatory hoping to meet the same man. He began to visit toilets to watch men masturbate; occasionally he performed mutual masturbation.

At 18 he was "picked up" by a man in a cinema and went to the man's flat. Mutual masturbation, intra-crural intercourse, and fellatio were performed. He began to visit homosexual coteries nightly, and 18 months before presentation had an affair with a 33-year-old man who re-introduced him to fellatio. That affair lasted a year. At presentation he was practising auto-masturbation with bisexual phantasy, including voyeristic phantasy of heterosexual sexual intercourse, fellatio, and kissing. He was particularly fond of kissing and said, "I will kiss anybody".

He was first sexually attracted to a girl at $13\frac{1}{2}$. At 16 he had managed to overcome his shyness and kiss a girl.

He engaged in "necking sessions" at 18 with enjoyment and had sexual intercourse at 19. He had taken out four girls *in toto*. When he immersed himself in the homosexual world there was neither time nor opportunity to see girls. His interest was such that he only looked at men in the street. At presentation his heterosexual interest was slight, and practice nil.

Personal History

He was illegitimate and never saw his real father, being brought up by his mother who remarried when the patient was 2. One year later his mother contracted pulmonary tuberculosis and was admitted to a sanatorium. The patient was admitted to a series of children's homes from the age of 3–11. He said: "They [the homes] were rotten, nobody cared for us— I wanted to go home, but I never cried. When I got home my stepfather was rotten, he didn't talk to me and he used to hit me for nothing."

He attended a variety of schools between 5 and 15 years but did very poorly and never learned to read or write. This difficulty appeared to arise from his personality: "I've always disliked being told what to do—I secretly think I'm better than other people."

From 15 he had a series of jobs, moving several times to better himself, once due to his illiteracy and once because an unreasonable (as he thought) request was made of him.

Personality

He appeared as a very smartly dressed young man of great verbal fluency. He was very ambitious and was deeply upset by his illiteracy, which he intended to remedy by attending night school. He showed features of a self-insecure personality abnormality which in previous years appeared to have disabled him, e.g. was the cause of his dismissal on two occasions.

He appeared to be emotionally stable and was successfully filling a junior managerial post in a supermarket. There was no evidence of psychosis, and his early traumatic years did not appear to have had major damaging effects. He lived at home.

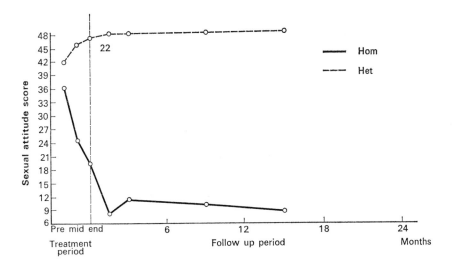

FIG. A10. Series case 22. SOM data.

Family History

His mother appeared to have a sensitive personality; her relationship with the patient was distant. His stepfather beat him a good deal in his early teens and was described as "hard, tough and explosive". There were five younger female sibs and one young male sib.

Treatment

He was admitted for treatment and had anticipatory avoidance aversion therapy. He responded rapidly. After 2 sessions he commented: "I've hardly thought about men and I'm masturbating less and thinking about women when I do." After treatment he reported: "I saw two queers in drag—thought about them and felt disgusted—later thought about them and was actually sick."

Follow-up

He had begun to take a keen interest in girls and no longer had to fight to prevent himself from thinking of and looking at men.

Two weeks after treatment he decided to leave home and to take a flat because of a disagreement with his stepfather. He went into a homosexual toilet "to see what I'd feel" and was nauseated.

Six months after treatment, he was well, working satisfactorily, and a week previously he had been to bed with a girl and had brought both the girl and himself to orgasm by partial penetration.

The month before review he had entered a homosexual toilet near to a homosexual pub. "There was a lad in there. . . . I felt nervous, got outside and ran. . . . I don't think I could have sex with a man now."

Fifteen months post-treatment he had maintained the change, reporting no homosexual interest. He was taking girls out, kissing and petting with strong interest. His auto-masturbatory phantasy was heterosexual.

SERIES CASE 27

Case 27 was a 41-year-old single clerk, one of six children.

Sexual History

He was first masturbated by an 8-year-old boy when he himself was 8. Mutual masturbation continued weekly for 2 years and then with another boy for a further 2 years. It is not clear when his auto-masturbatory phantasy became homosexual. At 14 he developed a transient interest in girls and attempted to seduce and have sexual intercourse with a 15-year-old girl, but she refused. He was annoyed and his interest in girls tended to diminish although he went out with a girl on three occasions during the years 14–18. He joined the RAF at 18, and at that time his auto-masturbatory phantasy was male and included mutual masturbation. From 20 to 23 he had satisfactory sexual intercourse with a female prostitute on three occasions. He began to practise mutual masturbation in a homosexual coterie in Cairo. On his return to the United Kingdom at 24, he continued to practise sporadic mutual masturbation, and began to drink heavily, up to 8 pints of beer per night.

At an Army party he was approached by another homosexual. This attempted "pick-up" disturbed him, and he consulted his MO who re-drafted him.

He began to experience very strong attraction to men, and began to wonder if people could tell he was homosexual by looking at him. He became persistently anxious, and was discharged from the RAF at 28. He joined a construction firm in a clerical job and continued casual homosexual sex. He was referred by another consultant.

On presentation, his sexual practices were mutual masturbation, fellatio, buggery, intra-crural sexual intercourse, and petting. As well as his homosexuality he complained of nervousness and a stammer which he had had from the age of 3. His physical health was good.

Personal History

He described his childhood as "poverty stricken. I was unhappy because I compared poorly with other children." His father seemed to the patient to be emotionally indifferent; he drank heavily and was strict with the children in contrast to the mother who was "weak willed" and tended to confide in the patient, telling him her personal worries.

He was a poor scholar, left school at 14 to become a page boy, and later became a bar waiter in an RAF officers' mess for 20 years. At 38 he suffered from marked anxiety and ideas of reference in relation to his homosexuality, and was discharged from the Service with a diagnosis of anxiety neurosis.

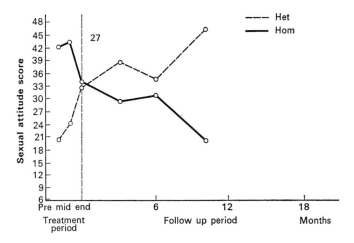

Fig. A11. Series case 27. SOM data.

Personality

He displayed lifelong sensitive and obsessional traits. He felt that his homosexuality had blighted his life, and he was prone to intermittent attacks of anxiety in which his sexual problem was the central theme.

Treatment

He was given anticipatory avoidance aversion. During his treatment he recorded a steady diminution in his homosexual interest and his interest in females was slightly increased; however, his auto-masturbatory phantasy was still male. After treatment he felt himself to be predominantly heterosexual in orientation.

Follow-up

At 3 months follow-up he reported three homosexual pick-ups. The first resulted in mutual masturbation, accompanied by strong guilt—a new feature. The other two were abortive.

Twelve months after treatment he described his situation as excellent. He had made two further abortive pick-ups and reported his interest in men was minimal. He had begun to date females and enjoyed their company and felt sexually aroused when with them. His auto-masturbatory phantasy was exclusively female. He felt more relaxed than before treatment because his mind was not constantly filled with sexual thoughts.

SERIES CASE 28

Case 28 was a 34-year-old secondary school teacher who referred himself with the following problem: "abnormal attraction to boys, chronic masturbation, and a difficulty in getting on with adults."

Sexual History

He was introduced to mutual masturbation at the age of $12\frac{1}{2}$ by the brother 3 years his senior. They practised this once weekly for 6 months. The patient commenced auto-masturbation, his mutual masturbation generalized to other boys at school and continued until he left school 6 years later. His auto-masturbatory phantasy consisted of mutual masturbation with his partners.

He joined the Navy at 19, where he had mutual masturbation once in the following 2 years. His auto-masturbatory phantasy continued unchanged.

He continued auto-masturbation for the following 4 years and refrained from homosexual activities. During this period he qualified as a male nurse, nursed in Canada, and studied at a teachers training college on his return to the United Kingdom. He also became a scout master, having been a scout from the age of 11. He practised mutual masturbation with scouts. At 28 he started teaching and practised mutual masturbation with a 14-year-old boy whilst on a walking holiday.

At 31, two 14-year-old boys visited his home regularly to practise mutual masturbation with him for a period of 2 months.

Eighteen months before consultation he "interfered with a scout". The boy was disturbed and the patient "realized that it was serious". He gave up scouting 6 months later so that he would not "pervert any more boys", although he continued to see one of the boys at home, when mutual masturbation was performed approximately once per month.

On presentation he was practising auto-masturbation 12 times a week and commented: "I felt I was getting depressed about all this, I've always been noted as being lively—it's always on my mind—the temptation is too great for me."

He had two girl friends at about 17. He had only slightly enjoyed holding hands and kissing, practices which were repeated with one girl when he was 19. Since that time he had felt no heterosexual interest.

Personal History

He was the youngest of five children, having two male and two female sibs. His birth and early years were unremarkable. His father was a very quiet, retiring, conscientious man who suffered from *petit mal*. By contrast his mother was "forceful—she wore the trousers, was authoritarian".

Personality

He was a small, diffident man with greying hair who was markedly obsessional, taking an hour to complete his dressing routine in the mornings. He was never late for appointments, and his main interest, besides scouting, was cine-photography. He was easily moved emotionally with a poor capacity for exteriorization. Apart from his paedophilia, he showed considerable strength of purpose. On examination he was thought to be slightly depressed. The depression of mood was thought to be part of a depressive psychogenic development which had occurred over the 5 years prior to treatment.

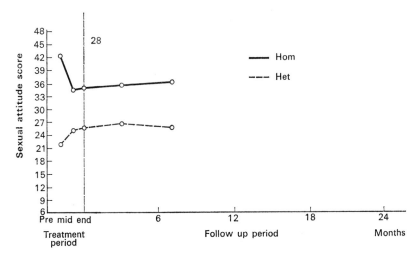

FIG. A12. Series case 28. SOM data.

Treatment

He was treated by anticipatory avoidance aversion as an outpatient. During the first month of treatment his masturbation rate halved.

Follow-up

Ten months after the start of treatment he had not performed any homosexual acts, and was masturbating five times a week with boys as phantasy material. He reported a virtual absence of heterosexual interest, and a further series of treatments was suggested. The patient failed to attend, although he rang the department several times to tender excuses. It was not possible either to try further treatment or to observe the patient's progression without it. It must be presumed that he relapsed.

SERIES CASE 31

Case 31 was a 33-year-old sales clerk who was referred by his factory MO because of his homosexuality. He had been charged with importuning 2 months prior to being seen, and had been the subject of a similar charge in October 1961.

Five months prior to interview his mother died, and he had been depressed during the interim period. He complained of drinking too much—to help him sleep. He felt that he was "too fond of myself—I don't feel that I am a good husband or father".

Sexual History

He was introduced to mutual masturbation at 7 by an older school friend. At this time he disliked games, and acquired the nickname of "pansy". He was led to believe that he was effeminate; he began to think that his voice and gait were effeminate.

He continued mutual masturbation with boys and was masturbated on three occasions by men in cinemas. At 24 he began to look for homosexual men in male toilets. He felt shy on these occasions but remarked that there were "no preliminaries"—in contrast to girls whom he began to date at 15. He felt extremely shy, and at this time noted a strong sexual attraction to men.

He met his wife when he was 16 and married at 23. He had no difficulty with heterosexual sexual intercourse which he preferred to his continued homosexual sexual acts. He developed an interest in singing and the stage, and at the time of interview was doubling his income by means of a singing act. He and his wife also were landlords of several flats.

Personal History

He was the younger of two brothers, born after a difficult breech labour. He remembered little of his father, who died of TB when the patient was 7. He described his mother as "wonderful", a very popular woman of high drive and strong personality, who ran a spirits off-licence for many years.

He left school at 15 and worked for 2 years as a clerk. He then served 2 years in the RAF as a corporal before returning to his previous employment.

Personality

He showed features of a self-insecure personality abnormality, with an abnormal psychogenic development concerning his appearance (which was normal). He had grown a beard to hide his face which he thought was effeminate.

At preliminary interview he was depressed and anxious. The psychic content was related to his court case, and there was no further feature of endogenous depression.

Family History

There was no familial psychiatric history.

Treatment

He commenced anticipatory avoidance treatment as an out-patient early in April 1965. His wife was interviewed a month later and she was found to be giving him good support. He had been placed on probation for 2 years.

Follow-up

By 15 June he said: "I am prepared to say something definite has happened—sex [with men] doesn't enter my head." He had begun to find females other than his wife attractive.

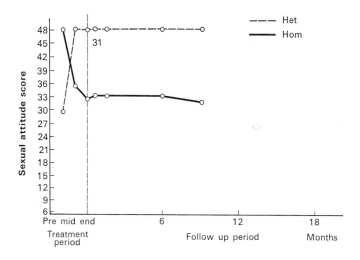

FIG. A13. Series case 31. SOM data.

In June 1966 he reported feeling "a return to square one". He noted an attraction to men in public lavatories and had been tempted to indulge in homosexual practice.

At this time he was depressed following a period of intense work associated with the production of a show. He reported early morning waking, impaired concentration and memory, and was drinking sherry to help him get to sleep.

He was prescribed nortryptilene 50 mg t.d.s., and 2 weeks later all his symptoms had much improved.

At follow up, a month later, he described his sexual interest as heterosexual once again. His depression had cleared and he was gradually weaned off his anti-depressant drug.

At final follow-up 16 months post-treatment he had no homosexual interest, phantasy or practice, his depressive symptoms were absent, there was no detectable abnormality in his life pattern and he was practising mutually pleasurable sexual intercourse with his wife.

Discussion

Subsequent experience would indicate that the homosexual interest was stronger than the patient acknowledged. It would perhaps have been wiser to prolong follow-up and use further aversion therapy if the patient suffered any further depression of mood ground.

SERIES CASE 41

Case 41 was a 33-year-old steel company middle-grade executive who presented of his own accord prior to a charge of indecent assault on a 17-year-old male.

Sexual History

When first seen he insisted that his only homosexual experience had been with the boy concerning whom he faced the charge and with whom he had been associating for the previous year. He stated that he had tried several times to break off the relationship but the boy had threatened him with blackmail. Finally, the boy informed his parents and they went to the police. The patient stated that the boy liked being hurt and that he used to hit him as part of sexual play. He was "trying to turn the boy into a man". The patient also stated that when he saw a good sportsman who was good-looking he liked him, but denied any other homosexual episodes apart from mutual masturbation for a brief period at school.

Personal History

He had served several years in the RAF and had completed pilot training. He was very keen on sport and "lived for sport" when he was not actually working. He enjoyed showing off and being the centre of attraction. He also enjoyed getting drunk and being in "punch-ups". His early family life had been happy and he had been attached to his parents, becoming severely depressed, with endogenous features, at the death of his mother. Whilst he was not strongly attracted to females at the time of presentation, he had had several affairs in his twenties and early thirties involving intercourse with females. He accounted for the affair with the boy of 17 in terms of his strong desire to make the boy more of a man. He was very strongly motivated for treatment, stating that he wanted to live a decent life without pretence. Several days later the patient felt able to give a full history of his homosexuality. This had started at the age of 10 when a man had tried to touch his genitals in the pictures. There followed several years of mutual masturbation at school, and for the next few years he was strongly attracted to various males. However, he still denied any further homosexual episodes during his Air Force career and, indeed, any further ones until the age of 26, when he was at a club dance and met an 18-year-old friend with whom he played soccer. The patient touched him by accident, and this led to mutual masturbation. The patient felt very protective towards the friend and the affair lasted 2–3 years until the friend met a girl. There then followed another affair with a young man he met whilst in another city. In each case the affair was terminated by the partner, and in each case the patient felt very upset by this. He stated that he seemed to feel much more deeply about the partner than vice versa and was always prepared to go out of his way to do favours for the partner. There was some evidence, therefore, of sensitive personality features. From the time of his late twenties he started picking up men in public conveniences. He also stated that for the previous 8 or 9 months he had almost no desire for a female. There was a gradual increase of homosexual desire and practice and a gradual decrease of heterosexual desire and practice.

Personality

He was assessed as a self-insecure disorder with attention-seeking, labile, and explosive abnormalities.

Treatment

After 5 sessions of treatment which was administered on an in-patient basis, the patient became involved in some horseplay in the ward with a female patient.

Follow-up

This led to his discharge from the ward, and although efforts were made to contact him subsequently, these were unsuccessful. It was felt that the prospects for a successful outcome here were reasonably good, and the termination of treatment was therefore particularly unfortunate in this instance.

2. THE TRIAL

Fifteen case histories have been selected, 5 from each of the groups randomly assigned to treatment by anticipatory avoidance, classical conditioning, and psychotherapy. The first 5 cases which follow are drawn from the AA group, the next 5 from the CC group, and the last five from the P group. Each group of 5 has been selected to illustrate the primary/secondary dichotomy and the part played by personality disorder. SOM data, data on avoidance latencies, and pulse rates are presented for all instances in which they were obtained.

TRIAL CASE 2

Case 2 was an 18-year-old drama student referred by his University Health Service because of mood swings and a homosexual problem.

Sexual History

He had been shown how to masturbate at school at the age of 11. Shortly afterwards he had had a prolonged illness (osteomyelitis of the knee), and during this time he masturbated himself, using the previous mutual masturbation as phantasy. On return to school be became fond of another boy, and had an affair with him, practising nudity and mutual masturbation over a period of 1½ years. From then on he developed crushes on a series of boys but was too timid to request overt sexual practice with them. At 13 he became interested in a girl of his own age. He would go and stand outside her home, but when she came out he was too shy to ask her to "be his girl". Other girls said that he was "too slow", and from then on he never tried to take another girl out. At 14 he was asked to take a car ride with him by an insurance clerk who called at his home. He agreed but ran off when the man wanted to fondle his genitals.

He then began to loiter in public conveniences and pick up homosexuals without allowing any practices; he also began to read about homosexuality in paper-back novels. At 15 he "realized" that he was homosexual and got himself a girl friend "because everyone else had one". He held hands, kissed, and tried nude petting without interest, but failed to get an erection. He felt unable to sustain the relationship because of his lack of sexual interest. He then took out another girl of whom he became fond. He attempted kissing and petting and went to bed with her but was unable to obtain an erection. He found touching her genitals to be distasteful, and also was disgusted when she attempted to masturbate him. At 16, whilst he was on holiday with his parents, he picked up a male Spaniard and practised fellatio in his hotel bedroom. Later the same year he met his current affair—a 28-year-old man whom he stated to be wealthy and influential in the theatre world. He was re-introduced to fellatio and was encouraged to be homosexually promiscuous. He went up to university at the age of 18, and 5 weeks prior to interview he met a fellow girl student whom he kissed with pleasure. He told her about his homosexuality and broke down and cried. He felt a great relief of tension at this point, and felt guilty. "After I told her, I didn't know where to put myself."

Personal History

He had a 26-year-old sister, and his early childhood was disturbed. His father was a publican and drank heavily, often hitting the patient, his sister, and mother. The father was described as having a "chip on his shoulder against well educated, wealthy and successful people". The patient's outlook has been coloured by his working-class upbringing and unhappy childhood. It was interesting to note that he considered his mother a snob. "She had had a wealthy childhood and is well educated. She often escapes into that world; she has a middle-class morality." Both parents had an "embarrassed" attitude to sex. His mother was often cruel to both children and was said to have had a "nervous breakdown" in her earlier life.

Previous Medical and Psychiatric History

He had osteomyelitis of the knee at the age of 11, and had become mildly reactively depressed on three occasions following the break-off of homosexual affairs.

Personality

He showed marked sensitive features and was judged to be suffering from a self-insecure personality disorder. On interview his manner became theatrical and anxious and he said he had difficulty in concentrating on his studies. He was very strongly motivated to change from being homosexual and was disturbed by his feelings for his current girl friend.

Treatment

He was treated with chlordiazepoxide whilst waiting to start therapy. He had 24 sessions of classical conditioning, and after therapy he noted a marked lessening in his homosexual interest and the cessation of his homosexual masturbatory phantasy. He was more interested in females and reported heightened pleasure in sexual contact with his girl friend. His SOM scores also showed a very marked shift. Treatment was therefore terminated.

Follow-up

At 2 weeks follow-up he began to relapse. He was attracted to a man at a party although he continued heterosexual petting with enjoyment and his general heterosexual interest was maintained. At 6 weeks he noted a definite resurgence in his homosexual interest, and his work began to deteriorate. His auto-masturbatory phantasy was male by 10 weeks post-treatment, he had become very tense over faulty exams, and described an episode in which he awoke screaming, his mind filled with homosexual thoughts. It was decided to give further treatment before the 3 month follow-up period had elapsed because it was felt that a change in his sexual orientation would improve his mental state. He was crossed over to anticipatory avoidance as an in-patient and made an immediate response both on his SOM scores and in his mental state.

Two weeks after his anticipatory avoidance treatment (post 12 weeks from classical conditioning) he had spent a weekend with his girl friend; they slept together and she masturbated him to orgasm.

Eight weeks after AA a new term had commenced and his work was going well; he did not feel tense or depressed and had no homosexual phantasies. His auto-masturbatory phantasies were female.

At 14 weeks post-AA follow-up his heterosexual interest was strengthening: "I see her every day, we hold hands and kiss—its lovely." At 16 weeks post-treatment he reported that he had met a man whom he thought had "fancied" him—this proved to be the case and mutual masturbation was performed. He went to talk to his girl friend but could not explain and "felt empty". After a difficult weekend at his parental home when his mother had attempted to be possessive, he went round a series of lavatories picking up men and then dropping them. Then he broke off with his girl friend and picked up with one of her friends and went to bed with her in her flat. He attempted intercourse 4 times but could not get an erection.

His auto-masturbatory phantasy switched to males, and he then tried to seduce a boy in the first-year course for 1 week. He then went back to his steady girl friend and started spending "warm, secure weekends with her".

Thirty-four weeks after second treatment he appeared a week early for appointment. He had suffered an acute depression of mood when trial patient no. 6 picked up a girl at a party which they both attended. He then went out and picked up a man but no homosexual act took place. He then went to see his girl friend and talked the situation through; his sexual orientation was heterosexual although he still had an appreciable attraction to homosexuality. He was assigned a follow-up Kinsey rating of 2.

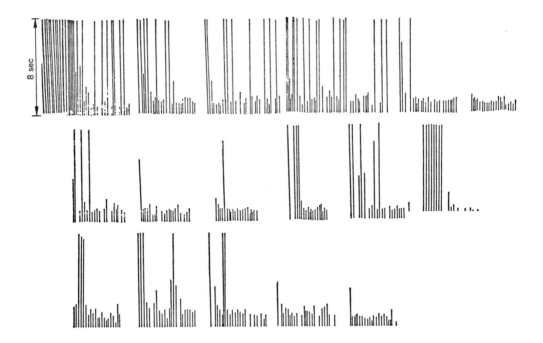

FIG. A14. Trial case 2. Avoidance latency data.

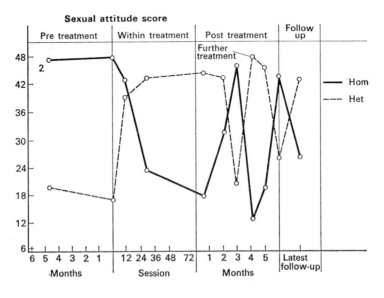

FIG. A15. Trial case 2. SOM data.

Discussion

There is as yet no clear indication of this patient's future sexual object choice; the overall impression is that he is bisexual, predominantly heterosexual. At presentation his personality showed labile traits, which were not fully appreciated at the time. He was undoubtedly a sensitive personality disorder with attention-seeking features. However, his lability of mood appeared to be the personality component which was mainly responsible for the varied response to treatment. The latter is reflected by the avoidance latencies (Fig. A14) which are characterized by interspersed long and short response times in sessions 1–4, followed by an abrupt change to short latencies in 5 and 6 (around 2 seconds), which are repeated throughout the rest of the treatment after a small number of early escape trials.

This patient has been included in the success group because he fulfilled the criterion of a drop of 12 points on the homosexual scale, both after initial treatment (classical conditioning) and at follow-up (43 weeks after the start of classical conditioning). There is SOM evidence that sexual reorientation took place during both periods of aversion therapy, the relapsing course was closely linked to mood, the changes in which were always reactive and disproportionately large in relation to the precipitating stimuli. It seems likely that this patient's personality will settle down, becoming less labile and less insecure; if he were able to continue to have support and possibly more aversion therapy, it seems likely that he would become a stable heterosexual.

TRIAL CASE 3

Case 3 was a 26-year-old Eurasian who was referred by another psychiatrist. At the time of referral the patient's marriage was about to break up because of his homosexuality.

Sexual History

His first homosexual experience took place at school when he was aged 14, and this was communal masturbation involving a number of boys. These meetings continued and later led him to attempt mutual masturbation which thereafter took place twice weekly. He was brought up in Hong Kong and was one-quarter Chinese. He joined the boys' army at $15\frac{1}{2}$ years and he formed a homosexual relationship which lasted a year. The homosexual practice was that of mutual masturbation. During an acute psychogenic reaction, he went absent without leave and was discharged from the Army. He had, in fact, stolen money. He then spent 2 years on probation and later 3 years at approved school for a second theft. At approved school he continued mutual masturbation. At 18 he was called up for National Service and at that time fell in love with a girl to whom he was engaged for a period of 3 months. He practised satisfactory sexual intercourse with her, but the engagement broke up because the girl's mother would not allow her to marry the patient. Following the break of this engagement, he became acutely depressed and married his present wife on impulse. At first, normal sexual intercourse took place over a period of 2 years until he again started homosexual practice. He had a homosexual "affair" which lasted 6 months and in which mutual masturbation was the main sexual practice. He continued to have sexual intercourse with his wife and also made numerous casual homosexual pick-ups. This latter practice continued at the rate of 3 times per month during the next 3 years, during which time he had also had three more homosexual affairs in which he was emotionally involved. Three months prior to admission, his increasing lack of affection for his wife led him to sleep apart from her, and later to leave home for a period of 2 months. He said: "I am not satisfied with my wife as a woman."

Personal History

He was the youngest of three sons of a tobacco planter who lived in Hong Kong, and he had one younger sister. His paternal grandmother and his maternal grandmother were both Chinese. He was said to have been jaundiced shortly after birth. He saw very little of his father during his early years but described himself as being very close to his mother. Shortly after the outbreak of the Second World War he was interned in a Japanese civilian camp and spent several years there with his mother. He summarized those experiences by saying; "I don't feel anything about it now." He came to the United Kingdom when he was 7, and although his parents both survived the war they split up when he was 9 years old. He recalls feeling that his father hated him and thought that this was because he looked Chinese. He had his early schooling in Scotland from 9 until 11, and then moved to Lancashire. He did poorly at school and later had a number of jobs after being demobilized at 21.

Previous Medical and Psychiatric History

He described attacks of reactive depression following the break-up of homosexual affairs at the ages of 18, 20, 23, 24, and 26. During these depressions he became retarded, suffered insomnia, lost interest in life, and had ideas of guilt, but the content of the depression was always that of the homosexual affair. There were no other biological features of depression. There was no significant family history of psychiatric illness.

Personality Classification

Self-insecure abnormality.

Treatment

He was treated by 24 sessions of anticipatory avoidance as an in-patient. Immediately after treatment he stated his homosexuality to be greatly diminished although as he had not seen anyone outside the hospital he could not "put himself to the test". Two weeks following discharge he said: "Everything is fine—home has never been better." Sexual intercourse with his wife was normal; he had changed his job. He stated that he was not looking at men in the street and had no homosexual thoughts, phantasies, or practice.

Follow-up

At 2 weeks, 6 weeks, and 12 weeks he reported a total lack of interest in men. His marriage was better than ever before, sexual intercourse was normal.

At 6 months the picture was the same; in addition he noted an increased interest in women in general. He was assigned a Kinsey rating of 0.

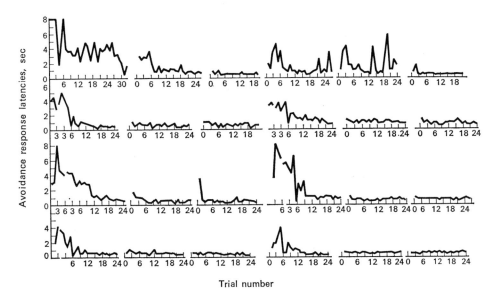

FIG. A16. Trial case 3. Avoidance latency data.

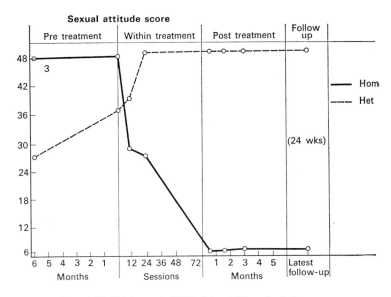

FIG. A17. Trial case 3. SOM data at 24 weeks follow-up.

Discussion

This patient's response to treatment was strikingly clear both clinically and behaviourally; the sexual orientation scale strongly emphasized the clinical impression. The avoidance latencies form classical learning curves without marked irregularity of latency times. Every fourth session, e.g. 1, 4, 7, 10, 13, 16, 19, and 21, shows an initial lengthening of latencies (Fig. A16), which indicates that the slide hierarchy was very accurate. (This factor largely depends on the patient.)

There did not appear to be any inconsistencies in any of the findings, in particular the clinical ones, and the patient was confidently discharged at 6 months follow-up when it became necessary for him to move domicile.

TRIAL CASE 4

Case 4 was a 19-year-old chemistry student who was referred by the consultant at his student health centre. His problem was tension and anxiety generated by strongly recurrent thoughts of himself being a "playboy model"; e.g. a woman, and in this role being masturbated by them. He was sexually interested on observing females, and had previously been sexually interested on thinking of females. His auto-masturbatory phantasy included women on occasions.

Sexual History

He was first shown auto-masturbation by a boy at school when he was 11, and at that time had a phantasy of heterosexual petting. He continued auto-masturbation for 4 years. At 14 he dreamed of lying on top of a naked boy. He began to use this image for auto-masturbation and became very anxious about the possibility of being homosexual. At 16 he first remembered imagining himself as a woman, i.e. in a sexual relationship with a man. This phantasy was the culmination of a year's auto-masturbation with phantasies of full body sex play with males and mutual masturbation. He had two homosexual approaches made to him which he rejected. He later used these events for auto-masturbatory phantasy.

He fell "in love" with two girls when he was 8, and was interested in girls from 11, and at 14 fondled a girl's breast. He had an erection, but was very disappointed by her refusal to let him advance the sex play. At 15 he made a date with a girl whom he had reason to believe would allow sexual intercourse. (He had a friend of 16 who was regarded as a Don Juan and he attempted to emulate his example.) The girl fondled his penis and produced an erection but then went off home. He attempted to see her again, but she refused to see him and he felt a strong sense of failure and resentment. He took a girl to bed at 16; he was very anxious and could only achieve a semi-erection. At $17\frac{1}{2}$ he took a girl to bed at a party after having a good deal to drink. He was completely impotent but did not experience anxiety, presumably because of the alcohol. He said: "I didn't really want sexual intercourse. I was beginning to be very hostile to girls." He always felt himself to be very shy, and his hostility to girls had been fostered by the relationship with his sister, who was 3 years his senior. At $17\frac{1}{2}$ he commenced cross-dressing with his sister's panties to heighten sexual tension and gain a stronger erection.

On presentation his current sexual practice was self-masturbation with male phantasy.

He found maintaining erection difficult, and on presentation he was convinced that he was heterosexually impotent.

In the few months prior to treatment he had had a girl friend whom he liked. There had not been any sex play at all. Four months prior to treatment he had attempted sexual intercourse with a nurse but was impotent and said: "I felt a nut; I did not see her again."

Personality

He was judged to show a sensitive disorder of personality with labile traits.

Personal History

He was the second youngest of four children. The eldest, 27, is male; the others, 21 and 18. female. His early history failed to reveal any significant features. He truanted a number of times to miss games as a junior, and feigned illness in his secondary school to avoid three examinations.

His father was a major in the regular Army, and their relationship was described as "off hand" in contrast to that with his mother which was "close". He did well at school, eventually qualifying for university entrance where he read chemistry. He failed his first-year examinations due to his inability to concentrate.

Treatment

Successful anticipatory avoidance which relapsed at 46 weeks. Second treatment, classical conditioning and anticipatory avoidance combined with anti-depressants. Final follow-up at 56 weeks post completion of first treatment.

Follow-up

Post-treatment: he was able to get an erection to female phantasy and had no homosexual phantasy or interest.

Six weeks post—more strongly heterosexual, but was impotent when he attempted sexual intercourse and became anxious. After this he began to recommence homosexual phantasy during auto-masturbatory phantasy.

Twenty weeks post—he continued to attempt sexual intercourse with success on one occasion, and a week later with more success, and his homosexual interests dwindled to nil.

Thirty weeks post—he broke off his friendship with his girl friend. She had refused sexual intercourse over several weeks and he noted a return to homosexual thinking accompanied by marked reactive depression.

He was readmitted at 46 weeks post first treatment. He was deeply depressed with loss of appetite, sleep disturbance, and a diurnal rhythm, he was treated with chlorprothixine 15 mg t.d.s. and nortriptilene 25 mg t.d.s. for 1 week followed by classical then anticipatory avoidance therapy.

Four weeks post second treatment he was practising auto-masturbation with heterosexual phantasy and reported strong interest in females. No homosexual interest, phantasy, or practice. His mood was normal and the biological symptoms of depression were absent. He was assigned a Kinsey rating of 0.

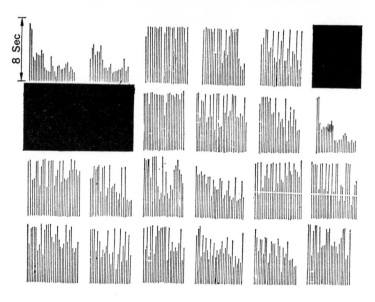

FIG. A18. Trial case 4. Avoidance latency data.

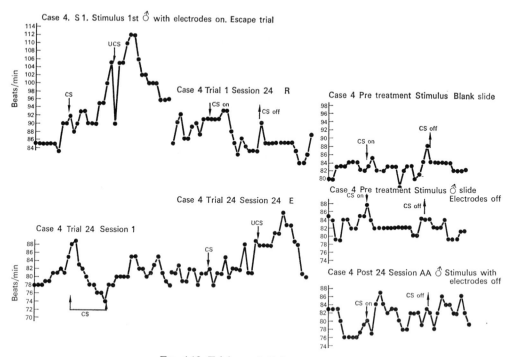

FIG. A19. Trial case 4. Pulse-rate curves.

Discussion

The avoidance latencies are long, in many cases of 8 seconds duration, and often mixed in length, e.g. sessions 5 and 22. However, there is some indication from sessions 1, 12, 14, 16, and 23 that some learning was taking place. Unexpected profiles, e.g. sessions 1 and 3, may indicate the effect of fluctuating mood on strength of sexual object choice. In a non-trial treatment situation therapy would have continued on each hierarchical step until short consistent latencies were established.

The pulse curves show a marked and progressive acceleration in response to trial 1, session 1, both conditioned and unconditioned stimulus onset result in a deceleration (Fig. A19).

Trial 24, session 1, shows an established acceleration and deceleration during the CS exposure which in this case was curtailed by an operant avoidance response.

Trial 1, session 24, by contrast with trial 1, session 1, shows a clear deceleration in response to the CS and the overall rate is confined to the 84–94 beats/minute range.

Trial 24, session 24, shows a lower average rate than trial 1, session 1, and trial 1, session 24, and the intra CS curve shape is irregular.

A comparison of pre-treatment blank slide minus electrodes and post-treatment slide minus electrodes demonstrates two points: (1) a homosexual stimulus pre-session 1 results in a higher rate modulation than a blank stimulus; (2) post-treatment presentation of a homosexual stimulus shows a conditioned cardiac acceleration and deceleration and a post-CS offset oscillation.

Aversion therapy clearly was helpful to this patient, but the major difficulty appeared to be his heterophobia which was extremely sensitive to any kind of failure in a heterosexual situation. His homosexual approach drive was heightened by depression of mood which was frequent and highly situation sensitive. Certain therapeutic success would appear to require prolonged supportive follow-up, perhaps incorporating further aversion therapy and heterophobia desensitization.

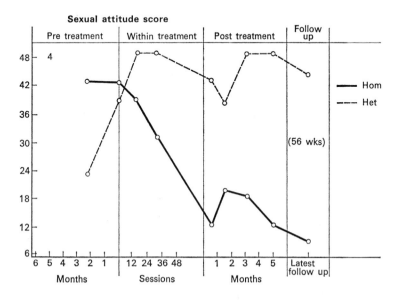

FIG. A20. Trial case 4. SOM data.

TRIAL CASE 5

Case 5 was a 33-year-old warehouseman who was referred by his general practitioner. He was complaining of anxiety centred on his homosexual practices and phantasy.

Sexual History

He was introduced to mutual genital handling at school at the age of 13. This continued with petting for 2 years. He left school at 15, and noted attraction to a number of workmates.

At 17 he commenced using male auto-masturbatory phantasy, which continued until he was 28. At this time he was picked up in a convenience and petting took place. He failed to keep a further assignation with the same partner because of fear of discovery by his parents and the police. Several other incidents took place over the following 9 months. At 29 he had homosexual intercourse when drunk. For 4 years prior to presentation he continued strong homosexual interest. His predominant wish was for a steady homosexual affair.

He never at any time achieved sexual arousal with a girl. He dated and kissed in his teens without real interest. He was anxious in case the girls realized that he was not sexually aroused. These sensitive ideas lessened his heterosexual activities.

Personal History

He was the only child of a bronchitic father whom he described as "weak", his mother being the more dominant parent. He was afraid of other children and found difficulty in mixing. His hobbies were music, reading, and art.

He described two depressive episodes which were precipitated by association with male friends. On both occasions he showed early morning waking, diurnal variation of mood, loss of weight and anorexia, albeit all to a mild degree. The content of his thinking always referred to the homosexual attachment. Therefore his depression could be described as endoreactive.

Treatment

He was diagnosed as a self-insecure personality disorder and was randomly assigned to classical conditioning treatment.

Follow-up

Two weeks post-treatment he reported an interest in girls and had commenced dancing lessons. His homosexual interest was minimal; he had mixed auto-masturbatory phantasy.

At 6 weeks post-treatment his heterosexual interest was steadily strengthening, which was maintained at 3 months. His auto-masturbatory phantasy was exclusively female, and his heterosexual relationships were much easier.

At 3 months follow-up he described sexual feelings toward girls, his interest in males was absent, neither did he look at them in the street any more. His auto-masturbatory phantasy remained exclusively heterosexual and he was going to dances weekly.

At 12 months follow-up he reported two incidents of mutual masturbation following heavy intake of alcohol. He was disgusted with himself on both occasions. He had been rejected by two girls at a dance with a consequent decrease in confidence. His overall

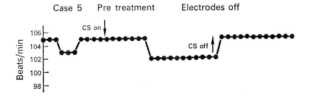

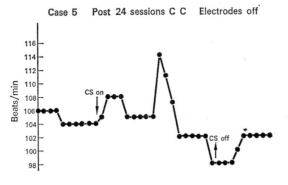

FIG. A21. Trial case 5. Pulse-rate changes.

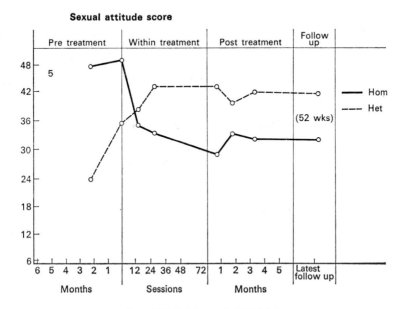

FIG. A22. Trial case 5. SOM data.

orientation was heterosexual, but he noted fluctuations, particularly if he was stressed at work. His auto-masturbatory phantasy remained heterosexual. He was assigned a Kinsey rating of 1.

Discussion

A comparison of the pre- and post-CC pulse curves shows a conditioned cardiac acceleration and deceleration. The sexual orientation scale scores at one-year follow-up indicate that a more prolonged period of aversion would have been helpful; although the patient's heterosexual score was high he was still appreciably heterophobic as determined by interview.

TRIAL CASE 7

Case 7 was aged 23, the son of an architect, and when first seen he was a commercial artist. His problem was auto-masturbation to strong homosexual phantasy.

Sexual History

He discovered masturbation for himself at the age of 10. Previously at the age of 8 he "hero-worshipped" a male school friend of similar age. No sexual practice took place. He saw a psychiatrist at a child guidance clinic for shyness and inability to mix. His auto-masturbatory phantasy was of boys from the outset, and he recalls being excited by babies of both sexes, wanting to see what they were like when undressed. From 8 to 10 he continued auto-masturbation with phantasy of mutual masturbation. Then he was taken for a drink by a man and later to bed where mutual masturbation and passive sexual intercourse took place. In the following 3 years he had mutual masturbation 3 times, and at 23 he practised passive fellatio once when he was drunk. His main problem on presentation was his intense preoccupation with homosexuality. "My problem dominates me—it's a nightmare. I wonder if they [other people] know I'm a queer. It holds me back." He never had any heterosexual interest or practice apart from the early desires to see naked female bodies.

Personal and Family History

Three older female siblings died from meningitis and two older male siblings died at birth. The patient was premature but thrived well. His early years were normal, but from 5 and even earlier he remembers mixing poorly. "I never played with the other children; I always felt tied to my mother's apron strings." At school he found mixing very difficult. His homosexuality rendered him more introverted and produced an abnormal psychogenic development. He studied at a local art school and later worked as a commercial artist. There was no family history of mental illness. His father showed sensitive personality traits, his mother obsessional traits.

Past Medical History

Tonsillectomy in childhood and operation for torsion of the testicle at 19 years.

Personality

He had always showed evidence of lifelong insecurity and was sufficiently disturbed in his childhood social relations to be referred to a child guidance clinic. He could not mix at school and was the recipient of extensive bullying. He was obsessional, and his methodical dressing was the source of much maternal chivvying. He had developed a psychogenic development about his homosexuality, feeling that he could never marry and have his own children. He was prone to quite marked mood swings which were always triggered off by rumination about his problem.

In interview, he appeared eccentric in manner and obsessional in his speech form. His embarrassment was acute; he was extremely introspective and prone to ruminate on diseases and the unfairness of cancer and its attendant suffering. He believed in thought-reading, and whilst he displayed sensitive ideas of reference there were no first rank symptoms of schizophrenia. He was judged to have a self-insecure personality disorder with an abnormal psychogenic development.

Treatment

He was assigned to anticipatory avoidance. After 24 sessions of therapy his SOM score was: homosexual 48, heterosexual 15. He was asked to attend for a further 24 sessions of classical conditioning but failed to attend. Repeated postal requests elicited a number of letters in which he stated himself to be greatly helped but too busy to attend.

Follow-up

He finally attended follow-up 58 weeks after treatment. At that time his SOM scores were homosexual 12 and heterosexual 39. He said that he derived benefit from the treatment 4–5 months after its completion.

Homosexual Status

He used no auto-masturbatory male phantasy and there was no sexual interest in men in the street.

Heterosexual Status

He had begun to take girls out, and his general level of confidence was greatly increased. He was anxious that girls would suspect that he had once been a homosexual. He kisses his current girl friend with enjoyment. He was assigned a Kinsey rating of 0.

Discussion

This patient had a long history of psychiatric disturbance, and apart from problems which arose directly out of his sensitivity, there was a degree of a parental rejection, particularly by his father who cherished unfulfilled hopes that his son would be an architect. In spite of a self-insecure personality disorder, he had established himself as a commercial artist, and he had limited his sexual deviation to auto-masturbatory phantasy with a few exceptions. He thus had attributes which may help to explain his sexual orientation change, high capacity to ruminate, and determination.

His motives for refusing to attend for CC or follow-up never became clear; however, his final interview at 58 weeks post-treatment, taken with his SOM score, left no doubt that he had become heterosexually orientated.

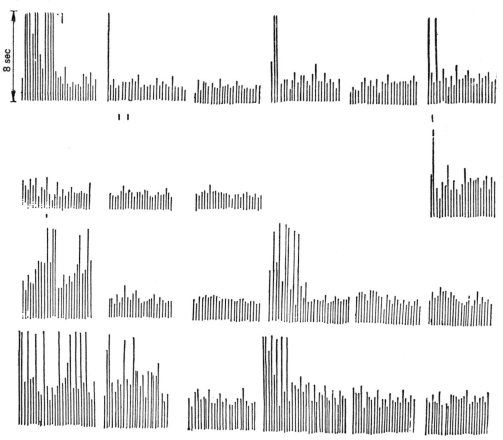

FIG. A23. Trial case 7. Avoidance latency data.

Avoidance Latencies (Fig. A23)

The best learning curves are seen in sessions 1, 4, 6, 16, and 22 which have some long initial latencies which give way to shorter latencies in the second half of the sessions.

Although this patient tended to avoid quite regularly, his later latencies were long (4 seconds) and tended to be mixed, long and short. Sessions 19 and 13 show two distinct reversed learning curves.

Pulse Data (Fig. A24)

Pre-treatment presentation of the male stimulus resulted in a minor cardiac acceleration and deceleration during the duration of the conditioned stimulus which gave way to a marked acceleration and later periodic oscillation at CS offset.

Application of the electrodes produced a higher basal rate, a larger intra-CS acceleration, and a massive CS offset swing.

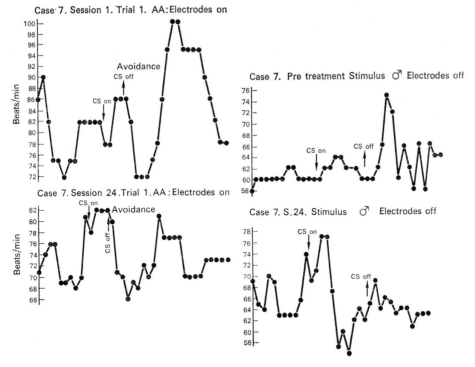

FIG. A24. Trial case 7. Pulse-rate curves.

In session 24, trial 1, the basal rate is lower than that in session 1, trial 1, and a clear acceleration and deceleration is produced by the CS. This pattern is seen in the post-treatment trial, and contrasts clearly with the pre-treatment trial. The post-CS offset oscillation is absent in the post-treatment trial.

TRIAL CASE 11

Case 11 was a 33-year-old married club steward who was referred because of impotence and strong homosexual phantasy.

Sexual History

He was introduced to mutual masturbation at school when he was 14. His partner was a school boy. One year later he became an apprentice plumber and practised mutual masturbation with an adult at work. He enjoyed it but felt guilty later. Following this incident he was sexually aroused at the sight and thought of males. He continued sporadic mutual masturbation. At 21, mutual masturbation occurred in a public toilet, and he began to seek out such situations and began to use this situation as auto-masturbatory phantasy material. He later met the same man and went back to his house where petting, intra-crural sexual intercourse, and mutual masturbation took place. He began to visit a homosexual pub and had his first "affair" at 18, which lasted 12 months.

He became intermittently depressed because of his homosexuality and increasingly afraid of being apprehended. On presentation his homosexual practices were mutual masturbation, fellatio, intra-crural sexual intercourse, nudity, and petting.

He began to take girls out when he was 17, "because it was the accepted thing to do". He met his wife at 18 and was attracted and sexually aroused by her. She refused pre-marital sexual intercourse, but kissing and petting occurred. After marriage sexual intercourse took place regularly until 5 years before consultation when he gradually developed impotency with his wife, although homosexually he was potent and his drive remained high. There was no psychotic depression. He saw a consultant psychiatrist one year prior to presentation and testosterone was tried unsuccessfully.

Personal History

He was the middle child of an artisan family of seven (four female, three male). His father was a cotton spinner, a strict, fairly aloof man. The patient left school at 15 and had a number of artisan jobs, and at one stage rose from shop assistant to manager. He then took his present post with his wife of caterer and steward to a golf club.

Personality

He was a meticulous man of habit with great difficulty in showing his feelings. He had a tendency to lability of mood, on occasions having bouts of depression clearly linked to homosexual events, and which displayed endogenous features. He was interested in the theatre and performed with "professional" panache in his capacity of club steward.

Treatment

He was randomly assigned to psychotherapy. He rapidly settled down and his personality was explored in detail. His self-insecurity was repeatedly revealed by each small incident in his life history and these points were explained. He was always timid and shy and exhibited a very marked difficulty in exteriorizing his feelings towards his parents, school-mates, and later his wife and 7-year-old daughter.

It transpired that his wife was exceptionally overtly affectionate and constantly touched and caressed him even during cooking, etc. (during their joint work at the club). It became clear that he was overfaced and swamped by his wife's emotion. As psychotherapy proceeded, the process of empathy was explained and taught to him, and it was suggested that he use such analytical and shaping techniques to understand and guide his wife in her relationship to him. He was encouraged to practise showing and verbalizing his feelings, and persuaded to be less self-critical about his sexual performance.

His potency gradually returned so that he was able to have sexual intercourse twice a week. His relationship with his wife vastly improved and there was less tension. He reported a great lowering in his own level of tension.

After 12 hours psychotherapy his homosexual score had diminished 6 points from 48 to 42; he was therefore randomly reassigned to anticipatory avoidance. After 24 sessions of AA therapy, his homosexual score dropped to 16 and treatment was terminated.

Follow-up

At 3 months post-treatment he reported himself to be "much happier". He had been practising auto-masturbation with a female pin-up, being slow to achieve full erection, whose completion coincided with ejaculation.

Between himself and his wife he described "a mighty great change—she thought that there was nothing wrong with her, but she's more humble and less aggressive now".

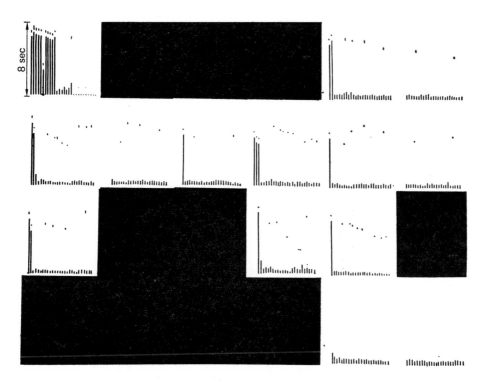

Fig. A25. Trial case 11. Avoidance latency data.

"She has tried to leave me alone after we'd had a long talk." There was an increase in satisfaction with their sexual intercourse, coincident with his wife's reduction in dominancy. He still retained slight interest in men.

At 17 weeks follow-up he declared his homosexual interest to be as strong as it had ever been, even to the extent of being unable to masturbate to a female picture. His improved heterosexual performance had been maintained largely because his wife had been persuaded to attempt sexual intercourse with the light on, thus aiding penetration with a partial erection. He tended to ejaculate before his wife reached orgasm.

At 25 weeks follow-up the homosexual position was unchanged—except that he did not now suffer from guilt in relation to his homosexual desires and thoughts. His complete heterosexual impotence had returned.

The situation was unchanged at a 42-week follow-up.

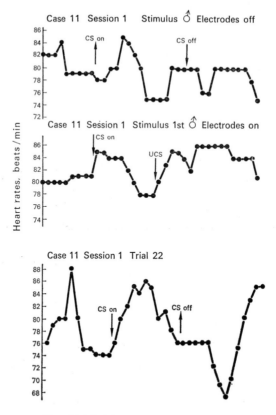

FIG. A26. Trial case 11. Pulse-rate data.

Discussion

This patient's problems were more than usually complex in that he had an intra-marital psychogenic development tending to inhibit heterosexual responsiveness because of his wife's behaviour: his impotence was probably not entirely dependent on sexual object choice and appeared to be based in part upon a waning sexual drive. Psychotherapy appeared to help him with his general marital and personality adjustment, and indicates that a thorough exploration of such cases at some time in the course of aversion therapy is an advantage. The avoidance latencies (Fig. A25) gave an early hint that treatment might not be fully successful. There are no S-shaped learning curves, a striking feature of this data is the extremely rapid avoidance—0·8 second.

Figure A26 shows the pulse-rate curves for session 1; the conditional stimulus produced a bimodal response in the absence of the electrodes which was repeated with the electrodes in position. Trial 28, session 1 shows an acceleration and deceleration more marked and sustained than in either previous condition.

There are insufficient data to confirm the presence of cardiac conditioning.

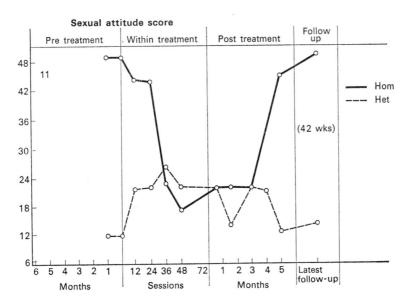

FIG. A27. Trial case 11. SOM data.

TRIAL CASE 13

Case 13 was a 21-year-old salesman referred from another psychiatrist because of homo-sexual phantasies.

Sexual History

At the age of 11 his next-door neighbour—a boy of 12—stripped him and handled his genitals under the pretext of teaching "the facts of life". He was excited by this procedure and concluded by masturbating himself. Following this incident, he used it as an auto-masturbatory phantasy, and shortly afterwards began to practise mutual masturbation at school, and used these experiences for his auto-masturbatory phantasies at home.

At the age of 15 he had the idea of hanging around in a public convenience and waiting to practise mutual masturbation with adult males. He did this daily from the age of 16–18, at which time he had an "affair" which lasted 2 weeks with an 18-year-old man. He claims to have been emotionally involved. Seven months prior to interview he spontaneously ceased homosexual practices following psychiatric consultation, but continued his phantasy life.

He became very interested in girls in his primary school aged 6, and had "girl friends". However, he had particularly prominent ears and nose and he felt it was increasingly difficult to be popular with girls. He developed multiple phobias at the age of 9 and was severely disturbed. At the age of 11 he became very depressed and attended a child psychiatry unit. His depressive state continued in a fluctuating fashion until he underwent plastic surgery on his ears and nose at the age of 19. During this depressive state he showed endogenous features and was treated with anti-depressants. At the age of 14 he took several girls out and practised kissing and petting. He was very anxious and failed to enjoy this. He felt that the sexual aspect of homosexuality was a substitute. At the age of 20 he went out with a girl sporadically, practising kissing and petting, and 6 weeks prior to interview he had been seeing another girl. He found it difficult to feel any enthusiasm for heterosexual relationships. His auto-masturbatory phantasy at presentation was one-third of boys, one-third men, and one-third women. He had frequent phantasies of "feeling another man's body".

Personality

He displayed features of a self-insecure personality disorder. He had dysmorphophobia *re* his nose and ears which led to an abnormal psychogenic development whose severity was heightened by his homosexuality. The sensitive ideas about his appearance were allayed by plastic surgery when he was 19. There was also evidence of weak-willed traits of personality.

Family History

He recalled early jealousy of his younger sister, aged 19, and felt that his parents had always been unhappy together. His mother suffered from an asthenic personality disorder with attention-seeking features. His father, who was an insurance broker, appeared to have a normal personality. There was constant parental bickering, mainly about his mother's laziness. He despised her and disapproved of his father's weakness. His older sister, aged 32, had suffered several attacks of psychotic depression, and one paternal uncle had committed suicide.

Treatment

He was assigned to psychotherapy and it emerged that there were three areas of stress: (1) his home, where there was constant parental disharmony; (2) work, in that he was employed as a traveller in ladies gowns and his employer relied upon him a good deal, asking him to undertake several duties after hours without extra remuneration: he found it very difficult to stand up for his rights; for instance, having a safe van for his rounds, and he was unable to express himself forcibly unless he actually lost his temper; (3) his homosexuality. This had ceased as a practice but he was extremely fearful that he should be found out. He developed marked anxiety from stress at work and was put on chlorprothixene 60 mg q.d.s. for 3 weeks. Further exploration showed that he had considerable interest in girls, but that he always felt anxious with them. He thought he was different, i.e. because of his homosexuality. When he kissed girls he felt guilty because he was homosexual, and that he was being unfair to the girls.

Three weeks after the start of therapy he had decided to leave his current employment. This proved to be a very stressing decision because he was unsure of himself and how he would fare in a fresh firm. He became depressed and retarded. He developed early morning waking, loss of concentration, and impaired memory. It was decided to continue psychotherapy but to add nortriptylene 25 mg q.d.s. For a week he worsened, and on the day that it was decided to give him ECT he changed jobs. He did better than he expected. One week later he was much improved, and at this point the 12 hours psychotherapy became complete. His SOM scores showed a small shift on the male side but not sufficient to terminate treatment. His female score showed a considerable improvement (6 points). He was reassigned for anticipatory avoidance conditioning therapy.

He continued on nortriptylene 25 mg t.d.s. during anticipatory avoidance conditioning and at the completion of 48 sessions of conditioning (24 AA followed by 24 CC) he reported that he had settled down well at his new business and relationships were improved at home. He did not suffer from disturbed sleep and there was no depression of mood.

Follow-up

He was unable to resist "looking at men with interest". This homosexual interest became stronger when his mood ground shifted towards depression which it did spontaneously approximately once a month. There had been no homosexual practice since the onset of treatment.

He had taken one or two girls out mainly in a crowd of friends; his interest in girls was desultory, although socially he could mix easily and well. His auto-masturbatory phantasy was male and had continued as such during aversion therapy.

Six weeks post-treatment he was using female pin-ups for auto-masturbation, which were successfully inhibiting male phantasy, his interest in men in the street had lowered, and he had kissed a girl accompanied by sexual excitement on two occasions.

Six weeks later (3 months post-treatment) he had recommenced utilizing some male auto-masturbatory phantasy, and his general interest in men was slightly increased. He had continued holding hands, kissing, and petting with a girl. His mood was still labile, his adjustment at home and work remained satisfactory, and he continued to take nortriptylene 25 mg t.d.s.

At 20 weeks post-treatment his homosexual interests were increasing and he was using male phantasy to obtain an erection prior to masturbation. His mood was more stable and the anti-depressant was reduced to 25 mg b.d.

At final follow-up 41 weeks post-treatment, it was possible to conclude that he was improved in his adjustment to non-sexual spheres. He was not depressed and much less labile than on presentation. He was in more settled employment and at home was tolerably good. Sexually there was no overall change in his orientation, he continued desultorily to meet and kiss girls, but his main interest was homosexual and his auto-masturbatory phantasy was male. He was still not practising homosexuality. He was assigned a follow-up Kinsey rating of 4.

Discussion

Groups of avoidance latency sessions (Fig. A28) show learning curves, e.g. 7, 8, 9, 19, 20, and 21, and where fresh slides are introduced avoidance latencies increase, e.g. 3/4, 9/10, and 15/16. However, there is much scattered inconsistency between sessions, i.e. 5/6 and 11/12, and in sessions, e.g. 6, 12, 14, etc. Moreover, short latencies are only consistently achieved on a limited number of sessions, e.g. 9 and 21. The avoidance latency picture is therefore mixed. The pulse rate changes are equally ambivalent (Fig. A30). In the pre-treatment situation there is a cardiac acceleration and deceleration in response to the CS which is not clearly repeated in session 1, trial 1. By session 24, trial 1, the average rate is lower than in session 1, trial 1, and the CS gives a high degree of rate modulation. Twenty-three trials later, session

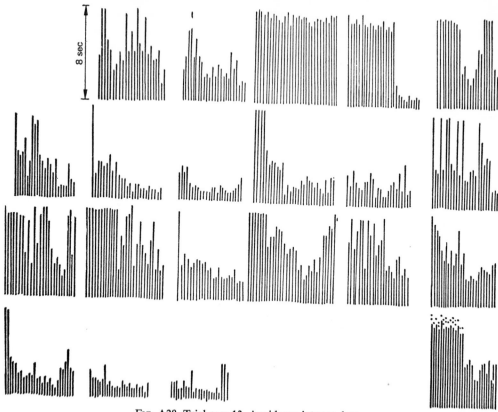

FIG. A28. Trial case 13. Avoidance latency data.

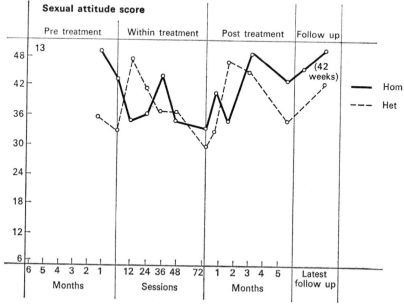

FIG. A29. Trial case 13. SOM data.

24, trial 24, the average rate is increased and the slight acceleration seen in session 24, trial 1, is abolished. However the post-treatment stimulation produces a cardiac acceleration which exceeds that seen in the pre-treatment situation and occurs from a background of a comparatively low, steady, resting rate.

The response to treatment as evidenced by the sexual orientation scale and the pulse and latencies is equivocal, containing components of factors predictive of both success and failure. Varying within-treatment SOM scores appear to be highly predictive of failure.

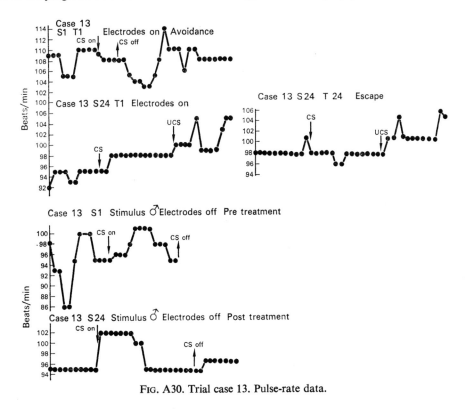

FIG. A30. Trial case 13. Pulse-rate data.

TRIAL CASE 15

Case 15 was a 22-year-old art college student who was referred by another psychiatrist because of homosexual phantasies.

Sexual History

At the age of 6 he was accosted by a man who took him to a wood, masturbated in his presence, and attempted to masturbate him. One year later a similar incident occurred with a park keeper. He remembers being frightened but curious and interested. At the age of 8 he developed a "crush" on a girl of similar age; no sexual practice took place. Between 9 and 11 he practised active and passive anal sexual intercourse with the son of his mother's daily help. The initial suggestion came from the other boy. He enjoyed this, and looked forward to his friend's visits. At the age of 12 he began to masturbate, and his phantasy was mainly of anal intercourse and partly concerned girls of his own age. This auto-masturbation and its phantasy continued until presentation. At the age of 16 he had a series of girl friends with whom he held hands and kissed. He enjoyed this at the time. In the 2 years prior to presentation he deliberately avoided homosexual practice so that "no one would get to know about me", but he maintained a strong interest in looking at men and phantasizing homosexual acts during his auto-masturbation. At college he was meeting girls socially, and estimated that he kissed a girl once per month without producing an erection or enjoyment.

Personal History

He had a brother 10 years his senior. His early childhood was unremarkable. His father was an engineer and a sensitive person who was dominated by the patient's much more outgoing mother. Both parents were "narrow minded" about sex and sex education. He did

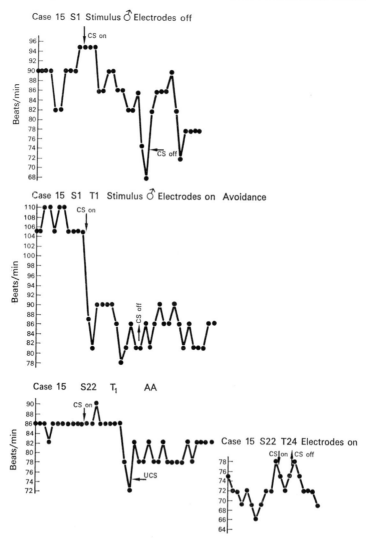

FIG. A31. Trial case 15. Pulse-rate data.

poorly at school until he passed the 13-plus and later went on to art college. He experienced great difficulty in mixing with people, and this symptom was his main complaint when he was first referred to his university health centre. It is noteworthy that his brother saw a psychiatrist for the same complaint (i.e. shyness) 5 years previously. He was unable to complete his second year's work schedule successfully, complaining that he was too slow and too perfectionistic. He started many projects but gave them up.

Treatment

He commenced therapy with 24 sessions of anticipatory avoidance conditioning. At this point he had increased his female score from 30 to 48, and then went away to Greece for 3 months after which treatment was to be recommenced.

Follow-up

In the interregnum there had been no sexual practices, but his phantasy had been predominantly homosexual. In interview he reported that his motivation during treatment had been ambivalent and stated quite clearly that he had not wanted to give up his homosexual feelings and thoughts when he had been confronted with the possibility of having to do so.

Three months after initial treatment the suggestion was made that he should cross over treatment by recommencing classical conditioning, but he moved away to a teacher-training college. At this point his marked insecurity and heterophobia were discussed at length, and a series of graduated heterosexual approach situations were suggested.

Six months after treatment he had made no heterosexual progress; he complained of depression of mood, but there were no biological features. Chlorprothixene was prescribed for tension.

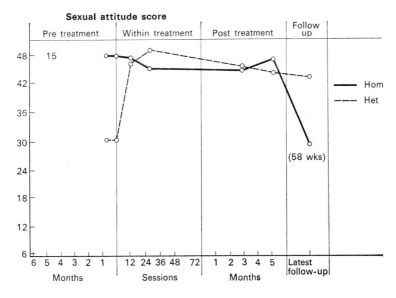

Fig. A32. Trial case 15. SOM data.

Thirteen months after treatment he declared himself to be "fed up of talking about myself". At final follow-up 58 weeks post-treatment he looked well and reported that he was successfully managing his course. He felt that his first instinct was towards men; his auto-masturbatory phantasy was homosexual, and he looked at men with interest. However, his heterosexual interest was strengthening, he had a steady girl friend for 2 months at college, and had sexual intercourse several times with enjoyment. He had begun to find other girls attractive but he had revisited two homosexual pick-ups in the 2 months prior to follow-up interview. He was given a Kinsey rating of 3.

Discussion

In retrospect this patient's personality deviation was gross in terms of obsessionality, and it is tempting to see his inability to decide either to embrace or reject homosexuality as evidence of a weak-willed personality disorder. His heterosexual score showed a marked and sustained upward shift in response to AA conditioning, and there was evidence of concomitant personality improvement 40–50 weeks after treatment. The trend of his homosexual score under the influence of increasing heterosexuality would have formed an interesting follow-up study.

The pulse-rate curves are mainly of interest because of their extreme lability. In the pre-treatment situation there is a cardiac acceleration followed by a very marked deceleration in response to the CS (electrodes off). The addition of the electrode deleted the acceleration, the deceleration was identically repeated, trial 1 of session 22* shows a reduced basal rate for session 1 and the cardiac deceleration remains. Later in the same session trial 24, the basal rate is 10 points lower, and, if the possibility of a "cue" response is admitted, the deceleration appears to have been converted to two small accelerations.

TRIAL CASE 17

Case 17 was aged 24 at referral and was one of a pair of identical twins. His twin was exclusively heterosexual. The patient referred himself via his general practitioner because he was finding the strain of maintaining a heterosexual "front" intolerable.

Sexual History

The patient's first sexual experience at the age of 13 was that of having another boy's naked body held against his at a swimming baths. He was excited by this; on other similar occasions he later came to admire the physique of other boys. He began auto-masturbation and phantasized males of his own age at the age of 17. He also bought physical culture books. At the age of 18 he was picked up by a male in a public convenience but declined to go with him for the purpose of mutual masturbation. Later he regretted this decision, and at the age of 23 he met a 35-year-old man under similar circumstances and practised intra-crural sexual intercourse with pleasure mixed with some anxiety and nervousness. Within weeks he began to make regular homosexual pick-ups and then began to go to another city specifically to make homosexual pick-ups. He did so in order to avoid recognition in his own town. He practised sodomy once at the age of 23, following a heavy intake of alcohol. At the time of the

*Session 24 was not recorded.

interview he was making homosexual pick-ups once per week and practised intra-crural sexual intercourse, kissing, and petting. His auto-masturbatory phantasy was of well-built males and various homosexual acts.

He played with girls a good deal as a younger child, preferring their company to that of boys, and he did not play games. He was never attracted to females but commenced hetero-sexual dating at the age of 15 "because it was the thing to do". He disliked holding hands. Six months prior to presentation he tried kissing and petting but, he said, "I just can't bring myself to put on a normal act. I dislike girls" (his sister-in-law did not attract him in any sense).

Personal History

The twin birth was uncomplicated and his upbringing unexceptional. He was described by the heterosexual twin as doing "girlish type things" as a child. There is a clear difference in their temperaments, the heterosexual twin being more outgoing and aggressive, the latter felt that the patient was more close to their mother and was shown more physical affection.

Personality

There was evidence of life-long self-insecure personality abnormality showing sensitive features and at times ideas of reference. The homosexuality was beginning to have a develop-mental effect. He showed obsessional features also. There was no hint of previous illness, and on examination his mental state was normal. His twin was interviewed, using the same initial questionnaire and the common parental history was confirmed. The twin was entirely heterosexual and had always been so.

Family History

His father was a foreman concreter and was a strict parent with sensitive personality features. The patient had little or no emotional contact with his father. His mother tended to complain of bodily ailments, and during the early years tended to smother the patient. On presentation he was tending to go out in the evenings in order to avoid listening to his mother's health complaints. She was, no doubt, the dominant parent.

Treatment

The patient received 24 sessions of anticipatory avoidance followed by 24 sessions of classical conditioning and showed no shift either clinically or by the SOM.

Follow-up

No change in sexual orientation had occurred at final follow-up at 66 weeks post-treat-ment. His final Kinsey rating was 6.

Discussion

Perhaps the most striking feature of this case was the complete discordance for sexual object choice and a more detailed discussion is shortly to be published (MacCulloch et al., 1970b).

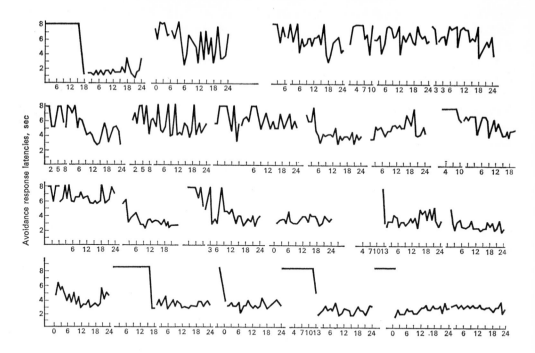

FIG. A33. Trial case 17. Avoidance latency data.

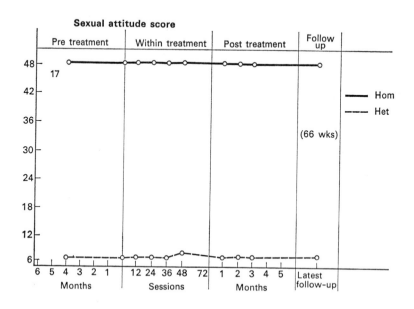

FIG. A34. Trial case 17. SOM data.

The avoidance latencies (Fig. A33) are extremely irregular and do not show any evidence of learning; short latencies in sessions 23 and 24 appear to be the result of elective behaviour to avoid punishment. The SOM figures totally fail to vary in response to treatment.

TRIAL CASE 18

Case 18 was a 26-year-old soft furnishings consultant. His problems were frequent homosexual phantasy of mutual masturbation and a ready sexual arousal by thinking of and looking at men.

Sexual History

His first homosexual act occurred when he was 14 years old. This was mutual masturbation and it was not repeated until 10 days prior to interview when he went to a party at the home of a man he knew to be homosexual. He said: "I wanted to see what it would be like. I've projected an image among my friends of being very heterosexual." On this occasion he indulged in kissing and mutual masturbation with a man and enjoyed it at the time but looked back upon it with mixed feelings.

Personal History

He was an illegitimate child—his real father lived next door to his mother. He had an unhappy schooling because he felt that he could not do games as well as the other children. He was a persistent school refuser, and consequently his academic progress was poor. His real father, who was a commercial traveller, visited him frequently, and at the time of presentation the patient daily visited his father. His mother appears to have been alternatively accepting and rejecting, being very warm and possessive one moment and cool and distant the next. He began dating girls at 16, and became emotionally attached to one when he was 18. However, he never felt any heterosexual interest or arousal. He left school at 15 and worked for a tailor. He later specialized in window display.

Past Medical History

Nothing of note.

Personality

He showed slight obsessive traits and evidence of an attention-seeking personality abnormality which was accompanied by a degree of lability of mood.

Family History

His father was very well known in the home district, being termed a "comedian". He tended to be forceful and argumentative in company. His relationship with the patient was a close one at the time of presentation. His mother was "not very intelligent, warm but not demonstrative". There was no family history of mental illness.

Treatment

He was assigned to classical conditioning and crossed over to anticipatory avoidance. Of the latter he said; "It's confusing. You don't always feel the pictures are in the right order." At the end of treatment he felt that the male slides were still interesting, his auto-masturbatory phantasy remained male. He was advised to use a female pin-up.

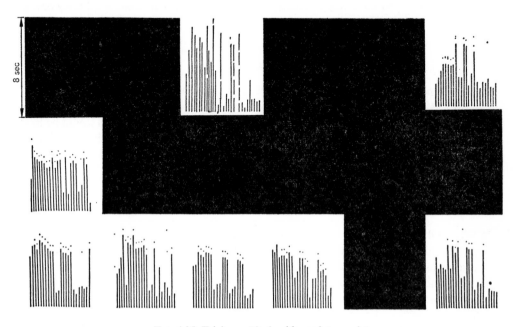

FIG. A35. Trial case 18. Avoidance latency data.

Follow-up

At 6 weeks post-treatment he was able to do this but he remained strongly heterophobic. He recounted how he would avoid giving a girl a lift home after amateur theatre in case she might expect a sexual advance from him. Twelve weeks after treatment he was using a good deal of sadistic sexual phantasy for auto-masturbation.

At final follow-up 66 weeks post-treatment he remained totally heterophobic and homophillic. He was assigned a follow-up Kinsey rating of 6.

Discussion

The available latency curves (Fig. A35) all show irregular long latencies, 9 and 21 show a few short latencies: taken overall there is little evidence of avoidance learning. This is borne out by the SOM scores and the clinical history. It is interesting to note that although he was strongly heterophobic, his female SOM scores were mainly in the 0–20 range which might imply that anxiety provoked by real life female approach behaviour was not in accord with his feelings.

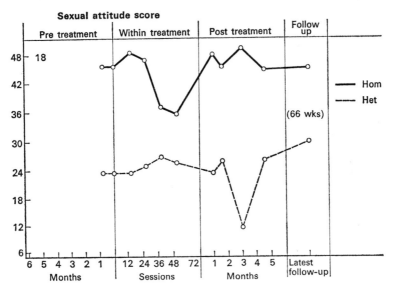

FIG. A36. Trial case 18. SOM data.

TRIAL CASE 20

Case 20 was a 20-year-old man on a court order for treatment. He was on probation for attempted buggery with two 12-year-old boys.

Sexual History

He was first introduced to mutual masturbation at school at the age of 12, and this took place several times. He developed heterosexual interest at the age of 14 onwards, but he was too anxious to approach girls. He felt his looks were poor, and it later transpired that he worried about the functional adequacy of his penis. He began to masturbate to a female image, and as he became older he did take out a number of girls but he was too afraid to attempt intercourse because he was afraid of pregnancy and could not bring himself to go into a chemist and buy contraceptives. He was unhappy and rejected at home, and spent long periods of time feeling lonely. At this time he began to be sexually aroused by looking at pubertal boys. When he was 18, his mother died and the family moved. He thereupon became more lonely. At the age of 18 he joined the Army, and during a leave he was involved in a friendly fight with another soldier. After they left, some young onlookers aged 12 were asked to fight with him in a similar way. During this, the patient fondled one of the boy's genitalia. This event happened during a period of reactive depression which had been precipitated by a row with his father. The boy cried, and the patient attempted the same manoeuvre with the second boy, who complained to the police. As a result of prosecution he was placed on probation. Six months later he had begun to think about pubertal boys in a sexual way, and he attempted the same act with two boys aged 13 and 14 respectively. He became excited and masturbated one of the boys. Four months later he apprehended two boys who were breaking into a garage. He took them home and attempted buggery with one of them. This failed but one of the boys was induced to masturbate him. However, the police were informed and he was charged and found guilty and put on probation with treatment as a condition.

At the time of admission, his masturbatory phantasy did partially include pubertal boys but consisted more of girls of his own age. He looked at boys in the street and was sexually interested in the possibility of mutual masturbation with them. He looked at females rather less, principally because he felt ugly and gauche. He noted that his desire to have mutual masturbation was very much heightened by depression of mood which was quite frequent, usually occurring when he was left alone in his father's house.

Personal History

He had a sister 10 years younger, for whom he felt a great deal of affection, and two elder sisters aged 27 and 23. There were no outstanding features in his early upbringing which he could recall. It appeared that his father was a selfish, attention-seeking person who drank heavily. The father seems to have been particularly cool towards the patient. For example, when the family went out for a car ride, the patient was not invited to accompany them, and he was too sensitive to ask to do so. There was no family history or personal history of illness, either physical or psychiatric.

Personality

He was markedly sensitive and displayed some obsessional features.

Treatment

The patient was randomly assigned to 12 hours' psychotherapy. It rapidly became apparent that he had all the secret desires to excel of the anankast. He had had several three-wheeler motor vehicles which he had tinkered with himself. Among his previous jobs had been one at a cycle shop and one at a grocery shop, where his polite and pleasing manner had no doubt assisted him. His sensitivity was explained to him in relation to the rather rejecting parental atmosphere, and this was linked with his feelings of inferiority based on his appearance. On further analysis it appeared that he had been "scruffily" dressed as a child, and at the age of 14 had found himself no sartorial match for one of his friends when it came to taking out girls. It was suggested to him that his heterosexual interest had been dampened by these considerations and had focused on an easy alternative, that is juvenile males, who required no suavity or maturity on the part of the seducer.

His feelings were further explored and it was decided that he was predominantly hetero-sexual in orientation; he felt that (a) he was not sufficiently smart or good-looking, and (b) he felt there was something wrong with his penis. He complained of pain when the foreskin was retracted, and there was a mild degree of paraphimosis. This was seen at the hospital by the genito-urinary surgeon who instructed him in hygiene. He was reassured that his penis was normal and he seemed greatly relieved. He settled down well in the ward and reported interest in the female nurses. At the conclusion of 12 one-hour sessions he reported the absence of homosexual interest with an increase in his overall confidence, together with a greater facility for heterosexual contact. His SOM scores showed a marked degree of change, and the treatment was therefore terminated.

Follow-up

At interview 2 weeks post-treatment he reported a great improvement in his level of confidence, and his masturbatory phantasy was exclusively heterosexual. Six weeks after discharge he started a job as an electrical salesman and was very pleased with it. He started going to dances and was finding approaches to females reasonably easy. His heterosexual orientation was still present at 3 months follow-up; however, he reappeared 24 weeks post-treatment complaining of depression of mood with suicidal ideas, psychomotor retardation, loss of weight, increased irritability and impaired concentration. There was no precipitating factor, and he was put on nortriptylene.

His homosexual desires had reappeared coincident with the development of his depression; his SOM scores were: homosexual 33½, heterosexual 48.

He was treated by anticipatory avoidance (not part of the therapeutic trial). His depression responded rapidly and his homosexual thoughts receded.

Four months after AA he was in good spirits, much more self-confident, and in steady employment. He had had a girl friend for 3 months whom he saw every night. They practised mutual masturbation; he reported a complete absence of homosexual interest and thought.

Discussion

At presentation this patient had an unusually high heterosexual interest level, which was inhibited by sensitive ideas about his face, body size, and penis. His initial homosexual

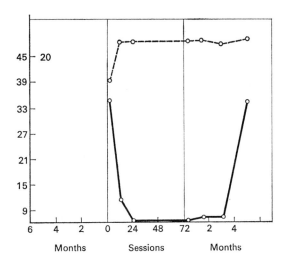

Fig. A37. Trial case 20. SOM data.

scores were 14 points below the maximum, so that a diminution in his heterosexual approach anxiety could be expected to produce a significant change in sexual orientation.

His relapse appeared to be due to a spontaneous depression of mood and was accompanied by very marked unpleasant ruminations about the possibility of a behavioural relapse.

A course of anticipatory aversion therapy was thought to be in the patient's best interest, even though it rendered the interpretation of results less clear.

TRIAL CASE 22

Case 22 was a 20-year-old sales assistant whose daily desire and phantasy was to have a permanent homosexual relationship. His homosexual practice was as follows: mutual masturbation, fellatio, buggery, intra-crural and sex play including petting and nudity. These acts were taking place several times per week at his digs, in public conveniences, and any other available place, e.g. fields, moors, and other people's motor-cars. He was sexually aroused by homosexual phantasy, observations, men, or male pictures. He described his heterosexual interest as thinking of and observing females, and he engaged in occasional heterosexual dates, with holding hands, kissing, and petting.

Sexual History

He discovered that his genitalia were bigger than those of his peers and said; "I used to masturbate in front of the boys to show them how male I was." When he was 10 he practised mutual masturbation with another boy at school, and he then re-enacted this in phantasy with pleasure. About the same time he commenced regular sexual acts with his brother who was then aged 13, and he said: "We had every homosexual act except he wouldn't kiss." This relationship ran *pari passu* with others for 5 years. At the age of 13 he had mutual masturbation with a 22-year-old male and was forcibly introduced to passive sodomy by a taxi-driver. He then started going to male conveniences and practised mutual masturbation with two adult pick-ups. He had four homosexual affairs and the first was for him a serious emotional relationship. Its break-up after 9 months heralded the onset of a depression of mood ground which reinforced that already existing which had started with his key experience. At 19 he contracted rectal gonorrhoea which was complicated by an ischio-rectal abscess.

By this time he was experiencing great lability of mood, often being deeply depressed—which he related to his homosexuality. On occasion he had ideas of reference "that people could tell about me". He was looking for a stable homosexual relationship because he felt that he needed such a relationship. His first job was that of an engineering apprentice, and he took this in order to prove himself masculine, but he was deemed unfit and became a sales assistant. At the time of referral he was a sales assistant in a large store.

He "dated" girls from 5 to 10, showing some degree of precosity, intellectually at least. Following his key experience he ceased heterosexual contact until the age of 17 when he fell in love with a girl. He had contracted VD homosexually and broke off the relationship because he felt it to be unfair on the girl. He had one other emotional heterosexual attachment at the age of 19, a girl whom he was still seeing at monthly intervals. He found kissing pleasurable but had no desire to "go any further".

Personal History

He was born one of four brothers—two older, one younger—and his early health and milestones were normal. He made good academic progress at school, but when he was 8 a girl teased him, saying, "Isn't he like a girl?" This proved to be a key experience and stuck in his mind; he was upset that he was thought of as being like a girl.

Personality

The patient was very markedly sensitive with anankastic features. There had been a key experience at the age of 8, and an abnormal depressive psychogenic development *re* his gender role since. He had sensitive ideas of reference and was highly emotional. There was lability of mood together with some evidence of weak-willed personality abnormality. On mental examination no abnormality was found except mild reactive depression of mood. Physical examination revealed no abnormality.

Family History

His parents both knew about his homosexuality and he had had a course of psychotherapy without benefit when he was 16. His father was a plumber who treated the patient "indifferently"; he was always in the background. The patient's father was described by him as insular, dedicated, and hard working. In contrast to this sensitive picture his mother was much more dominant and extroverted—"kind, strong-natured and lovable". He received no sexual education, but both parents expressed the hope that he could be helped by therapy. There was no family history of mental illness.

Treatment

He was assigned to psychotherapy and his case was initially formulated as follows: a self-insecure personality disorder predominantly of the sensitive type, showing a depressive abnormal psychogenic development following a key experience in which he was told that he was like a girl. There is evidence from 5 onwards of the "turbulent sexuality of the anankast". He was only mildly heterosexual in orientation and very actively homosexual. In spite of the lability of mood and some weak-willed features, he was occupying a moderately senior sales post.

The patient received 12 hours' psychotherapy in hourly sessions. Verbal exploration was used, and later free association. Later still he was able to gain insight into his own personality structure. The psychotherapeutic theme was as follows: he was constitutionally sensitive, e.g. sensible to events with a tendency not to exteriorize feelings. Much time was spent on this concept, and clear examples were abundant in his history. He related the key experience and saw that it fastened in his mind. Many of his later acts, e.g. his attention-getting exhibitionism and later the engineering job, could be explained in terms of sensitivity. There was a strong sexual drive firmly established in the homosexual mode by practice with his brother between the ages of 10 and 15, and thereafter a shrinking from females because "it wasn't fair on them". He developed "camp" mannerisms and affectations, and every trait which heightened his effeminacy became ready fuel to strengthen his growing conviction that "I was different". His sensitive personality disorder also meant that, even discounting his homosexuality, he was timid of females. He accepted this theme and he found it helpful. At the end of 12 hours' psychotherapy his female score was increased but the male score was unchanged. He crossed over to classical conditioning with no effect and finally crossed over to 24 sessions of anticipatory avoidance with a marked improvement in both male and female scores. At this point of treatment he felt that his heterosexual feelings were stronger and his homosexual interests were considerably diminished. He was unable to imagine himself having a personal sexual relationship with a male any more. His masturbatory phantasy was mixed but consistently became heterosexual at or near orgasm. He felt that psychotherapy had been helpful: "He made me realize why I was a queer." He was still suffering quite marked mood swings.

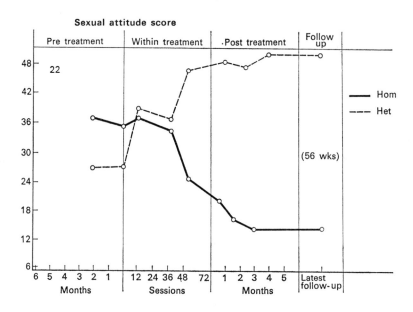

FIG. A38. Trial case 22. SOM data.

Follow-up

Two weeks post-treatment he said: "I feel great, I really do. I can cope. I don't get het-up, I manage better at work." He was not interested in homosexual sex and had rejected one offer but had occasional homosexual thoughts. He had also put on a stone in weight. Three months post-treatment he had developed a very strong emotional relationship with a girl and was having full heterosexual relationships with her with great pleasure on both sides. One year post-treatment the patient wrote to say that he had a strong stable relationship with a girl and their wedding plans were under way. He briefly outlined a strong heterosexual development; he said: "Our relationship is far, far better than anything I have experienced before—it's remarkable the amount of confidence . . . has given me. I don't feel quite the Monster I thought I was." He was assigned a follow-up Kinsey rating of 0.

TRIAL CASE 23

Case 23 was a 21-year-old machine-tool fitter who was referred by a consultant psychiatrist because of homosexual phantasy and practice.

Sexual History

He developed an interest in girls at 13. From 15 he took them out, held hands, petted, and kissed. He had sexual intercourse once at 17 and enjoyed it. He said that heterosexual sex was difficult to obtain in contrast to homosexual sex. The latter commenced with mutual masturbation in a garage toilet when he was 18; his partner was an older man. It occurred on a number of occasions, and he picked up a man in a London toilet and practised mutual masturbation. At this time he began male auto-masturbatory phantasy. His first homosexual affair occurred at 19 and lasted 3 months. It was followed by another three in which he was introduced to fellatio and began to prefer passive buggery. At this time he became reactively depressed over a period of several months when his mother was ill, but his homosexual activity continued until presentation, at which time he was practising mutual masturbation, passive sexual intercourse, intra-crural sexual intercourse, nudity, and petting, all at least once a week. His auto-masturbatory phantasy was mixed, male and female. He was also interested in women, and had been seeing a girl over a 2-week period, holding hands and kissing with enjoyment. His "girl" had fixed up with his general practitioner to see about the homosexual problem.

Personal History

His father was in the Army and absent for part of the patient's first 5 years. He disliked school, preferring play to lessons. He had one sister, 3 years his junior, who appeared to have enjoyed slightly preferential treatment from the parents who were, however, reasonably warm and supportive. Both parents were felt by the patient to regard sex as "dirty".

Personality

He did not display any abnormality of personality on presentation. He was well motivated for treatment. Later interviews revealed that he was shy with females and displayed some sensitive features.

Treatment

He was assigned to classical conditioning.

Follow-up

After 24 sessions he reported absence of interest in men in the street and an increase in his interest in females and in particular strong sexual arousal with his girl friend. His auto-masturbatory phantasy was female.

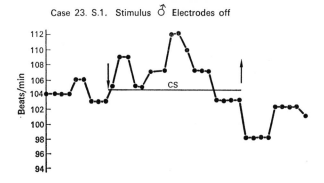

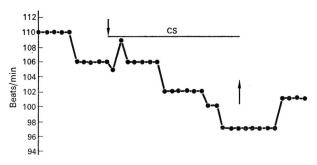

FIG. A39. Trial case 23. Pulse-rate data.

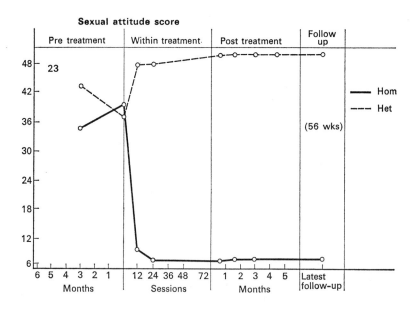

FIG. A40. Trial case 23. SOM data.

He made steady progress by increasing his heterosexual interest and experience, and remained untroubled by homosexual phantasy or practice. Sixteen weeks post-treatment he was exclusively heterosexual. He was reviewed 56 weeks after treatment and he was completely heterosexual. He was assigned a Kinsey rating of 0 at final follow-up.

Discussion

Although this patient was very active homosexually on presentation, he had a marked interest in girls which was inhibited by shyness. His comment that heterosexual sex was harder to get than homosexual sex was very revealing; his homosexuality would appear to have been a learned pattern influenced by two behavioural shaping factors: (a) ease of homosexual approach, and (b) difficulty of heterosexual approach. The effect of CC on cardiac rate (Fig. A39) after treatment appears to have been to convert an acceleration/deceleration response to a deceleration response.

TRIAL CASE 25

Case 25 was a farm-worker who was admitted for treatment of homosexuality as a condition of a 3-year probation order.

Sexual History

He began auto-masturbation at the age of 14, having discovered the practice himself. He was masturbated at the cinema at the age of 23 by a man, and although surprised and nervous he enjoyed the experience. Having watched the rest of the film, he was invited to masturbate the man concerned. He did so and was paid 10s. He met the same man several times and was introduced to a third homosexual who told him about "toilets". He later visited local lavatories when he was feeling "sexy". On his fifth visit he had mutual masturbation, and on the sixth visit active buggery which he enjoyed. He noted no sense of revulsion. He continued this form of practice for the next 4 years. Three years prior to admission he was found guilty of buggery with a farm hand. The offence which led to his admission was also buggery, for which he received 3 years probation and treatment was made a condition of probation.

He developed an interest in females at the age of 16 onwards, but was greatly hampered by his shyness. He was in the Army from the age of $17\frac{1}{2}$–$20\frac{1}{2}$, and during this time went drinking (heavily) and dancing "with the lads". He felt less reticent with a group and also after 5–8 pints of beer. He had, in fact, achieved heterosexual intercourse on a number of occasions but only after drinking 8 pints of beer or more. He remained sensitive about his looks, particularly his glasses. His pre-morbid psychiatric history was non-contributory.

Personal History

He was the middle child of two female sibs, and his father died when he was 3 years of age. At the age of 7 he recalls being particularly sensitive about his appearance and his spectacles in particular. He was so sensitive about his appearance that from his teens onwards he was unable to approach females socially without having drank several pints of beer previously or being in a group of males. His early childhood and schooling were otherwise unremarkable. At the age of 16 he developed asthma and since that time he had taken ephedrine tablets regularly. He took up farm work "to be like my father was", and apart from 3 years in the Army his occupation has been mainly concerned with farm work.

Personality

His personality was of the sensitive type and was judged to be a disorder. In addition he had an abnormal psychogenic development concerning his glasses.

Treatment

The patient received 24 sessions of classical conditioning as an in-patient. At post-treatment interview it was felt that he had been helped a great deal. He stated his interest in men had almost disappeared, his masturbatory phantasy had become heterosexual, and he felt much more attracted to females and less shy. In particular, he described how he had been helped in this by the close proximity of attractive female nurses. He was sufficiently emotionally involved with nurses and nursing for him to decide to take up a nursing career himself.

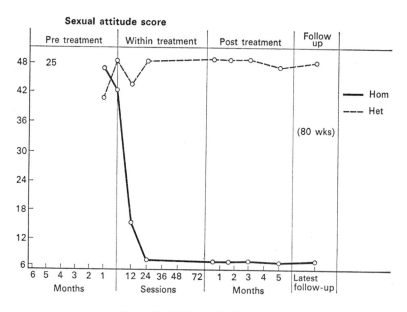

FIG. A41. Trial case 25. SOM data.

Follow-up

Three months post-treatment he had settled down well at a hospital as a state-enrolled nurse and he was taking female friends out alone. He reported total absence of homosexual interest and a sustained and increasing heterosexual interest. He was reviewed at 3-month intervals. No further homosexual problems recurred; the situation remained satisfactory at final follow-up at 80 weeks post-treatment. He was assigned a Kinsey rating of 0 at final follow-up.

TRIAL CASE 27

Case 27 was a 33-year-old unmarried clerk who was referred by another consultant psychiatrist because of his homosexual practice.

Sexual History

His later childhood was uneventful until the age of 9 when his 20-year-old cousin slept with him and performed mutual masturbation. He enjoyed this experience, which took place whenever his cousin returned home on Army leave.

At 14 he began to practise mutual masturbation regularly with a boy of his own age. At this time he developed an interest in girls and took a number out. He had sexual intercourse on a number of occasions but had very little genuine heterosexual interest until the age of 16. During this time—14 to 16—he maintained his mutual masturbation with a school mate.

At 17 he formed a deep attachment to a girl and became serious. She "let him down" and he wept. During later psychotherapy this emerged as a key experience. He "kept off them" (girls) from that time. When he was overseas, at 18, he went to Egypt with the Air Force and practised fellatio for 2 years. He joined the Kenya Police on demobilization (in case his parents should ever find out) and continued mutual masturbation with a male of his own age. On return to the United Kingdom at 23, he had an 18-month affair with a boy of 15.

At 24 he returned to South Africa with his friend and was betrayed to the police by another 15-year-old boy following homosexual activity (mutual masturbation). He ceased homosexual practice and had to return to the United Kingdom.

Twelve months later he began to frequent homosexual coteries and was betrayed to the police in 1959 and charged with indecent assault on a boy of 15. He continued to practise mutual masturbation, intra-crural intercourse, fellatio, and petting until Easter, 1966, when he was again charged with indecent assault on a boy of 14 and placed on a 2-year probation order.

At Interview

He was using homosexual phantasies and observing males with sexual interest. He sought help because he had become afraid of the consequences of continuing homosexual practice which he was unable to stop. He had been an active church worker and was seeing his vicar twice weekly at the time of presentation. He expressed a desire to become heterosexual and saw his ideal future as that of being married with two children. When his single state was questioned, he stated that it would be unfair to marry any woman because he was homosexual.

Personal History

He was the middle child of a family of three. His two sisters were aged 36 and 23. His mother died when he was 4, and his father re-married 12 months later.

Personality

He was an intelligent, meticulously dressed man with a pleasant manner. He showed features of a self-insecure personality and a psychogenic development *re* women following the key experience when he received a rejecting letter from a girl friend. At that time he was aged 18 and serving in Egypt. (In psychotherapy a weak-willed side of his personality emerged, which should have emerged from his case history.)

Family History

He remembered being taken to see his dead mother when he was 4, and he then lived with a godmother for a year. His father drank a good deal and was emotionally distant. His step-mother displayed little affection towards him, and at 14 he recalled feeling very censorious towards his father for having a mistress. His father worked away from home a good deal and there was constant strife between his father and his mistress. His elder sister ran away from home aged 16 because of a quarrel with the "mother" over a boy friend. His relationship with parents in his teens was very distant. In latter years there had been a rapprochement with his father.

There was no significant family history of psychiatric illness.

Treatment

This patient was judged suitable for inclusion in the trial and was assigned to psychotherapy.

A relationship was quickly established which rapidly strengthened. He experienced fears of being left in sexual limbo and pointed out that "homosexual sex is easier to get than

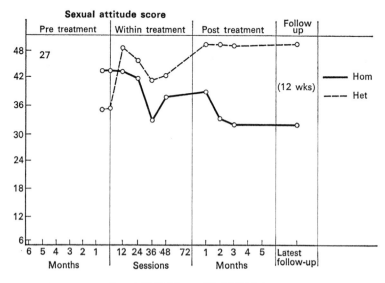

FIG. A42. Trial case 27. SOM data.

heterosexual. You are not so liable to become involved with an individual. Relationships are O.K. if sex is not involved." This was seen as an important point by the therapist because this patient had had at least three affairs of 6 months or over, and at the time of therapy had a relationship with another homosexual. He alleged that there was nothing sexual in this but showed great resistance to the idea that the relationship should be dropped. He said that his friend was in financial difficulties and could not cope with life without him.

From the patient's description it was concluded that his friend had a callous, attention-seeking personality disorder and the ultimate breakdown of the relationship was accepted by the friend with characteristic indifference.

Much time was spent discussing vulnerability and sensitivity to illumine the insecurity engendered by the rejection by his girl friend. His abhorrence of relationships was related to this traumatic experience. Further time was spent in talking about his inability to show his feelings.

After 12 hours' psychotherapy he crossed to classical conditioning which reduced his male score by 6 points.

Follow-up

He was given a post-treatment interview which showed that his homosexual interest was minimal. He had no homosexual phantasy and his heterosexual interest was heightened. He reported depression of mood following an incident at church in which a member of the congregation advised the vicar to get rid of the "queer" in his congregation. It was decided to terminate treatment and not cross over to anticipatory avoidance. This decision was in part vindicated by a continual fall in homosexual SOM score to 30 at 12 weeks follow-up, when he was regularly dating a girl with considerable reduction in his heterophobia. He said: "You get used to the idea of taking a young lady out—I put my arm around a girl's waist in the store the other day and she put her head on my shoulder." He was assigned a follow-up Kinsey rating of 2.

Discussion

This patient's problem clearly shows heterophobia and there was evidence that hetero-sexual approach was becoming more easy for him; on balance the correct treatment decision would have been to cross over to AA.

A CONDITIONING EXPERIMENT ON TWO NORMAL VOLUNTEERS

FOLLOWING the development and successful use in treatment of the second generation of aversion therapy equipment using the modified method described in Chapter 5, it was decided to subject two normal volunteers to a conditioning experiment, using the same learning programmes as employed with patients, to see if they would develop conditioned instrumental and autonomic responses comparable with those seen in successfully treated patients. The experiment was carried out as part of a BBC television programme on the application of conditioning techniques to abnormal behaviour. The producer of the programme was concerned to establish the applicability of such techniques to non-patient subjects. We were sceptical of the likelihood of successful conditioning in the 2 or 3 sessions available, but agreed to make the attempt.

A number of volunteers from a Midlands university were interviewed, and one male and one female, both aged 19, were chosen as subjects, primarily because they did not appear to show any disorder of personality. Both, however, showed self-insecure abnormalities of personality; they thus fell into the group of subjects in whom conditioning was most likely to occur (MacCulloch and Feldman, 1967b).

METHOD

The CS1 was a slide of a squirrel and the CS2 the slide of a toad; both subjects reported feeling a positive effect for the squirrel; in the case of the female volunteer there was a slight negative effect for the toad, the male volunteer being neutral to this slide.

The subjects were physically examined and found to be healthy. The nature of the experiment having been explained to them at the initial interview, the shock electrodes were applied to the left calf of the subject. The use of both buttons (CR1 squirrel avoidance, and CR2 toad request) was described, partly verbally and partly by operational example using blank slides. The shock thresholds of the two subjects were measured and conditioning was commenced using programme 1 (see Chapter 5).

RESULTS: FOR THE MALE SUBJECT

Figure B1 shows the avoidance latency curves of both subjects; both showed the classical S-shaped curve although it is of interest to note that the female subject made more escape responses than did the male subject before her avoidance responding commenced. The male subject had 2 sessions of treatment, and the female subject 3 sessions.

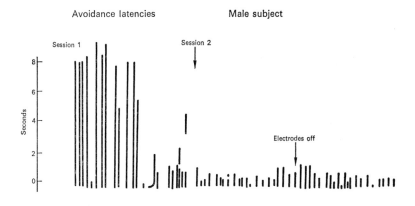

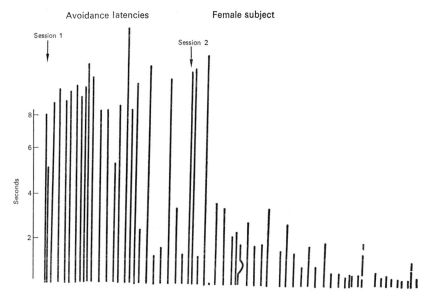

FIG. B1. Avoidance latencies to the slide of a squirrel (CS1) by male and female volunteer subjects (sessions 1 and 2 only).

Figure B2 shows session 1, trial 1, for the male subject. The CS1 was exposed (channel 6) 8 seconds before shock was administered (channel 3). The subject then escaped the shock by switching off both shock and CS1 concurrently (CR1 channel 4).

Channel 1. The EMG shows an early muscular response (0.9 second after the onset of the CS1) which persists up to the onset of the UCS and increases thereafter. This result shows the existence of an anticipatory muscle response from the beginning of the first session.

Channel 2. Respiration was recorded *via* a Nelligan thermocouple, so that it is not possible to comment on amplitude. However, if rate alone is considered, no change occurs during the major part of exposure to the CS1. The onset of the UCS coincides with a fresh inspiration, altering the preceding rate from 14 to 22. It is concluded that in session 1, trial 1, for the male patient, the presentation of the CS1 did not in itself alter the respiratory rate.

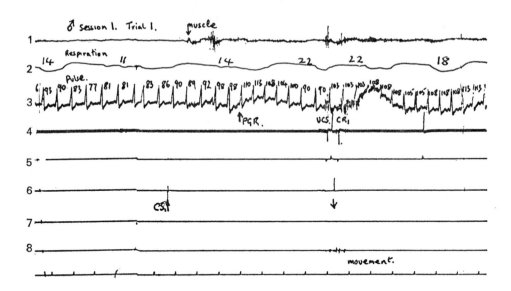

FIG. B2. Session 1, trial 1, for the male subject. The measures corresponding to the channel number are the same throughout Appendix B. Channel 1 is right forearm EMG. Channel 2 respiration (thermocouple). Channel 3 pulse plus GSR. Channel 4 CR1. Channel 6 CS1. Channel 8 ballistic bed. (The artefact is due to a ripped record page.)

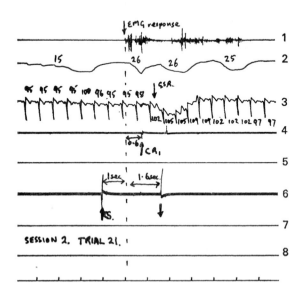

FIG. B3. Session 2, trial 21, for the male subject.

Channel 3. The PGR shows only a small response, quite compatible with the effect of light stimulation alone; however, there is a marked cardiac acceleration and deceleration which is completed before the UCS. The cardiac acceleration recurs due to shock. Thus the cardiac rate pattern was labile even before the onset of the CS1. This finding is difficult to explain, except that it is noted in passing that the subject knew that the shock would occur, had previously experienced shock, when his thresholds were being established, and it is probable that his anxiety was at a high level at the start of conditioning. The pre- and post-CS1 cardiac rate variability is also noteworthy.

Channel 8. There is no bed movement until the shock is administered.

Figure B3 shows trial 21 of the second session for the male subject. It can be seen from channels 4 and 6 that the subject has avoided with a latency of 1.6 seconds. The EMG (channel 1) latency is 1 second. There has been a marked tachypnoea (channel 2); the GSR response is present and marked, although it follows the CS1 offset because of the rapid avoidance (MacCulloch *et al.*, 1965).

The cardiac acceleration (channel 3) starts at about the time the CR1 response is made, is moderate in size (95–109 beats/minute), and is bimodal. It is worth noting that the pre- and post-CS variability of cardiac rate seen in Fig. B2 had disappeared. Figure B4 records the effects of showing the male subject the slide of the toad (CS2—see section A of Fig. B4) and the squirrel (CS1—see section B) at the end of session 2, after the leg electrodes had been removed and the subject knew that he could not be shocked.

1. *Section A of Fig. B4.* There is no EMG burst within the first to the fifth second after CS2 onset (channel 1) nor an increase in the muscle spindle activity.

There is no change of respiratory rate (channel 2) nor any change of GSR response (channel 3). There is, however, an acceleration of 10 beats/minute in pulse rate, but the overall impression is that the pulse rate is again labile. This lability might have been due to the changed conditions—that is the removal of the electrodes. There is no CR1—i.e. no attempt to remove the slide of the toad (channel 4) and no body movement (channel 8).

Section A of Fig. B4 shows, therefore, that the patient showed no autonomic activity of any marked kind to the presentation of the slide of the toad.

2. *Section B.* The picture now differs markedly from that shown in section A. There is an EMG burst 0.3 second after the onset of the CS1 (channel 1) followed by generalized tension in the right forearm. There is a CR1 in channel 4—that is the subject switched off the slide of the squirrel 0.6 second after the onset of the CS1. A clear and moderately large GSR occurs 2 seconds after the onset of the CS1 (channel 3) and is accompanied by cardiac acceleration (channel 3) which is not characterized by the pre- and post-CS1 lability shown in section A (channel 3). Finally, channel 8 shows body movement synchronous with the performance of the avoidance response CR1.

It is quite clear, therefore, that the male subject was both avoiding the slide of the squirrel and showing concomitant autonomic activity *after* the electrodes have been removed.

Samples of the pulse rate throughout the 2 sessions are shown in Fig. B5 for the following CS1 presentations. Section A: session 1, trial 1. Section B: session 1, trial 21. Section C: session 2, after the end of trial 24; CS2 is presented with the electrodes off. Section D: session 2 after trial 24; CS1 is presented with the electrodes off.

Section A shows a considerable pulse-rate acceleration and deceleration after the onset of CS1 and prior to the onset of the shock. Following the shock, the pulse rate again accelerates. This is the expected pattern of response when a subject "sets" himself in order to face an impending shock, which he does not avoid by making the appropriate response.

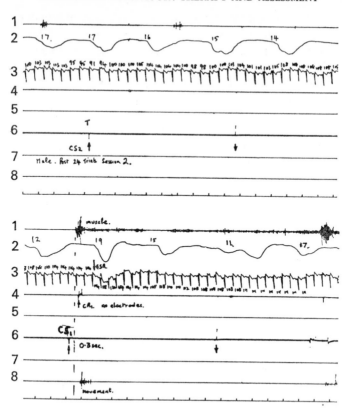

FIG. B4. An exposure of the CS2 (toad) following the end of session 2, and after the shock
electrodes have been removed.

The result for section B is reminiscent of the pattern of pulse-rate response shown by the
successfully treated patients, pulse-rate data for whom was presented early in Chapter 6.

The shape of the acceleration–deceleration curve is much the same except that because the
avoidance response (shown in section B as the upward-pointing arrow) occurs so soon
after the onset of CS1, the time relationship between the acceleration–deceleration curve and
the switching response is such that the peak of the curve occurs after the patient has avoided.
In both sections C and D the subject has had the shock electrodes removed. Section C shows
the pulse-rate response to the presentation of the toad—which has never been associated
with shock. Whilst there is a degree of rise, this is considerably less than in section B, and
can be attributed to the patient's overall autonomic lability—that is his tendency to display
spontaneous swings in his autonomic measures. By way of contrast, in section D when he is
presented with the slide of the squirrel, there is a fairly clear pattern of acceleration–deceleration which is similar to the patterns shown in the successfully treated patients, the data for
which are presented early in Chapter 6.

We conclude that there is considerable overall evidence that the male subject had become
aversively conditioned to the slide of the squirrel by the end of session 2, and that the instrumental avoidance response, together with concomitant physiological indicants of "anxiety"
persisted even *after* the electrodes had been removed, and there was no possibility of the
subject receiving the shock.

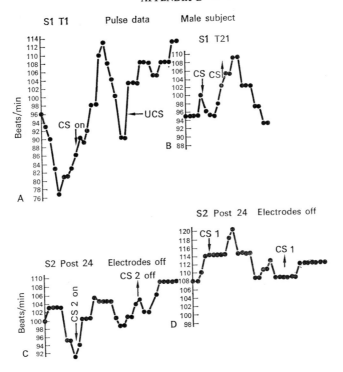

FIG. B5. Pulse data for the male subject on session 1, session 2, and after the end of session 2.

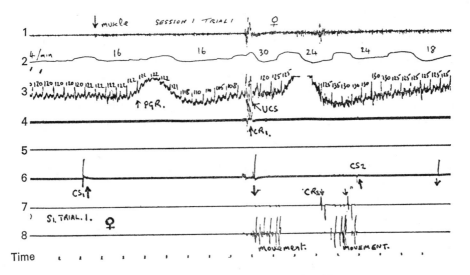

FIG. B6. Session 1, trial 1, for the female subject.

RESULTS: THE FEMALE SUBJECT

Figure B6 shows session 1, trial 1, for the female subject in which she performed an escape response. A CR1 (channel 4) is made in response to the UCS (channel 3). That is, the subject failed to avoid within the statutory period of 8 seconds, and hence received a shock, upon which she performed an immediate escape response. There is a slight increase in muscle tone (channel 1) at the onset of the CS1, and no respiratory change (channel 2) until the UCS occurs, when the rate almost doubles. There is no anticipatory body movement (channel 8), only that accompanying shock, CR1, and CR2. The PGR (channel 3) shows a response to the onset of CS1 which is almost as large as that associated with the shock. The pulse response (channel 3) consists of a 10 beat/minute deceleration, prior to the acceleration generated by the UCS. The deceleration has been noted previously by ourselves (MacCulloch et al., 1965) as well as by Deane (1964), who reported its occurrence in subjects facing unavoidable shock, and was explained by him as representing a "setting" response to the impending shock.

Figure B7 shows an escape response in session 2, trial 2. The record indicates a marked response to an unintentional sound which served as a cue to the subject. It can be seen that there is a respiratory acceleration (channel 2), a marked GSR response (channel 3), and a cardiac deceleration. However, there is no EMG response at the onset of the CS1. The marked cardiac deceleration, as seen in Fig. B6 has been converted to a slight acceleration, and the CR1 is insufficiently large to produce detectable general body movement (channel 8). Once again, the subject failed to avoid prior to shock onset, performing instead an escape response almost immediately shock occurred.

Figure B8 shows session 3, trial 13, for the female subject. She performs an avoidance response (channel 4) at a latency of approximately 3 seconds. This avoidance response is preceded quite clearly by a burst of muscle spindle activity (channel 1) marked by the arrow after a latency of 0.6 second. The respiration rate doubles (channel 2), and there is a cardiac acceleration and a GSR response (channel 3). Body movement (channel 8) consequent upon the performance of the CR2 (channel 7) is also noticeable. The energy involved in the second conditioned response (CR2) exceeds that involved in the first (CR1).

Figure B9 shows session 3, extinction trials 7, 8, and 9, after the end of trial 24, following which the electrodes were removed. During the latter part of session 2 and the whole of session 3, the female subject continued to avoid rapidly (see the second half of the learning curve for session 2, Fig. B2). Following session 3, trial 24, the electrodes were removed. The subject was then exposed to a series of extinction trials in which the CS1 (squirrel) was projected at 10-second intervals. The subject was given no instructions other than being told that she could not be shocked. The first point to note from Fig. B9 is that the subject avoided rapidly (channel 4). The instrumental responses indicate that the avoidance was very rapid, and the unnecessarily high effort used by the subject is clearly shown by the ballistic bed sensor (channel 8). In each trial there is a respiratory acceleration 2 seconds after the CS1 exposure (channel 2). The numbers accompanying the respiration trace indicate the increase in respiration rate consequent upon each exposure of the squirrel (CS1). The PGR response is clearly present (channel 3) on trials 7 and 8, $2\frac{1}{2}$ and 2 seconds after each onset of CS1; in trial 9 it is virtually synchronous with CS1 and is replicated once at $2\frac{1}{2}$ seconds after the onset of the slide of the squirrel (CS1). All three extinction trials show clear-cut cardiac accelerations accompanying the onset of the CS1. The final feature of note is the occurrence of a number

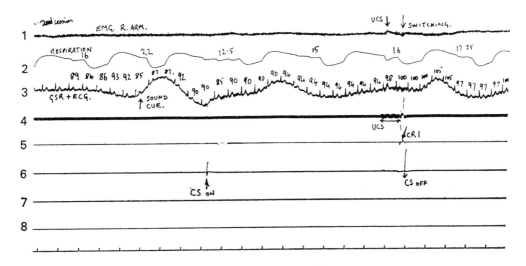

FIG. B7. Session 2, trial 2, for the female subject.

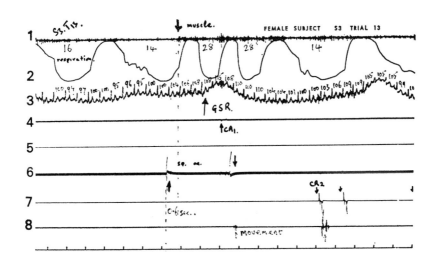

FIG. B8. Session 3, trial 13, for the female subject.

of requests for the toad slide (CR2), again replicating the behaviour shown by this subject while electrodes were worn, when the exposure of the slide of the toad meant a postponement of the squirrel slide, and hence of possible shock.

Some pulse-rate samples have been plotted so that they may be compared to similar data available on the trial patients, and these are shown in Fig. B10.

It is clear that a conditioned avoidance response with concomitant physiological responses has been established in the female subject by the end of session 3, and both were maintained with great intensity after the electrodes had been removed.

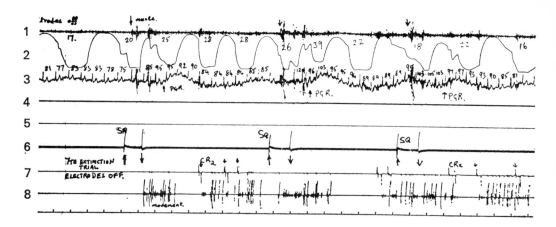

FIG. B9. Data for the female subject, showing the extinction trials 7–9 after the completion of session 3, and the removal of the electrodes.

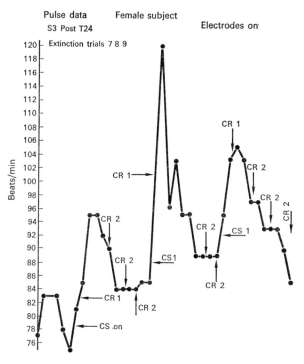

FIG. B10. Pulse data for the female subject on extinction trials 7–9 following the completion of session 3, and electrodes had been removed.

DISCUSSION

It might have been suggested that the learning and physiological results that were obtained on a number of homosexual patients would differ from data obtained from normal subjects; this suggestion is no longer tenable. Clear and unequivocal evidence of instrumental avoidance learning and conditioned anxiety has been obtained in the male subject after 40 minutes of conditioning, and in the female subject after 1 hour. It is reasonable to assume that the attractiveness of the CS1 (homosexual slides) for the patients was greater than the slide of the squirrel used for the experimental subjects; hence the relatively more rapid learning of the latter. In addition, of course, we intended that the learning of the patient should generalize into reality, hence we used a rather large number of learning trials. We had no such aim in the case of the volunteer subjects; on the contrary, our intention was the opposite.

The behaviour of the experimental subjects during learning replicated that of the successful patients in all respects, even down to the increasing rate of requests for the relief stimulus (CS2—the slide of the toad) as conditioning proceeded. In the case of the patients there was ample evidence that the responses acquired in treatment generalized to real life. This possibility was not tested for the experimental subjects (see above). Indeed, one objective of continuing exposure to the CS1 after the electrodes had been removed was to extinguish the conditioned avoidance response, and more particularly, the accompanying anxiety. In fact this extinction procedure was stopped for both subjects when it began to appear that the opposite effect than that which we intended was in fact occurring—namely the phenomena of incubation, or increment of response even in the absence of the UCS—as discussed in detail in Chapter 8. A verbal report from the subjects several days later was to the effect that neither displayed any ill effect, and that neither had come into contact with squirrels. This stimulus was chosen because of the comparative rarity of its occurrence in the busy Midland streets.

There are considerable ethical problems in research on normals—even if they volunteer—which attempt to condition potentially permanent responses, particularly to naturally occurring stimuli. Nevertheless, in so far as it seems likely that a learning process, not dissimilar to that described in the present book, underlies much real-life learning—particularly of anxiety-reducing relief stimuli which then become important cues for approach behaviour—further experimental work seems desirable.

REFERENCES

ADCOCK, C. J. (1965) A comparison of the concepts of Cattell and Eysenck, *British Journal of Educational Psychology* **35**, 90–97.

ALLEN, C. (1958) *Homosexuality: Its Nature, Causation and Treatment*, London, Staples Press.

ALTMAN, J. A. and DASS, G. (1964) Auto-radiographic and histological evidence of postnatal hippocampal neurogenesis in rats (unpublished manuscript, 1964). Cited by J. Money, Hormones and sexual behaviour in sex research, in Money, J. (ed.), *Sexual Research; New Developments*, New York, Holt, Rinehart & Winston.

AMSEL, A. (1958) Drive properties of the anticipation of frustration, *Psychological Bulletin* **55**, 102–19.

AMSEL, A. (1962) Frustrative non-reward in partial reinforcement and discrimination learning: some recent history and a theoretical extension, *Psychological Review* **69**, 306–28.

ANTROBUS, J. S., COLEMAN, R., and SINGER, J. L. (1967) Signal detection performance by subjects differing in predisposition to day dreaming, *Journal of Consulting Psychology* **31**, 487–91.

APPEL, K. E. (1937) Endocrine studies in cases of homosexuality, *Archives of Neurology and Psychiatry* **37**, 1206–7.

ARGYLE, M. and KENDON, A. (1965) The experimental analysis of social performance, in Berkowitz, L. (ed.), *Advances in Experimental Social Psychology*, Vol. 3, New York, Academic Press.

ARONFREED, J. (1965) Conduct and conscience: a natural history of internalisation, in Hoffman, M. L. (ed.), *Character Development*, New York Social Science Research Council.

ARONFREED, J. and REBER, A. (1965) Internalised behavioural suppression and the timing of social punishment, *Journal of Personality and Social Psychology* **1**, 3–16.

BANCROFT, J. H. J., JONES, GWYNNE, H., and PULLAN, B. (1966) A simple transducer for measuring penile erections, with comments on its use in the treatment of sexual disorders, *Behaviour Research and Therapy* **4**, 239–41.

BANDURA, A. and WALTERS, R. (1963) *Social Learning and Personality Development*, New York, Holt, Rinehart and Winston.

BANKS, J. H. JR., MILLER, R. E., and OGAWA, N. (1966) The development of discriminated autonomic and instrumental responses during avoidance conditioning, *Journal of Genetic Psychology* **108**, 199–211.

BARLOW, D. H., LEITENBERG, H., and AGRAS, W. S. (1969) Experimental control of sexual deviation through manipulation of the noxious scene in covert sensitization, *Journal of Abnormal Psychology* **74**, 596–600.

BARRACLOUGH, C. A. (1961) Production of anovulatory sterile rats by a single injection of testosterone propionate, *Endocrinology* **68**, 62–67.

BARRON, F. (1953) An ego-strength scale which predicts response to psychotherapy, *Journal of Consulting Psychology* **17**, 327–33.

BARTLETT, F. C. (1932) *Remembering: An Experimental and Social Study*, London, Cambridge University Press.

BAUER, J. (1940) Homosexuality as an endocrinological, psychological and genetic problem, *Journal of Criminology and Psychopathology* **2**, 188–97.

BEECH, H. R. (1960) The symptomatic treatment of writers' cramp, in Eysenck, H. J. (ed.), *Behaviour Therapy and the Neuroses*, London, Pergamon, pp. 349–372.

BENE, EVA (1965a) On the genesis of male homosexuality: an attempt at clarifying the role of the parents, *British Journal of Psychology* **3**, 803–14.

BENE, EVA (1965b) On the genesis of female homosexuality, *British Journal of Psychiatry* **3** (8), 815–21.

BERLYNE, D. E. (1960) *Conflict, Arousal and Curiosity*, New York, McGraw-Hill.

BLACK, A. H. (1959) Heart-rate changes during avoidance learning in dogs, *Canadian Journal of Psychology* **13**, 228–42.

BIEBER, B., BIEBER, I., DAIN, H. J., DINCE, P. R., DRELLICH, M. G., GRAND, H. G., GRUNDLACH, R. H., KREMER, MALVINA W., WILBER, CORNELIA, B., and BIEBER, T. D. (1963) *Homosexuality*, New York, Basic Books.

BRADY, J. D. (1958) Ulcers in "executive monkeys", *Scientific American* **119**, No. 4.

BREHM, J. and COHEN, A. R. (1962) *Explorations in Cognitive Dissonance*, New York, Wiley.

BRIERLEY, H. (1964) Electrical aversion therapy, *British Medical Journal* **1**, 631.

BRIERLEY, H. (1965) Personal communication.

BROOKS, J. (1969) The insecure personality: a factory analytic study, *British Journal of Medical Psychology* **42**, 395.

BROWN, P. T. (1964) On the differentiation of homo- or hetero-erotic interest in the male; an operant technique illustrated in the case of a motor-cycle fetishist, *Behaviour Research and Therapy* **2**, 31–37.

BYRNE, D. (1964) Repression—sensitization as a dimension of personality, in Maher, B. A. (ed.), *Progress in Experimental Personality Research*, Vol. 1, New York, Academic Press, pp. 115–68.

CARLIN, A. S. and ARMSTRONG, H. E., JR. (1968) Aversive conditioning: learning or dissonance reduction, *Journal of Consulting and Clinical Psychology* **32**.

CARMENA, M. (1934) Ist die personliche Affektlage oder 'Nervositat' eine ererbte Eigenschaft?, *Z. ges. Neurologie Psychiatrie* **150**, 434–45.

CATTELL, R. B. (1965) *The Scientific Analysis of Personality*, Penguin Books, London.

CATTELL, R. B., EBER, W. E., and DELHEES, K. H. (1968) *A Large Sample Cross-validation of the Personality Trait Structure of the 16PF with Some Clinical Implications*, Multivariate Behaviour Research Monograph, Special Issue, p. 107.

CATTELL, R. B. and MORONY, J. H. (1962) The use of the 16PF in distinguishing homosexuals, normals, and general criminals. *J. of Consulting Psychology* **26**, 531–40.

CATTELL, R. B. and SCHEIER, I. H. (1961) *The Meaning and Measurement of Neuroticism and Anxiety*, Ronald, New York.

CATTELL, R. B. and STICE, G. F. (1957) *Handbook for the Sixteen Personality Factor Questionnaire*, Champaign, Ill., Institute for Personality and Ability Testing.

CAUTELA, J. R. (1967) Covert sensitization, *Psychological Reports* **20**, 459–68.

CLARKE, D. F. (1963) Fetishism treated by negative conditioning, *British Journal of Psychiatry* **109**, 649–52.

COATES, S. (1962) Homosexuality and the Rorschach test, *British Journal of Medical Psychology* **35**, 177–90.

COATES, S. (1964) Clinical psychology in sexual deviation, in Rosen, I. (ed.), *The Pathology and Treatment of Sexual Deviation*, London, Oxford University Press.

COOPER, A. J. (1963) A case of fetishism and impotence treated by behaviour therapy, *British Journal of Psychiatry* **109**, 649–52.

CRESPI, L. P. (1942) Quantitative variations of incentive and performance in the white rat, *American Journal of Psychiatry* **55**, 467–517.

CRUM, J., BROWNE, W. L., and BITTERMAN, M. E. (1951) The effect of partial and delayed reinforcement to extinction, *American Journal of Psychology* **64**, 228–37.

CURRAN, D. and PARR, D. (1957) Homosexuality: an analysis of 100 male cases seen in private practice, *British Medical Journal* **1**, 797–801.

DEANE, G. E. (1961) Human heart rate responses during experimentally induced anxiety, *Journal of Experimental Psychology* **61**, 489–93.

DEANE, G. E. (1964) Human heart rate responses during experimentally induced anxiety: a follow-up with controlled respiration, *Journal of Experimental Psychology* **67**, 193–5.

DEANE, G. E. and ZEAMAN, D. (1958) Human heart rate during anxiety, *Perceptual Motor Skills* **8**, 103–6.

DESIDERATO, O. and WASSERMAN, M. F. (1967) Incubation of anxiety: effect on generalisation gradients, *Journal of Experimental Psychology* **74**, 506–10.

DOLLARD, J. and MILLER, N. E. (1950) *Personality and Psychotherapy*, New York, McGraw-Hill.

DYKMAN, R. A., REESE, W. G., SALBRECHT, C. R., and THOMASSON, P. J. (1959) Psychophysiological reaction to novel stimuli: measurements, adaptation and relationship of psychological and physiological variables in a normal human, *Annals of the New York Academy of Science* **79**, 43–107.

EBER, H. W. (1966) *Multivariate Analysis of a Vocational Rehabilitation System*, Multivariate Behaviour Research Monograph No. 1.

ELLIS, A. (1956) The effectiveness of psychotherapy with individuals who have severe homosexual problems, *Journal of Consulting Psychology* **20**, 58–60.

ENDLER, N. S. and HUNT, J. M. V. (1966) Sources of behavioural variance as measured by the S–R inventory of anxiousness, *Psychological Bulletin* **65**, 336–46.

EPSTEIN, S. and TAYLOR, S. P. (1967) Instigation to aggression as a function of degree of defeat and perceived aggressive intent of the opponent, *Journal of Personality* **35**, 265–89.

ESTES, W. K. (1944) An Experimental Study of Punishment, *Psychological Monographs*, 57 (whole No. 263).

EYSENCK, H. J. (1952) The effects of psychotherapy: an evaluation, *Journal of Consulting Psychology* **16**, 319–24.

EYSENCK, H. J. (1956) The inheritance of extraversion–introversion, *Acta Psychologica* **12**, 95–110.

EYSENCK, H. J. (1959) *Manual of the Maudsley Personality Inventory*, London, University of London Press.

EYSENCK, H. J. (1960) *The Structure of Human Personality*, London, Methuen.

EYSENCK, H. J. (ed.) (1965a) *Experiments in Behaviour Therapy*, London, Pergamon.

EYSENCK, H. J. (1965b) Personality factors in conditioning: an introductory note to two papers, *Behaviour Research and Therapy* **2**, 271–2.

EYSENCK, H. J. (1967) Single-trial conditioning, neurosis and the Napalkov phenomenon, *Behaviour Research and Therapy* **5**, 63–65.

EYSENCK, H. J. (1968) A theory of the incubation of anxiety/fear responses, *Behaviour Research and Therapy* **6**, 309–22.

EYSENCK, H. J. and EYSENCK, S. B. G. (1964) *Manual of the Eysenck Personality Inventory*, London, University of London Press.

EYSENCK, S. B. G. (1956) An experimental study of psychogalvanic responses of normal, neurotic and psychotic subjects, *Journal of Psychosomatic Research* **1**, 258–72.

FELDMAN, M. P. (1963) A reconsideration of the extinction hypothesis of warm-up in motor behaviour, *Psychological Bulletin*, **60**, 452–9.

FELDMAN, M. P. (1966) Aversion therapy for sexual deviations: a critical review, *Psychological Bulletin* **65**, 65–79.

FELDMAN, M. P. (1968) The treatment of homosexuality by aversion therapy, in Freeman, H. L. (ed.), *Progress in Behaviour Therapy*, Bristol, John Wright.

FELDMAN, M. P. and MacCULLOCH, M. J. (1965) The application of anticipatory avoidance learning to the treatment of homosexuality: I, Theory, technique and preliminary results, *Behaviour Research and Therapy* **3**, 165–83.

FELDMAN, M. P., MacCULLOCH, M. J., and MacCULLOCH, MARY, C. (1968) The aversion therapy treatment of a heterogeneous group of five cases of sexual deviation, *Acta Psychiatric Scandinavica* **44**, 113–24.

FELDMAN, M. P., MacCULLOCH, M. J., MELLOR, VALERIE, and PINSCHOF, J. M. (1966) The application of anticipatory avoidance learning to the treatment of homosexuality: III, The sexual orientation method, *Behaviour Research and Therapy* **4**, 289–99.

FENICHEL, O. (1945) *The Psychoanalytic Theory of the Neuroses*, New York, Norton.

FERSTER, C. B. (1965) Reinforcement and punishment in the control of homosexual behaviour by social agencies, in Eysenck, H. J. (ed.), *Experiments in Behaviour Therapy*, Oxford, Pergamon, pp. 189–207.

FESTINGER, L. (1957) *A Theory of Cognitive Dissonance*, Evanston, Ill., Row, Peterson.

FISHER, A. E. (1956) Maternal and sexual behaviour induced by intra-cranial chemical stimulation, *Science* **124**, 228–9.

FOSS, G. L. (1951) The influence of urinary androgen on sexuality in women, *Lancet* **2**, 667–9.

FRANKS, C. M. (1956) Conditioning and personality: a study of normal and neurotic subjects, *Journal of Abnormal Social Psychology* **52**, 143–50.

FRANKS, C. M. (1960) Conditioning and abnormal behaviour, in Eysenck, H. J. (ed.), *Handbook of Abnormal Psychology*, London, Pitman, pp. 457–87.

FREUND, K. (1960) Some problems in the treatment of homosexuality, in Eysenck, H. J. (ed.), *Behaviour Therapy and the Neuroses*, London, Pergamon Press, pp. 312–26.

FREUND, K. (1963) A laboratory method for diagnosing predominance of homo- or hetero-erotic interest in the male, *Behaviour Research and Therapy* **1**, 85–93.

FREUND, K. (1965) Diagnosing heterosexual paedophilia by means of a test for sexual interest, *Behaviour Research and Therapy* **3**, 229–35.

GEBHARD, P. H. (1965) Situational factors affecting human sexual behaviour, in Beach, F. A. (ed.), *Sexual Behaviour*, New York, Wiley, pp. 483–92.

GELDER, M. G. (1968a) Desensitization and psychotherapy research, *British Journal of Medical Psychology* **41**, 39–46.

GELDER, M. G. (1968b) Indications for behaviour therapy, in Freeman, H. (ed.), *Progress in Behaviour Therapy*, Bristol, John Wright, pp. 51–58.

GLASS, S. J., DEVEL, H. J., and WRIGHT, C. A. (1940) Sex hormone studies in male homosexuality, *Journal of Clinical Endocrinology* **26**, 590–4.

GOLD, S. and NEUFELD, INGE L. (1965) A learning approach to the treatment of homosexuality, *Behaviour Research and Therapy* **3**, 201–4.

GOLDSTEIN, A. P. (1962) *Therapist–patient Expectancies in Psychotherapy*, New York, Pergamon.

GOLDSTEIN, A. P., HELLER, K., and SECHREST, L. B. (1966) *Psychotherapy and the Psychology of Behaviour Change*, New York, Wiley.

GRYGIER, T. G. (1957) Psychometric aspects of homosexuality, *Journal of Mental Science* **103**, 514–25.

HADFIELD, J. A. (1958) The cure of homosexuality, *British Medical Journal* **1**, 1323.

HARRIS, G. W. and LEVINE, S. (1965) Sexual differentiations of the brain and its experimental control, *Journal of Physiology* **181**, 379–90.

HEBB, D. D. (1955) Drives and the C.N.S. (conceptual nervous system), *Psychological Review* **62**, 143–54.

HESS, H., SELTZER, L., and SHLIEN, M. (1965) Pupil response of hetero- and homosexual males to pictures of men and women: a pilot study, *Journal of Abnormal Psychology* **70**, 165–8.

HUMPHREYS, L. G. (1939) The effect of random alternation of reinforcement on the acquisition and extinction of conditioned eyelid reactions, *Journal of Experimental Psychology* **25**, 141–58.

HUNDLEBY, J. D. and CONNOR, W. H. (1968) Interrelationships between personality inventories: the 16PF, the M.M.P.I. and the M.P.I., *Journal of Consulting and Clinical Psychology* **32**, 152–7.

JAMES, B. (1962) Case of homosexuality treated by aversion therapy, *British Medical Journal* **1**, 768–70.

JENKS, R. S. and DEANE, G. E. (1963) Human heart rate responses during experimentally induced anxiety: a follow up, *Journal of Experimental Psychology* **65**, 109–12.

JINKS, J. L. and FULKER, D. W. (1970) A comparison of the biometrical, genetical, MAVA and classical approaches to the analysis of human behaviour, *Psychological Bulletin* **73**, 311–49.

JONES, E. (1964) *The Life and Work of Sigmund Freud*, London, Pelican Books.

JONES, A., BENTLER, P. M., and PETRY, G. (1960) The reduction of uncertainty concerning future pain, *Journal of Abnormal Psychology* **71**, 87–94.

JOST, H. and SONTAG, L. W. (1944) The genetic factor in autonomic nervous system functions, *Psychosomatic Medicine* **6**, 308–10.

KALLMAN, F. J. (1952) Comparative twin study of the genetic aspects of male homosexuality, *Journal of Nervous and Mental Disorders* **115**, 283–98.

KELLY, G. A. (1955) *The Psychology of Personal Constructs*, New York, Norton.

KENYON, F. E. (1968) Studies in female homosexuality, *Journal of Consulting and Clinical Psychology* **32**, 510–13.

KIMBLE, G. A. (1955) Shock intensity and avoidance learning, *Journal of Comparative and Physiological Psychology* **48**, 281–4.

KIMBLE, G. A. (1961) *Conditioning and Learning*, London, Methuen.

KIMBLE, G. A. (1964) *Conditioning and Learning*, 2nd edn., London. Methuen.

KINSEY, A. C. (1941) Criteria for a hormonal explanation of homosexuality, *Journal of Clinical Endocrinology* **1**, 424–8.

KINSEY, A. C., POMEROY, W. B., and MARTIN, C. I. (1947) *Sexual Behaviour in the Human Male*, Philadelphia, Saunders.

KOCKOTT, G. (1970) Psychiatrische und Lerntheoretische Asppekte der Transsexualitat, in *Sexual Forschung: Kritie und Tendenren* (in press).

KOENIG, K. P. (1965) The differentiation of hetero- or homo-erotic interests in the male: some comments on articles by Brown and Freund, *Behaviour Research and Therapy* **3**, 305–7.

KOLVIN, I. (1967) "Aversion imagery" treatment in adolescents, *Behaviour Research and Therapy* **5**, 245–8.

KRAFT-EBBING, R. (1934) *Psychopathia Sexualis* (rev. edn.), Brooklyn, Physicians and Surgeons Book Co.

LACEY, J. I., BATEMAN, D. E., and LEHN, R. VAN (1953) Autonomic response specificity, *Psychomatic Medicine* **15**, 8–21.

LACEY, J. I. and LACEY, B. C. (1958) Verification and extension of the principle of autonomic response stereotypy, *American Journal of Psychology* **71**, 50–73.

LACEY, J. I. and SMITH, R. C. (1954) Conditioning and generalisation of unconscious anxiety, *Science* **120**, 1045–52.

LACEY, J. I., SMITH, R. L., and GREEN, A. (1955) The use of conditioned autonomic responses in the study of anxiety, *Psychomatic Medicine* **17**, 208–17.

LADER, M. R. and WING, L. (1966) *Physiological Measures. Sedative Drugs and Morbid Anxiety*, Oxford, Oxford University Press.

LANG, P. J. and LAZOWICK, D. A. (1963) Experimental desensitization of a phobia, *Journal of Abnormal Social Psychology* **66**, 519–25.

LEVIN, S., HIRSCH, I. S., SHUGAR, G., and KAKAR, R. (1967) Treatment of a homosexual problem with avoidance conditioning and reciprocal inhibition (unpub. manuscript), Lafayette Clinic, Detroit.

LEVINE, S. and MULLINS, R., JR. (1964) Estrogen administered neonatally affects adult sexual behavior in male and female rats, *Science* **144**, 185–7.

LEWIS, D. J. (1960) Partial reinforcement: a selective review of the literature since 1950, *Psychological Bulletin* **57**, 1–29.

LOVIBOND, S. H. (1969) The aversiveness of uncertainty: an analysis in terms of activation and information theory, *Australian Journal of Psychology* **20**, 85–96.

LYKKEN, D. T. (1957) A study of anxiety in the sociopathic personality, *Journal of Abnormal and Social Psychology* **55**, 6–10.

MACCOBY, ELEANOR (ed.) (1967) *The Development of Sex Differences*, London, Tavistock.

MCALLISTER, J. (1968) Foulds' "Continuum of Personal Illness" and the 16PF, *British Journal of Psychiatry* **114**, 53–56.

MACLEAN, P. D. and PLOOG, D. W. (1962) Cerebral representation of penile erection, *Journal of Neurophysiology* **25**, 29.

MCCLELLAND, D. C. and MCGOWN, D. R. (1953) The effect of variable food reinforcement on the strength of a secondary reward, *Journal of Comparative and Physiological Psychology* **46**, 80–86.

MACCULLOCH, M. J. and ATKINSON, JEAN (1968) A simple method for adapting portable EEG machines for use as polygraphs, *Acta Psychiatica Scandinavica* **44**, 410–41.

MACCULLOCH, M.J., BIRTLES, C. J., and BOND, SARAH (1969) A free space-time traversal data-logging system for two human subjects, *Medical and Biological Engineering* **7**, 593–9.

MacCulloch, M. J., Birtles, C. J., and Feldman, M. P. (1970a) Anticipatory avoidance learning for the treatment of homosexuality: recent developments and an automatic aversion therapy system, *Behaviour Therapy* (in press).

MacCulloch, M. J., Feldman, M. P., and Emery, A. E. H. (1970b) The failure of aversion theory with a monozygotic twin discordant for sexual object choice and a theoretical formulation of aetiology of homosexuality, unpublished manuscript, University of Birmingham.

MacCulloch, M. J. and Feldman, M. P. (1967a) Aversion therapy in the management of 43 homosexuals, *British Medical Journal* **2**, 594–7.

MacCulloch, M. J., Feldman, M. P. (1967b) Personalities and the treatment of homosexuality, *Acta Psychiat. Scand.* **43**, 300–317.

MacCulloch, M. J., Feldman, M.P., and Pinschof, J. M. (1965) The application of anticipatory avoidance learning to the treatment of homosexuality: II, Avoidance response latencies and pulse rate changes. *Behaviour Research and Therapy* **3**, 21–44.

McGuire, R. J., Carlise, J. M., and Young, B. G. (1965) Sexual deviations as conditioned behaviour: a hypothesis, *Behaviour Research and Therapy* **3**, 185–90.

McGuire, R. J. and Vallance, M. (1964) Aversion therapy vs. electric shock: a simple technique, *British Medical Journal* **1**, 151–3.

McGuire, W. J. (1966) The current status of cognitive consistency theories, in Feldman, S. (ed.), *Cognitive Consistency: Motivational Antecedents and Behavioural Consequents*, New York, Academic Press, pp. 1–46.

McNamara, H. J. and Wike, E. L. (1958) The effects of irregular learning conditions upon the rate and permanence of learning, *Journal of Comparative and Physiological Psychology* **51**, 363–6.

Mahl, G. F. and Schultze, G. (1964) Psychological research in the extralinguistic area, in Sebeck, T. A., Hayes, A. S., and Bateson, M. C. (eds.), *Approaches to Semiotics*, The Hague, Morton.

Mandler, G. and Kremen, I. (1958) Autonomic feedback: a correlational study, *Journal of Personality* **26**, 388–99.

Marks, I. M. and Gelder, M. G. (1967) Transvestism and fetishism: clinical and psychological changes during faradic aversion, *British Journal of Psychiatry* **113**, 711–29.

Masters, W. H. and Johnson, Virginia E. (1966) *Human Sexual Response*, London, Churchill.

Maurus, J. M. (1964) Unpublished manuscript cited by J. Money, Hormones and sexual behaviour in sex research, in Money, J. (ed.), *Sexual Research; New Developments*, New York, Holt, Rinehart & Winston.

Max, L. W. (1935) Breaking up a homosexual fixation by the conditioned reaction technique: a case study, *Psychological Bulletin* **32**, 734.

Merbaum, M. and Kazaoka, K. (1967) Reports of emotional experience by sensitizers and repressors during an interview transaction. *Journal of Abnormal Psychology* **72**, 101–5.

Meyer, A. E. (1966) Psychoanalytic versus behaviour therapy of male homosexuals: a statistical evaluation of clinical outcome, *Comparative Psychiatry* **7**, 110–17.

Meyer, V. and Gelder, M. G. (1963) Behaviour therapy and phobic disorders, *British Journal of Psychiatry* **109**, 19–29.

Milgram, S. (1963) Behavioural study of obedience, *Journal of Abnormal Social Psychology* **67**, 371–8.

Miller, N. E. (1959) Liberalization of basic S–R concepts: extensions to conflict behaviour, motivation and social learning, in Koch, S. (ed.), *Psychology: A Study of a Science*, Study 1, Vol. 2, New York, McGraw-Hill, pp. 196–292.

Miller, N. E. (1960) Learning resistance to pain and fear: effects of overlearning, exposure and rewarded exposure in context, *Journal of Experimental Psychology* **60**, 137–46.

Miller, N. E. (1969) Learning of visceral and glandular responses, *Science*, **163**, 434–45.

Money, J. and Hampson, R. (1957) Imprinting and the establishment of gender role, *Archives of Neurology and Psychiatry* **77**, 333–6.

Morgenstern, F. S., Pearce, J. P. and Linford Rees, W. (1965) Predicting the outcome of behaviour therapy by psychological tests, *Behaviour Research and Therapy* **2**, 191–200.

Neumann, F. and Elgar, W. (1966) Permanent changes in gonadal function and sexual behaviour as a result of early feminization of male rats by treatment with an anti-androgenic steroid, *Endokirnologie* **50**, 209–24.

Notterman, J. M., Schoenfeld, W. N., and Bersh, P. J. (1952) Conditioned heart rate response in human beings during experimental anxiety, *Journal of Comparative Physiological Psychology* **45**, 1–8.

Oliver, W. A., and Mosher, D. L. (1968) Psychopathology and guilt in heterosexual and subgroups of homosexual reformatory inmates, *Journal of Abnormal Psychology* **73**, 323–29.

Osgood, C. E., Succi, G. L., and Tannenbaum, P. (1957) *The Measurement of Meaning*, Urbana, Ill., University of Illinois Press.

Ostrom, T. M. (1969) The relationship between the effective, behavioural and cognitive components of attitude, *Journal of Experimental Social Psychology* **5**, 12.

Ovesey, L., Gaylin, W., and Hendin, H. (1963) Psychotherapy of male homosexuality, *Archives of General Psychiatry* **9**, 19–31.

Ovesey, L. and Willard, G. (1965) Psychotherapy of male homosexuality: prognosis, selection of patients, technique, *American Journal of Psychotherapy* **19**, 382–7.

Patterson Brown, W. (1964) The homosexual male, in Rosen, I. (ed.), *The Pathology and Treatment of Sexual Deviation*, London, Oxford University Press, pp. 196–314.

Pavlov, I. P. (1927) *Conditioned Reflexes, An Investigation of the Physiological Activity of the Cerebral Cortex*, London, Oxford University Press.

Pfaff, D. W. (1965) Cerebral implantation and auto-radiographic studies of sex hormones, in Money, J. (ed.), *Sexual Research; New Developments*. New York, Holt, Rinehart & Winston, pp. 219–31.

Pfeiffer, C. A. (1936) Sexual differences of the hypophyses and their determination by the gonads, *American Journal of Anatomy* **58**, 195–222.

Phillips, J. P. N. (1968) A note on the scoring of the sexual orientation method, *Behaviour Research and Therapy* **6**, 121–3.

Rachman, S. (1961) Sexual disorders and behaviour therapy, *American Journal of Psychiatry* **118**, 235–40.

Rachman, S. (1965) Aversion therapy: chemical or electrical?, *Behaviour Research and Therapy* **2**, 289–99.

Rachman, S. J. and Teasdale, J. (1969) *Aversion Therapy and Behaviour Disorders: An Analysis*, London, Routledge and Kegan Paul.

Ramsey, R. W. and Van Velzen, V. (1968) Behaviour therapy for sexual perversions, *Behaviour Research and Therapy* **6**, 233.

Renner, K. E. (1964) Delay of reinforcement: a historical review, *Psychological Bulletin* **61**, 341–61.

Robinson, J. and Grant, W. H. (1947) The orientating reflex (questioning reaction): cardiac, salivary and motor components, *Johns Hopkins Hospital Bulletin* **80**, 231–53.

Rubenstein, L. H. (1958) Psychotherapeutic aspects of male homosexuality, *British Journal of Medical Psychology* **31**, 14–18.

Sandler, J. (1964) Masochism: an empirical analysis, *Psychological Bulletin* **62**, 197–205.

Schachter, S. and Lattané, B. (1964) Crime, cognition, and the autonomic nervous system, in M. R. Jones (ed.), *Nebraska Symposium on Motivation*, Lincoln, Nebraska, University of Nebraska Press.

Schachter, S. and Singer, J. E. (1962) Cognitive, social and physiological determinants of emotional state, *Psychological Review* **69**, 379–95.

Schmidt, Elsa, Castell, D., and Brown, P. (1965) A retrospective study of 42 cases of behaviour therapy, *Behaviour Research and Therapy* **3**, 9–20.

Schneider, K. (1959) *Psychopathic Personalities*, 9th edn., London, Cassell.

Schofield, M. (1965a) *The Sexual Behaviour of Young People*, London, Longmans.

Schofield, M. (1965b) *Sociological Aspects of Homosexuality: A Comparative Study of Three Types of Homosexuals*, Longmans, London.

Scott, P. D. (1964) Definition, classification, prognosis and treatment, in Rosen, I. (ed.), *The Pathology and Treatment of Sexual Deviation*, London, Oxford University Press.

Scott, T. R., Wells, W. H., Wood, Dorothy Z., and Morgan, D. I. (1967) Pupillary response and sexual interest re-examined, *Journal of Clinical Psychology* **31**, 433–8.

Sebeok, T. A. and Hayes, A. M. (eds.) (1964) *Approaches to Semiotics*, New York, Mouton.

Segal, S. J. and Johnson, D. C. (1959) Inductive influence of steroid hormones on the neural system: ovulation controlling mechanisms, *Archives d'anatomie microscopique et de morphologie expérimentale* **48**, 261–73.

Shapiro, D., Tursky, B., Gershon, E., and Stern, M. (1969) Effects of feedback and reinforcement on the control of human systolic blood pressure, *Science* **163**, 588–9.

Shapiro, N. B. (1961) *Manual of the Personal Questionnaire*, London, Institute of Psychiatry.

Skinner, B. F. (1953) *Science and Human Behaviour*, New York, Macmillan.

Silverman, J. (1968) A paradigm for the study of altered states of consciousness, *British Journal of Psychiatry* **114**, 1201–18.

Solomon, R. L. and Brush, E. S. (1956) Experimentally derived conceptions of anxiety and aversion, in *Nebraska Symposium on Motivation* (ed. Jones, M. R.) Lincoln, Nebraska, University of Nebraska Press, pp. 212–305.

Solomon, R. L., Kamin, L. T., and Wynne, L. C. (1953) Traumatic avoidance learning: the outcomes of several extinction procedures with dogs, *Journal of Abnormal and Social Psychology* **48**, 291–302.

Solomon, R. C., Turner, Lucille H., and Lessac, M. S. (1968) Some effects of delay of punishment on resistance to temptations in dogs, *Journal of Personality and Social Psychology* **8**, 233–8.

Solomon, R. C. and Wynne, L. C. (1953) Traumatic avoidance learning: acquisition in normal dogs, *Psychological Monographs* **67**, No. 4.

Solomon, R. L. and Wynne, L. C. (1954) Traumatic avoidance learning: the principles of anxiety conservation and partial irreversibility, *Psychological Review* **61**, 353–85.

Solyom, L. and Miller, S. (1965) A differential conditioning procedure as the initial phase of the behaviour therapy of homosexuality, *Behaviour Research and Therapy* **3**, 147–60.

Sommer, R. (1967) Small group ecology, *Psychological Bulletin* **67**, 145–52.

SPENCE, K. W. (1964) Anxiety (drive) level and performance in eyelid conditioning, *Psychological Bulletin* **61**, 129–39.

STEVENSON, I. and WOLPE, J. (1960) Recovery from sexual deviations through overcoming non-sexual neurotic response, *American Journal of Psychiatry* **116**, 737–42.

SUTHERLAND, E. H. C. (1955) *Principles of Criminology*, 5th edn., revised by D. R. Cressey, Chicago, Lippincott.

SWYER, G. I. M. (1954) Homosexuality: the endocrinological aspects, *The Practitioner* **172**, 374–7.

TAYLOR, JANET A. (1953) A personality scale of manifest anxiety, *Journal of Abnormal and Social Psychology* **48**, 285–90.

TAYLOR, JANET A. (1956) Drive theory and manifest anxiety, *Psychological Bulletin* **53**, 303–20.

THORPE, J. G., SCHMIDT, ELSA, BROWN, P. T., and CASTELL, D. (1964) Aversion-relief therapy: a new method for general application, *Behaviour Research and Therapy* **2**, 71–82.

THORPE, J. G., SCHMIDT, ELSA, and CASTELL, D. (1963) A comparison of positive and negative (aversive) conditioning in the treatment of homosexuality, *Behaviour Research and Therapy* **1**, 357–62.

TURNER, LUCILLE, H. and SOLOMON, C. (1962) Human traumatic avoidance learning; theory and experiments on the operant–respondent distinction and failures to learn, *Psychological Monographs* 76, No. 559.

ULRICH, R. E., HUTCHINSON, R. R., and AZRIN, N. H. (1965) Pain-elicited aggression, *Psychological Records* **15**, 111–26.

VALINS, S. (1966a) Cognitive effects of false heart-rate feedback, *Journal of Personality and Social Psychology* **4**, 400–8.

VALINS, S. (1966b) Emotionality and information concerning internal reaction, *Journal of Personality and Social Psychology* **6**, 458–63.

VALINS, S. (1967) Emotionality and autonomic reactivity, *Journal of Experimental Research and Personality* **35**, 41–48.

VANDENBERG, S. G., CLARK, P. J., and SAMUELS, I. (1965) Psychophysiological reactions of twins: hereditary factors in galvanic skin resistance, heartbeat, and breathing rates, *Eugenics Quarterly* **12**, 7–10.

WALTON, H. J. (1968) Personality as a determinant of the form of alcoholism, *British Journal of Psychiatry* **114**, 761–6.

WEST, D. J. (1968) *Homosexuality*, 3rd edn., London, Penguin Books.

WESTWOOD, G. (1960) *A Minority: Homosexuality in Great Britain*, London, Longmans.

WHALEN, R. E. (1969) Hormone induced changes in the organization of sexual behaviour in the male rat, *Journal of Comparative and Physiological Psychology* **33**, 327–9.

WHALEN, E. E. and NADLER, R. D. (1963) Suppression of the development of female mating behaviour by estrogen administered in infancy, *Science* **141**, 273–4.

WILSON, G. T., HANNON, ALMA E., and EVANS, W. I. M. (1968) Behaviour therapy and the therapist–patient relationship, *Journal of Consulting Clinical Psychology* **32**, 103–9.

WILSON, J. G., YOUNG, W. C., HAMILTON, J. B., and YALE, J. (1940) A technique for suppressing development of reproductive function and sensitivity to estrogen in the female rat, *Biological Medicine* **13**, 189–202.

WOLPE, J. (1958) *Psychotherapy by Reciprocal Inhibition*, Stanford, Stanford University Press.

WOLPE, J. (1962) Isolation of a conditioning procedure as the crucial psychotherapeutic factor: a case-study, *Journal of Neurology and Mental Disorders* **34**, 316–29.

WOODWARD, MARY (1958) The diagnosis and treatment of homosexual offenders, *British Journal of Delinquency* **9**, 44–59.

WOODWORTH, R. S. and SCHLOSBERG, H. (1960) *Experimental Psychology*, New York, Holt, Rinehart & Winston.

YOUNG, W. C., GOY, R. W., and PHOENIX, C. H. (1964) Hormones and sexual behaviour, in *Sexual Research: New Developments* (ed. J. Money), New York, Holt, Rinehart & Winston, pp. 176–96.

ZEAMAN, D. and WEGNER, N. (1957) A further test of the role of drive reduction in human cardiac conditioning, *Journal of Psychology* **43**, 125–33.

AUTHOR INDEX

SUBJECT INDEX

OTHER TITLES IN THE SERIES IN EXPERIMENTAL PSYCHOLOGY